We Must Love One Another Or Die

We Must Love One Another Or Die

The Life and Legacies of Larry Kramer

Edited by
Lawrence D. Mass

CHRISTOPHER BRAM • JOHN M. CLUM • ALFRED CORN
JOHN D'EMILIO • MICHAEL DENNENY • ANTHONY S. FAUCI
ANDREW HOLLERAN • ARNIE KANTROWITZ • TONY KUSHNER
LAWRENCE D. MASS • RODGER MCFARLANE • PATRICK MERLA
MARK MERLIS • MICHAEL PALLER • GAIL MERRIFIELD PAPP
CANAAN PARKER • GABRIEL ROTELLO • DOUGLAS SADOWNICK
MICHELANGELO SIGNORILE • CALVIN TRILLIN • SARAH TRILLIN
DAVID WILLINGER • MAXINE WOLFE

CASSELL
London

For a catalogue of related titles in our
Sexual Politics list please write to us at the address below.

Cassell
Wellington House
125 Strand
London WC2R 0BB

First published 1997

British Library Cataloguing-in-Publication Data
A catalogue record for this book is available from the British
Library.

ISBN 0-304-33545-2

Typeset by BookEns Ltd, Royston, Herts.
Printed and bound in Great Britain by Creative Print
& Design (Ebbw Vale, Wales).

Contents

Acknowledgments

Steve Cook has been the guiding light of Cassell's gay and lesbian studies series. As with Larry Kramer, it is presently impossible to gauge the extent of his influence and achievements. For now, I can only liken his impact on my own life as a writer to be like Larry's—immeasurably great.

There aren't words to convey the love and gratitude I feel for my life-partner, Arnie Kantrowitz, who has so unceasingly sustained and inspired me in every aspect of my life and work.

I am deeply indebted to Rodger McFarlane for his down-to-earth wisdom, tart humor, indomitable cheer, and daily help.

Special thanks to Roz Hopkins, Angus Killick, Rictor Norton, Alan Worth, Maura Burnett and their staffs at Cassell and St. Martin's, to Norman Laurila for his guidance, and to Michael Denneny for his editorial suggestions.

*You can't not go forward
and say what you think
just because of what you fear
might or might not happen.*

—Larry Kramer
"Interview with a Writer"

Works by Larry Kramer

Dates and inclusiveness are approximate and attempt to indicate the main period of commencement and/or activity, of both composition and completion.

1965–66 *Here We Go Round the Mulberry Bush*. Based on the novel by Hunter Davies. Directed and produced by Clive Donner. Released by United Artists. "Additional dialogue" credit and associate producer.

1966 *The Rich Get Richer*. Unproduced original comedy screenplay.

1967 Untitled screenplay set in the Paris fashion world. Director, Jim Clark. Unproduced original comedy screenplay.

1968–70 *Women in Love*. Based on the novel by D. H. Lawrence. Directed by Ken Russell. Released by United Artists. Screenplay and producer.

1969 *Hands Across the Sea*. Unproduced original comedy screenplay.

1968–69 *Forbidden Colors*. Based on the novel by Yukio Mishima. Optioned by Columbia Pictures. Unproduced screenplay.

1970 *Sissies' Scrapbook*. Original unproduced screenplay. Untitled New York Play. Unproduced.

1971 Untitled New York play. Unproduced.

1971 *Lost Horizon*. Based on the novel by James Hilton. Produced by Ross Hunter. Directed by Charles Jarrott. Released by Columbia Pictures. Music by Burt Bacharach, Lyrics by Hal David. Screenplay (uncredited rewrite by John Gale).

1972 *American Classic*. Based on the novel *A Sea Change* by J. R. Salamanca. Producer and director, Arthur Penn. Unproduced screenplay.

1972 *Stay Hungry*. Based on the novel by Charles Gaines. Producers Robert Chartoff and Irwin Winkler. Unproduced screenplay.

1973 *Sissies' Scrapbook*. 2 Act Play. Directed by Alfred Gingold. Produced by Playwrights' Horizons.

1973 *A Minor Dark Age*. Unproduced 3 Act Play.

1974 *Four Friends*. Revised version of *Sissies' Scrapbook*. Directed by Alfred Gingold. Produced by Michael Harvey. Theatre de Lys.

1974 *The Big Three at Yalta*. Unproduced original comedy screenplay.

1975–78   *Faggots*. Novel. Published by Random House, Warner Books, Presses de la Renaissance, Minerva (UK), Plume.

1978   *Late Bloomers*. Unproduced original comedy/screenplay.

1978   *The American People*. Novel. Commenced writing.

1982   Founded Gay Men's Health Crisis with Nathan Fain, Dr. Lawrence Mass, Paul Popham, Paul Rapoport, and Edmund White.

1983–85   *The Normal Heart*. 2 Act Play. Directed by Michael Lindsay-Hogg. Produced by New York Shakespeare Festival, Joseph Papp. Published by Plume, Methuen (UK), Nick Hern Books (UK).

1987   Founded ACT UP.

1988   *Just Say No*. 2 Act Comedy. Directed by David Esbjornson. Produced by WPA Theatre. Published by St. Martin's Press.

1989   *Reports from the holocaust: The Making of an AIDS Activist*. Non-fiction. St. Martin's Press, Penguin (UK).

1989   *The Destiny of Me*. 3 Act Play. Directed by Marshall Mason. Produced by Circle Repertory Company, Rodger McFarlane, Tom Viola, and Lucille Lortel. Lucille Lortel Theatre. Published by Plume, Nick Hern Books (UK).

1994–95   *Reports from the holocaust: The Story of an AIDS Activist*. (Updated and expanded version). Non-fiction. St. Martin's Press, Cassell (UK).

1994   "Mrs. Tefillin." Short story, excerpt from *The American People*. Published in *The Penguin Book of Gay Short Stories*. Edited by David Leavitt and Mark Mitchell. Penguin, US and UK.

1985–96   *The Normal Heart*. Approximately fifteen drafts for, among others: Barbra Streisand, Columbia Pictures, David W. Picker, Paul Maslansky, Derek Granger, Jeffrey Taylor, John Schlesinger.

Preface

Without any introduction, many will have already gleaned the thrust of this collection simply by looking at its list of contributors. Though that roster includes several distinguished AIDS activists and a number of writers who write about AIDS and are otherwise activist, it is dominated by writers. It may be true that Larry Kramer is more widely known as an AIDS activist than as a writer *per se*, but the principal source of that renown has been his writing. Even his most fiery orations have caught hold primarily in their published versions, as collected in *Reports from the holocaust*. This thrust would seem appropriate for another reason. Although there is now a consensus—whatever the caveats—about Kramer's colossal place in the history of AIDS, there has been less consensus (notwithstanding his commercial success) about his place as a playwright, novelist, short-story writer, essayist and journalist, in the gay as well as in the greater literary communities. Of course, it is ultimately impossible to completely disentangle the activist from the writer, just as it is inevitably impossible to completely disentangle the personal from the political—in the life and work and times of Larry Kramer, certainly, as well as in our own.

Just as the confrontation between Ned Weeks and his brother over what's "normal" is at the heart of *The Normal Heart*, the first version of *Reports* concludes not with Larry on Mount Olympus giving his most powerful speech to the largest crowd, but with a comparably messy, intimate, irresolute confrontation between Larry and his sister-in-law about their real *feelings*—attitudes, resentments, prejudices. The message is clear. Confrontation and dialogue with those closest to you is the foundation of greater change. The political begins, concludes and must continue with the personal.

Just as there is no simple, linear progression of comprehension in our real lives and times, there is none in this book. There is, instead, a zig-zagging progress in the unfolding and fleshing out of a preoccupation with the entanglement of the personal and the political. Among the themes that intermesh in this regard, but which have not been much considered heretofore are: Kramer's impact on the trajectory of the gay movement; his ethnicity as a factor in his work, viewpoints and reception; his experience as a gay writer; his place in the history of gay and American literatures and theater; his impact on medical research, policy and care; his work in progress.

We Must Love One Another Or Die is organized in thematic segments. The first parts attempt to introduce Larry Kramer by combining my own story of our thirty-year relationship and Patrick Merla's biography with broad overviews and largely historical perspectives by John D'Emilio, Gabriel Rotello and Arnie Kantrowitz. The anthology then proceeds to the realms of literature and theater. Though a number of these pieces are topical and scholarly, they likewise collectively engage or are otherwise revealing of this individual/universal, private/public, personal/political dynamic. "Psychology, Politics and Literature" thus ranges from Andrew Holleran's tale of the literary life and world of Larry Kramer through Michael Denneny's evaluation of polemical writing as literature. In the course of this journey, we experience the personally contexted, comparative literary and psychological analyses of Christopher Bram, Mark Merlis, Alfred Corn and Douglas Sadownick. With the literary preceding it, as *Faggots* preceded Kramer's first critically and commercially successful plays, the section on theater commences with Tony Kushner's consideration of the role of the dialectical in eliciting "truth," in art as in life. It then proceeds with John Clum's critique of Larry Kramer's theatrical voices and audiences, and continues through dialectical discussions of Larry's role and place in regional, mainstream and community theater by David Willinger and Michael Paller, culminating in Gail Papp's history of Larry Kramer and the Public Theater. The last section opens with the title piece by Rodger McFarlane, which sustains but inverts this dynamic by commencing with a history of AIDS activism and activists and proceeding to intimate, literary reflections on the value and meaning of Kramer's life and work. Continuing with the political and historical but fundamentally intimate reminiscences and commentaries of Maxine Wolfe, Michaelangelo Signorile, Canaan Parker, Anthony Fauci, Calvin Trillin and Sarah Trillin, the collection concludes with an interview in which the subject of this book literally becomes personal. Not so unlike the conclusion of the original *Reports*, we are left, just the two of us, Larry and me, in confrontation dialogue about our lives, experiences and feelings.

It seems appropriate to conclude this Preface with a word about my own personal journey in the course of working on this collection. When I began my activism, around the time *Faggots* was published, I believed, like most of the gay political community, that Larry was a retrogressive figure. While we were abandoning the shrinks that had pathologized us for so long, Larry was still in therapy, still working to take personal responsibility for what we liberationists saw so clearly to be entirely the fault of society. Like an emerging consensus of others, however, I have come to realize that Larry was right about quite a bit. It wasn't all society's fault. We do have to look to ourselves and our own lives. Being responsible *is* a moral imperative. Meanwhile, even as I worked on this collection, I—a cofounder of GMHC and the writer of AIDS guidelines—had evaded retesting for HIV. For years. Finally, unable to sustain the cognitive dissonance of affirming Larry's work while failing to take action with regard to my own life, I took the plunge. Getting the result was one of the most difficult and frightening experiences of my life. I don't often cry, but I did so then, not because of the result, but in relief of the fear and shame that evasion had compounded. Today, I am grateful to Larry Kramer for inspiring me to keep trying to be responsible, to myself as well as my community, but most of all, for giving me the courage to keep trying to stand up to my fears, to stand up to and for myself.

Larry Kramer may always be characterized as controversial. And opinion about him may always be divided. Yet there is one observation, as captured by Arnie Kantrowitz in "An Enemy of the People," with which we may forever concur: "Where would we be without him?"

Lawrence D. Mass
New York City

June 1997

For Arnie Kantrowitz
In memory of Vito Russo

Introduction:
Larry versus Larry:
The Making of a Writer/Activist

Lawrence D. Mass

PERIODICALLY, I'M ASKED ABOUT WRITERS who have influenced me. I could tell you about my adolescent infatuation with Anatole France. At the age of twelve, I wrote my first and very adult book review, of *The Crime of Sylvestre Bonnard*, which I banged out with two fingers on our old black Underwood. It was a page and a half, and I remember how much I loved it and that the paper was like parchment. Then there was my first great love affair with another writer—Shakespeare. My senior honors thesis in English at the University of California at Berkeley (1969)—hailed that year as the finest overall university in the world, but whose graduates wore gasmasks to protest Ronny Reagan and Shirley Temple Black—was on the subject of the "romantification," as I called it, of Shakespeare's plays, as exemplified by the Shakespeare operas of the nineteenth century, with Verdi's *Otello* as paradigm. I had been especially interested in *Othello* ever since my Chicago junior high school English teacher, who was British and Jewish (and gay?), was fired for teaching it to us. It had been on some kind of official list of censored/forbidden works. But there was more to his dismissal. Not only did he have us study the play, he had us read the parts in class. And according to testimony before the school board by the class Barbie Doll everyone called a "JAP" (not my first encounter with this epithet, but my first with its standing for "Jewish American Princess"), his direction had required us to engage in such inapporpriate activities as kissing. In reality, his efforts to help us make contact with our burgeoning sexuality gave the largely Jewish class something of the libidinal atmosphere of the private school classes Patrick Dennis recalls in *Auntie Mame*. Little did I know how much pain I would later experience over the anti-Semitism of *The Merchant of Venice* (even if it's no worse *per se* than the racism of *Othello*), but that's the stuff of another of my stories, *Confessions of a Jewish Wagnerite*. Going off on tangents the way I'm already doing here, being discursive and parenthetical, came naturally to me and I always regarded this tendency as an impediment, as I was always told it was, until I read Larry Kramer, who demonstrated with his own work and who later told me directly and without qualification—and he remains the only mentor to have told me this— that this was an asset rather than a liability.

Many years later, I fell in love with Robert Musil's novel-without-end *The Man Without Qualities*, coincidentally though not surprisingly a favorite of Larry's. But the literature I became most involved with was that which dealt with homosexuality—covertly, by implication (I, too, wondered about Iago before rejecting that theory as unfounded and homophobic), or directly. Beginning with James Baldwin, Jean Genet, Tennessee Williams, Gore Vidal and Patrick Dennis, I read to try to find myself, though buying the books of these authors involved lies—to the booksellers about my age, and risk— with my parents and teachers, from whom they had to be hidden. It seems a little funny to list Dennis with these masters, but *Auntie Mame* and its sequel—which I was caught reading in my eighth grade class, for which I was sent to the principal, who called and told my mother, who was bemused—made a strong impression, alongside *Giovanni's Room, Our Lady of the Flowers, The Thief's Journal, The City and the Pillar,* and *Cat on a Hot Tin Roof*. When my mother half-heartedly forbade me to see *Night of the Iguana*, which featured Bette Davis with exposed boobs, I went anyway. At some point in this journey, I commenced my own writing in earnest. Prior to that time, my efforts had consisted mostly of course work. The only really creative and independent writing I had done, beyond letters and some frighteningly primitive lurches at keeping a journal, was as a reviewer of opera performances, for the newspaper of the University of Wisconsin at Madison (I think it had "Badger" in its name) and subsequently for the *Daily Californian* at UCB. In 1979, when I began writing my first pieces—in academic medicine, as well as for the gay press—who and what was I reading? Who were my influences? Coincidentally, they were two people with whom I was to become deeply and intimately involved, but whose viewpoints could not have been more divergent. One of them, Arnie Kantrowitz, was someone I had never met and whom I otherwise knew nothing about. But his pieces in *The Advocate* were a revelation to me. Never had I realized that being gay could be so affirmative, and affirmed. Not only were these essays about me, about who I was, how I felt, about the life I was living. They manifested something else, something we were starting to call gay pride and which we would also later designate as gay spirituality.

The other writer, Larry Kramer, was someone I had known socially since 1966, five years prior to the APA declassification of homosexuality as a mental disorder. I met Larry through my first lover—an Episcopalean priest, Jungian analyst, real-estate baron and sometime Hollywood actor whom Larry had once had a crush on. At the time, I was an undergraduate at UCB and was coming out in the bars and baths of San Francisco, a city and time of my life wherein I was so happy and which I still love so reflexively that I quake with nostalgia every time its name comes within earshot. There was this whole circle of these people—"gay society" as I tried to conceptualize it then. Its Perle Mesta was Tom H., a legendarily "endowed" (do people still say this?), brilliant German-American who had earned degrees in political science from Harvard and Columbia, but whose real dream was to be a *danseur* and who actually did a semi-classical gig in a Broadway show, albeit at the cost of abandoning his doctoral studies. Like so many gay men of his time, he lost heart about having a public career when he saw how much self-compromise, how much closetedness, would be involved. Meanwhile, by virtue of his international connections with the rich and famous, and with an army of sexy and sexually active folk, "Waldi," as he's called in my *Confessions*, was something of a cross between Jerry Zipkin and Heidi Fleiss.

Chief among the celebrities with whom Tom was close was one of the world's richest men, Leon Lambert, a Rothschild baron who was one of the founding intellects and architects of the European Economic Community and who was to become the Lambert of Drexel, Burnham, Lambert, the investment conglomerate that was at the center of one of the biggest financial scandals of modern times. Home base for Leon, the top floor of the ultramodern, palatial Banque Lambert in Brussels, featured one of the world's greatest private collections of modern and contemporary art. From a framed photo on a side table, Leon looked out at the French impressionist and post-impressionist masterpieces that festooned his library's walls. The black and white moment was from one of his legendary parties. On one arm was Mrs. Onassis, on the other was her sister, Princess Lee Radziwill. But the truth about Leon, who still nurtured the dream that Tom had given up of meshing comfortably with straight colleagues and sustaining a career, was that he was a chronically depressed—"neurasthenic" was the very archaically appropriate word we were using—closet case who eventually died of AIDS. The speakers at his funeral at St. Thomas's in New York (though Leon was half-Jewish and raised Catholic, he was an honorary WASP) included David Rockefeller and Henry Kissinger. At the service, which I attended with Larry Kramer, whose birthday it coincidentally was and whose pleas to Leon and his cronies high up in the worlds of fashion and finance (e.g. Calvin Klein) to help out in the first years of the AIDS crisis had gone unheeded, no one mentioned that Leon was gay, half-Jewish or that he had had AIDS. As I recall in my *Confessions*, Larry and I exited the church civilly during a refrain of "The Christian Life." Several years later, Tom also died of AIDS.

I guess Leon, the basis of a character in an early draft of *Faggots*, was the most famous horse in Tom's stable, but Larry was a close second. At the time we met, in London in the late 1960s, Larry was preparing the screenplay for his film *Women in Love*. The sensitive gentleman I met there, on my second trip to Europe, seemed to be in real contrast to the hellraiser I had been warned about by Tom and "Andy," as the priest is named in *Confessions*. Larry was always very unhappy, I was told, and the reason, they said, was his inability to find love. But they—with me parroting them—were certain that that was because of his inability to accept people and circumstances on their own terms, to *give* love himself. He was self-important and *so* critical, they said. "Tantrums" and "screaming" were words you heard a lot whenever Larry was talked about, which he always was. At the time, I had no idea how much of their resentment was based on envy, and on Larry's exposure of the truths of their lives. But Larry was also, it was gleanable between the lines and sometimes grudgingly conceded, extremely talented, interesting and challenging, even generous; and for better or worse, like it or not, Larry was a member of our community, of our extended gay family, and here to stay.

□ □ □

Everybody was always up in arms about Larry. Who *was* this person? What struck me most about our first meeting—he took me to a private party and escorted me on a tour of London pubs that were gay or partly or sometimes or maybe gay (this was still the 1960s)—was his genuine interest in and respect for my relationship with Andy, notwithstanding what was apparently some degree of interest in me. Larry's own infatuation with Andy hadn't evolved, but beyond that, Larry's critics were partly correct in citing his preoccupation with what he generalized to be the failure of love in gay life. He really was concerned about love—about finding it for himself, of course, but also as a writer, critic and observer. The recurrent question of why it is so difficult for gay men to love is the theme of *Faggots*, the novel he would eventually "vomit up," as Rodger McFarlane would later characterize Larry's creative process, and the main question and challenge it posed. At a personal level, I had experienced the deepest life-transforming love, the stuff of Shakespeare's sonnets, with another man, Andy. At least that's how I felt about it at age twenty. Projecting my good fortune onto all of gaydom, I could not see the bigger picture that so preoccupied Larry. I couldn't help but agree with Larry's critics that he was fundamentally wrong, that gay love wasn't so elusive. It's with this viewpoint, that of Larry's critics, that the narrator of my *Confessions* overviews the life and work of "D. J. Love," the character I based on Larry, before finally conceding the substance of Love's concerns and perspectives. At the end of the chapter, "Wicked Love," the narrator, after vomiting up the most wildly Krameresque angry, over-the-top satire and criticism of Love and his work, reveals that Love has replaced Andy (who was twice my age and a father figure, but also a refractory conservative and closet case) as a premiere figure of paternal example, authority and esteem.

It's not that I couldn't see that a lot of gay life and sex and relationships were troubled. But while so many of us were comfortably situated in our embrace of what we called the sexual revolution and our assurance that whatever dysfunction there might be in gay relationships was society's fault, the result of internalized homophobia from patriarchal beliefs and systems, Larry had the sense that he was seeing something like the opposite. "The gay leaders who created this sexual-liberation philosophy in the first place have been the death of us," says Ned Weeks in *The Normal Heart*. And thus continued the dialectic Larry and I have sustained for nearly thirty years.[1]

What I didn't realize until recently was the extent to which my involvement with Larry, and his influence on me, had to do not with social connections or politics, but with writing. Larry was, in fact, the first writer whom I counted as a friend. After meeting him, I developed friendships with a number of other writers, without realizing why—why was I hanging out with these people?—without realizing that I was doing a kind of apprenticeship. Though not a musician myself, I had always written music criticism—the principal outlet for my writing prior to my first pieces for the academic medical and gay presses—and some of my strongest feelings were about opera. Like the two leading music critics, Peter G. Davis and Richard Dyer, who became my two closest friends during the 1970s, and from whom I did learn positive values of discipline, objectivity and professionalism (especially from Dyer, whose refusal to ever indulge in any kind of self-pity was granitic, and inspiring), I was an opera queen who was primarily concerned about performance values, within the art-*uber-alles* aestheticism that still reigns supreme. None of us—neither myself nor the music critics—had any real, genuine involvement with social or political issues or concerns, though we certainly regarded ourselves as liberal, and we all shared this bond of gayness and an awareness of homophobia. Having very little self-confidence or consciousness of the strength and primacy that that identity—as a writer—would eventually assume in my life, and never having been really encouraged in that regard by my family or friends, including the critics (who would never condescend to read the gay press, not even with the onset of the epidemic; rather, they would try to get the information directly from me, at which point I terminated our communications), I was observing and learning my craft from these people, but especially from Larry, and largely unconsciously. (Larry, incidentally, is the first writer from whom I learned that you could write just like you talk, that you could write things like ". . . that that . . ." and that that would be appreciated. Just as I learned from Richard Dyer that you could end sentences in prepositions, regardless of the fact that that's one of the things that people had repeatedly criticized you for.) Though I didn't realize it at the time, Larry was my first mentor.

For some years during the 1970s, the Baron rented an old colonial house overlooking the bluffs in Welfleet, Mass. This was in addition to his homes in Ostend and Gstaad. Leon was there only for August, and Tom maintained it and lived there the rest of the year. Larry and I were among its periodic visitors. My strongest memory is of one evening when we played some kind of game—charades or Scrabble—which found Larry preoccupied with a word I had never heard of but that would crop up in *Faggots*: "poultice." There was a lot of discussion about it and several dictionaries were consulted before Larry would let it go. Why did Larry care so much about this stupid word? Was it just because he was crazy, obsessive Larry, always trying to overanalyze and dominate everyone and everything? At the time, I hadn't the faintest inkling of why I found this so intriguing. Now, I realize that what I was observing was a real writer struggling with language, weighing things like color and nuance. (Sound is so important in *Faggots*, which can truly be said to have its own music; certainly its own rhythms.) Is this what real writers do—struggle and obsess to this degree? If my unconscious were beginning to ask such questions, the immature opera queen who had next to nothing in the self-awareness, assurance and esteem departments most certainly was not. And whatever complexity and genuineness of observation my unconscious may have appreciated in Larry was overridden by the consensus of certainty that he was simply trying to draw attention to himself, by being eccentric . . . and/or "narcissistic"—another word we would find ourselves frequently using to describe him with what was felt to be real justice and appropriateness in view of his very psychiatric background and our own coming of age in the psychoanalytic 1960s.

From 1973 to 1979 I lived in Boston, where I felt very unsettled. Some of my malaise had to do with the demands of my training in high-tech anesthesiology at the legendary MGH (Massachusetts General Hospital, aka "Most Greatest Hospital"), and as a clinical fellow at Harvard Medical School, during a time when I had yet to tap into my potential for more personal and creative work. Mostly, however, it was a combination of my desire to live in New York—where I was so comfortable I began calling it home long before I had any certainty that it ever would be, and where I finally moved in 1979 without having a job—and my growing discomfort in a city whose prudery, grimness and provincialism sat like granite beneath its veneer of being one of the most concentrated centers of brain power, youth and political liberalism in the world. There is one sense, however, in which I will be forever grateful to Boston, for having lived there in 1977, the year of the great fire at the Everard Baths in New York, wherein nine people, regulars like me, lost their lives. Had I been living in New York at that time, it's a lot more likely that I would have been among the casualties.

With increasing frequency during the 1970s, I visited New York whenever I could. Much of that time was spent at the opera, in the bars and at the baths, but I did have friends I saw from time to time. One of them was Larry. Following the success of *Women in Love* in 1970, Larry had begun work on a new screenplay, an adaptation of Yukio Mishima's *Forbidden Colors*. I no longer remember what Larry told me about Mishima and his novel, but whatever it was, it made me interested enough that I purchased and read a book that was to have more influence on me than perhaps any other—*Confessions of a Mask*. Never had I read such a clear, honest and persuasive story of the development of a homosexual consciousness and identity, and the time-and-place-transcending problems that came with them. Without ever becoming conscious of the connections to Larry, I embarked on one of my first independent and most precocious literary endeavors—a screenplay of Mishima's *Confessions*.

In the mid-1970s, just when Larry was becoming immersed in the auto-biographical *Faggots*, the APA declassified homosexuality as a mental disorder, and I began moving away from people and artworks that saw homosexuality through lenses of pathology. To a very real degree, psychiatry itself had been the problem, not the answer. I knew a lot of the people Larry was writing about, and couldn't help but feel that they were primarily the victims rather the perpetrators of their oppression. Even Barry F., the Eurotrashy expatriate snot Larry was so in love with. I don't think I've ever met a phonier person. And "Anthony Montano." And . . . (Was I a character? Apparently not, though I would be one of the models for "Mickey Marcus" in *The Normal Heart*.) The truth is that most of the people who became caricatures in *Faggots* were even worse than Larry's portraits. But in those days, I just felt sorry for them, as for myself. The idea that they—that we—might be responsible for our lives and problems was repellent, and as I smoked my daily joints and two-plus packs of cigarettes a day and drank my alcoholic levels of drinks, I joined those who resented, even hated, the messenger with that news. One of the moments I recall feeling the depth of that resentment—so much of it centered on envy of his success and freedom—was when Larry tried to console me about the difficulty of my circumstances of trying to write while having to earn a living. That's when he told me the story of Joseph Heller running a full-time business during the writing his first novel.

Another such moment came in the immediate fallout of the premiere of *The Normal Heart*, wherein the sources of my hospitalization for burnout—my major depression from, as I saw it, the stress and strain of having to maintain a job that limited my freedom to write (which at that time consisted almost exclusively of covering the epidemic), compounded by substance abuse—were reduced in the play to several unrelated and what seemed to me at the time absurdly simplistic and exaggerated premises: Mickey's fear that being more political about the epidemic could cost him his job which was being funded by the city; his inability to compromise his sex revolutionary ideals; and his core inability to know what to tell people, or to be willing to tell people what they needed to be told. In reality, though I now wish we had been a lot more outspoken much earlier about getting people to just "stop having sex" altogether, to "just say no," as Dr. Brookner proposes to Ned Weeks early in the play (though even now it's questionable how much credibility such an approach could ever have achieved), as I saw it, I had never waivered in my commitment to present the best information and advice available in a sex- and gay-affirmative context—the best information and advice from leading public health officials and researchers—however complex, however contradictory. And in fact, that commitment and approach have been widely recognized and praised, most recently in Rodger Streitmatter's *Unspeakable: The Rise of the Gay and Lesbian Press in America*. In retrospect, however, Larry was right: safe and safer sex guidelines needed to be stronger. Meanwhile, Larry's reduction of my role to what seemed this caricature in *The Normal Heart* was the source of the worst anger and resentment I ever felt toward him, and which found expression in the early aftermath of the play's success.[2]

Whatever the unperceived or disregarded danger of Larry's gift for satire and writerly commitment to tell on and about those he knew, *Faggots* had a lot more impact on me than anything I could even begin to realize. As had been the case with Mishima's *Confessions*, I was profoundly impressed with the work. While resenting and condemning the book for what I felt to be its homophobia and erotophobia, I was knocked out by the power of its writing. Notwithstanding the allegation of "run-on sentences," which I myself would be criticized for, *Faggots* contained some of the most dazzling prose, bar none, I had ever encountered. And notwithstanding the surrealism and theatricality that are its *mise-en-scène,* the language and cadences of *Faggots* were so genuine. It's the way people really thought and spoke. Not in short clear sentences, though the case for that can certainly be made—by Yukio Mishima, Arnie Kantrowitz and Edmund White, among others—but in intermerging feelings, and observations, in fragments of thought, in flashes, in whorling eddies and great flowing streams. More to the point, it's the way *I* thought and spoke. Mishima's *Confessions,* which I came to via Larry, may have been the first book to show me that I could tell my own story. But although I didn't realize it at the time, *Faggots* was the first book to let me know that I could tell my own story in my own language; in my own voice.

One of the techniques I learned from *Faggots* without realizing it at the time was the Walt-Whitmanesque technique of conjuring atmospheres and environments with lists. *Faggots* is full of shorter and longer lists: of individuals at various parties and events, of famous "faggots" (also in *The Normal Heart* and *The Destiny of Me*), of handkerchief codes, of ethnic groups, of sexual positions and activities, of gay bar and sex club names, of movie stars and divas, of drugs, of songs and musics, of fashion accoutrements, of great moments/scenes from movies, of audio equipment, of ex-tricks, of tricks within the preceding year, of lighting instruments and effects, of junk foods, of film production companies, of items left over from the "Toilet Bowl" blow-out, of Jews, of discos, of the names of houses in Cherry Grove, of the names of some of the Jewish women who wanted to park their yachts alongside the gay ones in the Pines, of tea dance attendees, of Fire Island costume accessories, of a lot of names—many of them Jewish and/or gay—for penis, of desperate fantasy sequences and options for a gay man trying to have sex with a straight woman, of Meat Rack party postures, of Nazi "party" regalia, of chocolates, of Fred Lemish's final vomiting up of the reasons for his anger (in case you still don't get it).

Another literary and theatrical technique I learned about from Larry but didn't fully appreciate—in fact, was very suspicious of—was hyperbole. Unlike the utilization of lists, this was a method that was as controversial as it was, ultimately, successful for Larry, but not something for others like myself, who weren't coming to it from their marrow, to try to emulate, toy with or otherwise indulge. Now that the word "faggot" has become vernacular among gay people ourselves in much the same way that "nigger" has among blacks, such street-talk and exaggeration seem true and funny. The narrator is people. In fact, in the light of its anticipation of the journey of gay minority vocabulary and phraseology as well as consciousness, *Faggots* can be seen as remarkably prescient. When the novel was first published, however, it created a firestorm of controversy, and I was among the critics. First, there was the issue of using the terminology of the oppressor. As recently as 1995, when I reread *Faggots*, I wasn't certain about how to feel about the title. I was staying at Parliament House in Orlando, Florida, perhaps the world's largest and busiest gay resort, a capital of sex, sleaze and sensibility you would have to go back to the *Satyricon* to find an equivalent of.[3] As I was reading *Faggots* by the pool, it occurred to me that many (most?) of the people there wouldn't have heard of Larry or his book. Though the PH, as it's called, does attract a national and international clientele, most of its visitors are locals, rurals, Southerners. Seeing the title, they might wonder whether I were reading something by David Duke. Perhaps they would think it's a publication of the "fundies" (as they call Christian fundamentalists, some of whom, because of inheritance from relatives who died of AIDS, became co-owners of the PH!), or of ultra-rightist/fascist groups that are anti-gay but that have gays in their leadership (a gay tradition—e.g., from Ernst Roehm to the neo-Nazi leader featured in the film documentary *Beruf Neo-Nazi*, to say nothing of the fantasies of Jean Genet, and the flirtations of Yukio Mishima, whose name, incidentally, is not mentioned in Ed White's biography of Genet). So uncertain was I about how the title might be misinterpreted that I created another dust jacket with plain paper.

But for me the biggest problem with Larry Kramer and his style was specificity. In my background of medicine and science, precision of terminology and maintaining standards of journalistic objectivity were of paramount importance. Granted Larry was an artist and satirist, and *Faggots* is fiction, but its stereotypes and caricatures and generalizations were being taken by many of us at face value, as representing "truths" we believed to be so much more complex, part of so much bigger a picture, that their validity was altogether questionable. In the aftermath of *Faggots*, when Larry began speaking of the large numbers of "friends" with AIDS (before it was being called that), of people he knew on Fire Island who might be affected, when he conjured up the worst gloom-and-doom and morally paradigmatic images of how bad things were, alarms went off. Was the distinction between Larry's art and what was actually happening becoming blurred? Worse, was this person who was still working his life out with a shrink while we were trying to better ours with community activism, some kind of homophobic psych case? On the one hand, he was right to be so concerned. From day one there was no question of the seriousness of the epidemic, and Larry and I worked together in multiple endeavors to inform and organize the community. But on the other, were the specifics of this concern being presented in the same manner as *Faggots* (at that time still so widely regarded by the gay community as homophobic)? Unfortunately, this mechanism of voice with which Larry has consistently expressed himself, hyperbole—the foundation of satire, the stuff of irony—would not be clearly understood and appreciated as such by most of us until many years later, and there would be countless instances when overstatement would have to be distinguished from fact. Eventually, Larry demonstrated his considerable journalistic skills in very accurately conveying information, facts, to the public, while still giving us the flavor and dimension of what was happening with examples and comparisons, and blunt statistics, that were as horrifying or worse than anything his art had conjured up, even at his angriest, but which were *not*, alas, hyperbolic. Larry's greatest predictions of catastrophe, or, for that matter, his equally grand and fierce beliefs in affirmative potentials and possibilities, no longer seem hyperbolic because so many of the earlier predictions have turned out to be true, from his earliest scenarios of the global holocaust AIDS would become to his belief in the possibility of developing a cure for a category of illness (viral) for which no cure has ever been realized, a goal toward which unprecedented progress has already been achieved. At the time, however, it seemed a shame that the same faculty that allowed Larry to see so profoundly into the malaise of his community in time and place and so broadly into the future with regards to AIDS and its treatments could not foresee the even bigger picture of a world in which sexuality would be better understood and its exigencies more efficiently and equitably engaged; a world in which equal rights for women and sexual minorities, sex education, contraception, and STD prevention and treatment would be transformative of humankind beyond today's most uninhibited hopes; the dream behind the front lines of what we called "the sexual revolution." In reality, Larry was never against those goals. The "sexual revolution" he was condemning was not the age-defining phenomenon ("The Birth Control Age") of the sexologists, but the no-responsibilities "love-in" ethos of the late 1960s and 1970s.

□ □ □

Among my earliest writings about the epidemic was a piece for *Christopher Street* called "Cancer as Metaphor" that held up Susan Sontag's "Illness as Metaphor" as a guidepost to how we should proceed in writing and speaking about AIDS. Tacitly, it warned against the likes of Larry Kramer. How wrong we were. Though Larry's metaphors have drawn a lot of criticism—most notoriously for his use of "holocaust" to characterize the scope and accountabilities of the epidemic—they have been inarguably successful in galvanizing responses that were vitally necessary and which were not otherwise being elicited.[4] Of course, the same can be said for Louis Farrakhan, and the accusation of demagoguery is difficult to evade completely. Today, we have a new edition of *Reports from the holocaust,* the title of which might be expected to cause some of the same kind of confusion as that caused by the titling of *Faggots*—i.e., if I go to Israel or the Catskills and decide to read *Reports* by the pool, should I put a blank sheet of paper over the cover? Likewise today, no one quotes "Illness as Metaphor" or even the updating of that essay, "AIDS and its Metaphors" (both essays were published as books), including Susan Sontag, who has otherwise maintained her very low profile on AIDS, and public (official) invisibility as lesbian, as has her longtime companion, Annie Liebovitz.[5] There can be no question that the future will cite what David Bergman has called "Larry Kramer and The Rhetoric of AIDS" as one of the richest chapters in the history of the metaphorization of illness.[6] Meanwhile, precisely what value Sontag's analysis has served—in what ways it has helped us—in the face of AIDS, remains to be determined.

The same might be said for Bergman's essay, which gets caught, as so many of us have been, in the lure of psychoanalyzing the messenger and his motivation at the expense of acknowledging and affirming the truth of his message. Using the metaphor of the great Quilt of the Names Project to reveal who and what Larry is not and has not achieved, or for that matter even been connected with (the fact of Larry's noninvolvement with the Quilt becomes tacitly suspicious), Bergman observes that

> the Quilt is quiet, and those who come to witness it are hushed by its magnitude, its seemingly unlimited detail, and its inescapable unity of effect. . . . The NAMES Project has struck a new chord in the American psyche: a way to incorporate gay people into the fabric of American society while recognizing—even commemorating—their contributions and sufferings. It forms the type of statement gay writers are only beginning to stitch together with words.[7]

What Bergman believes he's demonstrating is that the voices that have been quiet, those of more ordinary, less conspicuous folk, those varied Americans whose stories have yet to be told, have more to tell us, and a much vaster panorama to reveal, than the shrill rhetoric that has dominated the discourse thus far. Tacitly, Bergman pits the powerful silence of the Quilt against the otherwise predominant metaphor of the epidemic: Silence = Death. Bergman thinks that he's envisioning the forest that surrounds the few large trees in the foreground of what has already become yesterday. But even in the face of what would seem to be as safe an assumption as could possibly be made, what he's actually doing may prove to be the opposite. While history may well affirm the complexity and humanity and individual heroism of gay people in our great crisis, which the Quilt monumentalizes, it is just as likely to emphasize how the Quilt fits into *Larry's* perspective: of gay men for the most part passively, silently going to their deaths, many of whose only nonsexual connection with a gay community, greater civil rights or AIDS organization, endeavor or project is their patch, donated by a relative or friend.

With the publication of *Faggots*, the problems associated with Larry's use of hyperbole first presented themselves to the public at large and the gay community in particular, for example, everybody in that novel is a grotesque; there isn't a single affirmative image of a gay man, except, perhaps, in the figures of the young newcomer to the city, the narrator and in the listed examples of famous gay people in history; and sex is consistently seen as exploitative and dysfunctional. (*These* observations are not hyperbolic.) This same feature of Larry's technique (and a key to his success) reemerged in *The Normal Heart*, which recapitulates the experience, at least as Larry recreated it, of the formation of GMHC and the early unfolding of the epidemic. I still wince at the many generalizations and literal inaccuracies the play perpetrates, but not at its greater truths, which I consistently recognized and acknowledged publicly, even then. Beyond the changing of facts and history—e.g., Mickey Marcus, the character that is partly based on me, is not a physician, one of the many distortions relating to my role that cut so deeply—Ned, the title character, would make all these Kramer-esque exaggerations: e.g., "Nobody with a brain gets involved with gay politics"; "Do you realize that you are talking about millions of men who have singled out promiscuity to be their principal political agenda . . . ?" But this was Larry's voice. This is how he spoke, how he made his points, how he got attention. Years later, at Vito Russo's memorial gathering, he began by saying "We killed Vito." Eventually, everyone understood that this was Larry's way, so that when he more recently participated in a panel at the Center for Lesbian and Gay Studies (CLAGS) and denounced his academic hosts and their theorizing as worse than the problems they were addressing, no one got too upset. As Larry himself patiently and generously clarified later, in response to the one questioner who called him on being ungracious: "Of course, what Marty (Duberman) and CLAGS are doing is wonderful," he said. Earlier, he suggested that "ACT UP started falling apart because people began theorizing so much it made everybody sick." Then, just as everyone was reassuring themselves that that was just Larry going off again, being crazy, he observed: "The entire continent of Africa has yet to get AZT!" Today, we understand, and appreciate, Larry Kramer.

When *Faggots* was published, my unofficial, and for the most part unwitting, apprenticeship took its biggest step to date. Under the angriest and almost unanimous criticism and rejection of a writer by a public that I had ever directly witnessed (and in fact participated in, however ambivalently), I learned what has proved, at least for me, to be *the* most important of lessons about writing and writers: that you have to believe in your work, in what you have to say, in yourself, even when others, even when the great majority of others, don't. The example of Larry's tenacity and courage in the face of what amounted to virtually total ostracism by the political gay community was one that would repeatedly refuel me over the ensuing years of my own struggles as a writer.[8] Though I never was or would be in Larry's league, I felt an equivalence, a parallel, of odds against me in my belief in the importance of remaining affirmative about sexuality as the epidemic worsened, but especially in my simultaneous efforts to press the worlds of serious music and opera to deal more forthrightly with homophobia, to say nothing of AIDS, as well as in my later efforts to get both the gay and music communities to engage the reality of the resurgence of anti-Semitism, and include this concern in our statements and agendas.[9] Time and again, in the example of Larry more than anyone else, of *Faggots* and its aftermath, I would find the courage to face rejection and failure and continue with my work (e.g., when I asked if I could write the program note for the first GMHC "Music For Life" benefit, CEO Richard Dunne, who later refused to allow me to dedicate the fourth edition of my *Medical Answers About AIDS*, published by GMHC, to Larry Kramer and Vito Russo, didn't even respond. The program did, however, feature a closety piece by Peter G. Davis.) Each of the many times I would have to endure such slights and setbacks, I'd think of Larry Kramer, of *Faggots*, of all the rejections *The Normal Heart* had endured (none of our community's leading agents would touch it) before being accepted by the Public Theater. It was ironic but a fact that the very person of whom I was so critical, who was a subject—often as nemesis— and motivation for a significant portion of my writing to come, was at the same time the mentor who was most inspiring to me, by living example, and in his sensitive and supportive responses to my early pieces for the gay press, even those that were "too academic" (as he and Arthur Bell kept trying to get me to understand; and they were right) or that he otherwise took issue with.

After reading the first version of "The Housemates Who Got Nailed," the penultimate chapter of my memoir but the first to be published, Larry couldn't have been more supportive, even though he must have recognized the reference to "D. J. Love," the character who states his belief that he has never himself, personally, experienced anti-Semitism, but who had had an affairette with an interior designer whose closeted but virulent anti-Semitism is the subject of that chapter and the pivotal event in the creation of *Confessions*. When I ran into Larry at one of the West Street bars that no longer exist, he said, "Keep going. Say more. Make it even nastier." He genuinely connected with my writing, and his advice was sincere. I took it, to the extent of going after Larry himself with no holds barred. It was the kind of honesty Larry inspired and respected. I had to do it. As each of several chapters of the book was published, in their earliest versions, in *Christopher Street*, Larry was among the few to give me real feedback and encouragement. The extent to which Larry had become a father figure was reflected in the power struggle that had evolved between us. A true father will inspire a son to confront all who stand in his way, even himself. Ironically, this mythic circumstance is most familiar to me in the relationships between Wotan and his daughter Brunnhilde, between Wotan and his grandson Siegfried, and, more recently, between the brutal father of *The Destiny of Me* and his queer son.

With Larry as my mentor, I completed my own story of the "real" Mickey Marcus. There was just one small problem. My agent, Norman Laurila, and I couldn't find a publisher. After sixteen rejections, I turned to Larry and told him that I needed to ask him for a favor that was difficult for me, and that would be even more difficult for him. Even though my book contained some extremely critical and satirical (albeit also loving and respectful) material on him (material he hadn't seen), could he help me find a publisher? More than any other writer colleague or friend, Larry responded. His very specific suggestion: contact Steve Cook, publisher of Cassell's developing gay and lesbian series. If it weren't for Larry Kramer, the most personally important endeavor of my life to date, my story, might never have been born.

After the book was published, Larry remained supportive and consoling. When I told him about some of the slights and hostility I had encountered—for exmple, having the book banned by Nathalie Wagner, the New York Wagner Society's chairperson and literature table Nazi (figurative, as in "soup Nazi" or "tofu fascist") at a Columbia University symposium on Wagner—he repeated an observation that has likewise consistently sustained me: "You care too much about what others think." You cannot be a serious writer if you worry too much about being taken seriously as a writer. The lessons and legacies of Larry Kramer.

But part of the power of Larry's observation here comes from the paradox of knowing how much he really does care about what others think. Most people have no idea how vulnerable and sweet the real Larry Kramer is, how easily hurt (if simultaneously inspired) by criticism and rejection, how childlike, though this fundamental aspect of his character should be clear from his work. Consider the metaphor of "the normal heart," the abuse of Fred Lemish in his pursuit of Dinky, and of Ned Weeks by his father in

The Destiny of Me. Yet people have this predominant image of Larry as this "seething bulldog" ("fierce" is a term I've used). You would think such a champion and scourge would be made of iron. On the contrary, the real person is the one with a heart that is as vulnerable to breakage as it is big. That's why the courage is so impressive. Larry will go after people whose opinions really do count—Dinky, to whom he is now, in real life, united; his brother (does he still think Larry's "abnormal"?); his father (who never came around, even on his deathbed); his closest friends and legions of other writers, artists, and personalities—people who really do affect him and his self-esteem, even at the price of much more seriously and/or permanently alienating them. Ultimately, what Larry Kramer really means to say with his advice is: You have to write/say what you must, not so much in spite of but *because* you care so much what others think and say.

□ □ □

Which brings us to the final consideration of Larry versus Larry: our individual, confluent and divergent experiences of Judaism, anti-Semitism and their relationships to homosexuality and homophobia. Anyone who has read *Faggots* knows how flavored it is with Jewish sensibility, vernacular, humor, color and lore, just as anyone who has seen *The Normal Heart* or read *Reports from the holocaust* understands how deeply Larry Kramer does feel the weight of Jewish experience, especially that of the Holocaust and its relevance to gay people in our great crisis of AIDS. Though there is virtually no discussion of anti-Semitism *per se* in these works, there is some reflection about the impact of this prejudice on his family in *The Destiny of Me*. When it comes to the presence and escalation of anti-Semitism itself, in our own time and communities, however, Larry Kramer has been—like the vast majority of Jews everywhere—remarkably silent. On the one hand, this is because Larry's principal concern is AIDS and its Siamese twin, gay politics. There's little room for other involvements. Criticizing Larry for not being more outspoken about the resurgence of anti-Semitism is like criticizing him for not being more involved in the women's or other civil rights movements, with Bosnia, the environment, nuclear safety or animal rights. Even leaders as grand as Larry Kramer cannot be everything for everyone in need. On the other hand, I believe that there is more to Larry's silence, that it reflects my own life's silence and that of the overwhelming majority of today's Jews; in fact, not so unlike the Jews Ned Weeks talks about in *The Normal Heart* who managed to relegate the first news reports of what was going on in Europe to small articles in the center pages of the *New York Times*. Like most assimilated Jews, we've been seeing ourselves as part of the mainstream, in which we seem so deeply and safely integrated (a recent feature in *New York* magazine made the claim that Jews have become so successfully mainstream and establishment that we no longer have anything to worry about). It's precisely the way Germany's Jews saw themselves in the

Weimar Republic. Even with Alexander Zhiranovsky, Louis Farrakhan and Pat Buchanan—*a presidential candidate!*—spewing, defending or otherwise representing the most extreme anti-Semitic poison and getting the historically predictable, enthusiastic large-scale followings, our denial prevents us from seeing this as part of a continuum and appropriately gauging its seriousness. Rather, we regard the tirades, bombings, cemetery defacements and murders committed by neo-Nazis, terrorists, fundamentalists and other fascistically inclined extremists and fanatics in Russia, the Baltics, Germany, Israel, Idaho, Istanbul and Buenos Aires as remote and isolated. Contrary to liberal naiveté, the anti-Semitism that has defined Jewish experience throughout its entire history is still blisteringly present. As the protagonist of Herb Gardner's play, *Conversations With My Father*, puts it: that 5,000 year experience isn't likely to all be over with on Tuesday.

The subject of Larry versus Larry with regard to Judaism and homosexuality is too sprawling to try to capture in full, but it would seem to be the appropriate subject with which to conclude this introduction. A good starting point is the first weekend of the first *New York Times* report on what later became known as AIDS. By the most extraordinary coincidence, it was that weekend that I had the first confrontation of my adult life with overt anti-Semitism, an incident that is the subject of that penultimate chapter ("Housemates") of my *Confessions*. As it says on the book's dust jacket, as the epidemic unfolded and every gay man was forced to confront his own mortality, the necessity to understand the even greater depths of fear touched by the anti-Semitic incident became imperative, and I began to face the fact that my life had been dominated by internalized anti-Semitism, even as I had come to grips with my identity as a gay man. I had begun a second odyssey of self-discovery, quite unintended and ill-timed, within an identity that had been in many ways even more deeply repressed and closeted than my homosexuality. It was during the time of that first writing for *Confessions* that Larry first confided to me that he couldn't recall ever having personally, directly, experienced overt anti-Semitism in his entire life. With his later reassertion of this claim (see "Interview With A Writer"), I realized that, notwithstanding Larry's often very extroverted Jewishness, and his Philip Roth-like status as a critic, observer and satirist, he was and in fact to some extent still is in denial about the depth and pervasiveness of *ongoing* anti-Semitism, in his own communities as well as in the world at large. As with the rest of us, unless it slapped him in the face, which apparently it hadn't (or if it had, he still hadn't noticed it), he was able to evade it. As this journey of discovery has continued, in fact, I have yet to meet a single Jew, anywhere, no matter how political, ethnic, religious or knowledgeable, who does not relatively quickly reveal some significant degree of internalized anti-Semitism. (Of course, the same is true of blacks, women and gays and lesbians with regard to internalized racism, misogyny and homophobia.)

So one truth about Larry Kramer, however aware of the metaphor of the Holocaust and however proud and magnificent an exemplar of Jewish morality, ethics and sensibility he may otherwise be, is that he is silent about anti-Semitism in the world today. In terms of his current work—his novel *The American People*, which is very much about Jews and American history—Larry's stance can be appreciated as being parallel to his position *vis-à-vis* gay people at the time he wrote *Faggots*: as a critic who had extremely important and valuable things to say but who did so from a standpoint of detachment, of not yet entering the fray himself (just as he didn't get politically involved in the gay community until AIDS, which followed *Faggots*, he has yet to be thus involved with Jews; hopefully, a comparable cataclysm will not force such a connection). But things have gotten so bad that it's not enough for us to just be—like Barbra Streisand, Philip Roth and Larry Kramer—visibly Jewish and tacitly affirming of Jewish concerns. The time has come when we have to be more outspoken about anti-Semitism. As we have against homophobia, we must protest. We must march, my darlings. Has Larry Kramer ever participated in a petition or march or demonstration for anything Jewish? I doubt it seriously. For the record, neither have I. As I point out in my *Confessions*, I've marched against apartheid, racism, nuclear proliferation, and for the Equal Rights Amendment, and of course for gay rights, but never for anything Jewish or against anti-Semitism. Unfortunately, the question that really needs to be asked is a lot more shocking and disturbing: Why, amidst the most seriously anti-Semitic assaults from the likes of Louis Farrakhan, other Nation of Islam representatives, Pat Buchanan, the Christian right, and a host of rock singers and entertainers including Michael Jackson, has there not *been* a single major demonstration? Overwhelmed in our marginality, tranquilized by delusions of assimilation and power, and once again terrified, we Jews are still in the closet.

Whence the liberal and gay recticence to speak out about anti-Semitism *today*? More than to any other factors, I believe it is attributable to two ideologies: (1) the traditional belief that art transcends and does not have to be accountable to politics or morality; and (2) the socialist inference that anti-Semitism is an understandable and to some extent justifiable or inevitable response to a white racist, capitalist (elitist and bourgeois), tribalist and monocultural entity. In the writing of this essay, I have felt a lot of pressure to moralize about Larry Kramer, just as Edmund White was pressured to moralize about Genet. When asked about this by the *New York Times*, White responded, "For me, there's something so impertinent about sitting in judgment on a genius like Genet .... I feel that biography as a form has become the revenge of little people on big people .... Little people who have little lives are able to condescend to those who are superior to them by saying, 'He was a cruel father,' and so on."[10]

Well, I, for one, entirely disagree. Through my experience of Wagner, I've learned the hard way the tremendous cost of what White is saying. For so many years, I was the stereotypical Jewish Wagnerite, adulatory of the art at the expense of deep personal pain and conflict over Wagner's very crucial role in the evolution of Nazism. Should we really not be making any judgments about Wagner? Or Eliot? Or Pound? Even if we allow for the quality—to the extent of greatness—of their art, should we not make any judgments because their status as artists raises them above the fray and renders them nonaccountable? By taking such a stand, White places himself firmly in the tradition of those who have failed to condemn Wagner, Eliot, Pound, Dickens, even holy Shakespeare, for their anti-Semitism. Not calling our leading artists and politicians to account is a mistake Larry Kramer has *not* made, by and large, in his life's work on AIDS and gay people, nor in his writings about any other groups, including Jews; and it's a mistake I'm no longer making with regard to Wagner, Shakespeare, Genet, or for that matter, with Edmund and Larry. Where judgment and condemnation are appropriate, as with anyone else (how elitist to postulate that artists are better, to the extent of not having to be accountable, than everyone else!), in the spirit of Larry Kramer, I've given it. I won't do the usual literary and European "civility" thing of pretending to keep myself out of it altogether, of pretending that art is above the fray when it is often enough a major instigator and perpetrator of it. Even though Larry Kramer and Edmund White are far more important and valuable figures than I, as artists as well as leaders, I'll call them on the things they say or don't say, do or don't do, when they hurt or seem wrong. Throughout history artists have repeatedly demonstrated the triumph of art over politics, a tradition Edmund White could not be more comfortably or conservatively ensconced within. Though I'm one of the "little people" Edmund—mimicking Leona Helmsley (apparently unwittingly)—is talking about, and my moralizing about Wagner, Larry Kramer and Edmund White is not likely to have any impact on their legacies, I know it's the right, the moral, thing to do. In the spirit of Larry Kramer, I reaffirm, conclude and commence with my most heartfelt if not always politic belief that Silence = Death.

Notes

1. For elaboration of my version of Larry's conflicts with GMHC, and with me *vis-à-vis* the epidemic, see *Homosexuality and Sexuality: Dialogues of The Sexual Revolution, Volume 1* by Lawrence D. Mass (Haworth, 1990), p. 113–88. Also see my introduction to *The Golden Boy* by James Melson (Haworth, 1992).
2. Though I quickly recomposed myself to offer the far more measured—to say nothing of sane—assessment of *The Normal Heart* that is quoted in Merla, p. 47, I probably outKramered Kramer's wildest outbursts in my first gut reaction to the play. Here's what I wrote to *New York* magazine—a letter to the editor that, fortunately, was never published—following *New York*'s profile of Larry Kramer by Dinitia Smith (June 3, 1985):

    Predictably, Dinitia Smith and her editors at *New York* Magazine have "distilled" what many of us feel about Larry Kramer and his play, *The Normal*

Heart (*New York*, 6/3/85). The lies that the public is being told by Kramer and his promoters are too many and too serious to try to engage in a letter to the editor. And most of us are too busy doing unpaid and unrecognized work for the community and for the epidemic to attempt to otherwise engage Kramer in the pages of a gossip magazine. Suffice it to say that the only written statement I provided Dinitia—in the presence of Federico Gonzalez, GMHC Education Director—is the following:

"I think that Larry [Kramer] is sincerely trying to do and be for the gay movement what Hitler was sincerely trying to do and be for the Germans. Just as Hitler said and did some superficially good things for Germany, so Larry Kramer has said and done some superficially good things for gay people. (Utilizing the out-and-out lies he calls hyperpbole, Kramer is inviting the public to SCAPEGOAT a few individuals and groups as 'MURDERERS.' Like Hitler, he is saying 'THEY are to blame for all our troubles.') On the surface, and if you happen to be among the dwindling minority of persons or groups Larry isn't villifying at the moment, it's all very powerful and persuasive, so much so that I myself, whom Larry twice refers to in the play as 'our first hero,' was initially swept away by it. (Even now I find myself thinking that if it will bring *any* attention to AIDS, it can't be all bad.) I'm afraid that underneath all the altruistic bluster, however, there's nothing but fire, brimstone, and pure, unadulterated evil."

New York Magazine was right about one thing. I was indeed "honored" to finally be included (by myself if not explicitly by Kramer) among the ever-increasing ranks of those often defenseless persons and groups that have been so savagely and vindictively maligned and slandered by a rejected loner named Larry Kramer.

3. See "The Sex Vacation" by Andrew Holleran, *Flesh And The Word 3,* edited and with an introduction by John Preston with Michael Lowenthal (Plume/Penguin, 1995), pp. 323–34.

4. An early critique of Kramer's use of the Holocaust metaphor to talk about gay experience and AIDS, of what he felt was Kramer's misunderstanding of Jewish experience and inappropriate analogizing of that with gay people and AIDS— was by Seymour Kleinberg in the *New Republic* ("Life After Death," August 11, 1986).

5. When publicly accused and reprimanded by Sarah Schulman for being a closeted lesbian, Sontag did not respond. Rather, she was suddenly a leading spokesperson for what was transpiring in Bosnia. The cause she was involved with was too great and urgent to mandate a response to something so comparatively unimportant and selfish as one's sexual identity (and someone so unimportant as Schulman), a questionable business in any event (from Sontag's very constructionist milieu and presumed orientation). Once again, the affirmation of being lesbian, gay or bisexual was relegated, albeit to concerns whose worth and priority could not be argued with. See "Why I Am Not A Revolutionary" by Sarah Schulman, first published in *Publishing Triangle News*, June 1993, pp. 4–5. See also *My American History* (Routledge, 1994). Likewise in Schulman's novel, *Rat Bohemia,* there is a closeted lesbian writer whose friend, dying of AIDS, was disappointed in her inability/unwillingness to come out. See also the discussion of Sontag in "Interview With A Writer," pp. 351–4. Michelangelo Signorile, *Outweek,* "Gossip Watch." For further details and discussion, see *Contested Closets* by Larry Gross (University of Minnesota Press, 1993), pp. 171–2, n. 114.

6. David Bergman, "Larry Kramer and The Rhetoric of AIDS," from *Gaiety Trans-figured: Gay Self-Representation in American Literature* (University of Wisconsin Press, 1991), pp. 122–38.

7. *Ibid*, p. 138.

8. In 1980, several years after *Faggots* was published, I told Larry what a colleague, with whom I had attended the Gacy trial in Chicago, had to say about *Faggots*. Though it was not my own assessment, it reflected my reservations: "It would be as if James Baldwin had written what was expected to be *the* novel of emerging black consciousness and affirmation in the early 1960s—a time when the overwhelming majority of portrayals of blacks were still mired in negative stereotypes—and *all* the characters turned out to be petty welfare chislers, pimps, alcoholics and heroin addicts who do nothing but victimize each other in a 'black' comedy that is patently a screenplay entitled *Niggers*."—From *Confessions of a Jewish Wagnerite: Being Gay and Jewish in America*, by Lawrence D. Mass (Cassell, 1994), pp. 45–6. The "unanimous" rejection and failure of *Faggots* I refer to was from gay community publications and spokespersons. As Larry himself often pointed out in rebuttal, he got a lot of positive fan mail from gay men and not one, he claims, negative letter. The book itself sold well, as it continues to do. And for the current British edition, I provided the following blurb: "A generation later, *Faggots* remains the funniest, most controversial and dazzling evocation in all of gay literature, and has become an American classic."

9. Though she quotes the Anti-Defamation League in *Virtual Equality*, and her respect for the reality and history of anti-Semitism can be inferred, Urvashi Vaid does not specify anti-Semitism as a concern in her book. Nor have I heard her do so in talks or panels. Another example was Tony Kushner's Prayer for AIDS Day, which he read at a CLAGS symposium, which appealed for an end to all the isms—classism, racism, sexism, elitism . . . and any and every other form of prejudice you can think of, except . . . You guessed it. When I asked Tony (who is so extrovertedly Jewish and who does after all deal substantively with Jewishness and anti-Semitism in both parts of *Angels in America*) about this omission after his presentation, he seemed surprised. Similarly, neither CLAGS nor Outwrite, despite the participation of many Jewish writers and scholars and a scattering of minor presentations (colloquia, readings) of Jewish-themed work, has ever officially presented an event that gave real visibility to Jewish concerns—e.g., a symposium in which anti-Semitism would be given the same prominence, the same explicitness, as racism, sexism and class. As I see it, the whole situation can be summed up as follows: the relegation of anti-Semitism is the socialism of fools. My efforts to get the worlds of serious music and opera to deal more forthrightly with anti-Semitism—as with homosexuality, homophobia and AIDS—is the subject of my next collection, forthcoming from Cassell: *Musical Closets: Homosexuality, Judaism, Music and Opera*.

10. From "The High Priest of Apostasy," a review of Edmund White's *Genet* by Isabelle de Courtivron, the *New York Times* Sunday Book Review, November 7, 1993, p. 26.

PART ONE

Biography

A Normal Heart:

The Larry Kramer Story

Patrick Merla

L ARRY KRAMER is a familiar figure to millions of people who watch
television or read periodicals. When Magic Johnson announced his
positive HIV status and retirement from basketball, Ted Koppel of ABC-
TV turned to Kramer for comment on *Nightline*. When Arthur Ashe revealed that he had AIDS, BBC-TV2's *Late Night* sought Kramer's reaction.
Since the early years of the epidemic, Kramer has been interviewed on
virtually every major news and talk program as an expert on AIDS. He is
a frequent guest on *Charlie Rose*. Profiles of him have appeared in *Time*,
Newsweek, *New York*, *People*, the *Philadelphia Inquirer*, the *Los Angeles Times*,
Tikkun, *Vanity Fair*, the *New York Times*, and countless other magazines, and
he has been the subject of an hour-long documentary by the BBC.

Kramer is the founder of the two most influential AIDS organizations in
America: Gay Men's Health Crisis (GMHC) and the AIDS Coalition to
Unleash Power (ACT UP). GMHC began in Kramer's living room in 1982
with a group of six gay men and is now the largest AIDS information and
services organization in the world, the model for government and private-
sector agencies alike, with thousands of volunteers, a multi-million-dollar
budget, and its own building in New York City. Six years into the epidemic,
when governmental response was still minimal and it was clear that GMHC
would never do the political work that Kramer believed needed to be done,
he founded ACT UP. The organization grew into 100 chapters in major
cities across the United States and in Europe and has been called the most
effective grassroots political movement since the anti-Vietnam War movement of the 1960s. ACT UP's combination of street actions and media savvy
helped bring about changes at the Federal Food and Drug Administration
affecting the lives of millions of people; its Treatment and Data Committee
became so well respected that scientists and government bureaucrats sought
them out for information.

Kramer is also a successful playwright, novelist, film producer, and scriptwriter. The first film he produced and wrote, *Women in Love* (1969), garnered him an Academy Award nomination for best screenplay. His first novel, *Faggots* (1978), caused a sensation with its explicit depictions of gay life and sex and received scathing reviews, but went on to sell a half-million copies in two years and is still in print in England and the US. His play *The Normal Heart* (1985), the longest-running hit in the New York Public Theater's thirty-year history, changed the way the *New York Times* covered AIDS and received over 600 productions around the world; at this writing a film version is in the works with an internationally famous director.

Perhaps the most dramatic element of Kramer's story is his transformation from a successful businessman with a lucrative career in the most glamorous industry into a dauntless (if reluctant) street fighter and master of political rhetoric constantly at the center of debate and sought after by the media; the recipient not only of fan letters but of boxes of feces in the mail, of death threats as well as accolades—a man loved and hated, praised and vilified, often by the same people. Mention Larry Kramer's name and the first word that comes to mind is *controversial*. People who know Larry either love him or hate him. People who simply have to deal with him often feel the same way. Friends are always giving Larry chocolates because they know he likes sweets. Others send him death threats. This is a man who received a love letter from a person who had just attacked him violently in print. A man who himself publicly called his own lover a murderer when that man refused to fight the AIDS battle according to Kramer's instructions. A man who, invited to address the Gay Synagogue, criticized the Jews. Who, in answer to GMHC's conciliatory invitation to speak at its tenth anniversary gathering, told the 5,000 people assembled to hear him that he was sorry he had ever started the organization. Kramer's best friends stopped speaking to him when he made them characters in a novel, but he received thousands of letters from strangers around the world thanking him for telling the truth about their lives. When he attended the Broadway revival of *A Streetcar Named Desire*, one fan approached him and insisted that Kramer sign the program; another thanked him for standing up, years before, to a man who raised millions of dollars for anti-gay politicians but was an avid participant in Washington's gay social scene.

Here is a man who relentlessly attacked the *New York Times* at every opportunity—on television, in print, in a play—then sat down with its editors and charmed them into doing what he wanted. ("Do you know how powerful you are?" he asked, stroking their egos and appealing to their sense of responsibility.) A man who turned down the chance to direct his own script of *The Normal Heart* and suffered through two years of costly, unproductive negotiations with Barbra Streisand, then went back to the table with her five years later despite her insistence on hiring someone else to write the script if she so chose. This is the same man who listened as Streisand asked him about Bette Midler's gay following—expressing wonder at what she claimed to consider a strange phenomenon—then patiently explained to the incredulous star/director that her own gay following was probably bigger than Midler's. The same man who, when a reporter friend told him about a fan she was close to who had AIDS and was refusing to eat properly, offered to call the fan and encourage him to fight for his life.

Is Kramer merely an egotist with an endless need to assert himself, or simply a man with a vision who is no good at handling the day-to-day details of putting that vision into practice? Is he just a tireless self-promoter who knows how to manipulate the media, or a modern-day saint whose eventual martyrdom will turn him from an outspoken figure of dissent into a revered icon? Or is he something else: a combination of contradictory forces?

Kramer set out, in 1982, to form a group made up of "normal" people to whom everyone could relate, as opposed to political "crazies," and came himself to be regarded as the most radical activist of all. "We must do nothing less now than remake the soul of our time," Kramer told listeners at a gay pride rally in 1983.

How did it happen?

Childhood and Youth: "Marry Rich"

Larry Kramer was born June 25, 1935, in Bridgeport, Connecticut, the second and last child of an American Jewish father and a Russian Jewish mother. The Kramers' first son, Arthur, was born eight and a half years earlier. It was the Depression; Larry's father, George Leon Kramer, was a mostly unemployed attorney who lived away from home for two years when he worked for the Port in Boston. His mother, Rea Sara Wishengrad, taught foreigners English, sold children's shoes, and did other odd jobs to help support the family.

Both sets of grandparents ran grocery stores. After throwing her husband out for philandering, Larry's paternal grandmother singlehandedly put her two sons through Yale, a remarkable achievement in any case, given the times, but even more impressive considering that Yale was not then known for its Jewish enrollment. Rea, too, was a college graduate, of Syracuse University. The Kramers lived with Rea's mother, above her store. Although his maternal grandmother spoke little English, Larry spent much of his early years in her care while his mother was out earning a living. His grandfather was a dour man who made Kramer feel like he was constantly under foot.

In 1941, George Kramer got a job with the United States Treasury Department and moved the family to Mt. Rainier, a small town in Prince George's County, Maryland, just over the district line from Washington. George, Rea, Arthur, and Larry lived in Kaywood Gardens, an ever-expanding complex of two- and three-story brick buildings connected by underground tunnels and filled with hundreds of identical apartments. Unlike the rest of the working-class town, Kaywood Gardens was occupied by white-collar workers, civil servants, and the families of servicemen (the Kramers' neighbors included an architect, a doctor, and a captain's wife and children). As Jews, the Kramers were in a minority.

Kramer attended grade school in Mt. Rainier, but otherwise the Kaywood Gardens residents kept to themselves. When he was eight years old, a friend invited him to a puppet show at the National Theater. Kramer was entranced; every other week thereafter he went back to the theater to see whatever was playing (the program changed every two weeks). Kramer still remembers seeing Boris Karloff in *An Inspector Calls*, Cornelia Otis Skinner in *Lady Windermere's Fan*, Henry Fonda in *Mr. Roberts*, and Ezio Pinza and Mary Martin in *South Pacific*. His mother gave him the ninety cents for a ticket in the second balcony, and car fare for the long bus rides into the District. His father called him a sissy and let him know how disappointed he was in Larry's lack of interest in sports and other "manly" pursuits.

After grade school, Kramer attended Langley Junior High in the northeast sector of Washington. He was happy there, working on the student paper and appearing in the school's theatrical productions. At the urging of his brother, he continued his studies at Woodrow Wilson High School, which was academically the best school in Washington but outside the Kramers' district. In order to gain entry, Larry said he wanted to learn German (Wilson was the only school which offered it). In 1950 the family moved into the city. Unable to afford an apartment within the upper-class area in which Wilson was located, the Kramers settled in a modest apartment in the northwest sector of town.

Kramer knew no one at Wilson when he began classes there; for the first couple of months he avoided the cafeteria and ate his lunch at a drugstore off the school grounds. Rea Kramer was now running the Prince George's County chapter of the American Red Cross and teaching at the Reform Temple of the Washington Hebrew Congregation, with whose well-to-do children she encouraged Larry to socialize. (His mother's salary paid for Kramer's tuition at the Temple. His father, in turn, would remind Larry that it was just as easy to marry someone rich as someone poor.) His parents insisted that Kramer become a member of Pi Tau Pi, a fraternity of rich Jewish kids, and he found himself regularly taking three buses, an hour each way, to attend meetings, which rotated among the mansions of the other members, or weekend parties at their houses—and living in terror of the day when it would be his turn to entertain his new friends at his parents' apartment "on the wrong side of the tracks."

Even so, Kramer's fearful social life was preferable to his troubled home life. He spent most of his time alone in the apartment. His parents worked from early morning until late evening; when they were at home, they bickered constantly, which drove his brother, whom Larry adored, to stay away, often for days at a time. Kramer managed to adjust to the contradictions in his situation; he went on to become president of the Honor Society and an editor of the Wilson newspaper, and graduated thirteenth in a class of 300 students.

While he had been at Langley, Kramer had become sexually involved with one of his male friends. The boy, however, was only interested in physical release and after two years dropped Kramer, which did little to bolster Kramer's confidence in his ability to connect intimately with another person. During his time at Wilson, Kramer went out with the rich girls from Pi Tau Pi's sister sorority. His mother was thrilled; she would wait up for him at night to hear details of his dates.

In September 1953, Kramer, like his father and brother before him, entered Yale. It had not been his first choice of schools. Two of Kramer's closest friends at Wilson were going to Harvard and Kramer had applied there as well. But he couldn't afford to attend without a scholarship. When Larry gave the financial aid forms to his father for signing, George Kramer tore them up. Larry had been offered a full scholarship at the University of Pennsylvania as part of their recruitment program, but his father let him know in no uncertain terms that he had to go to Yale.

Kramer did not adjust well to the academic life at Yale. Desperately unhappy, he developed a mysterious cough and spent his first three weeks as a freshman in the infirmary. As part of his scholarship requirements Kramer had to work in a school dining hall. A star pupil at Wilson, he found himself getting failing grades at Yale. He fell behind in his studies. He switched from French to German, with a professor who had been a friend of Arthur Kramer's when he had been at Yale.

In November, Arthur got married and Larry tried to kill himself by swallowing 200 aspirin. Larry was confined to Grace–New Haven Hospital and required to talk to a psychiatrist if he wished to remain at Yale. The following April Larry's German professor seduced him and gave the willing boy his first taste of reciprocal affection from a man. The experience felt wonderful, but also frightened Larry. The professor had been awarded a Guggenheim fellowship to do research in Europe and he invited Larry to join him for the summer. Kramer said yes; then, out of fear, made arrangements instead to return to Kamp Kohut in Oxford, Maine, where he had worked before as a swimming counselor. The affair ended when the professor left for Europe without Larry. When Arthur Kramer, who remained friends with the professor, pressed Larry for an explanation as to why he had stayed behind, Larry confessed to Arthur about his relationship with the teacher. Arthur convinced his brother and their parents that Larry should go into analysis, which Rea Kramer paid for (their father would have nothing to do with it). Thus began decades of psychiatric work which would have profound effects not only on Kramer but on the lives of many other people.

What saved Kramer at Yale was singing. Early in his freshman year, he tried out for a part in the school production of a musical version of *The Great Gatsby*. When he was offered only a place in the chorus, he joined the Glee Club instead, as a second tenor. He did so well that he was accepted to the world-famous Varsity Glee Club in his sophomore term—a year earlier than usual—and to the Augmented Seven, a popular group that sang calypso and entertained at girls' schools on weekends. The Glee Club rehearsed two or three times per week and did Christmas, spring, and summer concert tours. In his junior year, Kramer starred in the production of Arthur Laurents's *Home of the Brave* at Branford College (his dormitory).

Kramer graduated from Yale in 1957 with a degree in English. Although the short story he wrote for his thesis was not well received, he didn't see it as a problem; he planned to become an actor or producer. He joined the RFA program of the army, which entailed six months active duty and five and a half years in the reserves, and did his basic training at Fort Dix, New Jersey. Afterward, he was stationed on Governor's Island in New York Harbor, in a company of 300 young men, 296 of them just out of college. On weekends, Kramer and his buddies went into the city.

Early Career: Becoming a Writer

In January 1958, Kramer began his first job, in the mailroom at the William Morris Agency in New York, at $35 per week. Six months later, after being promoted to second secretary to the head of the film department with a ten-dollar raise, he was fired. It was Kramer's twenty-third birthday; he had moved from the flat he shared with four friends from Yale into his own two-room apartment on East 50th Street and he desperately needed another job. He answered a *New York Times* ad for a "motion picture trainee" which proved to be a job running the teletype machine at Columbia Pictures. Thinking it would be a step in the wrong direction, Kramer hesitated to accept the position. When the personnel officer pointed out that the teletype room was opposite the president's office and only the top executives sent or received messages, Kramer took the job.

Kramer worked at Columbia for nine months, during which he asked for a promotion. Offered placement in either the story or advertising departments, he chose the former. He was assigned to advertising, where he discovered he had a flair for copywriting. Things went well until he pointed out that Kim Novak did not wear a bathing suit in *Bell, Book, and Candle* as depicted in the ad for the film. It was revealed that Kramer's superior had been taking credit for the copy Kramer was writing; after an investigation, Kramer was fired.

Kramer became a secretary at another agency and studied acting at night with Sidney Pollack at the Neighborhood Playhouse; he also took dance and voice classes. Then he was hired to assist Morton Gottlieb, business manager of the Cambridge Drama Festival in Massachusetts. Kramer worked with Gottlieb on three plays, including a production of *Much Ado About Nothing* starring John Gielgud and Margaret Leighton which later moved to Broadway.

At the end of the summer, Columbia Pictures offered him a job in their story department. Kramer became Columbia's "inside reader," working in a space enclosed by three filing cabinets and a mound of scripts and galleys with a man named Albert "Johnny" Johnston. Johnston taught Kramer how to evaluate material for film and to see cinematic possibilities in stories that might not immediately be apparent.

Occasionally, Kramer would sneak into the company projection room during an executive screening. Once, Mo Rothman, head of Columbia's European sales, was viewing *One Night of Love*, an old Grace Moore vehicle, spurred by the success of Columbia's romantic biography of Liszt, *Song Without End*, which was then playing to sold-out crowds at Radio City Music Hall. When the lights came up, Rothman demanded that the young man identify himself. "What do you think of remaking it?" Rothman asked. Kramer hedged a bit, answered "I'll let you know tomorrow," then stayed up all night writing a report for Rothman. The film wasn't remade, but Rothman was impressed. He recommended Kramer to M. J. Frankovich, the head of Columbia's London offices.

It was 1961. Frankovich invited Kramer to set up a story department in London. The 1960s saw the emergence of some of the major movie talents of our time and Kramer worked with many of them, on projects as different and important as *Lawrence of Arabia* (1962) and *Dr. Strangelove* (1964). During this period he met people who would become world famous, with whom he would keep in friendly touch. He was given the unprecedented license of taking properties directly to producers, directors, and stars, which resulted in such films being made as *The Collector* (1965), *The Night of the Generals* (1967), and *Accident* (1967). After Frankovich left Columbia, his successor divested Kramer of autonomy, nixing a book titled *In the Heat of the Night* which Kramer had shown to actor Sidney Poitier.

Kramer returned to New York to work as assistant to David Picker, the president of United Artists. One of the first projects he set up was *In the Heat of the Night*, starring Poitier; the film went on to win several Academy Awards. Picker, however, was used to doing things himself and Kramer quickly became bored. Expecting to be fired, he asked for a job in production. Picker gave Kramer the choice of working on a project with John Schlesinger or one with Clive Donner. Kramer had a hunch the Schlesinger movie wouldn't get made (he was right) and went with Donner. Picker phoned Donner in London and asked him to do him a favor and hire Kramer as associate producer on *Here We Go 'Round the Mulberry Bush*, a comedy about teenage sex. As severance, Picker gave Kramer "a wad of cash and a ticket back to London."

Kramer's first obstacle was the writer's unacceptable script. In those days UA did not pay for second drafts, and decided not to go forward with the film. Kramer saw his chance of becoming a producer going down the drain when Donner went off to scout locations for another project. He spent the Christmas holiday rewriting the screenplay, then put it on Donner's desk without a byline. When Donner returned and read it, he thought the script was terrific. Kramer admitted writing it and Donner sent the script to Picker for approval. The finished film was the biggest hit of the 1968 British season, outgrossing even the current James Bond installment. Kramer received screen credit for "additional dialogue."

Women in Love

While he had been at Columbia, Kramer had been instrumental in getting director Silvio Narizzano a three-picture deal. The first film had been *Die! Die! My Darling* (1965), a horror movie starring Tallulah Bankhead which became a cult favorite. The second film was *Georgy Girl* (1966), a huge hit starring Alan Bates which established the career of actress Lynn Redgrave and assured Narizzano control of future projects. Narizzano wanted to repay Kramer for his help. He told him about D. H. Lawrence's novel *Women in Love*. Kramer read the book, then paid £1,500 ("all the money he had in the world") for a one-year option, with the understanding that Narizzano would direct when the time came to film.

Narizzano left for the United States to direct *Blue*, a Western starring Terence Stamp. Kramer hired David Mercer, a Marxist with working-class roots in the same region as Lawrence, to write a script for *Women in Love*. Mercer turned in a draft that drew too heavily on his politics and not enough on his personal background. Kramer had not yet set up the film with a studio, having planned to put together a package which would get him a better deal. (In addition to Narizzano as director, he had Alan Bates for one of the leads.) Once again, he found himself faced with the possibility of a project not getting done because it had no script.

Kramer sat down to write. He showed both Mercer's script and his own (again unsigned) to Picker, who now recognized Kramer's work. Picker agreed to pay Mercer off and acquire the rights to the book, and gave Kramer a "very generous deal" to write and produce.

Suddenly Kramer found himself in a bind. Narizzano, who had brought the project to Kramer, had been plagued by personal tragedy (the breakup of his marriage and the accidental death of the male lover for whom he had left his wife), and *Blue* had turned into that year's major fiasco, running way over budget. As a result, UA would not agree to let him direct *Women in Love*. Picker advised Kramer to try to set up the deal with another studio and come back to UA if he was unsuccessful. Since Kramer had now been working on the project for two years, Narizzano agreed to bow out for a specified price, which Picker paid. The parting was friendly.

Kramer then asked, in succession, Jack Clayton (*The Pumpkin Eater*, 1964), Stanley Kubrick (*Dr. Strangelove*), and Peter Brook (*Marat/Sade*, 1967) to direct. His fourth choice was Ken Russell, director of the films *French Dressing* (1963) and *Billion Dollar Brain* (1967), but best known for his BBC biographies of composer Frederic Delius, dancer Isadora Duncan, and other artists. Russell signed on, with Bates in the role of Birkin. Kramer wanted Glenda Jackson for the role of Gudrun and Edward Fox for the role of Gerald. The studio said he could have only one. Fox, who had starred in *The Jokers* (1967) and fit Lawrence's description of the character ("blond, glacial, and Nordic"), was known to film audiences but not considered box office. The studio wanted the swarthy Oliver Reed. Jackson was a prominent member of the Royal Shakespeare Company who had gained attention in the role of Charlotte Corday in *Marat/Sade*, but she had yet to do a lead in a film. Kramer chose Jackson, on the condition that she have the varicose veins in her legs, which were "big as doorknobs," removed before filming. Jackson also had her teeth fixed for the part.

The character Ursula, Gudrun's sister and Birkin's wife, proved hardest to cast. Every actress who was offered the part, from Vanessa Redgrave to Faye Dunaway, wanted to play Gudrun, a far showier role. Finally, the costume designer told Kramer, "If you don't have your Ursula to me by Monday, she's not going to have costumes by the first day of shooting."

Kramer and Russell were screening footage of another actress when the projectionist mistakenly showed them Jennie Linden's 1967 screen test with Peter O'Toole for *The Lion in Winter*, a part she didn't get. Russell and Kramer had never heard of Linden, but were impressed enough with the screen test to drive three hours down to Reading to meet with her and offer her the role of Ursula. (Linden had just had a baby and was still nursing; coincidentally, Jackson became pregnant during the shooting of the film. "That's why there are such big breasts in *Women in Love*," explains Kramer.)

Kramer found the filming a painful experience. Reed initially said he could not work with Jackson, asserting he "could never fall in love with a girl who looked like that" as the script required, then found her to be more than a match for him as an actor. After financing the preproduction period out of his own pocket, Kramer was now obliged to risk his entire salary as producer as a completion guarantee for the film. (The production budget of $1,550,000 was tight and the movie required extensive location work; if sickness or bad weather intervened, Kramer would lose not only his money but two years' worth of effort.) The cast and director were all volatile, and having to work in isolated towns under arduous conditions and stay at uncomfortable hotels did not make things easier.

Kramer proved to be a resourceful producer, convincing Reed and Bates to defer part of their salaries, stretching the shooting schedule from thirteen and a half to sixteen weeks, and still bringing the picture in $150,000 under budget. Troubles didn't end, however, once the film was completed. The Rank theater chain, which released UA products in England, refused to book *Women in Love*. A heated clash ensued over the ad campaign (Kramer had shot his own logo—a nude couple in abstract form "*à la* Brancusi/ Rodin"—which UA wouldn't use). Although the ABC theater chain picked up the film, Kramer came away weary of the "endless chicanery" and studio politicking, feeling that producing was "a pain in the ass" and averring that "contracts are not worth the paper they're printed on ... it's all based on personal relationships, because you need them more than they need you."

"It's still not a very nice business when creative people continually have to battle with businessmen who have little understanding of their problems," Kramer told *Interview* magazine after the movie was released in the United States. "If a film turns out well, it's generally in spite of, rather than because of those responsible for its making. That's the system, and you have to work within it ... but I sometimes think I might just go off and try writing short stories or a play.

"I've cooled off a lot," Kramer continued. "I used to be very emotional, a real hothead, and I still hate all the figures—the business end of it—and someday, I'd like to be free of all that." (In later years, such remarks would become standard.)

Women in Love was released in 1969 to mixed reviews. Kramer was thirty-four years old. In 1970, the film received four Academy Award nominations: for Best Direction (Russell), Best Cinematography (Billy Williams), Best Actress (Jackson—her first Oscar), and Best Screenplay (Kramer). *Women in Love* established Russell as an innovative director and earned him a three-picture deal with UA. The film continues to earn money, and, with its frank handling of sex and love, proved to be a signal work in Kramer's writing career.

After completing *Women in Love*, Kramer spent eighteen months trying to mount a film of Yukio Mishima's novel *Forbidden Colors*, which Kramer describes as being about "homosexuality, power, and the difficulties between men and women, the story of an enormously fat heterosexual writer of genius, an old man who is very wise, and a beautiful, sexually ambivalent boy who wants this man's knowledge. The writer uses the boy as an instrument of revenge on all the women who have given him a hard time." Kramer wrote a script for Columbia, transferring the action from Japan to London; he was also scheduled to produce and direct. But the project proved too frightening for any studio and the film was never made. Kramer went on to write scripts for Arthur Penn and Chartoff/Winkler which also were not produced.

First Love and Other Fiascos

At a party in New York in 1970, Kramer met Barry Fifield, a young expatriate American, and fell hopelessly in love. Kramer was still living in London; Fifield lived in Rome. Kramer returned to the United States and settled on Long Island, in Bridgehampton. When he was nominated for the Academy Award, he and Fifield drove across country to Hollywood. (A paperweight in Kramer's living room bears the inscription "I knew before we started that it would be an interesting trip . . . Barry 6-25-71.")

Once they arrived in California, Kramer went to producer Ross Hunter to pitch an idea for a comedy set in the Parisian fashion world. Hunter wasn't interested. He opened the bottom drawer of his desk and pulled out a photograph. "The most exciting thing is happening," Hunter whispered conspiratorially. "I have obtained the rights to *Lost Horizon*. I'm going to make a musical, and I'm going to make it *here*." He pointed to the picture: the Mormon Tabernacle in Honolulu, surrounded by palm trees. Kramer had to bite his tongue to keep from laughing. "I want you to write the script if Robert Bolt isn't free, and if Erich Segal isn't free," explained Hunter.

Bolt had written the scripts for *A Man for All Seasons* and *Lawrence of Arabia*, Segal the script for *Love Story*—three hits. Like Kramer, they were represented by the William Morris Agency. Kramer's agent told him that neither Bolt nor Segal would be doing the script and pressed Kramer to accept the job. When the agent conveyed Kramer's negative response, Hunter took it for a bargaining tactic and offered more money. The more Kramer said no, the higher the offer went: $200,000 for the script (an enormous amount at the time), ancillary rights including music royalties (an unheard-of concession to a writer), and first-class air fare between London and Rome (so Kramer could be with Fifield) and Los Angeles, with lodgings in luxury hotels and all expenses paid.

Meanwhile, Kramer's home life was stormy, full of fights and breakups, with Fifield threatening to leave. Kramer accepted Hunter's offer, hoping that would save the relationship with Fifield. It didn't.

The finished film was also a disaster, critically and at the box office, despite the presence of Liv Ullmann, John Gielgud, and Michael York in the cast and songs by Burt Bacharach and Hal David. Kramer left the Morris Agency. With the help of his brother, he invested his earnings wisely and never had to hold a nine-to-five job again.

Kramer returned to New York in 1972, moving into a spacious apartment on lower Fifth Avenue in Manhattan where he still lives. In 1973 his first play, *Sissies' Scrapbook*, was given eight showcase performances at the recently founded Playwrights Horizons, which then shared space with a dance company in a gymnasium at a YWCA on Eighth Avenue and 53rd Street, with bleachers for seats.

Sissies' Scrapbook is the story of three straight men and one gay man who have been best friends since their days together at Yale. All four are emotional cripples; one of them becomes physically crippled in the second act. Kramer describes the play as being about "cowardice and the inability of some men to grow up, leave the emotional bondage of male collegiate camaraderie, and assume adult responsibilities." The immediacy of live theater and the audience response confirmed for Kramer that writing plays, rather than film scripts, was what he wanted to do. ("I was hooked," he later wrote. *"Something I had written* had been able to touch the audience. After each performance, I could see them leave the theater crying. Some of them would seek me out, still in tears. I had made people feel what I had felt, for my characters, for their stories, for what had happened to them. Heady stuff.") A revised version of the play was mounted a year later at the Theatre de Lys in Greenwich Village under the title *Four Friends* (the producer insisted on the change). "With friends like these you don't need enemies," wrote Clive Barnes in his *New York Times* review—although he arrived a half-hour late for the performance—and the producer decided to close the play.

Kramer took the play's failure as a personal rejection and vowed not to write again for the stage. He returned to film, turning out *The Big Three at Yalta* (a discotheque where the film's last scene is set), a comedy about two brothers—one straight, one gay—and their love relationships. Kramer showed the script to his agent at International Creative Management. She took it to the head of the film department, who told Kramer he could get him a million dollars if Kramer would move to Los Angeles. Kramer rented an office at MGM and waited. When nothing happened, he had anxiety attacks, which he tried to alleviate by jogging around the perimeter of the UCLA campus. That didn't work. He called his old therapist in New York, who told him to come home.

Faggots

Kramer wanted to write about gay life—the world he knew best—and no one in theater or in films thought the subject could make money. His therapist suggested he try a novel. Kramer spent the next three years writing *Faggots*, a Swiftian account of gay discotheques, bathhouses, high fashion, and pornography set in Manhattan and Fire Island Pines.

Faggots tells the story of Fred Lemish (Kramer's fictional alter ego), the author of a successful film who is trying to find a producer for a gay script and at the same time make sense out of his life in the four days before he turns forty. The novel is at once appalling and hilarious, a *tour de force* about sex without love and one man's efforts to find commitment in the face of overwhelming odds. During the writing, Kramer met the second great love of his life and found himself reenacting his first disastrous affair on an even broader scale (his new lover wanted not only to continue playing the field, including S/M, but to take Kramer with him). With the writing of Evelyn Waugh as a model, Kramer used the novel in part to work out his conflicts about the life he and most of his friends were leading. He wrote four drafts, two of which were 1,000 pages long, reducing the action from a year to four days, and dedicated the finished book to his therapist. He hoped readers would "laugh and learn."

When it was published in 1978 by Random House, *Faggots* received some good reviews but mostly was trounced in the gay and mainstream press alike: "Revolting" (*Washington Post*); "Reads like the quintessential homosexual 'how-to' manual; you cannot begin to imagine any sexual variation or game that's been left out ... quite depressing" (*Publishers Weekly*); "An outrageous look at the intricacies of gay life ... a kind of National Lampoon Guide to Gays .... In an age where gays are looking more and more for acceptance and understanding, Larry Kramer will bring them only loathing and contempt" (*Los Angeles Times*). The *New York Times* dismissed the novel as mere bad writing. One gay reviewer summed it up thus: "Unfortunately, Kramer's search [for love] is done with his eyes closed and his fly wide open.... appalling" (*Gay Community News*, Boston).

Kramer found himself shunned by his friends, who would cross the street to avoid him or ignore him at the few (and growing fewer) parties to which he still was invited. On a visit to Fire Island it was made clear that he was no longer welcome there. His best friend stopped speaking to him for years. Kramer's wounds were hardly assuaged by the fact that his novel sold 40,000 copies in hardcover and was bought for $150,000 by Warner Books, which sold 400,000 copies of the paperback edition. (The book was also published in the UK and France, where it was favorably reviewed, and has never been out of print in English.)

Despite his criticisms of the freewheeling gay sexual lifestyle, Kramer personally found it difficult to give up. "I [still] go to the baths, which I find useful," he told an interviewer. "I don't enjoy backroom bars. I love to dance. It is very, very hard to give up the life; and, especially, the deeper and deeper you get into it—it's like a narcotic."

For the next three years Kramer kept a low profile, using the time to work on a new novel. He kept in close touch with his editor about the sales of the paperback edition of *Faggots*, urging Warner to convince retailers to restock the book when it invariably sold out (some dealers had problems with the title). He corresponded with his French publisher about the translator, insisting that he have final approval of their choice even though he didn't read French, relying on friends such as poet and translator Richard Howard for guidance.

Birth of an Activist

In the summer of 1980, Kramer witnessed a disturbing sight on Fire Island: a man carrying his delirious lover in his arms, asking people, "Does anyone know what's wrong with Nick? I've been to doctors and hospitals and no one knows." Nick subsequently died of cat scratch fever, an unusual condition rarely fatal to humans. A year later Kramer read an article in the back pages of the *New York Times* headlined "Rare Cancer Seen in 41 Homosexual Men." He called up Lawrence Mass, a doctor friend who wrote about medical issues for the *New York Native*, a recently founded newspaper targeted to the gay and lesbian community. Mass was the first reporter— medical or other—to write about the AIDS epidemic in any media. He suggested that Kramer go to see Dr. Alvin Friedman-Kien, the dermatologist at New York University Medical Center who had treated many of the cases and who was quoted in the *Times* article. At Friedman-Kien's office Kramer encountered two friends who had been diagnosed with the "rare cancer" (Kaposi's sarcoma, an uncommon and atypical form of malignancy in the US, where it usually afflicted the elderly and was seldom fatal). Both friends would be dead by the end of the year. Friedman-Kien told Kramer these cases were just the tip of the iceberg and suggested that Kramer, because of his high visibility as the author of *Faggots*, should warn the gay community about the impending danger. Kramer agreed to hold a meeting to help raise money for Friedman-Kien's research.

On August 11, 1981, Friedman-Kien addressed eighty men assembled in Kramer's apartment; $6,635 was raised. On Labor Day weekend, with 15,000 revelers on hand the most profitable three days of the summer season,

Kramer and several dozen men attempted to raise more money at Fire Island. A six-page brochure including a reprint of a feature article by Mass from the *Native* was placed in front of every door in the Pines and Cherry Grove, the island's two predominantly gay communities, with instructions on how to contribute to Friedman-Kien's research. Kramer and two friends stood at the door of the Ice Palace, the most popular discotheque in the Pines, with a box for donations. Thousands of men passed by going in and out of the disco; Kramer and his friends collected $126. The total take for the weekend was $769.55.

The following week a "personal appeal," written by Kramer with the input of Mass, appeared in the *Native*, asking readers for money for Fried-man-Kien's work. "It's difficult to write this without sounding alarmist or too emotional or just plain scared," Kramer wrote. "It's easy to become frightened that one of the many things we've done or taken over the past years may be all that it takes for a cancer to grow from a tiny something-or-other that got in there who knows when from doing who knows what."

Kramer was immediately attacked in the *Native*'s letters column. "Read anything by Kramer closely," wrote Robert Chesley, citing *Faggots*. "I think you'll find the subtext is always: the wages of gay sin are death."

Chesley was a playwright who had interviewed Kramer at the time *Faggots* was first published. The two had wound up in bed when they finished talking; Kramer regretted it immediately and decided not to sleep with Chesley again. When Kramer discouraged his further advances, Chesley published a long, highly unsympathetic piece in *Gaysweek* (a now-defunct periodical), despite the fact that, during their meeting, he had told Kramer he agreed with the stance taken in the novel—and reiterated the same in a note he sent to Kramer with a gift after the interview appeared. Three years later, Chesley was attacking him again.

Kramer complained to his therapist about Chesley's hypocrisy; the therapist counseled Kramer to "stop *kvetching* and do something." Kramer responded with a long letter in the *Native* exposing his relationship with Chesley, detailing the fund-raising efforts on Friedman-Kien's behalf, and quoting from rave reviews of *Faggots* in the British and French press.

"I'm not interested in sin," wrote Kramer. "I am interested in the difficulties people have in loving each other; I am also interested in how we use sex as a weapon, and I think anyone will find that all my writing, including my adaptation of *Women in Love*, concerns itself with explorations of these subjects....Why is Bob Chesley attacking me? Why is he not attacking the CDC [Centers for Disease Control] for taking so long to prepare their epidemiological studies? Why is he not attacking the National Cancer Institute and the American Cancer Society for showing so little interest in KS and forcing Dr. Friedman-Kien to wait months and possibly years for them to fund his research, which has already produced interesting results?"

The CDC had declared an official epidemic in June. Kramer's letter appeared in December. By that time, $11,806.55 had been raised for the NYU Medical Center's Kaposi's Sarcoma Fund, most of it on that first night in August and half of it from a few individuals. Kramer realized that there was more to be done than simply raising money for one doctor's research.

GMHC

On January 4, 1982, Kramer held another meeting in his living room, which was attended by Lawrence Mass, Nathan Fain (a writer/editor), Paul Popham (a publishing executive and former Green Beret), Paul Rapoport (a rich investor and the lover of one of the two men from Friedman-Kien's office who had died), and Edmund White (another novelist who would become famous for his writing). When Kramer suggested they broaden their activities and form a new organization, Rapoport observed, "Gay men certainly have a health crisis."

"That's our name!" responded Kramer.

Thus Gay Men's Health Crisis was born. An organization started, not by the "political crazies" prevalent in other gay groups, but by attractive, socially active, successful gay men with whom most other gay men should easily be able to relate. An organization that would let those gay men know that what they were doing sexually might be endangering their lives, and that they could take action to end the epidemic and stop the spread of disease. An organization that would not only change the lives of individual gay people for the better, but also force the government to respond to their health crisis—and in the process accept gay people as part of society. At least, that was Kramer's vision for GMHC.

The six founders immediately went about recruiting members for their organization. One of these, Rodger McFarlane, set up a telephone hotline to answer questions and established the organization's patient services, an area in which GMHC would become a model for hundreds of other organizations. GMHC published a newsletter (which subsequently was requested by the Library of Congress), held public forums for disseminating information, and created a training program for crisis-intervention volunteers which has become world famous.

Not without difficulties, Kramer arranged for his brother's prestigious law firm to represent GMHC on a *pro bono* basis. Arthur Kramer felt that an illness affecting gay men was not his issue; Larry insisted that the law firm take on GMHC for exactly that reason. The brothers fought; Larry threatened to stop speaking to Arthur. One of Arthur's partners gave Larry what Arthur wouldn't.

On April 8, 1982, GMHC held its first fund-raiser—at the Paradise Garage, a discotheque that had seen better days. It was Good Friday; only 500 tickets had been sold, which had the event's organizers worried. But crowds started arriving well before the doors opened, queuing up in lines down the block. Within a few hours, the benefit committee had taken in $52,000. In February 1983, GMHC published the second issue of its newsletter, edited by Kramer, which was sixty-two pages long and numbered 25,000 copies. On April 30, the organization held another fund-raiser, a sold-out performance of the Ringling Bros. Barnum & Bailey Circus at Madison Square Garden.

Sixteen months after its founding in Kramer's living room, GMHC had become the largest AIDS services organization in the world. But Kramer was no longer associated with it. What had caused them to part company?

Kramer's vision of GMHC as an "advocacy group to spread information and fight in every way to help the living keep living" was not shared by his fellow board members. Instead, GMHC had evolved into a social services agency run by people who did not wish to call attention to themselves. (Some of them were still in the closet at work and feared losing their jobs— including Paul Popham, GMHC's first president, who once suggested crossing out by hand the word *gay* in the organization's name on 10,000 envelopes because he feared his mailman would realize he was homosexual.) Kramer advocated confrontational tactics; the rest of GMHC's board shied away, or found them distasteful. Kramer insisted that the organization issue safe-sex guidelines, and was unhappy when the guidelines they did issue weren't more explicit and seemed overly concerned with appearing alarmist or anti-sex (the viral cause of AIDS had not yet been discovered).

As the only board member willing to be publicly identified with GMHC, Kramer had become their media spokesman by default, although he relished the job and probably would have wanted to do it anyway. His angry attacks on the mayor (he called Ed Koch a pig on the *Today* show) and other government officials for their lack of response to the health crisis were seen by the other board members as counterproductive. Kramer had found himself fighting with the board, agitating for them to become a powerful pressure group and force the city into providing services gay people were paying for with their tax dollars but not receiving. After each fight someone would quit the board and be replaced.

Kramer's main opponent was Paul Popham, the former Green Beret who had been elected president of GMHC. Popham, a handsome father figure with Everyman appeal, was adamant about keeping a low profile and working within the system. ("I'd been a producer," Kramer later explained. "I thought I was producing GMHC. He'd been an army officer. Both of us were accustomed to getting results and, in very different fashions, having our own way.") It didn't help matters that Kramer had a crush on Popham, which made Popham uncomfortable.

Seasoned activists and newcomers who shared Kramer's desire for more aggressive, political tactics felt left out of GMHC, which had become known as an elitist organization. Together with Kramer, these people had formed the AIDS Network. They met once a week at 8:00 a.m., after which members went to their day jobs. On March 3, 1983, the AIDS Network had sent a letter to Mayor Koch outlining twelve requests and demands, from the mayor's announcing a public health emergency and allocating funds for research, to his putting pressure on the state and federal goverments to do likewise, to establishing a special office to address the health crisis and providing public assistance and private insurance for those afflicted. Written mostly by Kramer, the letter also called for the city to donate a building to house the rapidly expanding GMHC and other gay organizations.

The mayor did not even acknowledge receipt of the letter.

Kramer decided something more drastic was needed. The front page of the March 14–27, 1983 issue of the *Native* carried a huge headline: "1,112 and Counting," the title of a long essay by Kramer delineating the spread of the epidemic, the inadequacies of the health care system, the lack of governmental response, and, perhaps most alarming of all, the apparent indifference of most people in the gay community.

"If this article doesn't scare the shit out of you, we're in real trouble," wrote Kramer. "If this article doesn't rouse you to anger, fury, rage, and action, gay men have no future on this earth. Our continued existence depends on just how angry you can get."

At GMHC's insistence, Kramer included a disclaimer that he was speaking only for himself, not for the organization. He ended the essay with a list of twenty of his friends who had died, and called for volunteers for civil disobedience. As a result, fifty people showed up for a training session with a man who had worked with Martin Luther King Jr. Although not the hundreds Kramer had hoped for, it was enough. On Sunday, April 10 (two weeks before GMHC's circus benefit), a group of twenty protesters stood in torrential rain picketing an AIDS conference being held at Lenox Hill Hospital on Manhattan's Upper East Side. Inside the building were Mayor Koch and Terence Cardinal Cooke; a letter from Senator Edward Kennedy was read aloud to the attendees. The conference got media coverage—and so did the angry picketers and their provocative placards.

After nearly two years of silence from the mayor and opposition from GMHC, Kramer's efforts finally paid off. The day after the pickets, Koch agreed to meet with ten people from the gay community to discuss the AIDS crisis, including two from GMHC. Knowing it was primarily because of his efforts that this meeting was taking place, Kramer assumed that he would be one of GMHC's representatives. When he arrived at the morning meeting of the AIDS Network where participants were to be selected, Kramer discovered he was wrong. GMHC's board was afraid he would yell at the mayor if given the chance; behind Kramer's back, they had voted to send Popham with a part-time volunteer.

Enraged and hurt by what he took to be personal betrayal, Kramer threatened to resign from GMHC's board of directors if he was not included in the meeting with Koch. The AIDS Network offered to let Kramer go as one of their representatives, but Kramer stood on principle and insisted he go with GMHC. Popham would not budge. Kramer resigned, although several gay leaders begged him to reconsider.

Kramer went back to work on his novel, tried it as a screenplay, then again as a novel. At the few GMHC social functions he attended, he found himself standing on one side of the room while the board stood on the other, avoiding him. So he sat at home feeling like a pariah, missing his involvement with GMHC. "1,112 and Counting" had been reprinted in nearly every gay newspaper in the United States, making it "inarguably one of the most influential works of advocacy journalism of the decade . . . irrevocably alter[ing] the context in which AIDS was discussed in the gay community and, hence, in the nation," as Randy Shilts would later write in his best-selling book about the AIDS crisis, *And the Band Played On*. Having lost his official soapbox, however, Kramer found that it was easier to be taken seriously by the media when he was affiliated with an established organization. He had been disenfranchised.

Realizing he had made a mistake, Kramer tried to regain his seat three times during the ensuing months, going so far as to commandeer the DJ's booth at a popular discotheque and urge the dancers on the floor to insist that he be reinstated to GMHC's board. His efforts resulted in a board vote in early February 1984, at which Kramer's request was overwhelmingly rejected. (Popham said Kramer would return to GMHC "over his dead body.") Kramer responded with a letter in which he called the board a "bunch of ninnies, incompetents, and cowards." The equally angry board would not be moved.

The board's wrath may have been fueled in part by the fact that, although every one of the 18,000 seats at Madison Square Garden had been filled at the benefit held nine months earlier and Leonard Bernstein had conducted the national anthem, the mainstream press had stayed away. Only gay periodicals covered the event. However disagreeable his methods, Kramer had been undeniably effective in attracting media attention for GMHC (which is not to say that he would have succeeded in getting the straight press to the Garden). At the benefit, Popham generously had announced that Kramer was leaving GMHC to take a rest, and thanked him on behalf of the board for all his efforts.

The Normal Heart

After resigning from GMHC, Kramer remained in New York until June 1983, when he had promised to address the Gay Pride Day rally. In his speech he railed against Koch, calling the mayor a "heartless, selfish son of a bitch," but apologized to anyone in the gay community whose feelings he might have hurt by his actions, explaining, "I am by nature an impatient man." As he would continue doing for years, he urged listeners to become involved, telling them, "We must do nothing less now than remake the soul of our time." After the speech, he took a plane to London, the site of his first great success, a city he loved. He planned to spend the summer there, hoping things would sort themselves out.

They did, but not as he expected.

In London, Kramer attended a lot of political theater and was reminded of how much he had enjoyed his experience with *Sissies' Scrapbook*. He began to think he could make sense of his experiences with GMHC by writing a play. He set to work. Then some "inner direction" told him to go to Germany. He wound up at Dachau, where he was amazed to find that the death camp had been opened in 1933. Where had the United States been until 1941? Had no one cared? Now the same disregard was occurring with AIDS. Kramer decided he must do something about it. He would make people care. He returned home and started researching, discovering parallels between the gay community during the AIDS crisis and the Jewish community in America during the 1930s. He rented a shack on the beach at Cape Cod and finished the first draft of his play.

Kramer gave a copy of his play to Rodger McFarlane (who was now the executive director of GMHC and Kramer's live-in lover) to read, and sent another to Peggy Ramsay, his London agent, who represented many of Britain's leading playwrights (including the late Joe Orton). Then he went off to a friend's log cabin two hours south of Washington to write a second draft.

Although Ramsay responded positively, no New York agent would agree to handle the play. Kramer personally sent the revised script to three top directors—Tommy Tune, Mike Nichols, and Arthur Penn—all of whom liked it but declined to direct. He submitted it to producers in New York and to regional theater companies, as well as to *American Playhouse* and PBS. Everyone turned it down. Then Kramer gave the play to Emmett Foster, a GMHC volunteer and the personal assistant to Joseph Papp, impresario of New York's Public Theater. Foster showed it to his boss.

When he didn't hear anything, the impatient Kramer started sending Papp letters: "Mike Nichols said this." "Why aren't you doing my play?" "Why don't I hear from you?"—what Kramer himself calls "the Larry

Kramer school of outreach." Finally, A. J. Antoon, who had directed the Public Theater's Pulitzer Prize-winning hit *That Championship Season*, said he would like to do Kramer's play.

Kramer worked with Gail Merrifield, the head of the Public Theater's play department and Papp's wife, on six or seven drafts, then with dramaturg Bill Hart on ten more. But the Public still had not committed to do the play, and Kramer continued showing it to other producers. Marshall W. Mason wanted to do it at Circle Repertory Company; Jack Lawrence offered to put it in the Broadway theater that then bore his name. Kramer decided to stay at the Public.

The play was eventually scheduled for an August 1984 opening, with Antoon directing. When it was postponed until November, Antoon had to step aside due to prior commitments. Then the play was postponed again, until January 1985.

Meanwhile, Kramer had not altogether given up AIDS activism.

In November 1983, not long after he returned from Europe, Kramer had written an article to be printed as an ad in the *Village Voice*: "2,339 and Counting"—more than twice the number of cases reported at the time of his *Native* article in March, with 945 people dead. Kramer blasted the *Voice* for its lack of AIDS coverage. He urged readers to attend another GMHC fund-raiser at Madison Square Garden—the rodeo this time—to which 12,000 tickets remained to be sold. Kramer wrote the article at the request of McFarlane. The $4,000 cost of the ad was paid anonymously by a GMHC board member and his lover who had kept in touch with Kramer.

While his American agent had been reading the first draft of the play (before declining to represent it), Kramer had gone to Atlanta, where one top staffer in the CDC's AIDS Activities Offices suggested that if gay men had married women, the AIDS epidemic would never have happened. Kramer also heard a lot about rivalry between the CDC and the National Institutes of Health. ("We don't even talk to them," admitted one CDC official.)

In January 1984, a congressional staffer had arranged for Kramer to visit the home of the director of one of the largest, most prestigious NIH institutes, who lived in a mansion on the NIH grounds in Bethesda, Maryland. During lunch, the director's top assistant confided to Kramer, "My friend and I loved *Faggots*. We'd love to have you to dinner next time you're in town." "Is that one of the reasons this institute has been so negligent with AIDS—because the director is in the closet?" Kramer asked. The embarrassed assistant did not reply.

For Kramer it was yet another example of an individual's self-hatred having disastrous results for the larger gay community. Perhaps the worst offender was Terry Dolan, the fund-raiser for the National Conservative Political Action Committee and therefore one of the most influential gay men in America. Dolan had personally raised ten million dollars for Ronald

Reagan's presidential campaign. At the time of Kramer's visit to Bethesda, Dolan had just completed an affair with an epidemiologist from the New York City Department of Health who was a friend of Kramer's. Although Dolan made his living supporting anti-gay candidates, he was an active participant in Washington's gay social scene. A few days before lunching with the NIH official, Kramer had spotted Dolan at a DC cocktail party. "How dare you come here?" Kramer screamed, throwing a glass of water in Dolan's face. "You take the best from our world and then do all those hateful things against us. You should be ashamed."

Five months later, in June 1984, Kramer had stood outside an AIDS conference at New York University distributing a letter addressed to the *New York Times*, GMHC, the National Gay Task Force, New York City's Commissioner of Health and Director of the Office of Gay and Lesbian Health, and Mayor Koch, all of whom he accused of being "equal to murderers" due to their lack of coverage of, and inadequate response to, the AIDS crisis. Kramer then went inside and disrupted the conference, telling participants they were missing the "really important" issues (as outlined in his letter). By his own admission, Kramer's reputation was now "completely that of a crazy man."

He applied the same intensity to his play, which needed a new director now that Antoon had dropped out of the picture. Kramer wanted Michael Lindsay-Hogg, who had directed episodes of the popular television miniseries *Brideshead Revisited* and the Broadway hits *Agnes of God* and *Whose Life Is It, Anyway?* After a frantic search Kramer finally tracked down Lindsay-Hogg, who was in New York for a day, and messengered the play to him. Lindsay-Hogg read it immediately and responded with passion. But Papp preferred using people he knew. Although Lindsay-Hogg's mother, Geraldine Fitzgerald, did have an association with the theater, her son had never worked at the Public. Kramer arranged a meeting between the producer and the director, and Papp agreed to hire Lindsay-Hogg.

By now Kramer and McFarlane had split up. Their personal relationship had made it impossible for McFarlane to win the complete confidence of GMHC's board, particularly Paul Popham. At one point, Popham even asked the board to evaluate McFarlane's performance (they found that McFarlane was doing the work of ten people). When Kramer's repeated attempts to regain his seat on GMHC's board all failed, he took his frustration out on his lover, angrily insisting that McFarlane threaten to quit unless the board reinstated Kramer. By 1984, McFarlane had had enough. "I am living with this man and then going to work and reading letters, in the press as well as to my closest colleagues and friends, saying that I'm a murderer," McFarlane explains. "I'd had two years of Larry Kramer screaming and I just couldn't take it any longer."

As the play finally went into rehearsal, Kramer called McFarlane and said, "I need you." McFarlane served as a consultant on the production and contributed a fact sheet on AIDS which was handed out with programs. This so angered Paul Popham that he recommended McFarlane be fired from GMHC. But Popham was only posturing. McFarlane had already tendered his resignation and was in the process of training a successor when Kramer called to ask for help—which was why McFarlane felt free to say yes. The play opened at the Public Theater on April 21, 1985, with Kramer's aged mother in the audience. Two months later, as planned, McFarlane was gone from GMHC.

The Normal Heart (the title is taken from a line in W. H. Auden's political poem "September 1, 1939") tells the story of a GMHC-like organization and the conflict between one of its founders, Ned Weeks, and the board of directors, set against the story of Weeks and his lover, Felix, a society reporter for the *New York Times* who is dying of the illness Weeks's organization was created to fight. AIDS is never mentioned by name; Kramer uses the condition to create a metaphor of how people respond to crisis, personally and bureaucratically.

Lest anyone imagine that the play is about something else, however, in addition to McFarlane's fact sheet, AIDS statistics were written in chalk on the blackened walls of the Public Theater and updated each week by crossing out the old number and adding the new, higher number below it. Also on the walls (as in the fact sheet) were details of the *New York Times*'s coverage of AIDS compared to other medical crises. During three months in 1982, the *Times* had printed fifty-four articles about the Tylenol-poisoning scare (four on the front page), in which only seven people had died. During the first fourteen months of the AIDS epidemic, with 958 cases reported throughout the United States and thousands more in Africa, Europe, and elsewhere, the *Times* had written about the situation only seven times, never on the front page. In 1984, the coverage was better (forty-one articles), but still woefully inadequate compared to the 163 articles published during the same period in the *San Francisco Chronicle*, in a city with fewer AIDS cases than in New York, which had the highest incidence in the country. Actual copies of the *New York Native*, referred to throughout the play, were used in the production.

The Normal Heart is as unflattering to Ned Weeks as it is to the perceived faults of the organization he is unable to shape to his wishes. It is also evenhanded and sympathetic in its portrayal of different positions on sexual freedom and promiscuity (Ned and Felix become lovers despite the dangers in their having sex), and a fierce indictment of the government's non-response to the health emergency because it is primarily afflicting gay men.

"I tried to make Ned Weeks as obnoxious as I could," Kramer explains. "He isn't my idea of a hero. He fucks up totally. He yells at his dying lover and screams and rants and raves at and against everyone and everything else and gets tossed out of 'the organization' on his ass. I was trying, somehow and again, to atone for my own behavior. I tried to make Bruce Niles, the Paul Popham character, the sympathetic leader he in fact was. I hoped Paul would come and see the play, which he would not do, and be honored. But I also wanted to show that these were our fights that kept us diminished and divided. I think they're fights not dissimilar to those in any growing organization, gay or straight, and that they probably can't be avoided, or afforded."

One fallout from the play (added to Kramer's other political writing) was his being pegged as an advocate of celibacy.

"I don't think I ever advocated that, or urged anything but caution, and 'cooling it,'" he later wrote. "Characters in *The Normal Heart* may have said other things (as they did and do in real life), but it's a selfish and vicious critic who can so yank a line or two of dialogue out of context to nail the author with it as his sworn message. I was against promiscuity long before *The Normal Heart*; I believe being gay offers much more than that. But proponents (even in this age of AIDS) of promiscuity—which is far different from sexual freedom, which I, of course, support—have made me their enemy. I do confess to not knowing where one draws the line between caution and disregard. That is everyone's personal decision to make when he or she is completely informed of all that is known. But I am not so dumb as to believe that an entire population can stop having sex. Nor do I think it's healthy for many that they do so."

In the end, Kramer says, he wrote *The Normal Heart* "to make people cry: AIDS is the saddest thing I'll ever know. I also wrote it to be a love story, in honor of a man I loved who died. I wanted people to see on a stage two men who loved each other. I wanted people to see them kiss. I wanted people to see that gay men suffering and gay men dying are just like everyone else."

Papp called *The Normal Heart* one of the most important plays he had ever produced in his thirty-odd-year career and said he would keep it running for as long as audiences came to see it. To Kramer he sent a personal note: "Once every ten years or so a play comes along that fulfills my original idea of what role my theater must play in society. *The Normal Heart* is that play—and it fills me with pride (and tears) in being the producer of this play. Thank you, dear friend, for your noble fire."

Audiences came to see *The Normal Heart* for nearly a year—longer than any other production at the Public Theater before or since. The play was, for the most part, favorably reviewed, except in the *Times* and the *Village Voice* (in whose pages one reviewer wrote, "Kramer argues that sexual adventurism makes intimacy impossible, and saps away the energy gays might use to fight for civil rights. This looks like the plague metaphor in drag"). A few gay periodicals accused Kramer of writing a self-serving revenge play with himself as the hero and the GMHC board as villains. Although the *Times* went so far as to print a disclaimer about Kramer's assertions at the end of Frank Rich's less-than-rave review, an argument can be made that the success of *The Normal Heart* and its revelations about the *Times*'s previous response resulted in the paper's fuller coverage of AIDS.

Kramer found the process of mounting the play a mixed blessing. Exciting as it was to hear his words brought to life on stage, the same vitality forced him to relive some of the most painful experiences of his life. At one point in rehearsals, watching Brad Davis as Ned Weeks hold his dying lover in his arms, Kramer was overcome by personal memories. He ran to the men's room and sank to the floor, sobbing. Suddenly he found himself cradled in Davis's arms; having finished the scene, the actor had gone to the lavatory, discovered Kramer, and sought to comfort him. The two of them huddled together on the floor, crying uncontrollably. (Davis and Kramer were close friends. The actor had appeared in *Sissies' Scrapbook* and *Four Friends* before moving to Los Angeles and becoming a film star.)

Kramer wasn't the only person affected by the play's verisimilitude. At an early preview, Lawrence Mass became so upset he had to be escorted out of the theater by his lover and friends, although he returned a few minutes later and attended a subsequent performance. When later interviewed by *The Advocate*, Mass admitted that as a co-founder of GMHC who had known Kramer for nearly twenty years and as one of the models for a character in the play, he couldn't be objective.

"As an historical documentary that purports to detail exactly how GMHC evolved, what this organization has or has not achieved, what other organizations did or did not do, and the complex role Larry Kramer actually played in it all, *The Normal Heart* promulgates a number of sometimes patently self-aggrandizing, sometimes stridently polemical distortions, simplifications, and untruths," observed Mass. "However, while broadcasting just how serious this epidemic is and how much worse it's going to get, *The Normal Heart* speaks more persuasively than any other book, film, or play of recent years about such long-standing and entangled crises as gay self-hatred, the closetedness of powerful homosexuals, the dearth of visible gay leadership, and the underlying homophobia of society at large. As a semi-fictional docudrama that reveals, sometimes unwittingly, the most devastating truths about the state of our so-called community today, *The Normal Heart* is, I think, explosively powerful and uniquely important."

The Normal Heart went on to receive over 600 productions in the United States, England, Ireland, South Africa, Israel, Russia, Australia, and Poland (where the play was shown on television). In addition to Brad Davis, the part of Ned Weeks has been played in major productions by Richard Dreyfuss, Tom Hulce, John Shea, Joel Grey, and Martin Sheen. Two years of negotiations with Barbra Streisand, who planned to produce and direct the film and act the role of Dr. Emma Brookner, resulted in no deal, although Kramer wrote two drafts of a script for her with no contract (and no payment) and spent $20,000 in legal fees in efforts to reach a mutually acceptable agreement. In 1989, Paul Maslansky, producer of the popular *Police Academy* series of comedy films, tried to set up a deal to shoot the film with Kramer as director; but Kramer felt that a Streisand production would

get more attention and decided to wait and hope that things would work out
with her.

ACT UP

With *The Normal Heart* safely launched on stage, Kramer began work on
several new plays and returned to agitating. At the invitation of *Village Voice*
editor Robert Friedman, an acquaintance of Kramer's who had been hired
by the new owner, Leonard Stern (himself the business partner of one of
Kramer's closest friends), Kramer had been submitting story ideas about the
AIDS crisis to the *Voice*, along with the names of possible writers. When
none of them was used, Kramer published an attack on the *Voice* in the
March 17, 1986 issue of the *Native*.

"For the life of me," wrote Kramer, "I can't understand why the *Village
Voice* is so stinking awful on gay issues in general and AIDS in particular. I
can see no reason for any gay person to read this paper; in fact, I think we
should avoid it at present." Kramer also called Richard Goldstein, the *Voice*'s
openly gay senior editor, an Uncle Tom. (Goldstein had veto power over all
stories about gay issues and AIDS; he went on to become the *Voice*'s executive editor.)

Unable to affect policy from inside the organization, Kramer used his
access to the *Native* (then arguably the most influential gay publication in
the United States and the only gay newspaper in New York City) to exert
pressure on GMHC from the outside. Paul Popham had been diagnosed with
AIDS in 1984 and was no longer bureaucratically involved. Although he and
Kramer still were not speaking to each other, mutual friends told Kramer
that Popham now supported his criticisms of GMHC, particularly of Richard
Dunne, McFarlane's successor as executive director. When a GMHC board
member with whom Kramer had kept in touch called him confidentially with
a list of complaints, claiming there was great dissatisfaction among GMHC's
staff and volunteers, Kramer published an open letter to Dunne and GMHC
outlining the complaints and calling for organizational changes.

The letter appeared in the January 20, 1987 issue of the *Native*; for weeks
afterward the paper's letters column was filled with responses from everyone
except GMHC. In the February 16 issue, Kramer followed up with an open
letter to Tim Sweeney, GMHC's deputy director for public policy. "When I
am asked why I write at such a high pitch of invective, my response is that
this seems to be the only way I can get anyone to hear me. Calmer letters
always go unanswered," wrote Kramer. He subsequently met with Dunne
and established a working relationship with GMHC's new board president,

Nathan Kolodner. As a result, GMHC created an Office of Medical Information, with Kramer's friend Barry Gingell, a doctor who had received national media coverage when he went to Mexico to get unauthorized drugs to treat AIDS patients, at its head. Gingell immediately began publishing *Treatment Issues: The GMHC Newsletter of Experimental AIDS Therapies*, in which he criticized the National Institutes of Health and Federal Food and Drug Administration. It was a small victory and Kramer remained unsatisfied.

The Normal Heart was about to be produced at the Alley Theater in Houston. Kramer received repeated invitations from Mary Lou Galantino, the physical therapy coordinator at the Institute for Immunological Disorders there, to come to Houston, see the play, and visit the Institute. Galantino convinced the theater to pay Kramer's airfare and expenses, and he gave in.

Kramer's visit to Houston coincided with an invitation from the New York Gay and Lesbian Community Services Center to address their monthly speakers' series at their building in Greenwich Village. Writer Nora Ephron had canceled at the last minute and they needed someone to fill in. Kramer had no idea what he would talk about, and didn't particularly want to make a speech. As far as he was concerned, he'd said everything he had to say too many times; there was nothing new to talk about. Then he went to Houston.

The Institute for Immunological Disorders was a brand-new hospital devoted solely to the treatment and research of AIDS. Kramer was given a tour by Dr Peter Mansell, who ran the Institute, and learned that only sixteen of the hospital's 150 beds were filled. Mansell explained to Kramer that in Texas the state did not cover medical costs of people who had no insurance; as a result, Mansell was treating patients for free and the hospital, a for-profit corporation, was in danger of going out of business (which it subsequently did). The Federal Government, which had awarded a school on Long Island $600,000 to study AIDS stress among college students, was doing nothing to save the country's only AIDS hospital.

Kramer had his subject. When he got back to New York, he called everyone he could think of and told them to be at the Center on Tuesday, March 10, to hear him make an important announcement. He called all his contacts in the media and notified the offices of New York's Governor Mario Cuomo, Senators Alfonse D'Amato and Daniel Patrick Moynihan, and Mayor Koch, all of which refused to send anyone. As in the past with so many important events during the AIDS crisis, only the gay media showed up. But word of mouth spread and the hall was packed with over 300 people.

Kramer began his speech by asking everyone on the left side of the hall—two-thirds of those present—to stand up. When they did, he told them they could all be dead in five years.

"Let me rephrase my *Native* article of 1983," said Kramer. "If my speech tonight doesn't scare the shit out of you, we're in real trouble. If what you're hearing doesn't rouse you to anger, fury, rage, and action, gay men will have no future here on earth. How long does it take before you get angry and fight back?"

Given Kramer's five-year struggle with GMHC, no one could accuse him of barnstorming. It was 1987; the epidemic which had started with forty-one cases now numbered over 37,000 cases and more than 16,000 deaths. Kramer went on to tell the audience about the unutilized Institute in Houston and to list the government's continuing incompetence and refusal to release possible lifesaving drugs.

"I came back from Houston and I called people I haven't spoken to in many years," said Kramer. "I called Paul Popham. Those of you who are familiar with the history of GMHC and with *The Normal Heart* will know of the fights that he and I had and the estrangement of what had once been an exceptionally close friendship. Paul is very ill now. He and I spoke for over an hour. It was as if it were the early days of GMHC again, and we were planning strategy of what had to be done. We talked not about the hurts that each had caused the other. He supported me in everything that I am saying tonight, and that I have been writing about in the *Native* in recent issues. He would be here tonight, except that he had chemotherapy today. He asked me to say some things to you. 'Tell them we have to make gay people all over the country cooperate. Tell them we have to establish some way to cut through all the red tape. We have to find a way to make GMHC, the AIDS Action Council, and the other AIDS organizations stronger and more political.'" (Popham's condition had prompted him finally to become politically involved; he had even gone to Washington to testify before a Congressional hearing on AIDS, something he would never have done when he was president of GMHC.)

Kramer told the crowd he had invited them to the Center to seek their input and advice on rethinking the structure of the gay and lesbian community.

"It's easy to criticize GMHC," said Kramer. "It's easier to criticize, period. It's harder to do things. Every one of us here is capable of doing something. Of doing something strong. We have to go after the FDA—fast. That means coordinated protests, pickets, arrests. Are you ashamed of being arrested? ...Well, until we do [get arrested], I don't have to tell you what's going to happen."

Seated in the audience was Martin Sheen, star of the London production of *The Normal Heart*, who was known for his anti-nuclear activism. Kramer introduced Sheen, explaining, "He uses his name and his fame to help make this world a better place. The best man at Martin's wedding, his oldest friend, died today, from AIDS."

Kramer's speech was followed by a discussion at which it was agreed to hold another meeting two nights later. At that meeting, the AIDS Coalition to Unleash Power (ACT UP) was established as an ad hoc community group to fight for the release of experimental drugs. A demonstration was planned for Tuesday morning, March 24, on Wall Street, to protest the FDA's inadequate response to the AIDS crisis. Joe Papp contributed an effigy (built at the Public Theater) of FDA head Dr. Frank Young, which protesters hung in front of Trinity Church. The 250 young men and women tied up traffic for several hours, passing out tens of thousands of fact sheets about the FDA together with copies of Kramer's op-ed piece "The FDA's Callous Response to AIDS," which had appeared in the *Times* the day before. The demonstration and consequent arrests made the national news that night. Weeks later, when Young promised to speed up drug testing and release, Dan Rather of CBS-TV gave the credit to ACT UP.

Kramer divided the next four years between his writing and ACT UP, putting himself on the line with other demonstrators and getting arrested countless times. The organization grew to have a membership of thousands, with 100 chapters across the country and in Europe staging demonstrations and sit-ins, meeting with AIDS scientists and bureaucrats alike. Committees were set up to address individual agendas and plan actions. The group's history-making victories included a settlement from Philip Morris after a prolonged boycott, the release of countless drugs due to ACT UP pressure, and a decision by a New York City judge that the group could continue distributing clean needles to drug addicts to prevent the spread of AIDS. Eventually, ACT UP's Treatment and Data Committee became so well respected that AIDS experts sought them out for information.

Unlike GMHC, ACT UP refused to become bureaucratized; its weekly meetings were notable for their democratic process. All decisions had to be voted on by "the floor" and everyone was entitled to speak. (The negative aspect of this was that meetings sometimes dragged on for hours as cliques jockeyed to be heard before substantial numbers of bored attendees departed for the evening, leaving important decisions in the hands of the few people remaining at the end to vote.) After two years, meetings at the Center became so crowded that they were moved to the Great Hall at Cooper Union, which seats 800 people.

Predictably, Kramer had his differences with ACT UP and the way it was run, although he would admit to being "infinitely moved" by the organization. "These are men and women, some barely in their twenties, who have a comfort with their homosexuality that I never had at that age, and a desire to be politically active that, at such a young age, for such large numbers, is actually historically new and important in the ongoing struggle for gay rights."

Burnout

Partly because of his own inclinations and partly because of the way ACT UP was structured, Kramer continued to make appearances independent of the organization. On April 27, 1987, he participated in a GMHC-sponsored event called "Epidemic, Center Stage: A Forum on the Role of Theater in AIDS," held at the Washington Irving High School in Manhattan.

"I am no longer particularly interested in plays and movies and books that are not *about* something meaningful and important," explained Kramer about charges of his being a "message queen." "I no longer enjoy going to a movie for entertainment or escape.

"However, I don't think it is the playwright's or the novelist's or the filmmaker's responsibility to deal in ideas or rhetoric or political mean-ingfulness. These people can express themselves any way they see fit ... I have no choice. I've tried, in the past few years, to write other things: plays and screenplays about non-AIDS matters. But I can't seem to. They seem unimportant. Nothing else seems as important as AIDS—what gay men are living through."

Kramer acknowledged the irony of GMHC inviting him to speak—and his accepting—then criticized them for asking Mayor Koch to speak at their Walkathon fund-raiser (now known as the AIDS Walk, and an annual event bringing GMHC millions of dollars).

"If only each one of us could say to himself or herself: If I'm going to go, at least I'm going to go out fighting. Perhaps—perhaps—we just might survive if only each of you could become a message queen too," concluded Kramer.

A month later, what was meant to be the first installment of "Journal of the Plague Years," a nationally syndicated column on AIDS, appeared in *New York Newsday*. Kramer had submitted a proposal to Max Frankel, then editor-in-chief of the *New York Times*, to Robert Gottlieb, then editor of the *New Yorker*, and to a friend from childhood and college, David Laventhol, then president of the Times–Mirror newspaper empire, publishers of the *Los Angeles Times* and *Newsday*. Frankel said no, but Gottlieb and Laventhol were interested. Kramer resisted vanity and went with his old friend, reasoning that the column would ultimately reach a wider audience through syndication than it would in the *New Yorker*.

Kramer researched his first piece in Washington. While he was there, he received word that Paul Popham had died and that the *New York Times* was hedging on running an item. A few days before, Kramer had spoken with Popham from his deathbed. The two apologized to each other for their fights. "Keep fighting," urged Popham repeatedly. Kramer called Frankel's office and threatened to do everything in his power to bring down the wrath of the gay community forever if the *Times* did not run a full obituary with photo. The *Times* grudgingly acquiesced.

Kramer's completed column, in a severely edited form, appeared in the May 31, 1987 issue of *Newsday*, pegged to Ronald Reagan's appearance that night at a benefit for the American Foundation for AIDS Research, at which the President was expected to mention AIDS for the first time since the epidemic had been declared seven years earlier, during his first term of office. (The closest he had ever come was saying that he was categorically opposed to funding anything—such as AIDS research or education—which could be considered as encouragement of homosexuality.)

"Tonight, the President of all the American people is finally going to make his *first* AIDS speech," began Kramer. After detailing the bureaucratic quagmire of the government's response to the health crisis and the preponderance of second-rate scientists involved in AIDS research, he ended: "The record convinces me that no matter what Reagan says tonight, no substantial battle for a cure will be mounted while he is in office. There's only one word to describe his monumental disdain for the dead and dying: genocide."

It turned out to be Kramer's last column as well as his first; the piece failed to be picked up by any of the 300 subscribing newspapers when the Times–Mirror attempted to syndicate it. The night it appeared, Kramer sat in the audience while the President praised heterosexual AIDS service organizations but never mentioned GMHC—indeed never mentioned the words *gay* or *homosexual*, although AIDS was still considered to be primarily a gay disease and some 21,000 of the people diagnosed since 1981 were now dead. Reagan announced that he was in favor of mandatory testing for the AIDS virus of prisoners, immigrants, and applicants for marriage licenses, but said nothing about research and treatment. Actress Elizabeth Taylor and Dr. Mathilde Krim, the co-founders of AmFAR, watched in silence while Kramer and others in the audience loudly booed. (Krim, an interferon researcher and the wife of the president of Orion Pictures, had stated before the event that she would walk off the stage if Reagan recommended mandatory HIV testing. When he did, she remained in her seat.) The President sat down, obviously displeased.

Vice-President George Bush was booed even more loudly the next day at the Washington Hilton, when he spoke at the opening ceremonies of the Third International AIDS Conference. That night on television newscasts across the country, millions of people heard Bush mutter: "It's those gay activists."

It wasn't enough for Kramer. On June 9, he helped kick off Boston's Gay Pride Weekend by addressing the Lesbian and Gay Town Meeting at historic Fanueil Hall.

"We have little to be proud of this Gay Pride Weekend," Kramer began, going on to relate his experiences in Washington when meeting with Gary Bauer, then the President's domestic policy advisor on AIDS (now head of the Family Research Council, a virulent anti-abortion lobbying group), and the all-around incompetence he had encountered during his visit to the National Institutes of Health and talk with Dr Anthony Fauci, the head of the National Institute of Allergy and Infectious Diseases, who was in charge of disbursing federal monies allocated for AIDS.

"Now you know why NIH stands for Not Interested in Homosexuals," said Kramer. "What the fuck is going on here, and what the fuck are you doing about it?

"If I use gross language—go ahead, be offended—I don't know how else to reach you, how to reach everybody. I tried starting an organization: I co-founded GMHC, which becomes more timid as it becomes richer day by day. I tried writing a play. I tried writing endless articles in the *Native* and the *New York Times* and *Newsday* and screaming on *Donahue* and at every TV camera put in front of me. I helped start ACT UP, a small bunch of too few very courageous people willing to make rude noises. I don't know what else to do to wake you up! ...

"Politicians understand only one thing: PRESSURE. You don't apply it— you don't get anything. Simple as that.

"And it must be applied day by week by month by year. You simply can't let up for one single second. Or you don't get anything. Which is what is happening to us.

"For six years I have been trying to get the gay world angry enough to exert this pressure. I have failed and I am ashamed of my failure. I blame myself—somehow I wasn't convincing enough or clever enough or cute enough to break through your denial or self-pity or death wish or self-destruction or whatever the fuck is going on. I'm very tired of trying to make you hear me."

Kramer called it tragic that there were so few voices in the AIDS struggle as strident as his, that no gay leader had national recognizability outside the gay and lesbian community.

"Why is that?" he asked. "Don't you ask yourselves quite often the Big Question: Why am I still alive? ... How have I escaped?

"Don't you think that obligates you to repay God or fate or whomever or whatever, if only your conscience, for this miraculous fact: I am still alive ... By not putting back, you are saying that your lives are worth shit, and that we deserve to die, and that the deaths of all our friends and lovers have amounted to nothing.

"I can't believe that in your heart of hearts you feel this way. I can't believe you want to die.

"Do you?"

Kramer received a standing ovation. Earlier in his speech, he had told the crowd that, because "the vast majority of the gay world will not listen to what is so simple and plain," he was "shutting up and going away." The speech was subsequently printed in the *Native* and other gay newspapers across the country. Kramer received letters from strangers as far away as France and Utah and Nevada, begging him not to quit fighting.

Return to Activism

Three months later he was back, attacking the government and the white middle-class male majority at a September 7 symposium sponsored by the New York Civil Liberties Union to celebrate the 200th anniversary of the United States Constitution. On September 9, Kramer testified before the Presidential AIDS Commission in Washington. Among the panel members was John Cardinal O'Connor, the Archbishop of New York and an outspoken opponent of gay rights often in the news. Kramer read aloud a list of famous gays throughout history, including Catholic saints and Popes, to the unperturbed prelate.

On October 17, GMHC president Nathan Kolodner presented Kramer with the Arts and Communications Award of the Human Rights Campaign Fund, at the organization's sixth annual dinner in the grand ballroom of New York's Waldorf-Astoria Hotel. In his acceptance speech, Kramer acknowledged his brother and sister-in-law, Arthur and Alice Kramer, as well as Joe Papp and his wife Gail and Lawrence Mass, all of whom were present in the audience. Then Kramer exhorted "closeted presidents of corporations and banks and the partners in law and accounting firms"— the very people who were honoring Kramer—to become politically active. "In this room alone tonight is an assortment of talent, brains, and money that should be enough to move mountains," said Kramer. He compared the gay rights struggle to that of the Jews for Israel, citing the Irgun (a terrorist organization) as a model to emulate.

The May 21, 1988 issue of the *Village Voice* included "An Open Letter to Dr. Anthony Fauci" in which Kramer blasted the NIAID head for not using the $374 million allocated to him for AIDS research. The letter was reprinted a month later in the June 26 issue of the *San Francisco Examiner*, to coincide with Gay Pride Week. In between, on June 16, Kramer had written to Max Frankel at the *New York Times* citing chapter and verse of the paper's still-inadequate coverage of AIDS. Frankel circulated Kramer's letter to all the desk editors and reporters Kramer criticized, with the result that the *Times*'s main AIDS reporter, Gina Kolata, and deputy science editor, Erik Eckholm, took GMHC's Dr. Barry Gingell to lunch and asked him to provide them with a list of important possible stories. In addition, metro-politan reporter Tom Morgan was assigned to do a feature article on ACT UP, reporter Bruce Lambert was assigned to cover AIDS full time, and

Washington AIDS reporter Philip Boffey was told to stay at his post. Meanwhile, Kramer registered surprise that "the editor-in-chief of the world's most powerful newspaper actually answers my letters, and with occasional sympathy, but always politely and quickly."

On November 6, 1988, Kramer's "play about a farce," *Just Say No*, opened at the WPA Theater in Manhattan (best known at the time for its production of the hit musical *The Little Shop of Horrors*). A scathing look at the non-response to AIDS by the New York City and Federal Governments, the play includes characters clearly based on Mayor Koch, Nancy Reagan, and Ron Reagan Jr. The action takes place in a house on the outskirts of Washington where the First Lady conducts extramarital affairs, and is set around her son's efforts to come out of the closet and her own attempts to reclaim an incriminating videotape of sexual shenanigans at the White House.

After a month-long rehearsal period in which Kramer essentially rewrote the play, *Just Say No* opened to vitriolic reviews and closed a few weeks later. The stress aggravated a congenital hernia condition; in December Kramer entered the hospital for surgery. Rodger McFarlane, now Kramer's closest friend, was present when the surgeon informed Kramer that the operation had revealed the presence of chronic active hepatitis B, apparently contracted during the 1970s, and told Kramer that he would be dead in two years if the condition could not be brought under control. The surgeon encouraged Kramer to be tested for HIV, since some of the medications for the hepatitis would be counterindicated if he was infected with the AIDS virus.

Kramer tested positive, setting off new anxieties and a sense of personal urgency with which he still has to deal. ("No amount of suspicion matches the actuality of discovering the truth," Kramer wrote in 1990. "Even though there is nothing different in my body except this new bit of information in my head, my life is changed forever. A new fear has now joined my daily repertoire of emotions, and my nighttime ones, too. But life has also become exceptionally more precious and, ironically, I am quite happy.")

With treatment, the cirrhosis that had resulted from the chronic hepatitis stabilized, though it remained a more immediate threat to Kramer's health than his otherwise asymptomatic infection with HIV. By November 1989, he was quoting Dr Samuel Broder of the National Cancer Institute, in a letter titled "We Must Make Tomorrow Happen Today" distributed at ACT UP's general meeting. Broder had said that AIDS could be cured. (Broder is the discoverer of AZT, a cancer drug shelved for decades which was reintroduced in the 1980s and for years remained the only AIDS treatment approved by the FDA, despite continuing controversy about its toxicity and effectiveness.) Kramer urged ACT UP to adopt a new agenda, including beginning a dynamic, orchestrated effort to demand full participation in the decision making and operation of government AIDS treatment protocols and, if that failed, refusing to cooperate with government studies and thereby forcing more humane drug trials. Kramer also recommended that ACT UP stage a series of local actions against New York test sites where toxic doses of AZT were being administered despite proof that lower levels were less dangerous and worked better. He warned that too few ACT UP members were doing the work of too many and that massive burnout was beginning to occur. He acknowledged ACT UP's historic victories and impact on the system, but worried that the group might be becoming more conservative, saying that ways had to be found to renew ACT UP's original energy and effectiveness.

"Personally, ACT UP gives me my greatest energy and my greatest reason for being alive," Kramer wrote. "We have already proved so much to the world and to our fellow gay men and lesbians. Mark Harrington [an ACT UP member] is fond of saying the world's revolutions do not happen when there is no hope. They happen when there *is* hope, and when the system can't keep up with the rising expectations of the maligned and the downtrodden. We have discovered there is hope that this epidemic, as Dr. Broder says, can be cured. We must clutch this hope every day to our hearts and use it, as we have done so often, to fuel our anger and our fury that what we are entitled to—what is just out there, over there—is being denied to us and we demand it—that it be ours. It's there, still out of reach, but coming closer. We can't stop now. We've started the revolution. We can't quit until we finish it. WE MUST MAKE TOMORROW HAPPEN TODAY. *AND WE SHALL!*"

ACT UP followed his lead, but Kramer's hopes were soon dashed. Some ACT UP members began to challenge him openly, saying he had no right to call himself the organization's founder. Kramer was not going to have this achievement denied him by people who thought they could rewrite history, and took every opportunity to reassert his claim. When the governmental changes he had hoped would result from a refocused ACT UP did not materialize by the following spring, Kramer called for riots at the Sixth International AIDS Conference scheduled to be held in June in San Francisco.

Kramer was denounced from the floor; articles in *People*, the *Los Angeles Times*, the *Philadelphia Inquirer*, and elsewhere quoted ACT UP members as saying he did not speak for the organization. Kramer sallied with an open letter to the gay and lesbian community of San Francisco which was printed in gay periodicals in New York, San Francisco, and Chicago and distributed at ACT UP meetings; other gay papers ran lengthy interviews with Kramer.

"I'm sorry my recent call for riots . . . has upset you," wrote Kramer. "But you see, I believe we have lost our war against AIDS. . . . We must start facing the dreadful fact that the world is not going to perform the humanitarian acts required to save us. No matter how hard we try (and some of us have tried very hard), the system simply will not move for us."

Kramer cited ACT UP's past year of intense dealings with the NIH, Congress, and the Federal Department of Health and Human Services, stating that it had become overwhelmingly clear to him that even if a cure for AIDS were found, the rigid, unyielding system would not test, approve, and make it available fast enough to save most of the people who needed it.

"My gay brothers and sisters and your friends and families in San Francisco: You are free not to riot and you are free to criticize my call to riot and I am free not to comprehend your criticism. And we are all free to die," concluded Kramer. He believed the time had come for the gay community to follow the example of the Jews in the Irgun who had forced the creation of Israel. He stayed at home in New York as a protest against what he took to be the sham proceedings in San Francisco, and called for volunteers to join him for gun practice when he next spoke at an ACT UP meeting.

Kramer quietly withdrew from active participation in ACT UP, while continuing to join as many demonstrations as he could.

"I didn't want to repeat the GMHC experience," Kramer had written in *Reports from the holocaust: the making of an AIDS activist*, a collection of his writing and speeches on AIDS published by St. Martin's Press in 1989, explaining his changed expectations. "I also now accept, albeit reluctantly, that, once started, there is little any one individual can do to control or affect an organization's development. It's like a person: It's more or less going to be what it's going to be. And, like a person, it wants to do it and get there on its own. And when I found that my suggestions were coming to be resented, not because of their content but because I was making them, I returned home to get back to my writing."

As in the past, the storm died down. On the last Sunday in June 1990, as the ACT UP contingent of New York's annual Gay and Lesbian Pride Parade reached the foot of Fifth Avenue, marchers turned to the third-floor balcony on which Kramer stood with McFarlane, their ailing friend and fellow activist Vito Russo, Lawrence Mass and his lover Arnie Kantrowitz, and a photographer from *People*. "Look, honey, these are our children," Kramer said to Russo as each ACT UP member raised a fist, chanting "Larry! Larry! Larry!" in salute to their beleaguered, but nonetheless loved, founder.

Disillusion and Hope: "Never Give Up"

On December 20, 1990, Kramer gave what he called "the hardest speech of his life," when he addressed the memorial service for Vito Russo, the noted film historian and author of *The Celluloid Closet*, who had died from AIDS complications on November 7. The service was held in the Great Hall at Cooper Union, the site of ACT UP's weekly general meetings (Russo had been an important member of the group). More than 800 people filled every seat and stood crowding the rear of the auditorium; many more had been turned away for lack of space.

"Vito asked me to tell you the truth," a visibly shaken Kramer told Russo's family, friends, professional colleagues, admirers, and fellow activists. "Here it is: We killed him [by not working hard enough to make the government respond to AIDS and find a cure]."

Russo's other eulogists spoke more gently. Less than an hour afterward, a smiling Kramer joined the smaller group of invited friends and mourners at a reception in the lobby of the Public Theater, beaming as other ACT UP members arrived. It was a stark contrast, evidence—if anyone needed it— that Kramer had become a master of rhetoric. (His remarks were subsequently published in the *Village Voice*.)

Six months later, Kramer dedicated his keynote speech for the 22nd Annual Lesbian and Gay Pride Rally to his dead friend, and to three other "fighting heroes" lost to AIDS in the time since Russo's death: activists Lee Arsenault and Tom Hannan, and Phil Zwickler, a reporter for the gay press and prizewinning filmmaker. This time Kramer reversed gears.

"I want to make a hopeful speech," he said to the cheering crowd packing Union Square Park, where the rally was held. "I want to send you away from here cheering our future and our successes and our victories."

Kramer acknowledged some of ACT UP's achievements and went on to read a letter from Russo's mother:

"Fight for what you believe in. If you truly loved Vito, don't let his hopes and dreams die in vain.... Don't ever give up."

Kramer encouraged his listeners to pledge to get involved in gay organizations and join ACT UP's Labor Day action against (now President) George Bush at his home in Maine.

"Storm Kennebunkport on September 1st!" urged Kramer. "Holding hands is holding ground. In this day and age, holding ground is a heroic act. And we must hold hands with someone who is standing next to us. That's how we gain ground...."

"We must believe this war will soon be over!..."

"And we must believe, we must always believe, we must never stop believing that, in memory of every single beloved whom we want back here in our arms, we can somehow find the energy to fight and fight and fight until we have won!..."

"ACT UP!"

The crowd roared their acclamation. Kramer descended from the stage, accepted the congratulations of friends, then walked eight blocks south to his apartment. After watching a rerun of *Out in America* on Channel 13, he packed up his computer and drove with his wheaten terrier, Molly, out to his summer rental at Sag Harbor. He would not be in New York the next day to watch the Gay Pride Parade pass below his balcony or receive the greetings of ACT UPers as they marched by.

On July 3, Kramer was a guest on "Blood, Sex, and Tears: Ten Years of AIDS," a special edition of *Geraldo* commemorating the tenth anniversary of the *New York Times's* first report on the "rare cancer seen in 41 homosexual men." Rivera's other guests included talk show host Phil Donahue, Jeanne White (the mother of Ryan White), Michael Callen (a nine-year AIDS survivor), and Sonia Singleton (a black woman with AIDS who would tell viewers of the lack of AIDS services for heterosexuals when she was diagnosed in 1986, and how she had received help from the gay community which had enabled her to live long beyond the one year predicted by her doctors).

Rivera began with a recap of ten years of AIDS statistics: from the *Times* report of forty-one cases and eight deaths as of July 1981 to US government estimates of a million people infected and 109,000 deaths by 1991. Among the footage was his own 1983 interview with Kramer for *20/20*, in which Kramer had asked Rivera why it had taken two years for network TV to do a story on AIDS. "How many people have to die before someone pays attention?" the younger Kramer asked calmly. Eight years later, when Rivera introduced him as a "controversial" activist "who by his own admission is preparing to die," an agitated Kramer challenged:

"What do I say that's controversial? I say a plague is taking place in this land. I've been saying it since 1981, when there were forty-one cases, and now there are ten million infected. [Kramer was citing the World Health Organization's estimate.] I say we need a general in charge of this. We can send troops to the Persian Gulf in ten minutes, but after ten years there is still no one in charge of AIDS. I don't think that's controversial."

The studio audience burst into applause; Rivera smiled and said, "I love you, Larry."

"I decided today I was going to be as obnoxious as I could possibly be," asserted Kramer to more applause. "It's very nice," he continued, "their response, but do you know that one out of every four households in America has someone infected? Why aren't they out there, too? It's a plague! A plague! A plague!"

"It would be helpful," Donahue interjected, speaking to Rivera, "to think of yourself as standing on a pier and someone you know is drowning. You're screaming for help and people are telling you not to be controversial. Who among us is going to tell people with AIDS that they have a responsibility to be decorous? *We* have a responsibility to understand."

"I would be screaming and yelling and lying down in the street on Fifth Avenue," acknowledged Rivera.

"Like my beloved ACT UP," said Kramer.

In September, Kramer was under attack again by his beloved children. He had not gone to Kennebunkport for the Labor Day action against President Bush. (When the time came, the democratic ACT UP floor had refused to let Kramer be one of the speakers at the demonstration, saying that newer members needed the experience. Kramer was sure he could force the issue if he insisted that ACT UP was taking an unnecessary risk of inadequate media coverage by leaving its message in the hands of unseasoned speakers without recognizability, but the thought of doing so was humiliating. He protested the floor's decision by staying away. Perhaps coincidentally, the protest received only seconds of coverage in TV news reports.) But Kramer had told reporters that he supported Liz Abzug's candidacy for New York's City Council, asserting that rival candidate Tom Duane (like Abzug openly gay) was being less than candid about a personal issue which had serious ramifications. As a result, Duane called a press conference to announce that he was HIV-positive, and returned Kramer's $1,000 contribution to his campaign. Meanwhile, it was learned that Kramer had helped conceal the positive HIV status of a famous friend.

The death of Brad Davis from AIDS on September 8, 1991, shocked the Hollywood community. Although Davis had been diagnosed as HIV-positive in 1985 (the year in which he played Ned Weeks in *The Normal Heart*), he had confided the news only to his wife and a few close friends, fearing that he would be unable to get work as an actor if he was perceived as having AIDS. (His wife, a casting director, agreed.) At the time of his death, Davis was planning to write a book about his experiences and the AIDS-phobic atmosphere in Hollywood; Kramer had helped him with a proposal.

Kramer found himself vilified in letters distributed at ACT UP's general meeting and printed in the *Village Voice*, and denounced from the floor for "outing" a political opponent while covering up for a friend. Angered ACT UP members followed Kramer around, shouting him down when he addressed an AIDS forum at NYU Medical School. In a September 23 letter to ACT UP, Kramer maintained that Duane's position as a candidate for public office required disclosure of his HIV status, whereas Davis's as a private citizen did not. ("Brad Davis . . . was not being elected to look after my welfare; it is heinous to compare him with Duane," wrote Kramer.) In any case, Kramer admonished, being HIV-positive should not have to be a dark secret; he had gone public with his own diagnosis as soon as he'd received it. (Duane's disclosure may have helped him win the election.)

On November 7, Kramer was on television again, as part of *Nightline's* coverage of Magic Johnson's announcement of his retirement from basketball due to a positive HIV diagnosis. While others praised Johnson for his courage and honesty, Kramer reminded host Ted Koppel that Johnson would die just as 109,000 people had died before him, then interrupted another guest to shout that AIDS is a plague, not an epidemic, that after ten years there was still no effective treatment or cure in sight. When Koppel chided Kramer that the show's air time was limited, Kramer responded, "That's why I need to be heard." (Kramer put off watching a videotape of the show until December, then was so dismayed by what he saw that he sent a note to Koppel apologizing for being so "over the top.")

November 22 found Kramer in the pulpit at the Cathedral of St. John the

Divine as part of "AIDS: 10 Years: Remember, Respond, Resolve," one in a series of events sponsored by GMHC commemorating a decade of AIDS and the organization's existence. Kramer recently had returned from a two-month research trip to Washington in connection with the novel he was working on, which he hoped would somehow make sense of the last ten years. With 600 pages written, he still wasn't sure he was on the right track. Despite the fact that Kramer and GMHC had long ago parted company and Kramer remained an outspoken critic of the organization, two GMHC officials had asked him to speak at the Cathedral.

Kramer's address came midway in the proceedings, after remarks by a member of GMHC's board of directors and prior to a performance by the New York City Gay Men's Chorus and an appearance by Peter Jennings of ABC News. The Cathedral was packed; 5,000 people sat in darkness, the only light the pin spot illuminating Kramer high up in the pulpit, wearing a smartly tailored black suit and tie. Kramer's image, projected on a huge video screen to the rear of the main altar, towered over everything. A persistent cough had him worried he wouldn't be able to speak; the plan was for Rodger McFarlane to read Kramer's speech if Kramer had a coughing fit.

Kramer's voice never failed him. If anything, the pauses to sip water to clear his throat added drama to his address.

"I tried every way to say what I have to say," Kramer began. "I tried angry. I tried funny. I tried sad."

Murmurs of recognition and sympathy from the floor.

"Well, here it is: pure Larry."

And he proceeded to detail at length the inexorable progress of the plague and the failure of education, telling them "it would not make one single bit of difference" if GMHC—and AmFAR and even ACT UP—weren't there, and that he was sorry he had ever founded two of the organizations. "You don't want to get your hands dirty," he castigated. "You only want to feel good and virtuous which comes from attending events like this and writing a few small checks. I don't want your dollars to help me die. . . . I want your dollars to help save my life and 40 million other lives and you can do that . . . with ten, twenty, 100 important powerful rich board members who are willing, finally and at last, to open their mouths! And it is up to all the rest of us everywhere to pressure them to do so!"

He ended bitterly: "Well, now you can go home and say, 'I heard crazy Larry going out of his mind again.' And you'll ignore me again until ten years from now when you gather here for another one of these tender meetings of 'Remember, Respond, Resolve' and you'll say, 'Oh, Larry Kramer, thank God we don't have him to listen to any more.'"

Applause exploded in the Cathedral, thundering through the immense vaulted spaces as the mass of humanity rose in the darkness. McFarlane, a tall shadow, gathered Kramer up as he descended the pulpit and ushered him from the building. They did not stay to hear the speakers who followed Kramer, did not attend the reception that followed. Instead, they ran through pouring rain to the West End Cafe, a student hangout on upper Broadway near Columbia University, as previously arranged. After dinner with his niece, Rebecca, his nephew, Andy, and Andy's wife, Linda, Kramer took a cab home.

A shortened version of Kramer's speech was printed in the *Village Voice* and a report on Page Six of the *New York Post* resulted in Kramer doing a radio call-in show during which he challenged openly gay Congressman Barney Frank on his AIDS record and Frank hung up on him. The letters column of the *Voice* in the weeks following publication was conspicuous mainly for the lack of anything resembling the outcry over Kramer's disclosure of Tom Duane's HIV status. (In fact, the *Voice* printed no letters at all about Kramer's speech.) Tim Sweeney, now executive director of GMHC and one of the people who had asked Kramer to speak at the Cathedral, sent a letter to GMHC board members refuting Kramer's allegations point by point.

In December, Kramer spent time with Scott McPherson and Daniel Sotomayor, members of ACT UP/Chicago who were in town for the opening of McPherson's play, *Marvin's Room*, which quickly became the hit of the Off-Broadway season. Kramer sat with his fellow activists in their little hotel room, watching as the emaciated lovers encouraged each other to eat, to force some nourishment into their wasting bodies. Danny, just off a round of chemotherapy, could barely speak (he died February 5, 1992). Kramer subsequently wrote an introduction when his own editor at NAL published *Marvin's Room*; but he was unable to convince anyone to issue a book of Sotomayor's political cartoons, as he had hoped to do.

At the end of the year Kramer received a package from an anonymous "admirer"—a box of feces. Would death threats be next? It had happened before. But even that could not dampen Kramer's pleasure in the fact that Z Collective, a small company of actors, was staging *Just Say No* in the Gazebo Theater adjoining the AIDS ward of San Francisco's Davies Memorial Hospital, to good reviews and sold-out crowds.

The Destiny of Me

In January 1992 Kramer was quoted prominently in *Premiere* magazine's article on AIDS in Hollywood; an item in *New York* magazine's Intelligencer column told of encounters between Kramer, his dog, and Ed Koch, who had moved into Kramer's building after leaving office as mayor. Kramer also spoke to the *New York Times*'s "On Stage, and Off" columnist about the production of his new play planned for the following season by the Circle Repertory Company.

Kramer had been working on his "companion play" to *The Normal Heart* for years. Originally titled *The Furniture of Home* (another phrase from Auden's "September 1, 1939"), the play continues the story of Ned Weeks. Now sick, Weeks finds himself at the National Institutes of Health, having used his connection to the man he has attacked for years to get himself admitted to that same doctor's protocol for a hopeful but unapproved experimental drug. The present-day story is intercut with scenes of Weeks's unhappy childhood and suicide attempt at college and his defiant battle to accept himself and make his family accept him, with searching portraits of his weak, abusive father whom he could never satisfy, his seductive, guilt-inducing mother, and his older brother who never understood him but whom he idolized anyway (and to whom he ultimately dedicated the play). Kramer meant the work to be his own *Long Day's Journey into Night* and succeeded to the extent that John Simon and other critics compared Kramer's play favorably to Eugene O'Neill's masterpiece when it opened.

The Furniture of Home had been given a reading at the Manhattan Theater Club in August 1990, to which only one outsider was invited. Five months later, retitled *The Tyranny of Blood*, the script was tried out in public before a packed house at the Bruno Walter Auditorium in Lincoln Center's Library of the Performing Arts, with Brad Davis in the role of Ned Weeks and Colleen Dewhurst and George Grizzard as Weeks's (Kramer's) parents, under the direction of Marshall W. Mason. The play still needed work and Kramer had continued to revise it, while also working on his novel.

In December 1991 Kramer had talked with actors Ron Rifkin and Vanessa Redgrave about the possibility of their doing the play, now titled *The Destiny of Me* (from Walt Whitman's poem "Out of the Cradle Endlessly Rocking"), with Mason again at the helm. Rifkin had recently received rave notices for his performance of another difficult father in Jon Robin Baitz's *The Substance of Fire* at Playwrights Horizons. Redgrave had called Kramer after the death of her ex-husband, director Tony Richardson, from AIDS complications; she hadn't known until she'd read Randy Shilts's book how important Kramer was in the AIDS activist movement. (Colleen Dewhurst, who had wanted to repeat the part of the mother, had died in August 1991; Brad Davis was dead a month later.)

Neither Redgrave nor Rifkin was in the cast when the Circle Repertory Company production of *The Destiny of Me* finally opened on October 20, 1992 at the Lucille Lortel Theater. (Rifkin wound up committing to another Baitz project, and the part of Kramer's mother was played by Piper Laurie, like Redgrave an Academy Award-winning actor with a career spanning decades.) But Kramer told friends that the rehearsal period was the happiest of his life, and he had reason to be pleased. Mason had wanted to direct

The Normal Heart in 1985, and the Lortel was the same venue in Greenwich Village that had housed the ill-fated 1974 production of *Four Friends*, when the site had been known as the Theatre de Lys. Rodger McFarlane, reconciled with Kramer after a personal dispute that had lasted several months, was one of the play's associate producers. In more than one sense, Kramer had come home.

And it was a propitious homecoming. *The Destiny of Me* won Kramer the best reviews of his career—near unqualified raves. "Overwhelmingly powerful ... scaldingly honest," wrote Frank Rich in the *Times* (a noteworthy contrast to his underwhelmed response to *The Normal Heart*), going on to call *Destiny* "a seismic jolt of visceral theatricality." "A mature work by a gifted American playwright in his prime," lauded the *Wall Street Journal*, while *Time* magazine cited the play as one of the year's ten best, saying that it gave "new hope to the American theater." *Vanity Fair* ran a feature-length profile of Kramer and the BBC filmed an hour-long documentary on the man and his career. Even the notices in the gay press were favorable—perhaps because, for once, Kramer had not criticized his own.

Predictably, the reactions of the people Kramer did put in his play were mixed. "My brother liked it, my sister-in-law didn't, my mother thought it was a work of fiction," Kramer subsequently wrote in the expanded edition of *Reports from the holocaust* published in 1994, "and Dr. Fauci, who's in it too, was more generous than he had to be." Typically, Kramer had invited Fauci to opening night (he came), and thanks him (among others) in his acknowledgments in the published text.

In his introduction to the published play, Kramer relates how in trying to make sense of his life he had to imagine himself into his family's lives, to tell his own story from their point of view, and that this enabled him to see how they could have behaved as they did. "I began arranging for the production of *The Destiny of Me* when I thought I was shortly going to die," writes Kramer, explaining the urgency of his need to sort out his personal history. *Reports from the holocaust* contains a long essay comparing the AIDS crisis and the treatment of homosexuals to the treatment of Jews during World War II, interspersed with revelations about Kramer's difficulties in getting his brother and sister-in-law to respect and honor him as a gay man, not just as a relative they have no choice but to love. Kramer had told part of the story in *The Normal Heart*—his struggles to make his brother see that homosexuality is not a disease, that gay people are human beings equal to heterosexuals. His essay reveals how he stopped talking to Arthur and Alice Kramer for months when his sister-in-law told him she "knew in her heart of hearts" that homosexuality is an illness, and of their eventual tear-filled reconciliation.

In the 1994 *Reports*, Kramer writes: "My family has certainly had a hard time of it from this writer amongst them. I've used them relentlessly in much of my work. I owe them all a debt of gratitude for allowing me to criticize them so publicly. I know it hasn't been easy for them, particularly for my sister-in-law, who felt particularly wounded by references to the early years of her marriage in *The Destiny of Me*. I'm sorry she doesn't hear the loving comments about her in the final scene.

"As I get closer to a death I fear is coming, I find I have less interest in the part of me that needed, for whatever reasons (many of them certainly valid), to push so much into their faces. By now we've worked out whatever it is we've had time to work out. Now we're on the end of our journeys with each other. I find myself urging that we get over whatever it was that bugged us about each other in the earlier days. And to enjoy what time we've left together."

Even so, three months after *The Destiny of Me* opened Kramer was reviling his brother, Alice, and their son and daughter for daring to plan a vacation in Aspen, Colorado after that state passed its Amendment Two, virtually mandating anti-gay discrimination. (Arthur Kramer, every bit as obstinate as his younger brother, proceeded anyway, visiting Colorado more than once after the amendment became law; Alice and Andy and Rebecca canceled their trips.)

An understanding of Kramer's relationship with his family is essential to any true understanding of the man, the artist, and the activist. "They worship the ground Larry walks on," observes Rodger McFarlane, "and he doesn't see it." The complexities implied in that simple remark may be the key that will unlock Kramer's contradictions for future biographers.

Happy Endings?

As of this writing, Kramer is still alive, angry and active as ever. ("The deathbed play remains to be written; now I have the chance to write a trilogy," Kramer remarks, not without humor, in his introduction to the published version of *The Destiny of Me*.)

In February 1992, while Kramer was worrying about dying and helping Marshall Mason put together their production of *Destiny*, Barbra Streisand (in the process of promoting her film *The Prince of Tides*) told TV interviewer Larry King that her next project might be *The Normal Heart*, which she called "a great play." In March, her attorneys contacted Kramer's lawyers to reopen negotiations.

This time, Columbia Pictures optioned the film for Streisand. But once again she dawdled, although she continued to mention Kramer's play in interviews as being close to her heart and, in April 1993, personally introduced a star-studded reading of the play (by Eric Bogosian, Stockard Channing, Harry Hamlin, Kevin Bacon, and John Turturro) at the Roundabout

Theater on Broadway, which was recorded for audio as a benefit for Broadway Cares/Equity Fights AIDS (of which Rodger McFarlane was executive director), an organization linked to the Actors Equity theatrical union. In 1994, Kramer wrote in the expanded edition of *Reports from the holocaust*: "Yes, Barbra and I somehow managed to get back together. Working with her on the screenplay of *The Normal Heart* was an exciting experience.... So far I've only said the nicest things [about her]. (And meant them.) But if she's reading this, let me say: Barbra, if you don't film *The Normal Heart*—and film it well—watch out!"

Columbia's option expired in January 1996 and they did not renew. In the spring, Streisand publicly withdrew from the project after Kramer criticized her for beginning to film *The Mirror Has Two Faces*. Almost immediately, *The Normal Heart* was picked up by John Schlesinger, the openly gay Academy Award-winning director with whom Kramer had almost worked decades before, and David Picker, Kramer's old boss at UA. As of this writing, they are still trying to make the film.

After the success of *The Destiny of Me* Kramer continued to rail against the inadequacy of individuals' and governments' responses to the AIDS crisis—in the press, on TV, in interviews, in speeches, in letters to friends and family and people in the media, in a column in the pages of *The Advocate*. Michael Denneny, Kramer's editor at St. Martin's, became the target of Kramer's ire when he hesitated to agree to reissue an updated version of *Reports from the holocaust*. Kramer wanted to include everything relating to AIDS he had written since the original edition; Denneny felt the material needed shaping. Kramer eventually convinced Cassell, the British publisher, to do the expanded book, at which point St. Martin's joined in with Denneny as editor. The new edition was published with the subtitle modified to "The Story of an AIDS Activist." In an article written by Kramer for the *New York Times Magazine* ("A Good News/Bad News AIDS Joke," July 14, 1996), he was able to report the hopeful outlook for AIDS sufferers taking combination treatments including protease inhibitors, despite the fact that governmental action remained as dismal as ever under the once-hoped-for Administration of a Democrat in the White House.

On June 14, 1996 Kramer received a Common Cause Public Service Achievement Award. Common Cause describes itself as "a nonprofit, nonpartisan citizens' lobby that works to improve the way federal and state governments operate"; their award is given to individuals "who by force of imagination, initiative, and perseverance have made an outstanding contribution to the public interest in the areas of government performance and integrity." One of five people honored, Kramer was cited for his "impassioned activism and art [which] have focused public attention, compassion, and government action on the AIDS crisis." Kramer admitted to a friend that he found the timing and source of the award perplexing. ("Why is this group giving me an award, and why now?")

More welcome, perhaps, was the distinguished Award for Literature bestowed by the American Academy of Arts and Letters. Kramer has never made it a secret that he hopes to be remembered for his writing, even though he knows it is his activism that has made him a familiar face to millions of TV viewers. He had recently begun quietly showing portions of *The American People*, the massive novel he'd been working on for years, to professional colleagues, all of whom praised it. Revisions were progressing apace. Kramer can only have been pleased to find himself sharing the stage with the likes of writers John Updike and Elie Wiesel, composers Stephen Sondheim and Ned Rorem, historians Arthur Schlesinger Jr. and John Kenneth Galbraith, and architects Philip Johnson and Maya Lin (famous for her Vietnam Veterans Memorial in Washington, DC), before an audience filled with hundreds of luminaries from all areas of the arts. Nonetheless, Kramer was unable to stay for the reception in the Academy's august 155th Street headquarters designed by Stanford White, that pleasant evening of May 15. He had a pressing engagement downtown—to meet with a tiny group of HIV-positive writers who had invited him to speak.

Perhaps most wonderful—to Larry and to others—Kramer was in the third year of a relationship with the man of his dreams. In 1993, Kramer had reconnected and fallen in love again with David Webster, the man on whom he had based the character of Dinky Adams, Fred Lemish's lover, in *Faggots*. ("We came back together, after some fifteen years, during which we never so much as ran into each other, though we live only a dozen or so blocks apart. It's over a year now and this time it seems to be working out," Kramer observed in 1994.) The couple spend as much time as they can in the house Webster, an internationally successful architect, designed for them in Connecticut. Although Webster shies away from Kramer's public life, he did agree to be profiled with Larry in the *New York Times*—a piece which, predictably, elicited mixed responses from Kramer's supporters and detractors.

In 1997, Kramer was infuriating people again. The May 27 issue of the *Advocate* published a commentary variously entitled "AIDS: We asked for it" (the cover), "Our bodies, ourselves" (contents page), and "Sex and sensibility" (the article itself), in which Kramer accused gay men of identifying themselves too little with their history and too much with their sexuality. Kramer focused his wrath on gay writers, damning everyone else for not telling the truth about gay culture, and going on at length about the proliferation of sex scenes in the new novel by GMHC co-founder Edmund White. "[S]o many faceless, indistinguishable pieces of flesh," wrote Kramer, "litter [*The Farewell Symphony*] that reading them becomes, for any reasonably sentient human being, at first a heartless experience and finally a boring one … Surely … White … did not spend 30 years with a nonstop erection and an asshole busier than his toilet." White's book was not to be published in the United States for another three months; Kramer had read a bound galley of the British edition. In the novel, White writes mostly about the New York gay scene in the 1970s, the same period covered by Kramer in *Faggots*, but in considerably less graphic detail than in Kramer's book (or, indeed, in his essay). Many readers found Kramer's thinking muddled and contradictory to the point of near incoherence, and his instruction "Wait for my new novel" (to find out the truth about gay life and culture) self-serving, especially since Kramer still hadn't finished *The American People*. Several of the contributors to the present anthology (whom Kramer had previously praised) felt personally attacked and considered revising or pulling their essays, but decided not to follow Kramer's example of hotheadedness (as they judged it).

Kramer's attack had an unintended result: other writers and readers, including many who don't like White's work, found themselves defending White. All summer, dog-eared bound galleys of *The Farewell Symphony* traded hands. Meanwhile, Kramer continued to fan the flames by referring to his essay repeatedly in public every chance he got—and writers continued to argue about what he had done. And Kramer found himself yet again being accused of being politically conservative and anti-sex.

In the second half of his *Advocate* commentary, Kramer revealed how Yale University, his alma mater, had rebuffed his efforts to leave several million dollars to them for the purpose of endowing one or two tenured chairs in gay studies and/or help build a gay studies center. Kramer used his experience as proof of homophobia at Yale and the need to establish gay studies on campuses throughout the country so that young gay men (Kramer confined his remarks to males) would stop falling into the trap of thinking with their genitals. He expounded on this theme in a Gay Pride address in San Francisco on June 29, exhorting his listeners to grow up and follow the example of their eminent gay historical forebears. ("What have you done to contribute anything positive to honor the memories of so many of us? How selfish and narcissistic can you be?") Some critics noted that Kramer had come late to this debate, citing the rise of gay studies for nearly three decades. The front page of the Metro Section of the July 9, 1997 issue of the *New York Times* was dominated by a center-page photograph of Kramer standing, hands determinedly fastened on his hips, in front of the dormitory where he had attempted to commit suicide in 1953. The boxed article carried the headlines "Playwright Is Denied A Final Act/Writing His Own Script, Yale Refuses Kramer's Millions for Gay Studies." While adopting a sympathetic tone, the *Times* revealed what Kramer had left out: that Yale's tenured positions were frozen and the school would have to replace an existing professorship to create the new one he wanted (an impossibility, in any case, barring the death of a seated professor); that Yale had returned a $20 million dollar gift from another (presumably non-gay) alumnus who "wanted to have a say in who would fill the professorships in Western civilization he had tried to create"; and that Yale has had a Lesbian and Gay Studies Center, founded by the late historian John Boswell, since 1987. The *Times* also printed an offer from the Center for Lesbian and Gay Studies at the Graduate Center of the University of New York to do what Kramer wanted, in return for leaving his millions to them. As if anticipating such responses, Kramer had written in the *Advocate*, "Many times I asked myself, *Larry, why are you spending so much time trying to make someone accept a present they don't want to accept* [Kramer's italics]? Surely there are places other than Yale I can give my money that will benefit gays . . . Do I have to ram gay people down everybody's throat? And, of course, when put this way, I have to answer yes." Meanwhile, Kramer was leading a new AIDS initiative—an Internet program for tracking HIV drug treatment data—and the *Advocate* reported that Kramer's essay had received more mail than anything they'd ever printed, seventy-five percent of it positive.

Kramer (the man himself or the mere mention of his name) continues to provoke controversy—passionate praise and heated rage, often from the same quarters. People still argue about whether he has the right to take credit for founding ACT UP, about the veracity of his version of what happened with GMHC. They argue about whether Kramer is a self-serving egomaniac or a self-destructive saint, whether his actions have helped or hurt the cause so clearly close to his heart, whether he will be remembered most for his writing or his activism—or not at all. One thing is indisputable: Larry Kramer is the role model for a generation of activists who have helped change the way people gay and straight think about themselves in the world, the way sick people regard themselves and are treated by others, and the way the world responds to people in crisis.

PART TWO

Sex, Politics and History

A Meaning for All Those Words:

Sex, Politics, History and Larry Kramer

John D'Emilio

MY ASSIGNMENT is to place Larry Kramer in historical context, to connect his career and his influence to the larger pattern of change that the gay and lesbian movement, the evolution of public queer communities, and the AIDS epidemic have provoked in American life. On the face of it, the assignment seems fairly straightforward, not unlike what any biographical profile by a historian should do.

In Larry's case, the task is perhaps somewhat more complicated, since his influence lies, as does his work, at the juncture of culture and politics. Think for a moment about what he is best known for. He wrote *Faggots*, a novel that received wide attention as a commentary on gay male sexual culture in the 1970s; *The Normal Heart*, a play that, through its many productions, brought the politics of AIDS to a national audience; and essays, such as "1,112 and Counting," whose polemical power galvanized the outrage of the gay and lesbian community into political action. Larry was one of the founders of Gay Men's Health Crisis in New York City, the first—and still the largest—AIDS service organization in the world. His speech at the New York Lesbian and Gay Community Center in March 1987 provoked the founding of ACT UP, an organization which changed the face of AIDS activism and initiated the most vibrant, media-savvy brand of direct action politics in the US since the late 1960s.[1] Add to this his op-ed columns in places such as the *New York Times*, interviews in the *Washington Post* and elsewhere, and appearances on television talk shows, and it is not unreasonable to claim for Larry a higher level of visibility and public influence than for anyone else associated with the gay freedom struggle.[2]

What have I left out? Just the fact that Larry is as passionately loved by his supporters in the queer world and as deeply reviled by his antagonists in this same world as it is humanly possible to be; that the split between passionate love and deep antagonism can often be found in the very same individual; and that Larry himself is capable of swinging between poles of self-praise and self-criticism that are as far apart from each other as are his most rabid loyalists and detractors.

As the passions he unleashes suggests, assessing Larry's place in history requires more than totaling his accomplishments and measuring his output. His words and his actions touch some very deep places of pain in many of us, particularly among the white, urban gay men of the Stonewall generation whose experience he has commented upon and whose tragedies he has chronicled. I may be a dispassionate historian of the gay and lesbian movement, but I am also a gay man whose life has intersected with Larry's and whose social and political worlds he has commented upon. It would be foolish to claim that I can approach this essay only in the guise of the former role and not in the latter. In what follows, I am examining Larry's work and the response to it in order to see what it can tell us about the larger context of historical change, but it is an analysis inevitably informed by my own experience.[3]

□   □   □

Like many others, I first encountered Larry long before I met him. Autumn 1978 brought into print two novels, *Faggots* and Andrew Holleran's *Dancer From the Dancer*, that were immediately recognized as breakthrough books. Each of them was set in the urban sexual culture of middle-class white gay men that had taken shape above ground in the wake of Stonewall; each described that world from the inside, without reticence or apology; and each of them was widely reviewed, not only in the burgeoning gay press but in mainstream papers and magazines as well. Just as many of us were coming out proudly as individuals in the 1970s, as the decade drew to a close our collective world was now finding its chroniclers and bringing our experience out en masse.

Despite these commonalities, as works of fiction the two novels were dramatically different. Holleran's was lushly romantic, eliciting the longings for love and emotional attachment that surrounded the pursuit of sexual pleasure. Though it lacked the self-hatred endemic to much of the gay "problem" fiction of the previous generation, it nonetheless played upon familiar tropes of desperate desire, unfulfilled longing, and doomed love that still circulated not only in the products of popular culture but in gay male life as well.[4] *Faggots* occupied another place entirely. Bitingly, viciously comic, it cast a satiric eye on the gay quest for love. None of the sexual institutions of the gay subculture were spared; no concessions were made to the libertarian principles of the so-called sexual revolution. Although the critique of a world in which physical attractiveness and orgasm counted for everything was fierce, the novel stood firm in the unspoken assumption that gay is good, even if the social world and sexual mores it sometimes produced were not. Fred Lemish, its erstwhile hero, was neither struggling to be heterosexual nor contemplating suicide.

Faggots and *Dancer* differed in another way as well: their reception. Holleran's novel attracted worlds of praise while Kramer's was savaged. Reviewing them together in the *New York Times*, John Lahr described *Dancer* as "superb." As for *Faggots*, Lahr called it "an embarrassing fiasco," containing "sentence for sentence, some of the worst writing I've encountered in a published manuscript." Martin Duberman, in the *New Republic*, described *Faggots* as "a foolish, even stupid book. . . . It has nothing of discernment to say about [the gay] scene nor, in place of insight, any compensating literary distinction." Duberman further damned it for "primitive moralizing." A reviewer in *Gay Community News* of Boston, one of the more radical of gay papers, called the novel "appalling" and "offensive." The examples could be multiplied.[5]

I'm no literary critic. But I remember reading both novels soon after they were published and reacting differently from the reviews—and my friends. *Dancer* immediately drew me in. I could hardly put it down, yet I responded to it with anger. Despite its dreamlike quality, it evoked the emotional landscape of gay male life as I knew it with razor-sharp accuracy. But, to my mind, it also lacked any critical distance from that world. The absence of a view from the outside left no room for escape; the quest for love and attachment was doomed—as gay men had always been doomed—to failure. *Faggots* at least rebelled. I confess: I never finished it because it seemed like a one-line joke, but at least its one line was on target. Many of us did find ourselves enmeshed, more than we wanted to be, in a circle of sexual encounters that had no exit. Instead of "both sex and love," we were left with "either sex"—but no "or love"!

What raw nerve had *Faggots* touched? The venom in many of the reviews in the gay press had little to do with Larry's skill as a stylist. They were content-focused, and came with accusations of betrayal of the "lifestyle" (a word that came into vogue in the 1970s) of a community that was just emerging into the open. It seemed not to be Larry's particular critique of gay male sexuality that provoked outrage as much as the fact that there was any critique at all.

For many, *Faggots* would continue to shape their reaction to Larry. As the AIDS epidemic hit in the early 1980s, Larry's warnings—his jeremiads—would be filtered through ears that had already judged the speaker. Larry, a relative newcomer to gay politics, was typecast as anti-sexual, a Puritan or a Victorian depending on one's historical frame of reference, someone whose internalized homophobia ran so deep that his judgment was always suspect. Someone, in other words, who stood at odds with the gay liberation tradition. Interestingly, Larry himself accepted a piece of this characterization in that his own commentaries during the AIDS era often identified gay liberation with the sexual subculture of the meat rack at Fire Island, the baths, and the backroom bookstores and bars that proliferated in American cities in the 1970s.

Before I move on to Larry and AIDS, I want to jump this story backward in time, and scrutinize the unexamined elision of gay liberation and the sexual scene of the 1970s. Something, it seemed to me, happened on the road from Stonewall to AIDS and it isn't often commented upon.

□ □ □

Gay liberation, in its immediate post-Stonewall incarnation, has already had its share of chroniclers.[6] Those wild-eyed radicals who picked up the banner of the Stonewall riots exist more as myth—or nightmare—than as flesh-and-bones historical actors. Some cast them as authentic revolutionaries, who threw off generations of oppression and opened a brave new world of human freedom and justice. Others brand them as impractical extremists, utopian anarchists who mixed too many radical causes into an unstable brew.

Let's leave aside whether we agree with them or not, whether we approve of their politics or don't, whether we consider ourselves their political heirs or claim another ideological mantle. One thing *is* certain: they elaborated a critique not only of the mistreatment of homosexuals, but of human sexuality in a society they defined as exploitative, hierarchical, and oppressive.

To be more specific: they did not simply say that gay was good, that notions of homosexuality as sin, sickness, or crime were wrong. They claimed that the expression of sexuality in a capitalist and patriarchal society was inherently deformed. Patriarchy structured a system of gender roles that produced males and females whose erotic lives were misshapen. Capitalism played with human sexuality every which way: it channeled men and women into heterosexual roles to reproduce workers; it repressed as well as incited sexual desire; it demanded that we defer gratification until our desires exploded outward. Sexuality under capitalism became another kind of commodity, to be bought and sold, as objectified and alienated as were the products of our labor.[7]

This perspective often led gay liberationists, in the immediate aftermath of Stonewall, to be as critical of the gay subculture as they were of the heterosexual dictatorship. They dissented from the gender norms of American society and the way those norms shaped the eroticism of gay men. Male socialization placed a premium on dominance, aggression, coldness, and competitive success; it taught men to manipulate and use others as objects. Gay men were oppressed in large part because they failed to fill their role within the patriarchal nuclear family. Not fully male, they were drawn into the orbit of sexism, and treated with the kind of contempt that women routinely received. At the same time, even as gay men were targeted for oppression, their socialization as men made them enact their own version of masculinist sexuality. Anonymous sex, the objectification of youth and beauty, and the endless tricking of the bar world all came under merciless attack. The heirs of Stonewall were as likely to "liberate" a gay bar—by disrupting the bar's grim cruising scene with a circle dance, for instance—as they were to "zap" a homophobic shrink. For them, the institutions of the gay subculture did not inspire reverence.

These radical gay liberationists also played with notions of sexual orientation. Even as they defiantly embraced a public gay identity, they treated both heterosexuality and homosexuality as suspect categories, the products of an oppressive society. Liberation meant the shattering of restrictive identities. How else is one to interpret the phrase of Allen Young, in his introduction to *Out of the Closets?*: "In a free society, everyone will be gay." Or the injunction of Carl Wittman, in *A Gay Manifesto*, to "Free the homosexual in everyone."[8]

Less than a decade separates the stormy politics of radical gay liberation from the publication of novels like *Faggots* and *Dancer*, but their respective sexual worlds couldn't be more remote from one another.[9] By the end of the 1970s hardly a trace of the former's sexual critique of gay male life remained. Instead, the subculture they had once defined as flawed had emerged into view, bigger, grander, glossier than before. Ironically, an anti-capitalist gay liberation movement had made this possible. By containing police harassment in major cities, gay liberation opened the door to legitimate investment in gay sex. Cleaner baths, palatial discos, a Fire Island summer undisturbed by intrusive cops: the sex scene these allowed had more allure than self-reflective ruminations about what our erotic lives would look like in a world without alienation, economic insecurity, or gendered oppression.

I am not sure why or how the transition happened. Some of it can be traced to who those Stonewall-era gay radicals were, and how they offered their criticisms. Most were young, with roots not in the pre-Stonewall gay world but in the movements of the 1960s. In other words, even though they were gay, they were writing as outsiders. Their commentary on gay male sex life, moreover, arrived with a prescriptive edge. A heated moralism often shaped their words, as did a naivete about how easily human sexual desire could be reshaped. They acted, in other words, as if a call to authenticity in human relationships (a New Left favorite), coupled with a bit of consciousness raising, were enough to rewrite the scripts of our eroticism.

But they also were no match for the force of a subculture rooted in both oppression *and* resistance. The gay world that predated them absorbed parts of their message—coming out and gay pride—while discarding others. Gay liberation served less to refashion the sexual ethics of gay male life than to allow the pre-Stonewall urban gay scene to grow larger, more secure, and more stable. It opened a path, in other words, not only for individuals, but for a whole social world to come out.

□ □ □

Oppression and resistance. We tend to see them as dichotomous concepts: there is oppression and there is resistance, and never the two shall meet.

I have come to believe that the line dividing them is not quite as sharp and clear as we would like to think, that there are times when acts of resistance can unwittingly reproduce, or at least give sustenance to, systems of oppression.

The best way I can find to explain what I mean is by playing with the concept of internalized oppression. Most of the time we use internalized oppression in a relatively flat, unnuanced way. Society has told us, monotonously and repetitively, that we are bad, evil, sick, perverted. When gays and lesbians act in ways that seem self-hating, we label it as internalized oppression, as mimicking the negative oppressive messages of the majority culture. When we speak or act in ways that assert gay is good, we are shedding these internalized attitudes.

But what if it is more complicated than the two poles of good and bad? For instance, the dominant culture also claims that we are different. When we proclaim our difference—even if we celebrate it—is this resistance, or does this simply recreate the conditions of our oppression? Gay and lesbian oppression also operates in ways designed to isolate and marginalize us from the rest of society. When we create vibrant, exciting—but thoroughly separate—social worlds, have we resisted our oppression, or merely created a more comfortable zone of isolation and marginalization? An oppressive society has defined us only by our sexuality and has defined our passions as uncontrollable. When we make our sexual desires the heart of our lives and our political movement, is this an act of resistance, or does it signify the acting out of the terms of oppression?

Let me push this further. What if the adaptations we've made to survive in a hostile world function as a tool of oppression, but one that we unwittingly wield? Battered as we have all been by a barrage of destructive lies, by a culture that once denied our existence and still denies our worth, we have understandably become distrustful, defiant, and defensive. For gay men, whose sexuality is so much the heart and soul of the hatred directed against us, is it any wonder that we are instinctively distrustful of any criticism of our sexual lives, that we defend ourselves against it, and that we defiantly assert our right to do whatever we please?

But when do these responses serve us well, and when do they fail us miserably? When do defensiveness, defiance and distrust become modes of resistance, and when are they the knee-jerk reactions of a people targeted for mistreatment? When, in other words, are they a form of useful skepticism wielded by us, and when are they the outcomes of a repertoire of responses severely restricted by oppression?

□   □   □

It matters very little whether or not reviewers react defensively to the fictional portrayal of gay life in *Faggots*. It matters a good deal more when one of the earliest, most public wake-up calls to AIDS elicits a similar response. Yet Larry's statements about AIDS have repeatedly evoked such angry, defensive denunciations.

Take one example, which Larry himself has commented upon. In late August 1981, the same summer that the first cases of what became known as AIDS were reported in the press and soon after Kramer and others had begun meeting to plan a response, the *New York Native* published an appeal from Larry for funds. One sentence read: "It's easy to become frightened that one of the many things we've done or taken over the past years may be all that it takes for a cancer to grow from a tiny something-or-other that got in there who knows when from doing who knows what." The sentence seems innocent enough; in fact, it describes with perfect accuracy how many gay men, myself included, felt in the early stages of the epidemic, before anyone knew anything about retroviruses, antibodies, and modes of transmission. Fear was a chronic condition, fed by endless, futile speculation. Yet, for many, the sentence hit a sensitive nerve, prompting them to write back in anger. "Read anything by Kramer closely," Robert Chesley, a New York playwright, warned readers. "I think you'll find the subtext is always: the wages of gay sin are death."[10]

Or, consider this paragraph from a review of *Reports from the holocaust*, Larry's collection of essays about AIDS, that Gregory Kolovakos published in *The Nation* in 1989:[11]

> Kramer equates sexual freedom with promiscuity and writes, "There's no question that the promiscuity of some gay men was unwittingly responsible for AIDS killing so many of us." There's the old wages-of-sin argument—those more sexually experimental killed "us." Sontag explicitly agrees with Kramer: "Promiscuous homosexual men practicing their vehement sexual customs ... could be viewed as dedicated hedonists—though it's now clear that their behavior was no less suicidal" than that of addicts sharing needles. Are such pronoucements so distant from Falwell's statement about reaping "a harvest of corruption"?

Kolovakos asks the question rhetorically, intending "no" to be the only answer. Yet surely there is a world of difference between Larry's statement and Falwell's. And isn't there something suspect about the way Kolovakos slides from "promiscuity" to "experimental"? For some gay men at some times, random, casual, indiscriminate sex (the dictionary definition of promiscuous) could be highly experimental. For other gay men at other times, there was nothing experimental about it. In fact, it was boringly, traditionally male, a textbook display of how male (hetero)sexuality has been described in the West for centuries.

The issue here is not whether Larry or his critics were "right." Rather, the reaction to Larry, from *Faggots* through AIDS, tells us something important about the dynamics of gay male sexual culture and sexual politics. To venture into this territory is like entering a minefield ready to detonate at any moment. I have no solutions as to how to clear the ground, but I know it doesn't serve us well when frank expressions of dismay or concern about our sexual lives set off such explosions.

◻ ◻ ◻

Without AIDS, Larry would be one among many gay novelists and playwrights. Some of us would be moved by his work; others of us wouldn't; and most gay men would have no idea who he is.

AIDS gave Larry a national profile. Because AIDS appeared early in his social circles, he could be among the first to act. Because he was a writer with skills as a polemicist, he could give an articulate voice to emotions of anger, loss and fear that circulated in the gay community. Because of the privilege that inhered in his class, his education, his race, and his gender, he expected to be heard. Because he was doing all this from New York, and not from Phoenix or Omaha or Cincinnati, he found a large audience.

The broad outline of Larry's career as an AIDS activist is easy to summarize and already familiar to many. Late in the summer of 1981, after the first articles about a deadly immune deficiency among some gay men appeared in the *New York Times*, Larry was one of the conveners of a meeting that led to the formation of Gay Men's Health Crisis (GMHC). The organization grew and inspired others as cases of sick and dying men appeared in other cities. Larry became the earliest and most public polemicist about the epidemic, writing essays for the *New York Native* that were reprinted elsewhere. His writing raised consciousness, and also raised controversy.

Larry and GMHC parted angrily by 1983. Unencumbered by organizational ties, he continued to write essays and op-ed pieces, characterized by a willingness to attack anyone, friend or foe, who seemed to stand in the way of a no-holds-barred response to the epidemic. His play, *The Normal Heart*, premiered in New York City in 1985. A polemical piece in the tradition of the agit-prop theater of the 1930s, it was taken seriously by reviewers, and became a favorite of local theater companies throughout the US. Indeed, it would not be unreasonable to argue that *The Normal Heart*, more than any other single cultural product, spread the politics of AIDS to a mass audience.

Though never completely removed from AIDS political activism, Larry returned to it in a big way when his speech at the New York Community Center transformed simmering anger and frustration into a new form of direct action politics. ACT UP chapters spread rapidly and gave AIDS activism the hard, determined, driven edge that it needed. As with GMHC earlier, Larry eventually found himself at odds with the direction of ACT

UP. He moved away from political action again, but continued to write—*Reports from the holocaust, Just Say No, The Destiny of Me*—and to speak out against government policy, and what he saw as the failure of gay, lesbian, and AIDS activism.

It's quite a resumé to ponder. What patterns of meaning can we extract from it?

The most obvious is the recurring oscillation between explosive bursts of energy mobilized toward making change and dramatic criticism of his peers leading to withdrawal from the fray. Larry himself has offered one interpretation of what might be called his "career development": "I wanted to be Moses, but I only could be Cassandra," he has the character, Ned Weeks, say in *The Destiny of Me*.

Let's leave Moses aside. But in reading *Reports from the holocaust* I was struck by the aptness of the Cassandra analogy. Most of the essays in the volume were familiar to me; I had read them when they were first published in the *Native* and elsewhere. Reading them again, I remembered my original reaction to most of them: overblown, overstated, Larry the prophet of doom. And I was shocked to realize that, in this encounter with them as historical documents, I found myself thinking: "Virtually everything that Larry said has turned out to be true; the worst-case scenarios have become fact." Or at least that was my reaction up to a point. The closer in time to the present an essay was, the less credible it seemed. What is this, if not the fate of Cassandra?

Beyond Larry's "predictive" powers, there is something else to be analyzed in his AIDS career—the thread of acerbic criticism that runs through his words and deeds. The criticisms—indeed, if one is ever the object of them they look more like frontal assaults—are fairly indiscriminate in their targets: mayors, public health officials, Congress, Presidents, drug companies, scientists; but also AIDS organizations, gay and lesbian organizations, and the individual men and women who lead them.

I am especially interested in the way Larry has repeatedly attacked those within the community and the movement. Sometimes the attacks are aimed at individuals; sometimes at an organization; and sometimes at the AIDS movement and the gay and lesbian movement as a whole. The themes are similar. A large collective "we" stand accused of failure. The movement and its members are second-rate, lacking power or afraid of it, unable to respond effectively to the challenges at hand.

If the measure of success is the end of the AIDS epidemic, then, of course, the criticisms are right on target. The epidemic is not over, the number of diagnoses continues to grow, and the deaths keep rising. But what are the assumptions behind that expectation? What baseline of political strength do we attribute to the gay and lesbian movement when we accuse it of failure? Underlying the negative assessment is a badly distorted view of the movement's history, and a confusion over the relationship between the gay and lesbian movement and the larger community of which it is a subset.

Just as Larry and others have tended to conflate the gay liberation impulse with the urban sexual culture that flourished in the 1970s, so the criticisms of the failure to respond adequately to AIDS conflate the collective political movement that developed in the 1970s with the much larger public community of urban gay men that coalesced during the same years. The two were not identical; in many ways they looked at one another with a mixture of wariness and resentment.

For those of us who were involved in the political world of gay and lesbian activism in the 1970s, the gains we had made were wondrous. Because we all remembered vividly a time in our own lives when the isolation was impenetrable, the fear pervasive, and the hopelessness overwhelming, every bit of change seemed momentous. Every street demonstration, every column of media coverage, every conference filled to overflowing, every public hearing by a government body: all were historic, all seemed to be evidence of profound change. And they were. But they were also barely beginnings. "Been down so long it looks like up from here" went the line from a popular song of the 1960s. It captures a perspective that describes what happened politically in the 1970s more accurately than either the self-commendations of the time or the retrospective criticisms of Larry and others.

The fact is that, were we to chart the trajectory of the gay and lesbian movement in terms of a human life cycle, we might say that the pre-Stonewall activism of the 1950s and 1960s represented birth and infancy; the decade after Stonewall was at best a childhood. Virtually all local lesbian and gay organizations in the 1970s were staffed by volunteers; they experienced an ebb and flow of effectiveness dependent on the volume of donated labor. Although organizations were popping up everywhere, only in the largest American cities and in some university towns was there anything like a sustained organizational presence. National organizations like Lambda Legal Defense and the National Gay Task Force had barely gotten off the ground. On the eve of the AIDS epidemic, New York City sustained fewer than a score of activists in full-time paying positions in the movement. Most of those jobs were to be found in national organizations based in the city, or in social service—not political—organizations, like Senior Action in a Gay Environment.

The real institutional gains of the 1970s—the repeal of many sodomy laws; the passage of municipal civil rights legislation; the removal of homosexuality from the medical profession's list of diseases; changes in federal employment policies; the curtailment of police harassment—had little to do with the strength of the movement. Rather, change was attributable to the weakness of traditional sources of institutional power in the wake of the upheavals of the 1960s. In other words, the relatively small amount of militancy we were able to muster in the 1970s went an unusually long way. To be sure, none of it would have happened without us. But the times were right for a small but determined holy band of warriors to achieve quite a lot.

By the time AIDS struck in the early 1980s, this favorable political environment was already history. A new conservative movement had reconstituted itself as a political force, in part by mobilizing against the gains of social movements based on racial, gender, and sexual identities. The free ride of the 1970s was over.

Framed in this way, the response to AIDS is nothing short of miraculous. Within a few short years, the community was able to build from the ground up an extraordinary network of service organizations that cared for many of the sick and educated the community. The only comparable organizational response I can think of is the creation of the CIO in the 1930s among working people bombarded by the Depression. A relatively weak national organization like NGLTF was able to spark a large cooperative lobbying effort that penetrated the walls of Congress and shook funds loose for research, care, and prevention in the face of a Reagan administration that cared about nothing except large defense budgets and even larger tax cuts. AIDS pushed open doors for us that had been closed in the 1970s. Make no mistake: we were still only visitors. But a dialogue had begun.

In an ideal world, AIDS would never have happened. In an almost ideal world, a politically mature, organizationally stable, and collectively powerful gay movement would have orchestrated a response to AIDS in which everything that could be done was done. In the real world we inhabit, AIDS built a gay movement that did not yet exist; it reconfigured our movement and our community in profound, irreversible ways.

Although an AIDS movement and a gay and lesbian movement are conceptually distinct, in practice the boundary proved porous. For instance, gays and lesbians of color by the end of the 1970s were creating their own autonomous organizations. Like their mostly white predecessors, these groups were volunteer-based, with an unstable existence. AIDS created a material base of resources to push forward this organizing impulse: witness the importance of AIDS-related funding to organizations like LLEGO, the national Latino/a organization, and the national Black Lesbian and Gay Leadership Forum. In smaller cities and towns, gays and lesbians in the 1980s often established their first stable organizational presence through an AIDS service group; political organizations were then a short step away. The massive 1987 March on Washington, whose energy flowed in part from the accumulated anger and frustration engendered by the epidemic, unleashed a major new round of grassroots gay and lesbian organizing around the country. And AIDS, by arousing from apathy an economically privileged segment of the community, tapped resources that have allowed us to make the transition from a movement of only volunteers to one with an ever growing number of full-time paid workers.

Viewed from this angle, Larry's role in the history of AIDS and the gay movement can be defined more precisely—and modestly. As an activist, he was one of many. Though he was in the right place at the right time on a couple of occasions—for the founding of GMHC and ACT UP—it would be hard to claim that he was at the forefront of the steady, patient work that builds a social movement. But as a polemicist, as a wielder of words which can rouse and motivate, his role may be unparalleled.

It's a role that cuts two ways. For even as his words mobilized, his verbal attacks have also stung and have consequently limited the influence he has had on the shape and evolution of AIDS policy and on the direction of the gay and lesbian movement. As a figure with cultural capital at his disposal, Larry has been able to mount a platform from which he can be heard. Yet the stance that he has taken—the cultural critic as outsider—necessarily creates boundaries around this influence. Perhaps this tells us something about the state of the movement even after the enormous growth and institutionalization of the last ten years. The person associated with the movement who has as much visibility as anyone remains an outsider.

□ □ □

There is more that could be said, of course. Larry's political writings brim with specific criticisms of decisions that were made and actions taken—or not taken—in the fight against AIDS. But I have chosen to focus on two themes, gay male sexual culture and the trajectory of the gay movement, not only because Larry's work draws attention to them but because they seem to me of particular importance. Debates about gay male sexuality continue to rage, in discussions about sero-conversion rates, for instance, or about the reappearance of commercial sex businesses. Likewise, in our press, our books, and our everyday discussions among ourselves, we spin endless spirals of analysis about what the movement can or cannot do. Behind all these words lie implicit assumptions about the movement's past, from which we draw conclusions about the present and the future. Larry's are the words of only one of us, but they open a window from which we can view the past and thus better imagine—perhaps even influence—what is yet to come.

Notes

1. For a vivid account of ACT UP's style of activism, written by a participant, see Douglas Crimp, with Adam Rolstom, *AIDS demo graphics* (Seattle: Bay Press, 1990). For a discussion of other direct action movements, see Barbara Epstein, *Political Protest and Cultural Revolution: Nonviolent Direct Action in the 1970s and 1980s* (Berkeley: University of California Press, 1991).

2. In making this claim, I am painfully aware of how little visibility and public recognition have accrued to *anyone* associated with the gay and lesbian freedom struggle. One person who comes to mind as a point of comparison—Harvey Milk—was hardly known outside California at the time he was assassinated in 1978; recognition and influence came to him more in death than in life.

Another, Audre Lorde, was deeply influential among feminists as a poet, essayist, and theorist of change. But, sadly, the gay men and lesbians who have distinguished themselves through their actions and writings in the gay and lesbian freedom struggle rarely have achieved a profile beyond the boundaries of the gay community.

3. Unfortunately, there is still no thoroughgoing history of the gay and lesbian movement in the decades since Stonewall. For overviews see Barry D. Adam, *The Rise of a Gay and Lesbian Movement*, 2nd ed. (Boston: Twayne, 1995); Margaret Cruikshank, *The Gay and Lesbian Liberation Movement* (New York: Routledge, 1992); and my own essay "After Stonewall," in *Making Trouble: Essays on Gay History, Politics, and the University* (New York: Routledge, 1992).

4. I am thinking of a tradition of writing about homosexual desire that includes such diverse products as Thomas Mann's *Death in Venice*, Tennessee Williams's *Suddenly Last Summer*, and Mart Crowley's *The Boys in the Band*.

5. *New York Times Book Review*, January 14, 1979, pp. 15, 40; *New Republic*, January 6, 1979, p. 30; *Gay Community News* review quoted in *New York*, June 3, 1985, p. 45.

6. For accounts of the gay liberation movement in the immediate aftermath of the Stonewall riot see Martin Duberman, *Stonewall* (New York: Dutton, 1993); Terence Kissack, "Freaking Fag Revolutionaries: New York's Gay Liberation Front, 1969–1971," *Radical History Review* 62 (Spring 1995), 104–34; Toby Marotta, *The Politics of Homosexuality* (Boston: Houghton Mifflin, 1981); and Dennis Altman, *Homosexual Oppression and Liberation* (New York: Avon, 1971).

7. For a collection of representative writings from radical gay and lesbian liberationists see Karla Jay and Allen Young (eds), *Out of the Closets: Voices of Gay Liberation* (New York: New York University Press, 1992; 20th Anniversary Edition).

8. Quoted in Jay and Young, *Out of the Closets*, pp. 29, 341.

9. I do not mean to suggest that Larry's novelistic diatribe against the culture of gay male sexuality was rooted in the left-wing anti-capitalist politics of gay liberation. Larry wrote from the vantage point of a romantic in a new world of sexual plenty, frustrated in his search for love. Yet, in penning his novel, he was hardly attacking something that other gay men hadn't already taken on. His criticism, in other words, was different; it rested on mainstream values of romantic love. But dissent from the practices of gay male sexuality had precedent in the recent past.

10. Quoted in Larry Kramer, *Reports from the holocaust: The Making of an AIDS Activist* (New York: St. Martin's Press, 1989), p. 10.

11. *The Nation*, May 1, 1989, p. 600.

Kramer as Prophet

Gabriel Rotello

THE WORLD IS FULL OF PROPHETS, most of them false. People
have been proclaiming the end of time since time began and yet here
we spin, neither earthquakes nor floods nor plagues nor wars able to keep
the world from its appointed rounds. But even though prophecy has a long
history of not coming true, doomsayers remain a dime a dozen. Every few
years some charlatan attracts a flush following by predicting that the end is
near. We smirk when the appointed day passes and he skulks off in his
Mercedes to recalculate. We smirk less if, like Jim Jones or David Koresh,
he takes his followers with him into some private holocaust. In either case,
we soon turn to the next headline, the only useful lesson learned being that
humanity never learns its lesson.

There is, however, one school of prophets who are as rare as false
prophets are common. The ones whose warnings come true. I say rare
because even the select company we call the Biblical Prophets were not
exactly accurate. It's true that Jeremiah foretold the Babylonian captivity
and then lived to see it, but he was a notable exception. More typical was
Jesus, who indicated in no uncertain terms that the world would end during
the lifetime of his followers.

We moderns haven't done much better. For every Churchill vindicated by
the specific disaster he thundered about, there are dozens who predicted a
bang and got a whimper. What ever happened to the people who predicted
that the Cold War would inevitably go nuclear? What ever happened to the
Club of Rome? If anything, it seems remarkable that given humanity's
unbroken string of both pessimists and disasters, the twain so rarely meet.
You would think the laws of chance alone would dictate that before each of
history's major train wrecks at least one reedy voice would have cried out in
the wilderness, trying vainly to draw our attention to the doom barreling
down the track. But who predicted the great influenza epidemic of 1919? Or
the Taiping Rebellion? Or the death of disco? Or even that most predictable
of unpredicted disasters to rise up on a summer's day, the First World War?

A genuine Jeremiah, someone who really hits the disaster nail on the head, is as rare as an accurate five-day forecast.

The question I put to you is whether Larry Kramer belongs to this august but disturbing company. Whether Larry Kramer is, for want of a softer term, the gay community's AIDS prophet. And the answer I put to you is, Yes.

□ □ □

"Prophet" comes from a Greek word meaning someone who delivers the word of the gods to mortals. Strictly speaking, prophecy does not have to concern future disasters or even future events. Prophets are merely conduits through which God or the gods convey his, her or their divine utterances, messages, encouragements, warnings and, sometimes, predictions. In some cultures prophets serve this role reluctantly or in an unconscious state of inspiration or possession. Such a prophet, said Philo of Alexandria, is merely a lute the gods play upon. But others, particularly those in the Judeo-Christian-Moslem tradition, are wide awake and gnashing their teeth through the dark night of the soul, propounding a theology so fierce it's downright scary. Hebrew prophecy in particular focused on the stark dualism between good and evil. It was interested in what you're doing in the here and now, as opposed to the next world. Hebrew prophets did not just foretell or divine, they lectured and hectored and warned and screamed. It's no accident that our popular vision of Israel's greatest prophet is Charlton Heston, thundering over the idolatrous apostates, shocked at the perfidy of humankind. Wind howls. Lightning strikes. Mr. DeMille gets his close-up, and the angry eyes are on fire.

Hebrew prophets directed the burning lasers of their moral vision to the spiritual improvement of their own kind. Their message was invariably that if their fellow Jews didn't shape up, they were going to be creamed by external enemies: Egyptians, Babylonians, Assyrians, Romans, whomever. One of the reasons so many prophets were so unpopular in their lifetimes— from Jeremiah to Jesus—was that most of their Jewish contemporaries wanted to focus on the sins of the oppressor, or focus on the injustice of the invader, or even focus on the injustice of God in allowing the invader to invade. But the prophets had a different agenda. They focused on how the failings of the Jews brought oppressors and invasions upon themselves. To them, the Romans or the Babylonians or the Egyptians were almost irrelevant, the harsh but inevitable side effects of homegrown moral failure. In modern parlance, they "blamed the victim." With a vengeance.

If we define prophecy as a strictly religious franchise, obviously Larry Kramer is ruled out. Although he has consciously drawn upon his Jewishness as a basis for his sense of morality, and although he sees parallels between the historic plight of Jews and of gays, he certainly does not claim a direct line to God, notwithstanding such of his exhortations as

"Oh, my People." In fact, in many ways he is hostile to religion, or at least to the aspects of religion that are hostile to him as a gay man. But to say that Kramer can't be considered a prophet because prophets have to be religious is a little like saying a secular person cannot expound moral values because morality was traditionally rooted in religion. It seems just as reasonable to flex our social-constructionist imaginations and argue that the link between religion and prophethood is merely an artifact of history, that you can have prophecy without necessarily having God.

But if a direct linkup to the deity isn't a prophet's main qualification, what is? Someone once wrote that the proof of prophecy was simply the acid test of history—did the predicted thing come true? But that seems to me only half the test, and the mechanical, rabbit-out-of-the-hat half at that. By such a limited definition, the Weather Channel could have a shot. Accurate prediction, impressive as it may seem, often requires something more like a good slide rule than genuine vision.

The real acid test of prophecy is not just an ability to predict something about the future, but to root that prediction in some spiritual or moral vision. The great prophetic voices, religious and secular, not only warned of disasters nobody else could clearly see, but warned that people were bringing these disasters upon themselves. Sometimes the problem was spiritual, sometimes ethical, sometimes practical, sometimes all three. Winston Churchill played the role of prophet when he urged the democracies to show moral fiber in their dealings with fascism, to show ethical fiber in standing up for their weaker friends like Czechoslovakia, and to show practicality by building up their armies just in case. The role of a prophet is not merely to announce impending doom, but to tell us how to get our act together to avoid it.

By this definition, then, Kramer needs to have fulfilled a few basic requirements to be considered a bona fide prophet. First, he needs to have identified a central moral problem in gay life, and done so not from a scientist's medical perspective—If you keep doing such and such you will spread germs—but from a moral perspective—If you keep doing such and such, you will diminish your souls. Then he needs to have specifically warned of a coming disaster and explained from a practical position how it could be avoided. And finally, he needs to have been right.

I would argue that Kramer fulfills all three conditions. I can even get precise and pinpoint his period of prophecy from 1978 until around 1985.

During the period in question Kramer produced three immensely influential pieces of work. The first was the novel *Faggots*, published in 1978 four years before AIDS was announced to the world. The second was a series of essays and letters he wrote for and to the *New York Native* from 1981 to 1983, in which he alerted us to the potential enormity of the epidemic and told us how to avoid it and how to fight it. This writing can be said to begin with the letter "A Personal Appeal" and includes the essay "1,112 and Counting."

The third is *The Normal Heart*, a play first produced by Joseph Papp at the New York Shakespeare Festival in mid 1985, which recapitulates the drama of Kramer's prophecy, enfolds it, and puts the prophet's spin on his own legacy.

After 1985 Kramer continued his advocacy, and some might argue that his single most influential piece of writing was the speech he delivered in 1987 that resulted in the founding of ACT UP. But although his post-1985 work has been extremely influential, it cannot really qualify as prophecy. Not because Kramer was any less prophetic, or any less right, but simply because by then the AIDS epidemic had become so huge and undeniable that it no longer took a prophet to see it coming. It had arrived. Afterward Kramer continued to exhort, prod, investigate, cajole, shame and scream. He does to this day. But we no longer needed him to foretell. The sky had already fallen.

□ □ □

Faggots never mentions disease or illness, and it does not predict a physical disaster if gay men do not mend their wayward ways. But it established the moral and ethical basis of Kramer's later ministry. Easily the most controversial gay novel ever written, *Faggots* depicts four hectic days leading up to the fortieth birthday of its narrator Fred Lemish, who bears more than a passing resemblance to Larry Kramer. Lemish has decided that he must find true love before the big four-oh arrives, hopefully in the person of his unattainably gorgeous on-again off-again boyfriend Dinky Adams. But the world Lemish, Dinky and their friends inhabit is too hectically hedonistic, too drug-saturated and sexually precocious and predatory, to nurture the kind of stable relationship Lemish craves. He rails against this wacky world even as he gorges himself in its absurd comedy.

The novel's characters are deliberately overdrawn and sometimes grotesque caricatures in the manner of Evelyn Waugh, and they hurtle through their discos and tea rooms and drug and sexual adventures like the Red Queen in *Alice in Wonderland*: they have to keep running faster and fucking harder simply to stay in the same place. In the end Lemish finally sheds his infatuation with Dinky, his love–hate relationship with hedonism, and simultaneously has an epiphany about his own burdensome self-hatred. Declaring that gay life on the wild side is the epitome of the unexamined life, and that "the unexamined life is unlivable," he literally walks off into the sunrise at the novel's conclusion, presumably to continue examining.

Faggots, the poet Ian Young has written, "is Kramer's warning to gay men that 'We're fucking ourselves to death!'" Its theme is the impossibility of love in a world in which people treat each other as objects. Its charge is that gay men have to grow up and stop doing that. Its challenge is that we can, but that in order to do so we have to take responsibility for our own fates. It tried to establish, in the most infertile pavement of the 1970s gay fast lane, the most unlikely thing: a prophet's seedling, a call to responsibility. And the fast lane whizzed by, hissing.

It's funny how those criticisms tried to have it both ways. On the one hand, *Faggots* was trashed as inaccurate, overdrawn, exaggerated; it was said that gay men did not act like Kramer's grotesques, or that maybe a few did, but just a tiny minority. But at the same time that some critics excoriated the book as a shameless lie, others called it unforgivable precisely because it rang so true: It was said to have betrayed the secret lives of gay men, allowing the general public a peek into our promiscuous playrooms (it became a national bestseller, after all, and certainly not on the strength of gay sales alone). It was the ultimate airing of dirty laundry in public, making us look like the sex-obsessed twits our worst enemies accused us of being. I remember my nervous sense of dislocation at the time, when a politically active gay friend who had long argued that gay promiscuity was something we ought to be proud of, our form of revolution, told me he was furious with *Faggots* because now the people in his hometown were going to have a bad impression of gay life.

But while many in the gay world took *Faggots* as a diatribe against homosexuality, in retrospect it seems to be an argument against equating homosexuality and sexual liberation with selfishness, self-indulgence and self-destruction. Although it did not predict physical annihilation, it implicitly argued that the price we would pay if we didn't get it together would be heavy; a spiritual extinction, the meat-rack of the soul. *Faggots* warned of the moral virus of non-intimacy and the spiritual disease of unlove. The primary thing we were not loving, it told us, was ourselves.

This, of course, did little to mollify the argument that *Faggots* was simply repeating what the homophobes have always said—that gay men are sexual neurotics who need to get a grip. In that view, *Faggots* was seen as a monumental act of self-loathing. But in rereading *Faggots* today on the other side of AIDS, I see a gaping chasm between homophobic self-loathing and the book's message. Homophobes tell gay men that, as gay men, we cannot love. *Faggots* tells gay men that, as gay men, we must love. Homophobes tell gay men that, as gay men, we can never grow up. *Faggots* tells gay men that, as gay men, we must grow up. Homophobes tell gay men we will always be defective victims. *Faggots* tells gay men we must stop being victims and seize control of our own destiny.

Its angry gay critics, however, did have one thing right. While *Faggots* was not anti-sex so much as pro-love, it certainly was anti-promiscuity. Particularly the sex radicalism that characterized much of the gay fast lane of the 1970s, the three-thousand-men-up-my-butt lifestyle of the baths and the meat racks. It is precisely because *Faggots* connected this lifestyle to spiritual desolation that it qualifies as the genuine and necessary first act in the prophecy of physical desolation that was to come. Prophecy, after all, is ruled by a sort of spiritual ecology—what happens in the physical world is seamlessly connected to the life of the soul. The gay men Kramer wrote about were, he said, committing an offense against love. In so doing he established a prophet-like moral claim upon them, whether they liked it or not (we mostly did not). "We're fucking ourselves to death" is not far from "We must love one another or die." And "we're fucking ourselves to death" as metaphor is not far from "no, we're *really* fucking ourselves to death."

Obviously no one could have recognized *Faggots* as an AIDS prophecy when it was published in 1978, since the announcement of AIDS was several years in the future. But it is oddly ironic (and prophecy should be tinged with oddness and irony) that some epidemiologists now date the AIDS epidemic to the very year *Faggots* was published. In that year researchers began a major medical study of the hepatitis B epidemic that was sweeping the gay male population, one of the many precursor epidemics to AIDS. As part of that study they began collecting and preserving the blood of thousands of gay male volunteers at six-month intervals. When HIV was discovered years later, researchers were able to go back and use these samples to determine where things began. So for all practical purposes, 1978, the year of *Faggots*, is Year Zero of AIDS, the year HIV can first be detected in a tiny proportion of gay men in San Francisco and New York. It would rise to infect over 50 percent of gay men in those same cohorts by the night *The Normal Heart* opened seven years later.

After *Faggots*, Kramer was virtually banished from the gay world. Close friends stopped speaking to him. He was made to feel unwelcome on the New York gay scene and on Fire Island, and he went into a sort of retreat from gay life, a symbolic sojourn in the wilderness. "I didn't know it then," he has written, "but I was learning—not originally by choice—that necessary lesson for anyone who insists on speaking his mind: how to become a loner." Jeremiah could not have said it better.

□   □   □

Kramer's walk in the wilderness lasted less than three years. On June 5, 1981, the CDC's Morbidity and Mortality Weekly Report published a brief item about a strange cluster of rare pneumonia cases among gay men, a report that was picked up by Lawrence Mass in the *New York Native*. A month later it reported an equally strange cluster of rare cancers in the same population, which was then reported by the *New York Times* and other papers. On July 29, three weeks after the *Times* piece, Kramer visited the physician who had tracked the KS cases in New York. Dr. Alvin Friedman-Kien urged Kramer to raise money for research, and when Kramer, a bit of a hypochondriac, asked how he could personally avoid getting the disease, Friedman-Kien said he knew what he would do. "I'd stop having sex." On August 11 Kramer hosted the meeting of eighty gay men in his apartment that led to the establishment of Gay Men's Health Crisis. And on August 24 he published a piece called "A Personal Appeal" in the *New York Native*, and his next phase of prophecy had begun.

"It's difficult to write this without sounding alarmist or too emotional or just plain scared," he began. Unschooled in epidemiology, Kramer displayed a strong grasp of the implacability of doubling time. "If I had written this a month ago, I would have used the figure '40.' If I had written this last week, I would have needed '80.' Today I must tell you that 120 gay men in the United States—most of them here in New York—are suffering from KS or PCP. I hope you will write a check and get your friends to write one, too," he concluded. "This is our disease and we must take care of each other and ourselves."

With those words Larry Kramer sounded the tocsin of the epidemic. It was only six weeks from the first report in MMWR to his "personal appeal." The bravery of that appeal can be measured by its response, which was immediate and savage.

"Basically, Kramer is telling us that something we gay men are doing (drugs? kinky sex?) is causing Kaposi's sarcoma," wrote playwright Robert Chelsey in his now-famous rejoinder in the *Native*. "We've been told by [experts] that it's wrong and too soon to make any assumptions about the cause of Kaposi's sarcoma, but there's another issue here. It is always instructive to look closely at emotionalism, for it so often has a hidden message which is the *real* secret of its appeal. I think the concealed meaning of Kramer's emotionalism is the triumph of guilt: that gay men deserve to die for their promiscuity. . . . Read anything by Kramer closely. I think you'll find that the subtext is always: the wages of gay sin is death."

This letter has often been held up as a great irony. The fact that its author eventually died of AIDS makes it seem even more poignant, an example not only of denial but of how wrong somebody can be. But from the perspective of Kramer as prophet, Chelsey was right. Kramer was indeed telling gay men that something they were doing was causing this strange malady. Kramer did indeed have a larger message: not that gay men "deserve" to die, but that they *would* die if they did not change, and change fast. He did not argue that the wages of gay promiscuity *ought* to be death, but that they *would* be, like it or not. It may be precisely because Kramer was a critic of promiscuity that he was able to see this so clearly so early. Even, as Chelsey scornfully notes, before the experts.

Some might claim today that to draw a connection between the ethical vision of *Faggots* and the epidemiological vision of "A Personal Appeal" is to give Kramer too much credit. They might argue that it was purely coincidental that the man who wrote *Faggots* also happened to find himself, a hypochondriac, in the middle of a cluster of close friends who were early AIDS victims, and that in the circumstances he did what almost anyone would do. Freaked out. They might object that it's ridiculous to suggest Kramer's early AIDS warnings somehow flowed from his pre-AIDS warnings, that all were a part of some seamless prophetic web. But tellingly, that's not what Kramer's critics said at the time. *They* saw a connection all right. Indeed, it was precisely because they saw a connection that they were so outraged. Kramer, they said, was using AIDS to advance his moral vision (just as, it bears pointing out, the prophets used the Babylonians or the Romans to advance theirs). Had Kramer been known as a sex radical, or simply as neutral about the state of the gay libido, his appeals would probably have produced a more muted response. It was precisely because they came from the man who wrote *Faggots* that they were so provocative.

For the next couple of years Kramer engaged in what you might call the ministry phase of his prophetdom. Instead of chiseling his commandments in stone tablets, he published them in the *New York Native*, producing a spirited series of letters, articles and essays calling on gay men to get their act together to fight AIDS on two fronts, politically and sexually. Much of this writing reflected Kramer's increasing battles with the leaders of GMHC, a group he co-founded and from which he was eventually exiled. This dispute became sort of the Ur Battle of AIDS activism, the primal scene, pitting the forces of caution and timidity against the prophet's uncompromising vision. It's a battle that's been enacted a million times in gay history. Between the closeted Mattachine apologists of the 1950s versus their radical founder Harry Hay, whom they eventually ousted. Between the equally meek Mattachines of the 1960s versus Young Turks like Frank Kameny. The gay world seems to seesaw incessantly between these two opposing forces, the meek and the loud, each one hurling the thunderbolt accusation of "self-loathing" at the other, each one sure the other is destroying everything.

In this case, the dance was heightened and illuminated by its backdrop, which was death on an epic scale. Because the stakes were as high as they get, the main points of bitter dispute, Kramer's insistence that GMHC become more of a political group (much as ACT UP later became) and that they issue much tougher advice about safe sex, take on an added significance. In both cases he was outvoted and outmaneuvered and ultimately pushed aside. And in both cases he was right. The AIDS movement could have really profited from a highly visible cadre of uncompromising activists right then. There is absolutely no reason to think that ACT UP's eventually brilliant deployment of media savvy, its inspired use of advertising techniques to drive home specific messages, its defiant willingness to brave arrest and shut things down, would have been any less successful in 1983 than it became in 1989. As for safe sex, the early 1980s were the very years when most gay men became infected with HIV, a fact we know from, among other things, those hepatitis B studies. Yet as Kramer later wrote, GMHC seemed initially determined not to issue sex recommendations "or anything that in any way could be construed as moralizing. . . . What if it was discovered that nothing infectious was going around. . . . We'd look like fools." Kramer, clearly, was afraid of a lot of things, but looking like a fool was not one of them.

Perhaps the most famous piece from this ministry period was "1,112 and Counting," published in March 1983 in the *Native* and reprinted in gay papers everywhere. Many gay men later said that that essay marked their own personal turning point, the moment in their lives after which the reality of what was happening could no longer be denied. The reason was that "1,112 and Counting" was a two-fisted assault on denial. Kramer attacked the idea that only promiscuous men get AIDS. He attacked the idea that AIDS was soon going to spread epidemically among straights. He attacked lax epidemiology, and the lack of information about treatment, and the terrible conditions for people with AIDS in hospitals, and the lack of drug research, and the problems with health insurance, and the inadequacy of the government's response. By three-quarters of the way through the essay, Kramer had so stormed the gates of denial that his readers had presumably stopped dancing around the golden phallus and were paying rapt attention to his vision of the medical damnation that awaits them. And then like a true prophet, he went for his main target—his own tribe.

I am sick, he writes, of closeted gay doctors who won't help. Of the gay press that won't pay attention. Of gay men who won't donate money to the effort. Of closeted gays, period.

"I am sick of everyone in this community who tells me to stop creating a panic. How many of us have to die before *you* get scared off your ass and into action?

"I am sick of people who say 'it's no worse than statistics for smokers and lung cancer,' or 'considering how many homosexuals there are in the United States, AIDS is really statistically affecting only a very few.' That would wash if case numbers hadn't jumped from 41 to 1,112 in eighteen months.

"I am sick of guys who moan that giving up careless sex until this blows over is worse than death. How can they value life so little and cocks and asses so much?

"I am sick of guys who think that all being gay means is sex in the first place. I am sick of guys who can only think with their cocks."

He went on to praise gay men as "the strongest, toughest people I know," and to issue a call for civil disobedience training, a call that would not be heeded for almost five years. "We must fight to live," he concluded, adding a very prophet-like description of his despair. "My sleep is tormented by nightmares and visions of lost friends, and my days are flooded by the tears of funerals. . . . How many of us must die before *all* of us living fight back?"

The answer was many, many, many.

□   □   □

Within weeks of that essay Kramer's dispute with GMHC had led to his resignation. Within months the epidemic had mutated into front-page news everywhere, and soon the services of prophets were no longer required. Now, surrounded by the disaster he had warned about, Kramer had one more prophetic ritual to accomplish—his chronicle, his book of prophecy, his spin. It took the form of *The Normal Heart*, a play that continues to resonate in the public consciousness long after most of the letters and essays from the early days of AIDS have become the province of libraries and specialists.

The Normal Heart is a dramatic retelling of Kramer's prophetic ministry, his Ur Battle with the meek and mild, his struggle to get everyone to listen, his failure, his exile. It is a passion play, a ritual reenactment of the central tragic turning point of gay life. Because of *The Normal Heart*, an obscure struggle between unknown antagonists in a community nobody cared about has become a titanic struggle between heroes and villains larger than life, and life and death itself. But it bears pointing out that it is also an extremely tender and extremely frank love story between two adult homosexual men. It connects their love and their growth and their strength to their homosexuality in a way no play had ever done before. Those who consider Kramer anti-sex or self-loathing have to contend with the fact that his play is a clear-eyed, head up, shoulders back, out and proud queer love story with no apologies.

And that, basically, is it. From *Faggots* to *The Normal Heart*, a seven-year sweep of homosexual agit-prophecy in the name of love. If that's not enough to qualify in the Modern Prophet's Hall of Fame—with the founding of ACT UP thrown in for good measure a few years later—I don't know what is.

In looking back on Kramer's record, I suppose skeptics are entitled one final nit-picking question. Namely, how right was he? It's an easy hurdle to pass, of course, since most prophets get a good deal wrong. And in fact, the main thing Kramer was right about, the primary area in which his prophetic voice continues to ring true, was his belief that sexual behavior was crucial to containing AIDS. Kramer's other prophetic charges, that government officials and drug companies and the media were literally murderers who kept a cure out of our hands by their criminal negligence, has not weathered the test of time so well. Many were horribly negligent, and the advocacy of ACT UP and later generations of treatment activists certainly jarred the drug-making machinery in important ways. But the advances in basic science required to cure AIDS have been ponderously slow in coming, and in retrospect it remains questionable whether, had things been done differently, many of the dead would still be among us.

But interestingly enough, it is his legacy of anger against the government and the drug companies and the *New York Times*, not against the meekness and myopia of his fellow gay men, for which Kramer seems best remembered in the gay community. And this, to me, provides a further proof of his true prophethood—because true prophets are almost always remembered for the wrong reasons. The biblical Jews often castigated their prophets during their lifetimes, then elevated them to greatness, stuck them in the Bible, called their prophecies the word of God and repeated them so that collective humanity would not, like an amnesiac child, keep making the same mistakes forever. But people did make the same mistakes over and over again. And so do we. The issues that consumed us then consume us now.

In that sense, Larry Kramer passes the final acid test of prophecy. He failed. He was not able to lead gay men out of the wilderness of unlove, or the furnace of AIDS. It was his Cassandra-like lot to foresee the coming disaster perhaps more clearly than anyone else, and to foresee how to avoid it more clearly than anyone else, and to communicate both to us, and then to be disbelieved. Interestingly, he has never been accused of gloating. When he addresses gay men, his message is always contemporary—what you must do today, what you must do next week, what you must do next year. Never "I told you so."

And yet he did tell us so.

Perhaps he feels no satisfaction in such an expensive vindication, since its price was the lives of half his world. Perhaps he does a bit, but feels guilty about it, or recognizes that to say so would be impolitic. Perhaps a bit of both: a natural pride in having been right, tempered by unspeakable sadness at what he was right about. But however he feels, it's not really about him anymore. It never has been. It's about us.

Larry Kramer's central point—that gay men need to love more and fuck less, that we need more of the hearth and less of the hunt—is still, like most prophecy, undigested and unaccepted by the very people who need it most. We tend to find him and his message tedious, audacious, overstated, bullying, moralistic, sometimes even hysterical, always uncomfortable. Just like Jeremiah. And so, while the gay world has yet to produce a genuine leader, in Larry Kramer we seem to have produced a genuine prophet. Troubled. Resented. Mostly correct. And tragically, still mostly unheeded.

An Enemy of the People

Arnie Kantrowitz

> *A prophet is not without honor, save in his own country, and in his own house.*
>
> —Matthew 13: 57

G REAT MEN ARE OFTEN DIFFICULT TO LOVE. The powerful passions that drive them and the dreams that inspire them make them anomalies. Exceptions to the rule, they must be dealt with on their own terms. Their sharper focus and higher expectations move them to create change, even when it is not wanted. Larry Kramer, for example, has made himself an outsider at odds with every community he belongs to. As a gay man at the height of the sexual revolution of the 1970s, he called for the end of promiscuity. As a political activist, he excoriated his own constituents as harshly as he assailed unresponsive government agencies. As a Jew, he upbraided and satirized Jews. As a member of his family, he publicly accused his relatives of failure to love. He stands apart from the crowd he writes about, choosing his own perspective from which he can judge others, while apparently remaining indifferent to how they judge him. The issues are what matters, he would have us believe, not the man. Yet much of his writing is autobiographical, apparently born out of personal wounds, and he has battled his way to center stage by sheer force of personality, underscored by a powerful intellect and artistic vision.

In the early 1970s, when gay activists (myself among them, as vice president of the Gay Activists Alliance) tried to rouse the community to awareness of their own oppression and to the political action that would remedy it, by his own account Kramer sat on his hands, a little bemused and slightly disgusted at our bad taste:

Everybody knew there were gay organizations in New York during the 1970s, but until only recently—1982 or 1983—it was all tinged with an "us and them" kind of thing. You just didn't want to get involved. It was not chic. . . . I can remember being at Fire Island in the 1970s, and when there was a news story on television about the gay pride parade, people would sit in front of the TV set and make fun of it. (Marcus, p. 422).

Although he was known by some as the screenwriter of the 1969 film *Women in Love,* his first great impact on the consciousness of the gay community at large was his novel *Faggots,* published in 1978. In his protagonist Fred Lemish's efforts to cope with approaching middle age while pursuing Dinky Adams, the self-involved, unresponsive object of his ardor, Kramer created an angry satire of the social mores we had newly invented for our post-Stonewall sexual Eden. It has not been uncommon for gay men to criticize what has come to be known as the "gay lifestyle" (even though it does not represent the activities of all of the gay male population). John Rechy described the guilt-ridden sexuality of the pre-Stonewall years in his *City of Night* in 1963, but if he depicted lurid sex, he did so with compassion, and he defended the compulsive behavior of the 1970s in *The Sexual Outlaw* the year before *Faggots* appeared. Dennis Altman in *Homosexual: Oppression and Liberation* saw our objectification of each other as a sign of our oppression, imposed on us by the larger society. David Goodstein, the publisher of *The Advocate* in the 1970s, assailed both anonymous sex and radical gay politics in an effort to win respectability; and in the 1990s, Bruce Bawer, in *A Place at the Table,* has carried on the same campaign, seeking to normalize homosexuality by hiding its more embarrassing features from an uncomprehending society. Daniel Harris criticizes commercialized values in *The Rise and Fall of Gay Culture.* Gabriel Rotello in *Sexual Ecology* and Michelangelo Signorile in *Life Outside* challenge gay men to abandon their promiscuity and evolve more hetero-imitative relationships for the sake of their medical and psychological well-being. Arthur Evans has spoken out against "masculinist" sensibility in *The God of Ecstasy.* He and other writers, such as Ian Young (in *The Stonewall Experiment*) and Douglas Sadownick (in *Sex Between Men*), have reassessed the experience of the liberated 1970s from historical, social, psychological—and even mythological—perspectives. Each writer presents the first decade of gay liberation in his own way, but Kramer's impassioned depiction remains the most vitriolic.

There were actually two intertwined but distinct revolutions occurring in the 1970s: one sexual, and the other political; and their adherents were often at odds with one another, even though many activists, like myself, supported both. Since Kramer was at odds with both the sexually liberated and the politically correct, people in both arenas were enraged by his attacks. The sexual celebrants found him homophobic. He had gone out of his way to reveal and ridicule some of the most exotic practices with which the new sexual pioneers were experimenting in the privacy of their public bathhouses. Turning on a powerful light while people are having unspeakably hot sex is not the best way to win new friends. If he didn't enjoy the party, that was fine, went the thinking of the day, but why did he have to ruin it for everybody else? He was castigating all of us, we said, because he had failed to find a lover for himself, and the community had failed to provide one for him. He knew neither how to be free nor how to have fun. He didn't understand the beauty of "recreational sex," of making love to all mankind in the abstract by embracing one stranger after another with fabulous finesse, but without commitment or responsibility. We ourselves had hardly begun to understand the implications of casual, anonymous sex, but at least we knew how good it felt. All he knew was how to air our dirty linen in public. In short, he was considered an embittered prude.

Like the sexual revolutionaries, the political people also greeted *Faggots* with rage, contempt and ostracism. Craig Rodwell, the principled founder of the first gay/lesbian literary store, the Oscar Wilde Memorial Bookshop, refused to carry the book. The movement of the early 1970s was already in serious decline, having fallen victim to its own fractiousness, which occurred along several faultlines. Middle-class white gay males, who formed the bulk of the Gay Activists Alliance (a nonviolent militant group which sought to reform the existing society to make it accommodate gay concerns) had faced criticism from women, racial minorities, sexual minorities (e.g. drag queens, transsexuals, bisexuals and leathermen), the rich, the poor, the radical and the conservative. Kramer's seemed to us a conservative, "assimilationist" voice, seeking to make us adapt to society's norms, yet we ourselves were labelled "assimilationists" by gay Marxists who dreamed of overthrowing the entire existing order. The movement had exhausted much of its energy on infighting, even before the backlash began. But a new wave of openness, evidenced by a huge swelling of the number of participants in the annual gay pride parade, had appeared in 1977 as Anita Bryant spearheaded what would become the decades-long juggernaut against the community by the religious right. Kramer came neither from the right nor the left. His attack was more moral than it was political. He wanted gay men to treat each other less callously, less objectively. The source of his indignation was personal, not revolutionary, yet many of us felt that his efforts to inspire self-criticism were ammunition for the enemy, and we reviled him as he did us. It was the political community—with its consciousness raised almost to the point of paranoia—that was, according to Kramer, the most vicious: "I did not receive one angry or 'hate' letter from the entire American gay community. The only hate letters I have received have been from the American gay 'political' press" [*Reports*, p. 16].

I agreed with his critics at the time, yet only two years later, in an article I wrote for London's *Gay News* in 1980, I found myself quoting from *Faggots* as I tried to describe my own experience in the wonderful world of promiscuous sex. Trying to recall my many partners was an impossible chore, and Kramer, however acidly, had said it concisely and well when he described Fred Lemish reviewing his sexual diary to reconsider the eighty-seven men he had dated in a single year:

He had been dismayed at how many of the names he no longer remembered: Who were Bat, Ivan, Tommy, Sam, Jellu, Beautiful Henry, Kelly
Hurt (or Kelly hurt?), Joe Johns, Francois, Watson Datson, too many of
the . . . 87 were now unrecognizable and obviously equally as unmemor-
able as the how many—100? 200? 50? 23?—orgasms he had forgotten to
tally. He had had sex with somebody or other one or two, maybe three
times a week for an entire year, including religious holidays but not
counting, hopefully, illnesses. He had spent a whole year (not to mention
all the preceding ones!) with a faceless group of sex objects. . . . And
who the hell was Tiddy Squire? Or was it Ditty Squirt? . . . How could he
not remember? How could he have made love with another human
being and not remember? The face? The body? Something? Anything?
A wart? A smell? BO? (Kramer, *Faggots*, pp. 28–29)

Veiled in humor, what he had said was dark and ugly; but some of it, I had
to accept, was true. The difference is that I was not disappointed or angry at
my experience in the sex bazaar, and Kramer was both. I wrote:

I, too, have my lists, but I am not reviewing them. I've had a dozen brief
infatuations and two or three more fully developed affairs. . . . Each of
them had its own lesson in intimacy. I remember much less about the
prodigious number of fleeting encounters in baths and bars. The features
of all those men dissolve into a single countenance. But I am not sorry
for having tried. For each forgotten name or face there was a moment of
human sharing. Our anonymity released our inhibitions, and we were
fellow explorers of the libido. Each encounter was a fantasy enacted into
reality, and together they add up to a grand season in Never-Neverland.
(Kantrowitz, p. 19)

Nonetheless, I did feel jaded, and when I found myself yawning with
boredom at the notorious sexual supermarket, The Mineshaft, I stopped
having sex for several months. Eventually, I returned to having multiple
partners, but I was a bit more judicious, and I continued to have a good
time. For me, the world of anonymous sex with everyone finally did lead to
a single long-term intimate relationship. I met my lover of fifteen years,
Larry Mass, in a dimly lit cubicle at the Everard Baths, and we are still
together. Promiscuity is not necessarily an ugly word.

Kramer turned his target from sex to politics later in 1978 when he wrote
an op-ed piece in the *New York Times*. Responding to the assassination of
Harvey Milk, the first openly gay member of San Francisco's Board of
Supervisors, and to the impressive outpouring of grief in a gay-led candlelight march there, he attacked the gay community of New York for not
having done its homework:

Several months ago, I listened to Lieut. Gov.- Elect Mario Cuomo speak to the Greater Gotham Business Council [an organization of gay retailers]. He said that until homosexuals organized, until we prepared accurate demographics on our numbers and our purchasing power, we would get nowhere, that political power—and therefore rights—is based on numbers and money.... The City Council was right [in rejecting a gay anti-discrimination bill]. We are not ready for our rights in New York. We have not earned them. We have not fought for them ... (Kramer, "Gay Power")

It did not sit well with the gay activist community that a man who had refused to join our political efforts nearly a decade earlier had the temerity to criticize us for the painstaking work we had done without his help. We had mobilized thousands of gays to attend meetings, "zapped" homophobic businesses and elected officials, raised the consciousness of both straight and gay society (including Larry Kramer's), and organized marches of hundreds of thousands of people. Now were we to be criticized for not being able to count a people who had purposely made themselves invisible? For us, Kramer had no credibility at that point. We knew how hard we had worked, and he didn't. We had certainly done our homework. We had traveled to Albany to lobby the state legislature. We had laboriously drawn up gay civil rights legislation and demonstrated and been arrested in front of City Hall in an effort to force action on its passage. Who was this upstart who thought we could count our constituents as easily as more visible minority groups? The closest we could come to a head count was based on Kinsey's 1948 study, which suggested that in America 10 percent of the population spent at least a year of their adult lives having sex with the same gender. We also knew in what areas of which cities we were concentrated, but no one believes movement statistics anyway. Our enemies were not about to concede such a large number to us. Their intelligence suggested that we were no more than 5 percent or as little as 1 percent of the population. Cuomo surely knew he was demanding the impossible when he asked for accurate numbers. His purpose was to gain either a reason to ignore us or the political leverage he would need if he decided to represent us. As an outsider to the gay political community, Kramer had made himself a tool of the establishment. Even though some activists believed that gay opposition to the movement was a form of internalized homophobia, and hence a symptom of our oppression deserving of our compassion, some of us also believed in Eldridge Cleaver's dictum: "If you're not part of the solution, you're part of the problem," and we saw Kramer as our enemy.

His *New York Times* piece did not limit itself to accusing gays of being incompetent. In a parallel attack, he also accused New York's Jewish organizations of being homophobic: "What temple here would open its doors [to homosexuals]? The [gay rights] legislation was actively opposed by Jewish organizations". (Kramer, *Reports*, p. 5) Members of the gay Jewish community, who belonged to two minority groups with Kramer, felt especially aggrieved, perceiving a manifestation of internalized anti-Semitism in his criticism:

> I particularly aroused the wrath of some Jewish members of the gay synagogue Beth Simchat Torah, who were offended by my criticism of "Jewish organizations"—by which, of course, I meant heterosexual Jewish organizations, and particularly Orthodox and Hasidic Jewish organizations. When I was invited to speak at Beth Simchat Torah, I was barely allowed to do so, so persistent was the heckling. (Kramer, *Reports*, p. 6)

While gay Jews saw Kramer as an outsider because of Jewish self-hate, others believed that the primary source of his energy was a gay self-hatred that extended to wholesale erotophobia. Robert Chesley, a talented playwright, who knew Kramer personally, challenged him in a *Gaysweek* interview:

> Doesn't the extremely negative portrayal of gay sex and promiscuity in *Faggots* fit all too well what anti-gay bigots say about us?
> Kramer responds: "I think that what people are responding to . . . is the terrible fear that 'What if the outside world knows we're doing this?' . . . There must be a heavy burden of shame underpinning this. And it's time to expunge the shame. . . . If we're not doing anything we're ashamed of, then no one should object to the book." (Chesley, p. 12)

People felt betrayed. Because of his own personal problems, we believed, he had made our lives harder. Not only had he exposed our private behavior to the examination of the nation at large, but he had forced us to re-evaluate and defend the underground pleasures we had come to assume were our right as sexual outlaws. He was asking us to alter our behavior so we could demand a legitimacy that not all of us were sure we wanted. Some of us just wanted the government and the police and our employers off our backs so we could be free from prying eyes and hypocritical judgments. We were like children playing a new game, and we weren't ready to assume the responsibility of adulthood.

Then came the epidemic. In the early 1980s, Kramer—along with my soon-to-be lover Larry Mass, who wrote the first articles sounding the alarm in the gay press—was among the first to realize the perils that lay before us. Kramer made an appeal in the *New York Native*, asking the community to contribute to the fight against Kaposi's sarcoma, speaking for the moment like a man of the people. Putting divisiveness aside, he identified himself as a part of the gay community, perhaps because he was speaking from his heart—or perhaps because it suited his rhetorical needs:

The men who have been stricken don't appear to have done anything that many New York gay men haven't done at one time or another. We're appalled that this is happening to them and terrified that it could happen to us. . . . This is our disease and we must take care of each other and ourselves. In the past we have often been a divided community; I hope we can all get together on this emergency, undivided, cohesively, and with all the numbers we in so many ways possess. (*Reports*, p. 9)

But when he and a small cohort of friends went to the Fire Island Pines in an attempt to raise funds to help those stricken with the mysterious "gay cancer," he ran into the same apathy that he had once been proud of in himself. With the publication of *Faggots* he had socially alienated the chic Pines crowd. Now he had become the political activist outsider in the community of the bored and privileged which he had once belonged to. Despite his own history, he was surprised that few people wanted to pay attention. It certainly wasn't because no one there had the money. It was a display of denial in a community whose bond was social and sexual, but not yet political enough to create some sense of shared responsibility. Not only did his enterprise have a decidedly unchic reputation in one of the capitals of anonymous sex, but its subject threatened the medical complacency that had helped to foster the licentiousness of the 1970s. Any sexually transmitted disease was supposed to be curable. It seemed a guarantee of the "clap doctors." For the men of the Fire Island Pines at that time, the sexual revolution was little more than an excuse to have untrammeled fun in the sand dunes at night and by the light of the next day pretend that it had never happened. Then along came this crazed queen, crying like Jeremiah that everyone was supposed to stop fucking and get politicized. Fat chance! He must have come from some other world. A few years later, their friends and lovers stricken and dying, they would turn their fabulous poolside parties into AIDS fundraisers—but only when the reality of what they were facing had struck home, not merely on Larry Kramer's say-so.

Robert Chesley continued to assail Kramer in the *Native*:

I think the concealed meaning in Kramer's emotionalism is the triumph of guilt: that gay men *deserve* to die for their promiscuity. In his novel *Faggots* Kramer told us that sex is dirty and that we ought not to be doing what we're doing. . . . Read anything by Kramer closely, [and] I think you'll find the subtext is always: the wages of gay sin is death. . . . I am not downplaying the seriousness of Kaposi's sarcoma. But something else is happening here, which is also serious: gay homophobia and anti-eroticism. (Kramer, *Reports*, p. 10)

Chesley's own work frequently championed sexual freedom. One play, *Pigman*, defended the rights of people with AIDS to unrestricted sexual activity and placed the responsibility for self-protection on the uninfected. (Chesley himself died of AIDS in December 1990.) Kramer responded to Chesley's attack, and the argument continued with issue after issue of the paper adding new voices to the debate. The lesson was not lost on Kramer:

> I was also beginning to recognize the usefulness of controversy. It was controversy that helped sell so many copies of *Faggots*; it was, and is, controversy that helps an issue stay before the public, so that more people join in debate, in this process becoming, one hopes, politicized. (*Reports*, p. 22)

Kramer, Mass and four others went on to found Gay Men's Health Crisis (GMHC) to tend to the needs of people with AIDS. The very name of the organization was a political decision, an effort to identify with the primary community from which the patients and their service providers would come, although it was clear that the disease would respect no boundaries of race, class, sex or sexual orientation. At last the community was mobilized. Defying the stereotypes of homosexuals, thousands of men and women showed up to raise funds, to help fill out insurance forms, to clean apartments and shop for food and wipe up vomit for the sick. Despite Kramer's insistence, the organization was unwilling to demand that everyone stop having sex, mostly because no leading medical authority such as the Centers for Disease Control (CDC) in Atlanta was making such recommendations. (The reluctance and slowness of the CDC to distribute more explicit safe sex guidelines earlier on is well documented in *And the Band Played On* by Randy Shilts.) But eventually safe (later "safer") sex, with its attendant concern for one's partner's identity and well-being, was taught as an alternative to anonymous promiscuity. It was a medical rather than a moral program. Moral arguments were almost a luxury in the face of the work that needed to be done. GMHC became the prototype for AIDS service organizations around the country.

Eventually, the numbers of dead and stricken grew so large that the arguments of self-hatred and erotophobia grew irrelevant, and Kramer emerged as a hero who had been right all along. When Larry Mass introduced me to him in 1982, Kramer asked me to write an essay for a GMHC publication about sex in the gay bathhouses. I was inspired by his crusade and wrote a piece that included accurate descriptions of men fucking other men and not stopping to wash their genitals before entering the cubicles of their next partners. I tried to be neither lurid nor moralistic, merely objective, but Kramer rejected it as too graphic! Considering the even less sanitary practices he had exposed in *Faggots*, I was surprised, but then I realized that the publication would probably be seen by prudish representatives of the agencies that might supply much-needed funds to GMHC. I understood then what a lonely tightrope he had to walk.

It was Larry Kramer's energy that was the primary force in reawakening the exhausted community to respond to the AIDS crisis, which until that point had left most people in stunned disbelief and depression. When he wrote an alarming article "1,112 and Counting," in the March 14, 1983 issue of the *New York Native*, he signaled the beginning of the end of the community's denial. He attacked the federal government, the medical establishment, the media, local politicians, and, of course, gays themselves, but because he was sounding the first call for civil disobedience, GMHC demanded a disclaimer. Playing the outsider once again, he also signaled the beginning of his own distancing from the organization he had created:

> I am writing this as Larry Kramer, and I am speaking for myself, and my views are not to be attributed to Gay Men's Health Crisis. . . .
> It is necessary that we have a pool of at least three thousand people who are prepared to participate in demonstrations of civil disobedience. . . . All participants must be prepared to be arrested. (*Reports*, p. 33)

This shift from education and service to politicizing the epidemic echoes the shift in the gay movement from the educational policies of the Mattachine Society in the 1950s to the confrontational tactics of the Gay Liberation Front and the Gay Activists Alliance in the 1970s. It led to a historic struggle between Kramer and GMHC, which he recorded in dramatic form.

□ □ □

Taking a breather from the hectic world of activism, Kramer used his experiences to write a play that has been performed around the world, *The Normal Heart* (which is being made into a film). Along with Robert Chesley's *Night Sweats* and William Hoffman's *As Is*, it was among the first dramas to deal with AIDS. A thinly disguised history of his own experience in the early days of GMHC, it is the story of Ned Weeks, outsider, an AIDS activist who angers not only the government but his family, his fellow Jews and the gay community in his effort to save his world from itself. He fights with his brother, refusing to speak to him until his homosexuality is accepted as normal. Comparing the inactivity of the uninfected gay community during the epidemic to the paralysis of American Jews who lived in safety during the Holocaust, Weeks, like Kramer, alienates himself still further from the Jewish community by accusing the Jews of moral failure, of fighting with each other rather than cooperating to ward off the threat that faced them. And, an outsider even from his GMHC colleagues, he attacks the board members for being too closeted to carry on the battle against AIDS in public and for their inability to accept his admittedly stringent methods. The board finally revolts against him and dismisses him in a public letter:

We take this action to try to combat your damage, wrought, so far as we can see, by your having no scruples whatever. You are on a colossal ego trip we must curtail. To manipulate fear, as you have done repeatedly in your "merchandizing" of this epidemic, is to us the gesture of barbarism. To exploit the deaths of gay men, as you have done in publications all over America, is to us an act of inexcusable vandalism. And to attempt to justify your bursts of outrageous temper as "part of what it means to be Jewish" is past our comprehending. And, after years of liberation, you have helped make sex dirty again for us—terrible and forbidden. We are more angry at you than ever in our lives toward anyone. We think you want to lead us all. Well, we do not want you to. In accordance with our by-laws ... Mr. Ned Weeks is hereby removed as director. (II, xiii, pp. 113–14)

By creating sympathy for Ned Weeks, Kramer was, of course, reporting this not only as a lesson in politics and personality but as a measure of retribution. In reality, he wrote an angry letter to the board members of GMHC after the incident dramatized in the play:

I did not believe that it would ever come to pass that I would grow to hate you, as a group, so much. But it has happened.

I am writing this so that the new members to your board will know that I think they are joining a bunch of ninnies and incompetents, cowards who do not have the courage and the foresight to return to the board the one member who pushed and shoved them, who pulled them by the hair, who bullied them into making this organization the inspiration that it is. I am furious with *all* of you for denying me the organization that I started in my living room, that I fathered into being in every conceivable way from the legal services of my brother's law firm to pressing into membership several of you reading this, and that is perceived by this community to have been fueled by my inspiration, devotion, and energy. . . .

I know I am not a team player, that I am impossible to get along with when I want something, but I know that each and every one of you knows that you would not be sitting there today if it weren't for me. It is a tragedy, for you, for me, for GMHC, for AIDS, that you are all so gutless and I frighten you so. . . .

In shutting me out so mercilessly, you are indeed murderers—of the spirit and in actuality.

Larry
(Kramer, Unpublished letter)

Acknowledging that he was not "a team player" was an understatement, but he *was* the captain. Larry Kramer was never capable of being an ordinary person, but his expectation that others would be willing to put up with his tempestuousness—and that he could get away with blaming it on his being Jewish, without offending other, more mild-mannered Jews—was presumptuous. Either he needed a position of absolute power, which even the exigencies of the epidemic did not grant him, or he needed to work as an individual among other individuals of equal force. Since there were few who could equal his power, it was his destiny, he believed at that time, to be alone.

Dinitia Smith's interview of him in *New York* magazine soon after the opening of *The Normal Heart* quoted Kramer's opinion of the gay political agenda as expressed in the play:

"The gay leaders who created this sexual-liberation philosophy in the first place have been the death of us," says Ned Weeks (Kramer's persona, played by actor Brad Davis). "Why didn't they fight for the right to get married instead of the right to legitimize promiscuity?"

Angered by his dismissal of work I had participated in, I wrote a letter to *New York*, excerpts of which were published in a later issue:

While I applaud Larry Kramer's call for more attention to the AIDS epidemic, I am appalled at his attacks on the gay community. This is a classic case of "blaming the victim," and that it should emanate from a gay man compounds the tragedy. . . .

We acted in the best of faith according to the best ideas of the times. Even the heterosexual marriage rate declined in the late 60s and early 70s. Nonetheless, GAA demonstrated at the office of City Clerk Herman Katz in 1971 when he threatened to put an end to the legally unrecognized "holy unions" of couples performed in a local gay church. It is all too easy to criticize with 20–20 hindsight. Where was Mr. Kramer's voice when these issues were being publicly discussed? Even after fifteen years of struggle we have not been able to secure our rights to housing and employment in this city, let alone the right to marry. [The first two rights referred to were legislated the following year.]

In the same interview, he claimed that he had not been able to find love because he had the wrong type of looks:

I am not the type whom homosexual men usually find attractive. This is a community that is for the most part obsessed with physical appearance, with youth, and with beauty. I am not attractive in gay terms. I am not blond. I am not young, and I have achieved professionally, which many gay men find threatening.

I retorted:

All American culture adores youth and beauty, and the gay subculture merely reflects those values. Has no one in America found love? I know many gay couples who do not appear fashion model perfect, but who are fulfilled human beings. There is nothing wrong with Larry Kramer's appearance. What's unattractive is his puritanical self-righteousness. To get love, one must give love.

To be sure he saw it, I sent a copy to him. The next time I saw him, several weeks later, he was perfectly friendly, as if he hadn't read my angry statement, so we didn't discuss it. It wasn't until a few years afterward when the subject of his lovability happened to come up in conversation, that he casually turned to me and asked with a smile, "Didn't you once write that there was nothing wrong with my looks?" He'd been aware of my response enough to remember it, but he'd been unfazed by it. A thicker-skinned public figure never existed, but there is a vulnerable person underneath, protected by the armor of his rage.

His anger at GMHC took more concrete form once it became clear that the organization would never act on his demand that it engage in political lobbying and demonstration because of the board's fear of losing its tax-exempt status. He wrote angry public letters to its leaders, insisting on the political nature of the epidemic. They were adamant, but the time was ripe. The gay public had begun to realize that this epidemic was not going to go away by itself and that caring for the sick was only part of the job. They saw the wisdom of Kramer's complaint, and, recovered from the early waves of nursing and burying their friends or discovering their own sero-positive status, they were ready to fight. Kramer seized the moment and agreed to speak at New York's Lesbian and Gay Community Services Center on March 10, 1987. Some 250 people showed up, including me. It was a historic moment. He was still the angry patriarch, but vulnerable, nervously—and paradoxically—smoking cigarettes outside before he spoke. His leadership was needed that night. Everyone sought his inspiration; everyone shared his rage. Word was out that a new group would be forming that would fight the political fight. GMHC sent a delegate, Tim Sweeney, to wish everyone well, and then Kramer spoke, using his words to unite himself with his audience:

Last week, I had seven friends who were diagnosed. In one week. That's the most in the shortest period that's happened to me. . . . Two-thirds of you—I should say of *us*, because I am in this, too—could be dead within five years. Two-thirds of this room could be dead within five years. (*Reports*, p. 128)

Hyperbole was his primary rhetorical device. Perhaps seven of his friends were diagnosed in one week, but I have lived amidst the epidemic, too, and even though the diagnoses and deaths almost invariably occurred in clusters, two or three would be a lot for one week. Similarly, Kramer liked to claim that he had lost 500 friends to AIDS. Could a man who bristled so intensely ever have so many friends? Could anyone? As an activist I've known many people in our community, but as I write this, more than fifteen years into the epidemic, I have lost just under 200 friends and acquaintances. (He explained himself in *Reports from the holocaust* by noting that if he didn't see some nameless person he used to see on the streets, he assumed that person had died and added him to the list. *Reports*, pp. 218–21)

That evening, the hyperbole worked. Two days later, the AIDS Coalition to Unleash Power (ACT UP) was born, and for the first time in history a disease was fought not just with magic or science, but with politics. Street demonstrations began within weeks. He had awakened the gay community from its torpor almost single-handedly, and just as his predecessors could ask him where he had been during the early 1970s, he could ask them: Where are you now?

Larry Kramer was at his peak as an orator. If he spoke to the gay community, it was usually to castigate them, never to celebrate their homosexuality. His tone became overtly biblical when he spoke as one of the tribe as he accepted the Human Rights Campaign Fund Communication Award at the Waldorf Astoria, only half a year after the founding of ACT-UP:

Oh my people, I beg you to hear me. We are woefully unprepared. . . .

Oh my people, I beg you to listen to me. I say all of this because I love you and I don't want to leave you or lose you. (*Reports*, pp. 187, 191)

In that speech, he called upon his audience to become terrorists in the manner of the embattled Jews of pre-Israeli Palestine, who had formed the *Irgun*. It is doubtful that he meant his exhortation to be taken literally, any more than he meant to implement the quotation from Malcolm X that he notoriously wore on a T-shirt some time later: "By any means necessary."
Like Moses reviling the Jews who worshiped the golden calf, Kramer made it his task to tell gay men that the sexual liberation they had celebrated with promiscuous abandon was a false god. In his role as leader, he was still not a member of the group he led. Rather, his position set him apart as spokesman, teacher and prophet. "*Sissieeees!*" he would underscore some of his speeches, panning the room with an accusatory finger while he hurled the one epithet that could most easily undermine the hard-won self respect of his gay audience, many of them newly out of their closets. If they didn't cringe before his wrath, he could always call them, "*Murderers!*" Like the Puritan Jonathan Edwards comparing each member of his congregation to a spider suspended by a slender thread above the pits of hellfire, Kramer terrorized, cajoled and assailed his listeners in an effort to rouse them to faith and from there to action. If he could make them feel angry enough, they would pour into the streets demanding an end to the AIDS epidemic.

And they did take to the streets, time and again, until the nation's consciousness was raised, albeit grudgingly, especially as AIDS stole more and more lives, and a greater number of people had witnessed their loved ones die. For their efforts, Kramer readily referred to his colleagues as "heroes," which they were, yet he remained exceptional among them, screaming at them, the media, the public and anyone who would listen. But, except for some window-dressing, from administration to administration the government remained unmoved—if ever it had had the will or the power to end the epidemic in the first place—and the dying continued.

Like all organizations, like all living things, ACT UP had a life span. After a few years, the troops, some of them ill and dying themselves, grew exhausted, their morale sapped. Eventually it became bogged down in factionalism and internecine squabbling like so many political groups before it. Kramer's rage and his call for extreme measures eventually came between him and ACT UP as it had between him and GMHC. When he called for rioting at the Sixth International AIDS Conference held in San Francisco in June, 1990, no one was interested. And when younger members of the organization refused to acknowledge his role as its architect and defied his efforts to control them, it was clear that his anger alone could not keep ACT UP going. Rather than contribute to its decline, he stepped aside and focused his energy on public appearances and writing instead of meetings. But then the word came out that he, too, had been diagnosed as HIV-positive. His earlier identification with the community of people with AIDS had proved not to be merely rhetorical. Perhaps he had known his status for some time before he announced it publicly, but in all probability, he did not know it when he set out to do his work a decade earlier. His words were resonant: "This is our disease, and we must take care of each other and ourselves," and, "Two-thirds of you—I should say *us* because I am in this, too—could be dead within five years." In one sense this made Kramer yet another kind of outsider. Since the inception of the epidemic the gay community had become divided into two subgroups: those who were HIV-positive and those who were HIV-negative. As close as dearest friends were, if their status was different, they were in one significant way separated. Larry Kramer was now an outsider from the uninfected community, but he remained exceptional in the infected community as well. Even with the additional bad news of a chronic liver disease, he continued his work, his force unabated.

He didn't always have difficulty relating to other HIV-positive heroes of the cause. He admired my good friend Vito Russo, the film historian turned AIDS activist. Shortly before Vito died in 1990, Larry invited us to his Fifth Avenue apartment to watch the annual Gay Pride parade from his balcony. As we watched thousands of ACT UP members fill the street below to pay homage to their heroes, chanting "Larry! Larry! Larry!" and "Vito! Vito! Vito! We love you! We love you!" he turned to Vito and said simply, "These are our children."

At Vito's memorial service later that year, I read a tribute that described our friendship of card games and movies and brunch. Larry also spoke, saying that that was not the Vito he had known. His Vito was the angry AIDS activist who was, according to the speech, "the only person who agreed with me unequivocally on everything I did and said." In a way that seemed wildly alienated at the time, he turned his eulogy into an angry AIDS speech before a bemused audience that included Vito's embarrassed mother:

> We killed Vito . . . Vito was killed by 25 million gay men and lesbians who
> for ten long years of this plague have refused to get our act together. . . .
>   And they [i.e. the government] shit all over us. Day after day they shit
> huge turds all over us. . . .
>   They haven't even done the basic science yet. . . . They don't do basic
> science for faggots and queers and niggers and spics and junkies and whores
> and bastards. And we let them shit all over us . . . (*Reports*, pp. 369, 371)

He explains his rhetoric almost disingenuously:

> I sensed the utter silence that I was learning occurred when I said things
> in an unexpected way. I could sense people almost holding their breath.
> What was I saying that was so shocking or unbelieveable? I always mean
> everything I say. I don't say it to shock, I say it because that's what I'm
> thinking.
>   There was a blasphemous amount of applause at the end, which totally
> surprised me. I'd expected people to throw spoiled tomatoes or rotten
> eggs. (*Reports*, p. 373)

He knows the uses of shock as he knows the uses of controversy. It is the ploy of the outsider to get attention. Angry children use it in the school-room.

□ □ □

In his next drama, *The Destiny of Me*, Kramer, in the guise of an ailing Ned Weeks, turned his anger on his family and the medical establishment, but he also went on to outrage Jews once again:

> *Ned*: All these old Jewish doctors—the sons of Sigmund—exiled from
> their homelands, running from Hitler's death camps, for some queer
> reason celebrated their freedom on our shores by deciding to eliminate
> homosexuals. (II, p. 85)

In this play he explores his personal history more deeply, dissecting his family relationships and the pain they have caused him. His mother is accused of being self-absorbed, too busy with her progressive social projects to pay attention to her children, and his father is accused of abuse:

> *Ned*: ... After my father beat me and Mom up and told me he'd never
> wanted me and after I told my brother I was gay and after my brother got
> married and before my first year's final exams that I knew I'd flunk, I
> pulled a bottle of some kind of pills which belonged to my roommate
> whose father was a doctor out of his bureau drawer and swallowed them
> all. I had wanted to take a knife and slice a foot or arm off. I had wanted
> to see blood gushing everywhere, making a huge mess, and floating me
> away on its sea. But there were only pills.... (II, p. 96)

Kramer did attempt suicide at Yale, and Ned's fantasies of violence show
what an act of rage it was. His self-loathing was inextricably entwined with
his alienation from every group he was supposed to belong to because he
had internalized their homophobia:

> *Ned*: ... Every social structure I'm supposed to be a part of—my family, my
> religion, my school, my friends, my neighborhood, my work, my city, my
> state, my country, my government, my newspaper, my television ... —tells
> me over and over what I feel and see and think and do is sick. (II, p. 96)

Only in the arms of the gay community could his feelings seem healthy, but
the gay community itself had grown physically ill, without the self-disci-
pline to change their "immoral" habits and prevent themselves from passing
along the infection, so they seemed weak in his eyes. They had failed him,
too.

But he was not left alone. His self assessment in *The Destiny of Me* happily
proved erroneous: "*Ned*: I don't fall in love. People don't fall in love with
me" (III, p. 104).

As if life were a novel (which is appropriate for one who has made a novel
out of his life), who should reappear but David Webster, on whom the
Dinky Adams of *Faggots* had been based. The news was so delicious that
the *New York Times* published a celebratory piece about it, called "When a
Roaring Lion Learns to Purr," and placed it in the Home Section! Their
original affair in the 1970s hadn't gone too well:

> The two tell a story about the time Mr. Kramer bought tickets to a
> Broadway show for Mr. Webster's birthday and was stood up.
> "I told him I was going to Fire Island, take someone else," Mr. Webster
> recalls. "So what did he do? He took a train to Fire Island, then the ferry,
> like Barbra Streisand on the boat in 'Funny Girl.' All to walk up to me at a
> dance and punch me in my mouth. Then he got back on the ferry to the
> train and came back to New York."

Now all is bliss. As Webster comments:

> Some parts of life should be fulfilling enough to tone the anger down.
> Larry found a necessary vehicle to use as a weapon for an important
> thing that he believed in. Privately though, he is quite lovable. Giving,
> gentle, childlike. (Witchell C10)

Now Kramer leaves messages on our phone answering machine saying,
"Why am I so happy? Oh yes, I'm in love," or "We're staining floors [in their
new Connecticut home]. I've never been happier in my life."

Some believe that his romance has robbed the movement of the fuel that
his angry energy provided, yet the movement had always spent as much of its
strength fighting his personal dominance as it did fighting its opponents. It
was time for him to move on. Being in love hasn't stopped him from being
provocative. In his work-in-progress, a novel tentatively called *The American
People*, he takes on the whole country, group by group. I read a chapter on the
Jews called "The Bloods." It is highly literary, imaginative, and witty. As a
symbol of Jews becoming part of America, Kramer has a *mohel* [circumciser]
planting foreskins in the soil of Washington, D.C. This should earn him the
right to join the likes of Philip Roth and Woody Allen in being denounced
as a self-hating Jew. He continues to antagonize one group after another as if
he needs the outrage of his fellows for his sustenance.

The strident demands of his ego have become so legendary that he was
satirized in an independent film in the form of a character named "Harry
Blamer," who appears on a TV talk show:

> *Blamer*: What about me? What are you doing for my needs? You're all
> wasted hunks of human flesh if you can't find a cure for me. I don't care if
> you're sick, too. Fuck you. You're not trying hard enough to save me!
> (Bordowitz)

At a recent panel discussion on gay politics, attended largely by leftward
leaning academics with "social constructionist" credentials, Larry Kramer
was one of the star panelists. Although the audience probably disagreed
with his politics, they listened intently as he denounced them, saying he was
not thankful to have been invited to speak. "I hate academic conferences," he
said. "The last thing we need is more theorizing." He spoke with an exhaus-
tion born of trying too hard for too long. "I'm sixty years old," he said. "I
can't keep doing this." Despite all his efforts no total cure for AIDS has yet
been found, but although he is tired, he does not give in to despair. Speaking of the need to revitalize AIDS activism using the methods of ACT UP
to inspire a disinterested public, he once again invoked his membership in
the tribe:

They're all basically sound ideas. Why is no one responding to them? . . . The basic experience is that we are brothers and sisters. . . . We're at a new crisis point. . . . You really have to go out and get every friend you have and get money from them.

A young man from the audience named Leonard Hirsch commented, "I almost always agree with what you say and disagree with your tone." Kramer responded, "My tone, my tone, I'll go to my grave with my tone."

A short conversation with him will easily reveal that in his private life, behind his public mask of angry prophet, Larry Kramer is, as David Webster observed, a kind, loving man. Like Dr. Thomas Stockmann in Ibsen's *An Enemy of the People*, he brought a warning that no one wanted to hear. The polluted water in the tourist baths of nineteenth-century Norway and the spread of HIV in the gay baths of twentieth-century America both meant the end of a dream of health and freedom as well as the end of highly profitable businesses. But it is unfair to blame the messenger. Some dreams simply cannot come true. For his own reasons, Larry Kramer has told us all a difficult truth: We cannot be healthy or free without being responsible. Posing as an outsider from the groups he belongs to, he has served his people well. Yes, he has been harsh and disruptive and accusatory and unforgiving, even egotistical, but in evaluating Larry Kramer, one simple question should be asked: What would we have done without him?

Works cited

Bordowitz, Gregg, *Fast Trip; Long Drop* (film), 1994.

Chesley, Robert, "It's Hard to Walk Away from a Good Blowjob," *Gaysweek*, January 1, 1979, pp. 12–15.

Kantrowitz, Arnie, "The Death of Peter Pan," London *Gay News*, No. 201, October 16–29, 1980, p. 19.

Kantrowitz, Arnie, partially published excerpts from letter to *New York* magazine, May 29, 1985.

Kramer, Larry, *The Destiny of Me*. New York: Penguin Books, 1993.

Kramer, Larry, *Faggots*. New York: Warner Books, 1979.

Kramer, Larry, "Gay 'Power' Here," Op-Ed page, *New York Times*, December 13, 1978.

Kramer, Larry, *The Normal Heart*. New York: New American Library, 1985.

Kramer, Larry, *Reports from the holocaust*. New York: St. Martin's Press, 1994.

Kramer, Larry, unpublished letter to GMHC Executive Board, February 10, 1984.

Marcus, Eric, *Making History: The Struggle for Gay and Lesbian Rights, 1945-1990*. New York: HarperCollins Publishers, 1992.

Smith, Dinitia, "The Cry of 'The Normal Heart,'" *New York*, June 3, 1985, pp. 42–6.

Witchell, Alex, "When a Roaring Lion Learns to Purr," *New York Times*, January 12, 1995, pp. C1, C10.

PART THREE

Psychology, Politics and Literature

Larry and the Wall of Books

Andrew Holleran

I MET LARRY KRAMER through a group of friends who lived on the Upper East Side of New York in the early 1970s and who all warned me about him. I don't remember the specific charge, but the general impression given was that Larry was someone who would, sooner or later, cause a scene.

Where this scene would occur, or when, or what it would consist of, I had no idea, but the meaning of all those rolled eyes, those scattered remarks, was basically: This is a man who will ruin your dinner party.

The dinner party nevertheless was exactly what I wanted to be asked to at that time—my problem was I hadn't been invited to one. That first year in New York I waited for the phone to ring, and when it finally did, and I went uptown to Donald Sullivan's I felt sure that he, and Larry, and the others were privy to a glamorous and exciting way of life I knew nothing of. Larry was a newcomer to New York too at that time, in 1971—but he had written and produced a film, *Women in Love,* and had lived already in London and Los Angeles, and spent time in Rome with the group on the Upper East Side: my friend Donald, the playwright Jerry Max, the Stanford heartthrob Barry F., whom everyone was in love with, including Larry. Rome was now just a photograph on Donald's table—of a terrace in Trastevere on which Donald sat, in dappled light, a wine-soaked gamin; but it spoke for a whole network of people who knew each other and who all conveyed the warning that Larry was a man who could be rude in a way they did not admire. They were all wary of him.

But I never saw the promised scene; instead, when I ran into Larry one day at the West Side YMCA, and he said he had heard I had completed a novel, he told me to give it to his agent. Not long afterwards my first novel came out at about the same time as Larry's first novel, and one day we found ourselves on a plane together going to Chicago to appear on a local television show.

All of this happened as in a dream —though I remember meeting a man at a cocktail party who told me that the sort of novel we had written could never have been published during the years he had spent as an editor; and that the reason my book and Larry's were getting the attention they were was that both were about a subculture which had not been a topic one could address in public till recently—the world of gay men. *Faggots* was a comic view of that world—written as a farce—though it seems to me (rereading it almost twenty years later) that it's rather true-to-life and actual—and this bleak, black send-up of clone culture did not sit well with some segments of the gay community, who reacted with the classic thin-skinned umbrage of a minority culture under attack. (By one of its own!) In fact, through the fog, the surreal experience of one's first novel, I became aware that Larry and I, or rather our two books, were being turned into Good Cop and Bad Cop, even though I thought my own book was in its way as critical.

No matter—*Faggots* was singled out for being sex-negative, for being the work of a man who felt profoundly unhappy about being homosexual, who hadn't a nice word to say about anyone. Like Truman Capote after the famous excerpt of "Answered Prayers" in *Esquire*, Larry was cut by people who considered themselves the models for his characters and who stopped speaking to him. This was the scene at the dinner party I had been warned against, I gathered, though it seemed to me all he had done in *Faggots* was hold a mirror up and let people see their own reflections—or at least some of the most grotesque obsessions and compulsions of gay life. Yet when we drove out that autumn to the Hamptons to address a gay group there, and went to stay with the novelist–playwright Jimmy Kirkwood afterwards, I was given the impression once again that I was traveling in the company of a social grenade; even if the dinner we had together that evening went off without a hitch, there was some memory of another dinner that had not, and *Faggots* was apparently, in their eyes, just another version of this.

I saw primarily a writer, however, as I got to know Larry that autumn and winter—a writer who was also a producer who had worked in Europe and Hollywood, a man who seemed to know an awful lot of people in both the gay and straight worlds, but a writer, nevertheless. With a writer's reflectiveness, a writer's fascination with character, hunger for stories and dish. He seemed to be done with his years in the film business. ("They're monsters!" he said once when I asked about certain celebrities. "No one who gets to the top like that isn't. They're monsters! You have no *idea*!") He'd worked with stars, he knew Ken Russell, Glenda Jackson, Alan Bates, he'd discovered Brad Davis, but they were simply on the Rolodex; what he wanted to know now was the identity of the man whose chiseled good looks held me in thrall one evening at the Eagle's Nest as I listened to him tell me about his life as an Army Ranger. (Paul Popham). It was odd to have someone who had lived and succeeded in a much larger world care about the gay demi-monde I now found myself immersed in; but clearly Larry was as fascinated with those men as I was. Because he was, like me, a writer. In fact, the only thing that interested, even awed him, as much as physical beauty or human personality was—books.

□ □ □

When I walked into his apartment on Washington Square the first time, I found an entire wall of books. I didn't ask if he'd read them all. His apartment was like a bookstore. I don't think he could run an errand without bringing back more; the latest novels were always on the table. And after the tour, the hubbub over our novels about these men in the Eagle's Nest, the Pines, the Everard, died down, it was that dull, quiet, bookish writer's life we both fell back into—faced, each of us, with the literary equivalent of the problem that made Warhol walk around the Factory asking everyone: "What should I paint next?" We couldn't write about the circuit again. In fact, by 1979 the culture—the world that produced the scenes and characters in both our novels—seemed dead already. It was not simply that we had already written them down—rather some staleness, some inevitable banality was now evident; and a way of life that in 1974 had been fresh, spontaneous, creative seemed by the decade's end, repetitive, habitual and exploitative. In 1979 a strange interregnum between the Age of Disco and the Age of AIDS was in place; gay life was both more crowded and more conformist, more frenzied and more vapid.

So vapid that some of the leading clones were now moving to Miami Beach: one winter, Donald, Larry and I went to Miami and shared a house in Kendall for a week. We even went to the Club Baths together one night. What eventually became AIDS must have been already in the air because I remember thinking, as we checked in, that this was a dubious thing to do, given what we knew. But it did not stop us from going. Nor was it the topic of conversation as we drove around the city—after strolling through Fairchild Gardens one afternoon, marveling at the trees and shrubs. I remember making fun of Larry and Donald because they toured the entire place a few steps behind me, so engrossed in a discussion of apartment rents and Manhattan real estate, they had not noticed a leaf. Then Larry, with the intuitive sense that leads writers to material, drove up to Palm Beach by himself one day, and when he came back he began writing a story about a Jewish woman in Florida named Mrs. Tefillin, and I thought: Well, that was what Larry found in Palm Beach—something to write about next. In other words, one of the innumerable small ironies of the plague is this: before it arrived, Larry was going to follow *Faggots* with a story about a widow in Palm Beach. Gay life seemed to offer us nothing new or interesting; it had, in fact, turned into the predictable carnival Larry had sent up in his first novel—only now there were roller-disco and gay cruise ships.

Then one day the summer after our vacation in Miami I was walking across the harbor of Fire Island Pines with a friend—the first one of mine to come down with the new gay cancer, it would turn out—when we saw Larry sitting on a folding chair at a small table next to the entrance to the ferry, handing out flyers to raise money for what would eventually be called Gay Men's Health Crisis. Unbeknownst to me, Paul Popham—the icon of the Eagle's Nest, the Clone Dreamboat—and some other men had formed a group to address the bizarre new disease called Kaposi's sarcoma. This surprising encounter—this alien subject, on that sunny Saturday in the harbor of the Pines—was followed not long afterwards with an article Larry wrote to warn people about what was happening, beneath a famous headline in the new gay newspaper, the *New York Native*: "1,112 and Counting."

It is now impossible to have a party in the Pines that is *not* a fund-raiser, but none of this was welcome in that community at the time; it seemed, in fact, an extension of the anger many felt was the motivation for *Faggots*. The *Native* article induced Robert Chesley, a gay playwright, to accuse Larry of promulgating the doctrine that the wages of sin are death. In other words, this was just Larry again—the hectoring kvetch everyone knew already to avoid.

Indeed, it seemed a replay of the commotion following his first novel. The fact that everything had flipped was not something people wanted to admit. Foucault reportedly laughed when he heard about this disease; another Frenchman, a friend in New York, said it was just one more instance of American Puritanism. Most people found it hard to believe that there was a fatal penalty for having sex with one person, one time. Donald asked that it not be discussed at dinner; it spoiled the ambience. The writers' group I belonged to, scribbling autobiographical novels—the next logical subject matter for gay writers: the family—disbanded. Larry abandoned Mrs. Tefillin in Palm Beach. And when we drove to Ithaca the following spring, to visit a friend of Donald's at Cornell, Larry startled us all by saying he felt sick the day we arrived and drove back to Manhattan. In fact, he was pregnant; with *The Normal Heart*. When I finally saw this play, we were still so shocked by what was going on, that when Larry turned to a friend and me at a restaurant after the performance, and asked what we thought of it, we were both speechless; it seemed to be nothing more than Larry's life the past few years. What could one say?

What could one say about any of it? AIDS truncated gay life as completely as the Civil War terminated the Old South, like the barbecue at Twelve Oaks in *Gone With the Wind* the day the war was announed; a Before, and After, separated by a fact so cataclysmic it resembled even more the sinking of the Titanic. Only Larry seemed to keep his head above water. Only Larry seemed to thrive. The other gay writers I knew were mute and stunned. But Larry's voice found a civic function. He was no longer needling guests at a dinner party of gay men; his acolytes were throwing blood on the floor of the Stock Exchange—like a figure in Plutarch whose traits are first seen in small scenes from private life, then matters of state. That there was a continuum between these two people, public and private, was not surprising, I suppose; what was, was the unforeseen catastrophe.

But then everything about AIDS was both unforeseen and continuous. Riding home on the subway one evening early in the 1980s, looking at the headlines in a *New York Post* someone was reading, describing the closing of The Mineshaft, I thought to myself: Well, they know everything about us now. The world described in *Faggots* was now a headline in the *New York Post*; all because of AIDS. Only AIDS flipped all of gay life on its head. The great good (sex) was now the great bad; the hot man now a potential murderer; the whole infrastructure of gay life (baths, bars, discos, drugs, Fire Island) as obsolete as cruising itself. One night I went to a meeting at the new gay and lesbian center on Thirteenth Street and heard Larry and Vito Russo ask the audience to stand up; and, when they had, say: "In five years, half of you will be dead." And: "There is a gun pointed at your head. Why aren't you angry?"

This of course became Larry's theme—the central question as the disease began mowing down, among others, the people who had introduced me to Larry on the Upper East Side. It split gay friends, generations, eras, the way the Dreyfus case had split French society in the previous century. Why aren't you angry? Or: Why *are* you angry? (And hysterical?) Larry was so angry he was thrown out of GMHC—because Paul Popham, the ex-paratrooper so many of us had a crush on, could not abide Larry's confrontational style. Larry, in the meantime, was reading Martin Luther King Jr. and Mahatma Gandhi.

And everyone had a different take on Larry. I would leave the apartment of a friend who equated him with Gandhi, and visit someone who considered him a drama queen replaying *The Way We Were*. (And the two could be mixed: the friend who rated him with Gandhi broke up laughing years later reading Larry's column in *The Advocate* describing his taking his first capsules of AZT one day in Barbra Streisand's bathroom.) But whether you thought ACT UP heroic or just a place to meet hot men (forget the Eagle's Nest), or a replay of 1960s politics, one thing was sure: a generation was having its moment, an adventure that did not, as ours had, revolve around sexual liberation but rather street demonstrations and zaps. And Larry was their icon.

"I don't see anybody from my generation at these meetings," he said to me one evening as we took a break outside the gay and lesbian center. I didn't either. Larry had responded to new data, changed times, in a way a lot of men my age had not. In a speech in Boston Larry asked his audience whether those who had been spared thus far did not have some moral obligation to fight AIDS. (The message on his answering machine asked the same question; and the ACT UP posters plastered to this day on his door.) It was a moral challenge to which the guilty answer seemed obvious: of course. Where people differed was what form that obligation would take. Some felt ACT UP was needed; others thought it a mistake. The point was that Larry had done something—had gone on the attack. "I don't know anyone who has the same friends after he's gone through this," he said in an interview—and then spoke to me about the intensity of the bond, the romances, among the cohorts he went down to Washington with on the bus to demonstrate: Whitman's camerados.

In retrospect it makes sense that the man who produced *Women in Love* and was constantly matchmaking on an individual level—author and editor, for instance: I was one of many—should start GMHC and ACT UP; these were the work of someone who brings people together, gets things done. Yet the writer activist is a species we associate more with Europeans than Americans; and almost always the balance tips one way or the other. The cliché is that the qualities that make a writer—detachment, alienation, the desire to observe—are the opposite of those that enable the man of action to influence events. With Larry the two fed each other. One day while I was visiting him at home, he went to his word processor, punched something up on the screen, and then left the room to get us drinks. I went to the computer screen and read some notes about a man with AIDS whose lover, etc.,—at which point it dawned on me: Larry, the man on Nightline, was still this other Larry, the writer who had been amassing, because he had been at the center of all this the past decade, all the stories. "You've got all the stories!" I said to him when he came back into the room. "You've got all those incredible stories!" A writer's capital, indeed. (Years later, after Donald died, I would learn the details of his death while talking to Larry one day— he knew a woman who knew the man who had found him, etc.—and I thought: who else?) During the Terror in France, the artist David would vote in committee to condemn people to the guillotine, then run home, get his sketchpad, and return to the street to draw the faces of the condemned as they passed by in the cart on their way to their execution. Two centuries later, in New York, our own Terror, Larry pressed a button, and the precious material vanished from the screen, perhaps returned to storage, but we both knew at that moment: he was sitting on a heap, a treasure trove, a mountain of a writer's most essential resource—stories—and it was all in his head, his computer, as it was in nobody else's.

□ □ □

The Destiny of Me played at the same theater on Christopher Street where, years earlier, *Sissies' Scrapbook*, a work about a group of friends from Yale, had flopped. (I guess Manhattan real estate *is* engrossing, since space is limited, and the same buildings are used at different times for wildly different purposes.) It was not the ground-breaking salvo in what was to become AIDS art that *The Normal Heart* was. But it draws more than the other play on the connections between the activist and the artist; the producer and the writer; or at least the child who became the man friends warned would spoil the dinner party. In this play we see the brother whose older sibling is the sports-minded, successful heterosexual he is not; the son of a father who screams at, rather than encourages, him, a mother whose critical faculties are as keen as his own, the anguish of growing up as that which is not expected, wanted, honored. A few nights after seeing Larry's play, I ran into him at a performance of *Jeffrey*, a more comic, light-hearted, crowd-pleaser—and we walked down to the Theater de Lys with Simon Watney (social Larry), and then I went to Ty's and stood there by its plate glass window waiting to see the expressions on the faces of the people who had been to *The Destiny of Me* when they came out (Old Testament Larry). I couldn't imagine their expressions. Larry after all is Jeremiah—full of anger at the failings of man. This rage against the father, whether it be his own, or a city-father like Mayor Koch, or a national father like the President—this confrontation with the failed man—lies at the heart of all his work; even of *Women in Love*, where, though they try, men simply cannot love each other, in the way we were trying to.

That way has consequences, of course, from the moment you grow up as someone's child to the moment you die. "I want to have what you have!" Larry told a straight interviewer once. That's all—everything he felt he had been denied, including, once AIDS came along, health and life. As I watched the audience step out of the lobby of the Theater de Lys from the gay bar across the street—a bar that had been popular in the Age of Clones—it struck me how difficult it is to be a gay man, period, much less a thorn in everyone's flesh.

But Larry had, with *The Destiny of Me*, tried to stitch together the two contradictory parts, the heterosexual family, the homosexual adulthood; that stunning change that seems to many of us a more radical disjuncture than being switched as babies in the hospital. *Faggots* had been directed at the men in Ty's. *The Destiny of Me* was directed at everyone else, or at least the dilemma of being homosexual. Some dilemma. The street I walked home on that evening, the quiet, wintry sidewalk from the west to the east Village, was so very different from the one I'd walked my first year in New York. Almost every member of the group on the Upper East Side who'd told me about Larry was dead. The city was a cemetery; even Larry had a worrisome cough a few nights later when I had dinner with him in a restaurant on University Place, where the chef, a lean, handsome young man who had been in ACT UP, came out and talked to us at our table. Larry had become like the professor I knew who, as we walked around the city, would constantly spot students of his. In Larry's case they were young men who had been in ACT UP. At Veselka's in the east Village this past autumn, it was a woman who had since moved to Michigan and started a chapter there.

By then Larry himself had moved, too, to a house his partner was renovating on a lake in Connecticut—a man who had been the inspiration for Dinky Adams in *Faggots*; the love interest who had led Fred Lemish to comic despair. Now, more than fifteen years later, the same man had resurfaced in Larry's life, and, in one of those happy endings we sneer at in film, they were reunited, like two victims of the same shipwreck. For whatever reason, Larry seemed calmer, quieter. Around us, in the back room of Veselka's, were reminders of why men move to New York: the handsome faces who had come to the city, like us, twenty years earlier, to find some version of what Larry had obtained: the career, the house, the life, the lover, the dog—momentarily tied to a tree outside where we could watch her charm passersby. He was at once the same Larry I had always known—the writer who had only recently read my own manuscript, given me advice, another writer a title, another an editor—and a man I no longer called casually because I assumed the Center for Disease Control, if not the White House, was on the other line.

For now, Larry was, I surmised, once more in the writer part of the writer–activist cycle, putting his energies into the reportedly very long novel he was working on. Another decade had just ended, somehow; we had lived long enough to see the 1970s give way to the plague years, and now the plague years turn into something else. Something hard to define, but no longer the 1980s. The 1970s redux? Ten or more years since Larry published "1,112 and Counting," it was becoming clear that AIDS had not totally changed the world he had described in *Faggots*. (As Larry said when faced with the Morning Party in the Pines—the annual mass of body-builders boogying on Ecstasy in the sun: "They're doing drugs in the Portosans.") A new party circuit had sprung up; the scenes in *Faggots* were being restaged by a new generation—as what a friend, on Ecstasy himself, called AIDS: The Party. The carnival had resumed. The plague years had not answered the questions *Faggots* had raised. And now this social grenade, who had begun by telling gay people what was wrong with them, and then straight people what was wrong with *them*, sat, having an egg salad sandwich at Velselka's while his dog waited outside, planning, I thought, only he knew what.

When I asked how the novel was going, he said he had written thousands of words, and then been unable to read more than a few pages of it—a familiar sensation. The problem, he said, was the problem all of us had faced; how to write about AIDS and be funny. (People forget that *Faggots*, which takes its epigraph from Evelyn Waugh, is as farcical as *Just Say No*.) He said he was wondering if his computer wasn't the problem; the ability it gave him to fiddle, to write a scene over and over, in slightly different ways. His editor, he said, had told him he was afraid he would have to retire before he ever saw the manuscript. "But doesn't that worry you?" I said.

"What?" said Larry.

"That you may die before you finish the book?"

"No," he said.

This struck me as so odd—so contrary to the proverbial urgency of the artist to complete his work before darkness falls—I forget now what he said next; but the impression I got was that of a writer who had not yet found a way of organizing, of dealing with, an overwhelming amount of stories from Life. The moment of quiescence was really a moment of digestion, as he showed us the photographs of the Connecticut house in *Architectural Digest*, telling us, over tea at his apartment later, the stories all of us star-struck queens wanted to hear; what working with Streisand was *really* like. The wall of books in his apartment was now supplemented with a corresponding wall of file cabinets, each drawer filled with folders stuffed with notes; the raw material of this epic novel. What was charming about Larry that afternoon was what had been appealing about him all these years: his honesty, his sense of humor, the omnivorous interest in every conceivable dilemma, personality, nook and cranny of the city that came his way, his Balzacian appetite for the human comedy. There was at the same time something sad about the wall of books this visit—like a real stone wall, it had collapsed in places, and novels were spilling onto the floor beneath the gaps, as if real rocks had come tumbling down—because, he explained, portions of it had been carted off to his new house in Connecticut. Sandwiched between the crumbling wall of books, and the undented wall of file cabinets whose voluminous data were proving hard to digest, he seemed to me almost becalmed by the enormity of the task that lay ahead; the production of the novel that, whether he finished it or not, could make him what all of us wanted to be: a great writer.

Faggots Revisited

Christopher Bram

THE TITLE ALONE WAS A SLAP IN THE FACE. The word has lost some of its sting, but imagine an African-American novel titled *Niggers* or one by a woman called *Cunts*. The book itself hit many gay readers like a slap in 1978. The angry responses ranged from George Whitmore declaring in *The Body Politic* that copies should be burned, to the graffiti I saw in the john of my local gay bar: "If brevity is the soul of wit, *Faggots* is witless."

Few novels make such an impact that they get reviewed on bathroom walls. This was one of those highly public books that people could judge without reading, yet it was a bestseller, read by many and often enjoyed. And it was remembered, branding Kramer with a reputation for hating his sexuality, or at least for hating sex. His satire of high ghetto life clearly treated the new sexual freedom as foolish, shoddy, even soul-killing. Three years later, when Kramer's first AIDS piece ran in the *New York Native*, "A Personal Appeal," skeptics used the novel to dismiss his proposal that 120 cases of a "gay cancer" might be the start of a catastrophe. As late as 1991, when the brutal fact of AIDS was undeniable, David Bergman argued in *Gaiety Transfigured*, in an essay that mixed occasional insights with irritable, unbending animosity, "Kramer could address AIDS with such speed and force because the disease served as an objective correlative for many of the ideas and attitudes he already had"—the unfortunate use of a term from literary criticism suggesting that Kramer would have "written" the epidemic if it hadn't already existed.[1]

Novels rarely sustain such long, controversial lives. If they irritate, they usually disappear forever, or drop from view for a few generations, like *The Bostonians*, Henry James's satire of the sex wars, or are quickly tamed into "classics," as happened with Richard Wright's raw racial thriller, *Native Son*. Certainly no gay novel has elicited such prolonged, strong feelings from its audience. If the book provoked so much anger, why didn't it simply go away? What does it mean to us now, eighteen years later?

□ □ □

We should go back to the novel itself, before it became a myth. After all, it began as just another work of fiction.

Faggots is a 384-page comedy about a Memorial Day weekend in the early 1970s among New York City's gay elite, an elastic aristocracy of libido, beauty, youth and/or money. At the center is thirty-nine-year-old Fred Lemish, a screenwriter trying to set up a motion picture about this new gay world while he pursues the love of his life, Dinky Adams. Around them are hundreds of other gay characters, the densely populated book suspended between two mammoth parties, one the opening of a new club, the Toilet Bowl, the other the first party of the season on Fire Island. Along the way are orgies, a fire in a bathhouse, a public fistfuck in the Pines, and much casual tricking.

Kramer has claimed Evelyn Waugh was his model, and there is evidence of Waugh in the floor plan, not *Brideshead Revisited* or *The Loved One*, but the perpetual party of "Bright Young Things" in his 1930 novel *Vile Bodies*. The book built on that foundation, however, has none of the restraint of Waugh's deadpan comedy, but belongs to the maximalist fiction of the 1960s, those inventive three-ring circuses overloaded with people, plots, subplots, speeches and wordplay, content overflowing form. The novel looks back to *V* and *Gravity's Rainbow* by Thomas Pynchon, the mega-narratives of John Barth, the word-drunk tapdance of *The Armies of the Night* by Norman Mailer. And it looks ahead to Tom Wolfe's 1987 novel *The Bonfire of the Vanities*, the resemblance so strong that one can't help wondering if *Faggots* were a model for Wolfe's book. Both are comic jeremiads, cartoon extravaganzas where New York City is treated as a vast stage set. Wolfe includes a broader range of class and race, and is more obsessed with fashion and furniture than his gay counterpart. Yet the chief difference between the two works, a profound one, is Kramer's self-critical awareness, an acknowledgment of complicity that's completely absent in Wolfe's zoo of rip-off artists. Wolfe stands at a safe distance from his prejudged characters, while Kramer scatters naked, contradictory pieces of himself throughout his cast.

Faggots employs a busy mock-eighteenth century narrative voice, a device rediscovered in the 1960s as an alternative to the button-down conventions of cinematic realism. The prose is full of deliberately absurd names, odd capitalization, eccentric punctuation, bits of S. J. Perelman punning and many jokes, both good and bad. Much of this sits heavily on the page while the first hundred pages while scene and characters are introduced. Kramer's talent is dramatic, not verbal, which is not to say that he's primarily a playwright, but that his art needs action, the bounce of opposing personas in collision to come to life. He needs the momentum of plot to keep his attitudes, caricatures and often heavy jokes airborne. It takes time for the carnival machinery of the novel to get underway.

This slow opening turned me against the book the first time I tried to read it. I have since learned that I am not the only person to put it down after twenty or so pages. And I disliked its sexual bluntness, the emphasis on the dirt rather than the poetry of sex. The epigraph from Waugh—". . . the ancients located the deeper emotions in the bowels"—is not there for nothing. I moved to New York the year that *Faggots* came out and the description of something called "felching" on page three wasn't what a young man from the provinces wanted to hear about. Not until several years later, when I had had enough sexual experience to get over my squeamishness and see past the scatology to the sheer energy of the book, could I actually read it through.

The novel doesn't fully take off until the arrival of Timmy Purvis, a sixteen-year-old boy literally fresh off the bus from suburban Maryland. Timmy introduces joy to the novel, a selfish exuberance with none of the bad conscience of Fred and his friends. As Timmy and the others carom from party to party, dick to dick, the novel develops a velocity that carries through to the end. An elaborate logistics of parties, chance encounters and copulations has been worked out to create an erotic Rube Goldberg machine. Timmy meets his dream lover, Winnie the Winston man; the two fall into a feckless dance of lust and distraction, until Timmy falls into the hands of the sadistic, closeted media executive, Randy Dildough. Fred pursues Dinky, Dinky pursues new thrills. Fred brings Abe Bronstein, his producer and the novel's straight father figure, to the Toilet Bowl and out to Fire Island to see this brave new world. Meanwhile Bronstein's gay son, Boo Boo, plots his own kidnapping to get ransom money from his father. A multitude of other characters plan conquests, romance, financial gain and just getting laid.

Soul-killing or not, casual sex among a huge all-male cast can't help but reduce characters to a faceless swarm. (The females are minor, although there's a surprisingly sweet subplot about a lesbian fling by Bronstein's ex-wife, Ephra.) The important figures read clearly, however, and this melding of identities is one of the novel's subjects. You have to go back to the gleeful absurdities of French eighteenth-century pornography to find a similar mix of slapstick, philosophy and fucking. The sex itself is rarely sinister. For all these men's macho role-playing, only the self-hating Randy Dildough is deliberately vicious, and even his cruelty comes out of a desperate romantic need. Despite their self-indulgence, these men usually *mean* well. The flood of diminutive nicknames—Dinky, Timmy, Boo Boo—conjures up a world of good little boys playing at toughness, escaping inhibitions with fantasies, costumes and drugs. (The novel's delirium is fueled by a remarkable intake of chemicals, more striking now than when it was published.)

We cannot forget that *Faggots* is a comedy, which should allow for exaggeration and unfairness. But comedy is slippery, subjective; it needs surprise to get away with the murder it seeks to commit. Kramer often succeeds, but his humor is uneven, with the hit-or-miss quality of rude jokes by a teenager suddenly free to say anything. The title, for example, is intended, in part, as a nose-thumbing joke, only who exactly will be laughing? The comic names can be obvious, stale or just plain silly. (Randy *Dildough*? *The Advocate* becomes *The Avocado*, an old chestnut even then.) As with most broad comedy, there is much stereotyping. Italians, African-Americans and WASPs all get caricatured—square-jawed blonds are mocked for their blandness, although they remain the standard of beauty—but the heaviest artillery, sometimes clever, sometimes crude, is reserved for Jews like Kramer himself. He's an equal opportunity mocker. (A detail that still disturbs me, however, is his "Ubangi lipped" urinal.)

This humor was of its time, when the joke was on propriety and just voicing the outrageous could seem funny in itself. The failed jokes here are no worse than those in other 1970s satires, such as *The Great American Novel* by Philip Roth or *Breakfast of Champions* by Kurt Vonnegut, two literary veterans. *Faggots* was a first novel. Kramer was forty-four when it appeared, yet it reads like the work of a much younger man, excessive and vulgar, but also lively, boisterous and passionate. It commits almost every literary sin imaginable, except the fatal ones of being either dull or trivial.

The mass of incident is held together by the chain reaction of sexual encounters, and a single issue, introduced early in the thoughts of Jack Humpstone, a teacher who's part-owner of a gay club: "Yes, sex and love were different items when he wanted them in one, and yes, having so much sex made having love impossible, and yes, sadism was only a way to keep people away from us and masochism only a way to clutch them close, and yes, we are sadists with some guys and masochists with other guys and sometimes both with both, and yes, we're all out of the closet but we're still in the ghetto and all I see are guys hurting each other and themselves." Jack was burned by the end of his six-year relationship with the elusive, thrill-obsessed Dinky. His ideas are the very ones that Fred will come to believe once Dinky finishes with *him*. Jack functions as an alter ego to Fred, who's already an alter ego of the author.

There are two novels here, or rather, two contrasting tones. The first, focused on Fred and supported by Jack, is full of dissatisfaction with the sexual feeding frenzy. The other, centered around the adventures of Timmy Purvis, is a sharp, irresponsible comedy that captures the sheer joy of humping any stranger who responds to your smile. Even Fred drops into this erotic pinball game now and then, and it can be very sexy. I've talked to men who found *Faggots* quite hot when it came out and used it for one-handed reading, despite its message.

There is no denying where Kramer himself stands in his satire, but he complicates his argument. In addition to the sexiness of the book is the comedy of Fred's hypocrisy and, by extension, the author's. Kramer recognizes the irony of writing a fat, sex-driven novel that denounces sex. He puts that comic hypocrisy in the foreground during the exchange between Fred and Dinky on the eve of the party at Fire Island, a dialogue that's the didactic center of the book, and frequently quoted by Kramer's critics. It's here that Fred tells Dinky gay men need to discover committed love, "Before you fuck yourself to death"—a line later read as a prophecy of AIDS. Fred wants Dinky to be his lover. Dinky wants only to be friends and accuses Fred of aping heterosexual marriage. While they talk, Dinky suits up for the night's orgy, slipping on cock rings, leather vest and boots. Fred can't take his eyes off Dinky while he delivers his big speech:

> I'm tired of being a New York City–Fire Island faggot, I'm tired of using my body as a faceless thing to lure another faceless thing, I want to love a Person!, I want to go out and live in that world with that Person, a Person who loves me, we shouldn't *have* to be faithful, we should *want* to be faithful, love grows, sex gets better, if you don't drain all your fucking energy off somewhere else, no, I don't want you to neutralize us into a friendship!, for all of the above! ... stop running away from me and yourself and answer me ... and ... uhn ... where did you say you bought the boots?

Because, despite his high-sounding words, Fred is excited by the sight of Dinky in leather. The appeal of that fantasy makes him wonder if his ideal of marriage is fantasy too. He fights his doubt and plunges on, but the comedy at his expense rattles his soapbox, makes him more human.

Kramer gives Dinky good arguments against romantic monogamy, including the fact that neither of them know any happy straight marriages. This is reinforced by our glimpses of Fred's parents, a cartoon version of the family that Kramer later explored with real pain and sympathy in *The Destiny of Me*. Even Abe Bronstein, the good, straight father, has had more marriages than he can keep count of.

But the strongest argument against Fred's belief that love is the answer comes not in words but action, in the most powerful scene in the book, the public fistfuck in the woods on Fire Island. Fred, still angrily in love with Dinky, watches with a hundred other men while the object of his affection is hoisted in a swing and fisted by Dinky's other resentful lover, Jack Hump-stone. The play-acted violence comes dangerously close to what both men actually feel: Jack would like to kill Dinky; Fred would like to see him die. Jack thinks, "Yes, I could punch a hole in your stomach just like you punched a hole in the last six years of my life." The reader holds his breath while Jack strains to keep his anger in check. Kramer prolongs the scene in a suspenseful knot of unrequited love and deadly anger. What kind of love is it, though, where you want to destroy the beloved if you cannot possess him? Such love is just as soul-killing as the obliteration of self in pleasure.

This is a novel written by a writer divided against himself, arguing with himself, a split that continues to give the book surprising power. In an anti-sex climate, it would still be controversial. For all its faults, *Faggots* remains alive as few books do so many years after publication.

□ □ □

Why were the gay press and many gay readers so enraged when *Faggots* first appeared?

Political timing was a factor. This was one year after the Anita Bryant campaign in Miami, when the religious right used fake statistics and accounts of bizarre sex acts to revoke Dade County's gay rights code. A similar battle was underway in 1978 over the Briggs Amendment in California, which would have barred gay people from teaching in public schools. At the very moment when activists were arguing that gay men were no kinkier than anyone else, a major publisher put out a commercial novel that opens with two men inviting the protagonist to piss on them. Reviews in the mainstream—the *Los Angeles Times* for example—harped on this bad public image as much as the gay press did. (To my knowledge, the religious right has never quoted the novel in its campaigns, although Midge Decter cited it in her smug 1980 *Commentary* essay, "The Boys on the Beach.")

Deeper than current events and fears about image, however, was the fact that *Faggots* hit a nerve with gay readers. If they were as comfortable with the sexual free-for-all as they claimed, they could have dismissed the book with, "Oh, Larry, relax." But their feelings were every bit as split as Kramer's. A friend hated the book simply because it told people like his parents what he did in the backrooms and the docks every weekend; he was ashamed to have his secret life publicized. Such embarrassment masked larger frustrations with this world of available skin.

At the time, the new pride of the 1970s seemed to be built on sexual freedom. To cast doubt on sex was to doubt the value of liberation. Yet we forget that gay promiscuity, anonymous sex, sex-for-the-sake-of-sex (none of the phrases feel right) was not a post-Stonewall invention. Read any account of the period between 1945 and 1969, the journals of Christopher Isherwood or Donald Vining, for example, or biographies of Frank O'Hara and Tennessee Williams. When sex was one of the few available social acts for gay men, there was plenty of sex. Gay liberation, along with the relaxing of liquor laws, the growth of bars and backrooms, and the pleasure revolution that affected everyone in the 1960s turned up the volume, transforming an established custom into a frenzied institution with its own ideology.

This ideology is difficult to discuss when it was more often implied than articulated. Sex is intensely subjective anyway, full of built-in guilt and anxiety. No matter what you do or don't do, it often feels wrong. During my first years in New York, I felt that I had failed as a gay man if I had too few partners, and like a loveless slut if I had too many. Monogamy was considered a blind aping of heterosexuals, despite the fact that the sexual revolution made fidelity less mandatory for them as well. Of course there were monogamous gay couples, and many men visited the fleshpots only in concentrated bursts. Sexual adventure can be exhausting, especially if you have a full-time job. Then came AIDS, which made monogamy acceptable, even respectable.

Nineteen seventy-eight was the miracle year of gay male fiction. *Faggots* appeared within months of *Dancer from the Dance* by Andrew Holleran and *Nocturnes for the King of Naples* by Edmund White, along with Armistead Maupin's sunny, lightweight *Tales of the City.* Kramer was singled out as the glum, self-loathing brother. Nevertheless, Holleran and White carry their own load of regret and unease. Holleran's discontent is expressed in romantic elegy over the impossibility of love; White internalizes his dissatisfaction in a wounded narrator who sleepwalks through an imaginary world that bears only traces of the 1970s. (White's self-chastisement continued in his next novels with less metaphorical plumage; it is especially strong in *The Beautiful Room Is Empty.* His essays reprinted in *The Burning Library* present sport sex as all fun and games, but his fiction paints a darker picture.) Kramer was not the only one with doubts about this artificial paradise, but he was more blunt than White or Holleran in his meanings, more raw and artless. Minorities are quick to attack the first pictures of their lives, demanding that they be both positive and universal. Gay critics may have pounced on the other novels if *Faggots* hadn't been there to serve as a lightning rod.

Eighteen years later, the secret war between domestic love and Dionysian sex has still not worked itself out. Put on hold during the epidemic, the debate became frozen, exaggerated. The ideology of sex was tamed in campaigns for safe sex, translated into a need for pornography, underwear parties and j.o. clubs. Recently, the war flared up again over fears that younger men are having unsafe sex again. The debate is complicated by the fact that different generations are involved. Men in their twenties and thirties do most of the fucking; older men do most of the writing, projecting ideological fantasies on the young. Gabriel Rotello righteously denounces the wild life he once enjoyed, while Leo Bersani and Frank Browning rhapsodize over it as the one true homosexuality.

Is promiscuity soul-killing? Or is it the keystone of gay identity? Monogamy or soullessness? Sexual freedom or surrender to mainstream hypocrisy? Such an extreme either/or, which is at the center of the *Faggots* controversy, resembles the all-or-nothing approach that alcoholics use with booze. There has to be a looser, more flexible way to think about sex. In the 1970s we took a perfectly human desire to fuck around occasionally and recast it as one of George Orwell's "smelly little orthodoxies." It was the most efficient defense against mixed feelings that included guilt and broken hearts. But the celebration of monogamous love as the chief aim of adult life is also a defense mechanism. Love is work, life in a couple isn't always sane or virtuous, and the world is full of lighter, brighter opportunities. I should say here that I've been with the same man now for sixteen years. I am continually surprised at the life we've made together, how we both feel better grounded in this thicker, heavier, shared existence. Yet I don't believe for a minute that our bond makes us better, or worse, than our single friends.

What is the answer? I don't know, unless it's simply that there is no answer. Any public declaration about something as personal and private as sex will be wrong. Dig deep enough into *Faggots* and you find a similar message. The book's attitudes are far more mixed than Kramer himself can now admit. Trust the tale, not the teller. Yes, the novel attacks the ideology of sex, but it also casts doubts on the ideology of love, and it makes sex-for-the-sake-of-sex look awfully good.

A romantic moralist, Kramer has an undeniable squint, but one that enabled him to see past false pride and nervous guilt to question customs still at the center of gay life. *Faggots* remains important as a tool for arguing about the role of sex in our cultural identity. It has become part of our common language. We improve our vocabulary by seeing the difficult, ambiguous, living book that's actually there, rather than the simplistic Paradise Lost/Paradise Scorned of its reputation.

The novel has also become important as a chapter in the ongoing work-in-progress that is the life of Larry Kramer. *Faggots* would not be nearly as meaningful, or as interesting, if its author had disappeared after writing it. We use this man in a variety of ways, as a spokesperson, scapegoat, guilty conscience, hero and villain. We use him to think about our own issues.

A public figure as well as an autobiographical writer, Kramer has shared more private life with the world than is safe for anyone. Two years ago, word went out in gay literary circles that he had found a boyfriend. He was setting up house with a man whom he had known years before: the very man, in fact, who was the model for Dinky Adams. Dinky didn't fuck himself to death after all. What next? How important is sex and fidelity to these two men now that they're older? What does requited love mean to someone who believed in it so fervently and wanted it for so long? Will the day-to-day compromises of domestic life make him looser, less certain and more flexible? Was love the answer?

Note

1. David Bergman, "Larry Kramer and the Rhetoric of AIDS," in *Gaiety Transformed*, (Madison: University of Wisconsin Press, 1991), p. 125.

GPT: Time and *Faggots*

Mark Merlis

S O: I HAVE REREAD *FAGGOTS*, after eighteen years.
It has been there on my shelves all along, has escaped the spasms of deaccessioning I go through every time I move. Most of its fellow survivors are books I mean to reread some day (or read the first time; my virgin Proust will probably accompany me to the nursing home). But some books hang on just as souvenirs, tokens of an earlier self. Until I agreed to write about *Faggots*, I had no more thought of cracking it open again than of looking, say, at *A Separate Peace*. Every time I pick up a book that mattered to me when I was younger, it crumbles in my hands, as if it were a pressed flower handled too roughly. I read a few pages and think, how could this ever have mattered to me? And this isn't a question about the book. It's a question about who I was.

People sometimes speak of books as friends. But friends change over time, just as you do. If you encounter an old acquaintance and find that you no longer have anything in common, it is because you have both grown older, different. But an old book doesn't change at all; it is more like a stopped clock. Now, just as a stopped clock is right two times a day, there are books whose time comes round again. (Henry James is right about once every two decades.) Maybe this will happen to *Faggots*. But there are people who think it was never right, that it told the time wrong even in 1978.

At any rate, *Faggots* is stuck in that year, and we are not. So it is mostly good for measuring the time that has elapsed, the distance we have traveled.

1978

I came out the same year *Faggots* did. Of course people don't come out the way books do. Coming out is a serial novel, and labelling 1978 my coming-out episode is arbitrary, hindsight, a way of organizing the times of my life. No, not hindsight: I applied the label at the time. That is, after years of resistance, rationalization, dipping my toe in the water and pulling it out again, I finally acknowledged in 1978 that I was gay.

This wasn't a discovery about my sexual preference. At twenty-eight, I was a Kinsey 5, at least. I had performed nearly all the acts in my current repertoire with dozens of men. I had gone no further than hand jobs and abortive, flaccid attempts at penetration with two or three women, the last of these left disappointed and self-questioning in my wake some years earlier. So I had no remaining illusions about what I would be doing in the future with my body parts. I was homosexual, but I wasn't gay, I wasn't like all those gay people. I was more like, say, Melville than the creatures at the bars I went to in Baltimore.

I can't remember, it has been so long I can hardly imagine what satisfaction I derived from this refusal. It was partly internal, the lifelong reluctance to join other people's clubs that had kept me away from flower power, Deadheads, any form of externally organized identity. And it was partly the dreariness of gay life in Baltimore. The A-list in Baltimore consisted of a car dealer with airs, a man who used a hand-puppet to do the weather on the local news, and a window-dresser who had risen to prominence as a walker for Rosa Ponselle. The B-list did hair, mostly. Everyone else, including me, was still essentially in the closet. Where I intended to remain. I couldn't see any way of making a life in this world.

I did join the club, finally. And of course what I had always anticipated as a weary surrender turned out, in the event, to be an enormous relief. I was out. I went to Nautilus and bought Lacoste shirts. I tried and failed to grow a moustache. I read *Nocturnes for the King of Naples* and *Dancer from the Dance* and *Faggots*. Three novels that arrived within a few months of one another and that are forever joined for me now, an accidental trilogy. Their appearance so nearly coincided with my own emergence from the closet I can't be sure, now, if I received them merely as a welcoming fanfare, or if they actually helped me come out.

Of the three, *Faggots* was the most important. Not as literature: the only other gay reader I knew at the time—a beaten-down community college lecturer named Sam who was later killed by a trick—preferred *Dancer*. Of course I could see, as Sam insisted, that the other two books wore the trappings of literature and *Faggots* didn't. If I had looked at any of these books as a model for my own writing (I never have), it would have been *Dancer* or *Nocturnes*. Small, rueful books with some amount of technical fireworks, self-congratulatory literary allusions, and a sensibility informed by the Moderns. This is the kind of book we read and write, what those in the trade call literary fiction, a specialty line as clearly demarcated as crime or sci-fi. While *Faggots* was—what? Some kind of heavy-footed satire: Juvenalian or Swiftian, some would have it, though Max Shulman is probably nearer the mark.[1]

But really none of the books mattered to me as literature. I was aware, even in Baltimore, that the near-simultaneous arrival of these volumes in our chain bookstores was an event, the belated dawn of post-Stonewall writing. There they were, bearing the names of reputable publishers, on the shelves with the other fiction—before there were enough gay titles to be quarantined in a section of their own. But I didn't respond to the books as works of art. What I gobbled up was their picture of the distant gay world of New York. And of course the fullest picture was in *Faggots*: still, despite all its weaknesses, the most nearly successful attempt at a panorama of gay life.

A hideous and distorted one, to be sure, and ugly in ways we can perhaps see more clearly now than then; its black characters, for example, are well-endowed cartoons. But nonetheless it presented a vivid parade of the varieties of the genus Homo, its very existence an affirmation of how far we had come. What I got from *Faggots* was the image of a rich and autonomous gay society: a Zion. I wanted to live in the city of *Faggots*.

Zion

I was, as I say, twenty-eight and living in Baltimore. I was ordinary-looking and extraordinarily shy. I had no close gay friends; the gay community to me was a dingy bar called Leon's where I went faithfully every Friday and Saturday night and, mostly, struck out. Down the street was a disco, the Hippo, but I rarely went there. I was too self-conscious to dance, and it was too noisy for me to try my carefully rehearsed opening lines on anyone.

But elsewhere there was Zion. One need only compare *Faggots* to earlier attempts at a panorama of gay life—*City of Night*, for example, or the even earlier *City and the Pillar*. In those books, a single character crisscrosses the continent. The gay world is the world of the Damron guides: a certain park in this town, a bar in that one (but only on Tuesdays). Despite the singular "city" in both titles, there was no city of gay people. Gay life occurred in cities that belonged to someone else, behind unmarked doors or groves of bushes, while the straight people who owned the cities strode by unaware.

But in *Faggots* there was one city that was entirely gay. Not a ghetto, though Zion and the ghetto are similarly homogeneous. But a city that was ours, in which straight people appeared only as disoriented tourists. Kramer's gay world was in full ascendancy, a point he makes at the very outset of the book by totting up the faggots—2,556,596—in the New York area. They were as numerous, settled, and ridiculous as the nineteenth-century middle class. And so ready to be mocked, as the emergent middle class was once mocked by Dickens or Thackeray.

Satire, it is common to say, measures the actual world against an ideal one. It is a token of how far we had progressed by 1978 that Kramer does not compare the homosexual world to a heterosexual ideal—the straight people in his book are just as neurotic as the gay ones. Instead he uses his picture of current gay life to suggest the possibility of a superior gay life. This was, I think, missed at the time by readers who thought he was condemning homosexuality itself. He wasn't, any more than Dickens rejected the bourgeoisie. Kramer's book was not a reaction to our progress, but the most potent evidence that our progress had occurred. There was a secure gay world that had come far enough to begin examining itself.

And this, perhaps, was the key message for me, reading it out there in the provinces, where gay life was still a ghostly appendage to the real, straight world. Where, accidentally crossing paths at night with someone from the office, you'd look away: I didn't see you, you didn't see me. Not two hundred miles away there existed a gay world, where men lived openly, if ineptly. Reading *Faggots* was like opening a message in a bottle, one that had drifted to me from a continent infinitely distant from my own.

Now of course it is funny that I thought I was reading about the promised land, while everyone in New York was reading a book about hell.

Partly it was just that *Faggots* was a roman to which I did not hold the clef. New Yorkers might recognize that so-and-so was a caricature of some prominent personage, while club X was the very place they'd been the night before. So for them *Faggots* was an amalgam of the reported, the distorted, and the invented. And I suspect much of the fury directed at the book focused on the middle category, the nearly true. While for me, far away, the book was more or less seamless: maybe nearly all true, maybe all fantasy. It didn't matter, either way it offered a vision of a better place.

Rereading it now, of course, I see that it was a horror story. Why did it seem hopeful, back then? Not, I think, because I missed all the digs at the compulsive and dysphoric faggots; I was naive but not stupid. But because behind that—taken by Kramer as understood, a given, and no great consolation—was the image of a community of friends. Fred Lemish and all his party buddies with the silly names, Bo-Peep and Mikie with the tambourine and the rest, who offered one another some support, who tried to cheer one another up in Kramer's bleak universe. It was this that caught me, and let me overlook the rest.

So it was earlier, when I was a kid reading Rechy's *City of Night*, the first depiction of gay life I ever stumbled across. I ignored the grotesque underworld Rechy's hero moved through and drew from the book the single, hopeful message: look how many people like me there are. Readers, if they are needy enough, get what they need from books.

Did I suppose, reading *Faggots* and the other books, that my problem was being in Baltimore? That if I could just get up the nerve to move to New York my life would suddenly blossom into one of witty friends and hot sex,

Fire Island weekends and never-ending brunch? I think not; I think I understood that in New York I would just have pressed myself miserably against the wall of some other dingy bar (Ty's, probably), trying to work up the courage to say Hi to someone from Queens. I used to read with trepidation and assent the grim lines of Cavafy, in his poem about a man fleeing from one city to another: "Now that you've wasted your life here, in this small corner, you've destroyed it everywhere in the world."

So they weren't guidebooks, these novels, directing me to a better place. They were the place. Their authors were the witty friends I didn't have; being inside these books was as close to the party as I was going to get. If the place they described was Zion, I was living in the Diaspora. There was no way to book passage to the place in those books.

Gay People's Time

Except: I was also there. The world of *Faggots* might have been very far from my own, but we were in the same time zone. It was 1978, even in Baltimore. And we were all on Gay People's Time.

I haven't heard this expression in years. You'd be waiting for someone in a bar, thinking you'd been stood up, and a friend would say, "Oh, honey, maybe she's just on GPT." Meaning that gay people were always late, partly because they were scatterbrained, partly because they had to try on every shirt they owned before they could step out the door.

But there was more to GPT than mere chronic tardiness. Gay life might sometimes seem as slow-paced as life in a Jane Austen novel, where people drive to a neighbor's for dinner and go home three months later. Yet it was also lived in a frantic hurry. We loitered, we wanted to stop time in its place, and yet we also rushed towards the next thing.

That is, there were several kinds of GPT, several different clocks running at once and at various speeds. And they all tick steadily through *Faggots*. The paradoxes and contradictions of GPT are the core of the book. I cannot fully reconcile them, cannot synchronize the clocks. So let me just list them, the parallel beats we seemed to march to back then. Even in Baltimore.

□ □ □

GPT was the speed with which we used to hurtle to bed, the haste with which affairs began, the equal haste with which they ended.

So many men, so little time—that was the slogan. Meaning either (a) we had to taste, in some fixed interval, every man on the planet; or (b) we had to audition and discard the legions of Mr. Wrongs before finding Mr. Right.

The two schools of thought, (a) and (b), seemed distinct enough at the time. Only in retrospect is it clear that their adherents left equal numbers of bodies in their wake. And that school (a), those for whom promiscuity was a vocation and not just a time-killer, was the more romantic. Its members did not really intend that, when the music stopped, they would be without a partner.

□ □ □

GPT was the interval implied in the old standard joke/complaint/putdown: he acted butch in the bar, but when I got him home he ...

The implication of that remark was that some deception had occurred, that what you saw in the bar wasn't real. But it was real. In the bar, during the moment you first saw him, he stood the right way, he held his long-necked beer at the proper angle, his speech was low-pitched and laconic. This was no illusion; you saw what you saw. Your mistake was supposing that you had seen everything of him in that moment, that he would be and act just the same way ten minutes, or ten years, later. What you really wanted to do was freeze time, or at least extend the initial moment indefinitely. Because time brings with it contradiction, complexity. Even John Wayne was butch only a few minutes at a time.

□ □ □

GPT was the little bit of time before you grew old and ugly.

The ticking of this particular clock, of course, was especially loud in those days, and it resounds throughout *Faggots*, from Fred Lemish's fortieth birthday to the lucky plummet of the Winston Man in the last instant before his face shows his true age. It is most poignantly rendered, perhaps, when the already used-up teenage hustler Paulie looks sadly at an even younger newcomer to the city: "so innocent and shy and inexperienced and was this what he himself had been like how many weeks ago?"

□ □ □

GPT was later. Not right now, but soon.

The central action of *Faggots* is the pursuit, by Fred Lemish and several other hopefuls, of the chameleon-like Dinky Adams. Dinky displays a different personality to each suitor and strings each of them along. His constant refrain is: later, later we will ... And what everyone is after is to seize his time. Not to possess or master his body, but to engage him, fill all the lines on his dance card, compel his continuous presence. Starting tomorrow, or the next day, Dinky will renounce all his other selves and stay with me, be forever the one Dinky that only I can see.

□ □ □

GPT was the hour you gained in the fall, the night they turned the clocks back.

In Baltimore the bars closed at two, so that serious hunting began around one. But one night a year, at one in the morning, the clock was turned back to midnight. Which meant—Saturnalia!—you had an extra hour before last call. I always thought of this night, not Halloween, as the true gay national holiday. For all the other kinds of GPT came together, their meanings interlocked, in that holy hour before last call.

Classic drama used to observe—or at least critics said it should—three unities. Unity of action, unity of place, unity of time. You can't have several plots going on at once. You can't start in Athens and wind up in Corinth. And everything has to happen in one day or, even better, during the length of the drama, more or less in real time. The chorus can fill everyone in on previous events, but you can't have one scene in April and the next in October, or even morning and afternoon. All the action has to occur in an hour or so; which means, sometimes, that the characters are pushed through the story at a pretty dizzying pace. The effect can be almost comical. People leave the stage and come back, having killed somebody, in about thirty seconds flat.

Faggots observes the unity of time, and with the same comic effect. The action takes a single weekend—not quite real time for the reader, unless you move your lips, but pretty close. And during this time romances blossom and wilt, plots are hatched and consummated, the fresh young thing stepping off the bus becomes jaded and used-up, Miss Yootha Truth rises from the streets to stardom. The temporal compression may seem reminiscent, not of Euripides, but of some bloated, multi-character farces of the late 1960s: *What's New, Pussycat?*; *Casino Royale*; and so on.[2]

But Kramer is clearly aiming at something a little more elevated. The climax of the book is ushered in with the line: "And here the convergence of all ill auguries . . . never ceases."

Everything can happen so fast in tragedy because it's all been prepared for, events over years reach their culmination in an instant, traps that destiny laid for us on the day the world was created snap shut, right now. Last call, when all the different clocks chime together. Followed, as the party breaks up, by some sort of insight, acceptance.

Last Call

The party ended. The one I once read about in *Faggots* and to which I thought I was not invited—though I can see now I was a guest, even in Baltimore—that party ended. And we have had a glut of literature that can be summed up as before/after. This is the whole, naked plot of Christopher Coe's *Such Times*, David Feinberg's *Eighty-Sixed*, and so on. So it is easy to think of *Faggots* as the equivalent of the first half of one of these novels: a naive picture of Before, its couples like the ones in the first reels of horror movies, parked somewhere and innocently necking, unaware that the monster is right behind that tree; the audience can already hear the eerie music. But of course it isn't that way: death may lurk in the Edens of before/after novels, *et in Arcadia ego*, but there is no such foreshadowing in *Faggots*.

Faggots isn't Before, it is Then-and-There, a relic and not a premonition. You cannot read it properly without putting out of your mind everything that has happened since. What people were doing in 1978 had consequences that were invisible at the time. But the easy irony to be derived from this knowledge is less valuable now than Kramer's central message: that what people were doing in 1978 had consequences that were visible, already. Rereading the book is a crucial antidote to the before/after novels, which posit that everything was dandy before the unfortunate interruption and will be again if the cure is found (as in Feinberg's *Spontaneous Combustion*, which concludes with a rather chilling fantasy of the post-cure bacchanalia).

We were enjoying in 1978 a (physical) freedom that may not come again in our lifetimes, and everything wasn't dandy. Not just *Faggots*, but *Dancer* and *Nocturnes* as well, have an elegiac tone. The party was already ending. Indeed, the very appearance of these books, while it may have represented the dawn of contemporary gay writing, was also the equivalent of the band striking up "Good Night Ladies." It was already last call; the life described in these books was unsustainable. Gay men were already moving away from it, walking away as Fred does at the end of the novel.

Walking away from what? Not leather or excrement or drugs. Kramer doesn't really judge these things; he merely reports them. It is true that all through *Faggots* he allows the Mosaic figure of Abe Bronstein to observe, with a sort of tolerant revulsion, that natural laws are being violated. But Kramer doesn't, finally, take Abe's side—here, I think, his New York critics misunderstood him. He does not condemn. Not even at the end, when his stand-in Fred Lemish is kissing goodbye to the world of faggots:

... All my friends. All sitting on the sand. Arms around each other. Touching. Holding. But not too close. Please, no hassles or involvements. Sharing this moment. No one speaking.

Yes, all my friends are here. It's hard to leave you. All this beauty. Such narcotic beauty. Yes, it's hard to leave.

What I want is better though!

No. Just different. I'm going to have enough trouble changing myself. Can't change everyone else too. Can't change those who don't want to change.

Please, no hassles or involvements. Surely Kramer condemns promiscuity, lack of commitment, if nothing else? But even this is too simple; the book is not a sermon on monogamy. Fred Lemish after all, has been a proponent of monogamy throughout the book—monogamy meaning Dinky staying with him forever, uncomplicated and unchanging. It is this vision, not the sexual circus, that Fred walks away from.

For the style of monogamy that Fred has been pursuing is not a bond in the present—there is not one instant in the book when Fred's and Dinky's hearts meet—but a hope for the future: Dinky will be here tomorrow, and the day after that, and one of these days we will touch. And then the holes in me will be filled up.

Fred's conclusion, that his problem is one of insufficient self-love, seems very seventies now, of a piece with EST or the Me Generation, as dated as the Village People. But it is the problem for everyone in the book: everyone is looking for someone to fill the holes in him. (As Dinky himself must literally be filled, by Jack Humpstone's arm, and then wants the other arm.) And this need is the motor that keeps the clocks of GPT running.

No one in the book, coupled or alone, has an autonomous and continuous sense of self. Most, like Fred, live for the past or future and can experience nothing in the present. Others—the no hassles or involvements crowd—cage themselves in the present. Avoiding commitment because it will inevitably end, the other will walk away leaving you with nothing. The two stances are, finally, indistinguishable. Faggots have no being that stretches from yesterday through tomorrow, no identity that is not contingent and mutable. You can't even begin to find that identity until you walk away from the party.

When last call came and the lights were turned up at Leon's, you could try to make some hasty connection in the minutes before you were hurled out onto the street. Or you could head for the baths. Or you could—most often I did—go home. Walking those few blocks to my apartment, I was still in Leon's for a while, sucking in my stomach, cruising passersby. Sometimes I would even take a long way home, stretching out those minutes before I would step into the elevator and watch the doors close and know that I was going to be alone for another night.

Other nights, there would be someone with me in the elevator and I would still be sucking in my stomach, straining to make conversation, being whoever I had to be so that my lucky catch would stay till morning.

Either way, there would never be more than one person in the elevator.

□ □ □

I have reread *Faggots*, after eighteen years. Years during which we were all hurled out of GPT and into real time, facing the one big clock. *Faggots* is a museum piece now, a timepiece to be relegated to the glass case along with the sundial and the hourglass. Its hands set permanently at 1978, marking forever that hour when Fred Lemish walked away from the party. The party broke up soon enough, the friends on the sand dispersed by a tidal wave. So we will never know how else it might have ended, or where Fred Lemish was headed as he walked down the beach. We can only see where he, and the rest of us, got to. That is what *Faggots* lets us measure, with unsettling precision.

Notes

1. The genre game went out with Northrop Frye, but if we must play I think we might assign *Faggots* to the category of Menippean satire, in which each character is the voice or embodiment of a single *idée fixe*, and the action consists of conversations in which the characters' assorted monomanias collide. This is the genre of Thomas Love Peacock; the nearest modern equivalent may be William Gaddis. Kramer merely substitutes fetishes for ideas, and sexual for verbal congress.

2. The similarities between *Faggots* and *Casino Royale*, filmed by Columbia in England while Kramer was an executive with the firm, might be worth examining by someone able to sit through *Casino Royale*.

Faggot Psychology:
Encountering the Gay Shadow and the Gay Soul Figure in *Faggots*

Douglas Sadownick

I F WE, AS GAY PEOPLE, wish to raise ourselves from our current level of psychological arrest, a good place to start is Larry Kramer's novel *Faggots*. Given Kramer's personal and intellectual connection with psychoanalysis and psychotherapy, it comes as no surprise that his text provides an unnerving psychological experience as much as it does a novelistic one. The book nastily confronts a reader's defenses—which explains why the book was greeted with disdain at its 1978 publication and why it works on a therapeutic level that is shocking, appalling and ultimately revolutionary.[1]

Kramer's variety of "inner work" begins with first things first. He names a terrifying psychodynamic truth of gay life, knocking the point home through scatological references and the evocation of horrible feelings by working resistances through to their underlying emotive themes. He calls attention to the *most* disagreeable aspects of gay life—its sexual greed, body fascism, hysterical extroversion, compulsivity, addiction, misogyny, superficiality, and bitchiness—to flush out the sewer contaminating gay psychic potential and wisdom these days.[2]

To speak authentically of gay potential and "ensoulfulness" (as we speak in depth psychology of the process of coming out inside), I must immediately reference its opposite, which is the nastiest side of gay life. I do this at a certain peril. Everyone has an inferior side, gay and straight, yet it often seems politically incorrect to speak of the inferior side of people who have too often been made to feel less-than. But to shirk from the task to name inferiorities so as to be free of their secret domination is to keep us in a regressed state, thus playing into the oppressor's hands.

I have nothing but respect for the gay liberationists of the 1970s. I came out in 1979, and feel no small proximity to this era. I was mentored by men

(Arnie Kantrowitz, Michael Callen, Mark Thompson) who made use of unbridled sexual celebration for the purpose of fighting a repressive postwar American culture, a society that supported the forms of psychic fascism we now call racism, sexism and homophobia. I continue to see gay love and gay sex as positive and good—certainly not just a narcissistic defense to cope with poor upbringing. Yet there is this problem side to gay love and sex that it is no longer so taboo to acknowledge. In fact, we've reached a turning point; we can no longer shirk from being self-critical, that is, if we seek wholeness. Like Kramer, we might explore the shadow side of what motivates our erotic behavior for the express purpose of developing an even greater sense of inwardness and sexual healing. This effort to separate excrement from gold is precisely the point behind Kramer's novel.

Kramer's tone and approach actually resemble that of an astute therapist —one who turns up the anxiety level until the patient either runs out of the consulting room screaming or opens up. To amplify Kramer's feeling approach, we will come at *Faggots* from a *thinking* attitude, and as such, because I am being slightly more scientific, I am constrained to define certain terms. By the "return of the repressed" I mean those childhood feelings of hate, shame, rage and envy stirred up by everyone's upbringing that were split off from everyday life and buried in the unconscious—but only for so long, for they eventually return in any intimate relationship.

They certainly return over and over again in *Faggots*, which provides psychological experience through the tireless evocation of AWFUL feelings. Like the shadow itself, these hideous feelings offer no possibility for escape while also exerting a mesmerizing attraction on the curious gay individual who yearns to go beyond neurosis to find an incorruptible value in his psyche.[3]

The "shadow" offers a way to name one's very own inferior self. Everyone knows this hated part of the personality. It forms the world of dark, judgmental feelings, jealous and desperate acts, addictive needs, self-hating cognitions and aggressive impulses. A person who is easily offended has a big shadow. So is a person likely to accuse another of a problem that actually lies in him. Shadow projections form much of the basis behind what constitutes homophobia, racism and sexism. A person hates something in himself and projects that vileness on another to manage his own dark feelings and terror of fragmentation. We underestimate how recent an acquisition consciousness is in human history and how inclined it still is to fragment. Projections manage such a disintegration of self. A person caught in his shadow may appear like an enraged child or a bully, two sides of the same coin. Most people engage in shadow projections all the time and unconsciously. Jung writes that shadow projections "change the world into the replica of one's unknown face."[4]

But lest a reader get too caught up with definitions, the shadow is nothing if it's not an experience: an embarrassment, a stupidity, a public fart, a moral inferiority, a desperate grasp for love, an ulcer or an unsafe sex act. In fact, Kramer's novel treats the shadow as a selfish monster inside that is paradoxically humanizing if only it can be related to on its own miserable terms. A person simply must take up his shadow if he is to own and objectify his Homosexual Soul as a being in His own right, as a living daemon, as a Spirit Within, the personification of homosexual libido. Kramer, in fact, opens with this quote from Evelyn Waugh, ". . . the ancients located the deeper emotions in the bowels," to suggest that no genuine look into gay life can proceed without a sniffing out of its shit. If one separates the shit from the inner relations in a good enough way, one can only then begin to sense and intuit the "cosmogonic principle" or "unending all of life" of homosexual eros.[5]

Whatever we want to call the rejected piece of the gay personality, there is no question for Kramer that the integration and assimilation of the split-off, alien part of the gay psyche is necessary if we wish to usher in the next step of gay liberation. "Why is there such a contrast between what I might be and what I continue to be?" asks one of Kramer's characters, who sees the centrality of love as a key to his personal myth. "Do I want . . . can I have . . . am I capable of . . . a friend?"[6] Only people striving toward wholeness through integrating their awful inferior sides can experience emotional intimacy with their sexual mate. Likewise, only those drawn to the passion of love can strive toward wholeness, which is to say reunion with one's own psychic patrimony and symbolic father: the Mysterium of Royal Incest.

□   □   □

But before we address the highest in gay life—the transcendent function; the spiritualization of homosexuality; reunion with the Primal Source—we must first address the lowest. *Faggots* came out in the year and city in which I came out: New York, 1978. It has always been a book that has rubbed my own face in my own emotional shit—my reliance on promiscuous coupling as a defense against facing my inferior feelings or potential for genuine love and individuality—and for that reason it is, to me, the most significant gay novel ever published. So rather than join in with the chorus of individuals who, at the time of the book's publication, saw Kramer as pathologizing gay life, I'd like to suggest that, like an alchemist (which is to say a true psychologist), Kramer creates a "holding environment," albeit a very rude one, for the gay reader to start a terrifying inner journey toward self-realization.[7]

In every psychological analysis, an individual will always meet up with his most hated and inferior self before he can make sense of more impersonal energies in the psyche. Kramer names this awful aspect of life in a collective, gay community way to show how little people have owned their shadows.[8] Whatever is unconscious is projected, so it's no wonder that the gay social scene of the 1970s has become a septic tank. Or that the hottest, new bar is the Toilet Bowl.

If the gay streets have turned to waste, no community effort can solve this problem. Each person must face this hell alone. No one can know another person's psyche. (Most people don't know their own!) The extent to which a gay person can bear and partner this dark twin, this terrifying piece of his or her own mind, is the extent to which he or she can separate out the *prima materia*, or shit, from contamination with his or her inner relations, and strive toward wholeness, or a relationship to the archetype of the Self, the supreme psychic authority to which the gay ego is appended, even if it doesn't yet know its own inner gay authority.[9]

When I speak of this "inner psychic authority," I talk about an incorruptible value a gay person can find within himself through an encounter with his own gay psyche.

I therefore speak of gay enspiritment and gay psychological wisdom as a uniquely personal and thus practical affair that has to do with the awakening of the inwardly felt source of life inside a gay person. It is a grassroots approach, really, although a person may find it helpful, especially at first, to acquaint himself with the powerful tools psychology has discovered to wrestle his own unconscious and defenses (via the assistance of someone who has gone before him to wrestle his own). But a gay person's unconscious, and the seizures it produces, are a person's very own. No analyst can take that away from him, nor should dare try.

For a divine seizure happens to each of us daily more often than we think. It happens when a gay man sees an image of a porn star or a handsome man in a bar (or on the street), a man he could love well if only he dared. But we do not own this inwardly-felt source; we split it off and project it, time and time again, on an outside person.

I shall hardly escape the charge of mysticism by suggesting that we, as gay people, begin to take our subjective feelings seriously (at least as seriously as the fellow who has provoked these feelings). I can't help but be continually mesmerized by the way intelligent men (in Kramer's novel as well as in the social world today) allow themselves to be carried away by other faculties than mere reason when they meet up with a man who earns the title (at least in one's private thoughts) of "stud," not to mention "angel."

Gay academic thinkers have monopolized intellectual discourse with a valuable but ultimately one-sided observation of class, gender and race and the attendant power discourses. With roots in feminism and Marxism, these thinkers call themselves "social constructionists" (alternatively, social constructivists). Social construction says that we are what our cultures makes us: nothing more, nothing less. The notion that people are born with the archetype to seek out a love object with a certain religious compulsion is repugnant to social constructionists, who say we are born *tabula rasa*. There is a certain irony here. For social constructionists argue against inborn religious programming with what can only be called religious fervor.

The spiritualists are no better in their intellectual reasoning. They often leave out the real facts of material reality and sexual greed in their sermons that insist that "you make your own reality," or "everything is for the best." Or worse, the New Age, post-Christians suggest that human nastiness can be willed away through meditation, good will or love. Never has the word "love" been so demeaned. A more psychologically minded person knows full well that psychic health hardly consists of repressing disagreeable feelings, but just the opposite: wholeness comes through accepting and working with evil thoughts. To reject unpleasant feelings in oneself, in service of some alleged act of love, is ultimately very hateful.

Torn between social constructionism on one hand and air-headed essentialism on the other, it is no wonder that gay thinkers have as yet to fashion a world-view that speaks to the whole gay person. After all, most people, including gay people, live in the *real* world, and by that I mean a world that incorporates psychic needs with material ones. Many gay people do not see the inconsistency between working to change a corrupt political system *while also* yearning for a personal sense of myth, meaning and reverie. Indeed, a world-view that does not try to bring spirit and matter into the same discussion can never reach gay people in their deepest selves, which is a place in the *heart*, a word few intellectuals have the guts really to utter and too few New Agers have the practical psychology to meet on its own terrifying terms.

Such cowardice will sabotage people in the long run. Life, after all, is at stake. So is a sense of gay-engendered and indigenous culture. Religious hunger in the form of sexual lust and romantic obsession will not be willed away through theorizing on power hierarchies. Not a few of the individuals who call themselves "social constructionists" actually engage in ecstatic gay sexual acts and gay romantic yearning; some even go in for domestic merging. They seek wholeness from eros with such an urgency you would think they were early Christians. I know a few of them and their clandestine lives. These "thinkers" do not consider themselves hypocrites. But anyone who has spent time at a gay academic conference will see that the energy placed on finding a boyfriend or a trick during the heady weekend far outweighs the lectures on how gay identity is a mere "social construct." (It's even possible to see that some of these individuals are constrained to give such talks to earn tenure). They say "the self is a fiction, a series of associations created by culture and power," while in the same breath uttering, at least to themselves, "I'd give anything for a man who could teach me about my self, return me to myself, through his beauty and touch." When the mind says one thing, and the heart and body another, a smart person ought to pay attention, even if it might expose himself as not being as smart as he thinks. In so many ways, Kramer's novel is about this very split between mind and matter (of which this long-standing and now re-escalating debate between radical essentialism and social constructionism, what we used to call nature/nurture, is one symptom), a split that has yet to be reconciled within gay life.

Kramer's novel lands us in the New York of the late 1970s. The thrilling and radical spirit of gay liberation following the Stonewall Rebellion has given way to an apolitical consumer sex culture: "A fuck here and there, a blow job, a jerk-off—once you've been to the White House, where's left to visit?" Gay urban life in the 1970s is militantly extroverted. By that, I mean the psychological attitude is focused on external, ever-stimulating, objects and *not* the inner life or inner figures of the individual. Staunchly materialistic, gay life has been equated with urban life; it has been colonized by general psychology: "Ah, the street, the Streets, *the streets*, let us pause for an Ode to The Streets, Gay Ghetto, homo away from home, the hierarchy and ritual of The Streets ...."[10]

This cult of extroversion makes sense given the need for gay people to come out of the closet and be visible. It shows how embedded the modern gay movement is in the American myth of individualism, action and the Protestant work-ethic. From Walt Whitman to Henry Miller to Ernest Hemingway and even to Allen Ginsberg, physical and emotional health is often equated with embracing the American streets and the boys who people them. Kramer continues and critiques that historical legacy of the "incessant, insinuating, impossible Streets, addictive, the herb superb, can't keep away from you, always drawn to you, STREETS ... !" For this ode to the streets reveals an inherent paradox. The streets, if they are addictive, can offer anything *but* freedom. The streets are another kind of womb and as such work as a block against separating and individuating from old, comforting ways. Individuation stands for an ability to break away from this symbolic mother, bear painful feelings *on one's own* and transform them into new attitudes.[11]

For life doesn't take place only on the streets. It also takes place in the mind. Here one refers not to the "mind" in a Western way, as it is divorced from the body, but as *psychic existence* encompassing the conscious and unconscious, spirit and matter. But who thinks of the "mind" in gay life, not to mention the "gay mind"? This is a great tragedy of gay life, as Kramer himself implies: "We have the ultimate in freedom—we have absolutely no responsibilities!—and we're abusing it." For by itself, extroversion all too easily can grow cruel: "All we do is fuck. With dildoes and gallows and in the bushes and on the streets."[12] Self-assertion without self-realization can never lead to freedom, where a certain value on non-attachment must be acknowledged as having at least some validity.

So, without a conscious integration of its opposite, extroversion exhausts anyone hysterically caught up within it, leading to a kind of psychosis that is not recognized as such: a serious *loss of soul*, which is to say, a loss of personhood and boundaries.[13] People then live in a temporary trance of sex, drugs and disco but without the benefit accrued to people who lived in tribal cultures. We gay moderns participate in group-think, yet paradoxically feel alienated from an abiding connection to the collective. ACT UP comes and goes; so does Queer Nation; so did the Gay Liberation Front and Gay Activists Alliance.

This is the torture of modern gay life. We have not yet created an indigenous community culture that invites a person to develop a sense of gay inwardness rather than just fit in. "You govern your emotions to fit the scene just like everyone else," one character tells Fred, the book's main character. Fred thinks he's special, but he has made his friends and acquaintances into parental objects and remains dependent on them for approval and acceptance: "You want to be part of things and go to all the parties and disco openings and Fire Island and have a lover more than anyone I know. Don't give me that Artist/Hero-as-Outsider shit."[14]

Fred, like the rest of us, has little awareness of the mind's ability to take threatening mental activities and project them into the world with the express purpose of controlling those objects (and thus the threatening mental activities). This is why we, as yet, have no authentic individuality. Only by facing one's hurt places, and providing them a certain regard (a kind of soothing), can one find a core sense of self that can sustain the most intense criticism (or praise). Only then can we begin to recollect projections of authority to people (lovers; bosses) who may have no interest in being represented as parental surrogates.[15]

We are in the middle of a historical transition. We are neither authentically individual (because we have not made an encounter with our psyche to differentiate our being as uniquely different from general psychology) nor are we fully collective (because we have lost our conscious sense of unity with history, myth and general psychology). The American and French Revolutions, the rise of technology, the two World Wars (and even the AIDS epidemic) have demystified collectivity, unbridled merging and religious hysteria of any kind (even the sexual kind) as being often antithetical to individualism. Yet we haven't separated psychologically from the extroverted values from which we come to truly appreciate what is collective in us. "Everybody knows what they want," main character Fred Lemish says to his infatuation Dinky Adams. "They just won't examine their behavior closely enough and see what it means."[16]

We have not yet discovered our minds as the perceiver of the streets. We think the street came before the mind. We have made matter into a supreme principle of reality. This is what the ancient monotheistic religions did with the God-Image, whereby they hypostatized the Self on an invisible figure in the sky, doing so with great emotion and dedication, so as to give vent and voice to an inner call from the Self. We do the same thing with the constellation of powerful feelings on sex and romance. And yet we say we don't believe in the God-Image in any form; we prize rather, these days, the primacy of the body and of material reality. But how do we know anything unless we perceive it with our own minds? Matter is itself a hypothesis. If we can acknowledge that the mind autonomously searches for an object onto which it can attach a high value—that object being a material item, a God-surrogate, a job, an ambition, a boyfriend, a dick—then we can start to say we know something about the reality of the mind. As one of the characters in *Faggots* puts it, "So we make up some new religion to excite us and get up our things."[17] Like all of the ego-centric characters in *Faggots*, he attributes too much power to the ego, when it is actually the unconscious that "makes up" religious symbolism of a homosexual nature, but he gets the point. The human psyche is an energy system that looks for divine meaning wherever it can, which, in our day and age, is often in the arena of physical and emotional love.

□ □ □

Gay-centered psychological thinking is not only new, but revolutionary, considering how American psychiatry pathologized homosexuality until 1973 and, in some quarters, covertly continues to do so. Traditional psychoanalytic theory says that male homosexuality is a pathological defense stemming from over-involvement with one's mother, leading to failure to resolve the Oedipal complex. Freudian analyst Richard Isay tells us, in his foundational *Being Homosexual*, that such an attitude is homophobic and biologically untenable. He quotes E. O. Wilson who suggests that homosexuality is an entirely normal trait "that evolved as an important element of early human social organization."[18]

Many others have exposed the violently regressive way in which psychoanalysis repudiated homosexuality. "This view of gay men," writes gay-centered depth psychologist Mitch Walker, "has come under increasingly critical attack by a new generation of analytic writers, both Freudian and Jungian, who question its assumptions and argue that as a scientific theory it is erroneous and deceptive, in effect serving both to misrepresent the nature and character of homosexuality and to invalidate it."[19]

In the last two decades, many gay psychologists of a variety of stripes insist, through clinical observation, that homosexuality is inborn, natural, and psychically different from heterosexuality. Isay says it is "constitutional in origin."[20] Walker says it is "intrinsic and meaningful, it is natural, good, growth-enhancing, creative . . ."[21] Isay and Walker stipulate that it is not the parents that make a child gay, but rather it is the four-year-old who projects his inborn romantic feeling on the first available man: "my clinical experience suggests that while the early environment has considerable influence on the manner in which sexuality is expressed, it has indiscernible influence on the sex of the love object."[22] Walker amplifies this notion of inborn homosexual libidinal programming: "it is father-son incest that preoccupies the earliest fantasy life, elicited by the inherent impulse itself, in a manner analogous to heterosexual love. For a gay boy, it is the father who is loved and yearned for as the expression of his libidinal striving, in the way that the heterosexual boy 'falls' for his mother."[23] Walker is interested in the teleological meaning of homosexuality, especially in terms of Jung's notion of individuation, namely that an individual's homosexuality has a unique and mysterious meaning to each gay man, and that psychological development involves the hard challenge of becoming conscious of this astonishing potential.[24]

Although Jung had little to say about homosexuality, a new generation of gay Jungians has tried to speak about gay soul from a gay-centered perspective, arguing that homosexuality is inborn, archetypal and expressive of a deep meaning and purpose in both public and private life. Two schools of gay Jungian thinking, centered in both San Francisco and L.A. have emerged in the last decade. San Francisco's Robert Hopcke wrote a ground-breaking book in 1989 analyzing Jung's five stances on homosexuality, trying to apply Jung's notion of the *anima* (the soul as *the* source of life and meaning) in gay male terms, as the "Male Anima."[25] L.A.'s Walker, who co-founded the Radical Faeries with Harry Hay, argues that the gay psyche is organized differently from the heterosexual one and that the soul figure cannot be an anima—that would be a homophobic castration. Every gay man knows that his greatest love is a masculine figure. Given the magnetic power of that attraction, Walker, in 1976, proposed an archetypal concept, the Masculine Double, "to cover a soul figure with all the erotic and spiritual significance attached to anima/us, but of the same sex, and not yet a shadow."[26] This "Gay Soul Figure" is so profound yet basic a notion that no one (least of all the other so-called gay Jungians) has caught up with it. Walker has been instrumental in cultivating a theory and a practice of gay-centered inner work in Los Angeles of which this essay, along with Mark Thompson's 1987 *Gay Spirit* and 1994 *Gay Soul*, are early manifestations.[27]

Before any gay man in *Faggots* gets a tangible awareness of this gay soul figure, the inner double, he must taste and process a good deal of shit from unfinished childhood and family business. I'm not just talking about paternal rejection. We are so caught up in the cult of extroversion that we do not see how our early mothering experience from the first several years of life also still lives inside us as a current affair. To see that, we must turn inside and partner the most primitive of anxieties about not being held or mirrored in a "good enough" way. But this is hard to do if the community standard says: "Extrovert yourself!" If a person didn't get good enough maternal eye-gazing because one's mother used the baby phallically to fill up something missing inside her, thus making the baby gaze at *her*, chances are that that grown gay man is hungry for food, touch and soothing. He needs to acquaint himself with his archaic feelings if he is to change.[28]

If you go to a lover to get mothering, as so many of us do, because you feel absent a secure mothering base inside, chances are you will one day resent the resultant smothering because the primitive injury isn't being seen for what it is. Such a person rests on a false self, not a solid self, and is poorly differentiated. He relies on an outside figure (or an outside value system) to provide foundation. Fred Lemish must do things not because he wants to, but because "it's part of the faggot life style—to find abandonment and freedom through ecstasy—fucking and being fucked and light s & m and shitting and pissing and Oh I want to be abandoned."[29] But this dependency on a replacement secure base (i.e. the faggot lifestyle) is deadly; no gay man can stand its apron strings for very long for it reminds him too much of the dominance of another over his individuality. The faggot lifestyle is as intolerant of feelings as family life used to be.

The "good breast" of gay sex turns into a "bad breast" if it represents the deadening of feeling life through too much escapism. After Fred gets dumped yet again by Dinky Adams he stops off at "four donuterias, two delicatessens, four grocery stores, one late-night A&P, one ice creamery" on his way to the Everhard. This self-medication poisons. Fred's not kidding when, on his way to see Dinky at the Toilet Bowl, he says to himself that "Tonight was obviously going to be, in all ways, a night for shit food."[30]

In other words, many people, including many gay people, don't know what they are feeling, especially if what they're feeling is rageful or shameful. So they self-medicate themselves in all manner of ways, only to find that the defensive maneuver—food in one case, sex in another—makes them feel even worse. The means to escape inferior feelings (food; sex; domestic life; travel) becomes itself a conduit for inferior feelings. In such a setting, there is no difference between nurturance and waste.[31]

□ □ □

This discussion of the gay inferior self and gay inferior feelings is not to diminish public life or even public sex – only its addictive and cultish exclusion of other modes of relating. From a sociological point of view, public sex *has* played an important role in gay life. Gay liberation activists sought to tear down the hypocritical distinction between private and public life when they came out in the early 1970s. "The head of one of America's major Stock Exchange companies is a faggot," Kramer writes, indicting the gap between social life and bedroom life.[32] Unlike the homophiles of the 1950s and 1960s, some of whom adopted aliases and even wives, Stonewall generation gays fought hard to close the difference between what they showed themselves and what they showed the world, by reclaiming their streets.

For a time, they succeeded. But, according to Kramer, what started as healthy Dionysian abandon—a radical, cum-spewing celebration of gay life—ended up losing its political underpinning. Public sex deteriorated into a public display of greed, scarcity and emptiness. Without realizing it, gays played into what Ian Young calls "The Myth of the Homosexual," a nineteenth-century classification that defined homosexuality as an act, a sexual function, "a psychic magnet" for forbidden sexual longing that suggested gay men were "oversexed and impotent, infantile and cunning." The medical model embedded in this myth made a huge impact on homosexuals. Scientists observed that gay men could only meet in public spaces, not taking into account how the modern world (and science) left no other option. So the medical model reified homosexual life as being about a certain kind of secretive behavior (a certain kind of public acting out). Somehow the means of homophobic oppression fit in with what many gay men presumed they needed: more and more sex, often of an anonymous nature. The Myth of the Homosexual discounted ways of being, feeling and expanded consciousness. "The notion of homosexuality," Young writes, "as a kind of amputated and misdirected sexual function led inevitably to the creation of 'the homosexual' as a subspecies of humanity whose very identity was dependent on his unhealthy state—a kind of walking disease."[33]

In Kramer's book, many, if not all, homosexuals identify with this myth, either consciously or unconsciously, through their reluctance—or simply inability—to bring intimacy and eroticism together. This is how the pathologized identifies with the pathology: "every faggot . . . considers his homosexuality as very special to him . . . like a pain he has lived with a very long time."[34] Yet this pain is rarely partnered, related to and made into a community discussion in *Faggots*. People get overwhelmed by their pain and done in by it. They do not know that the ego has the ability to pull away from a feeling without disowning it, and thus to objectify, classify, and relate to a feeling like an actual fact of nature.

I mean this as an actual technique. This empathetic pulling away from a feeling's stranglehold is an actual way of working with and differentiating unconscious material. Unless this lifelong partnership (and thus separation) between the ego and the shadow is engaged in, one will always unconsciously merge with pain, become it, and then, as a defense against the pain, act it out in an extroverted manner. A gay-centered inwardness is necessary if we are to develop a sense of "I" that is not continually contaminated by secret hurts and resentments, but instead breaks free through inner relating.[35]

Only a minority of individuals take this wasted feeling as a wake-up call to take up the shadow. They are the lucky ones. For they can then enter consciously into the depression and worthlessness they have been viciously pushing away, and then can see, once and for all, that the inner shadow world can actually be worked with, wrestled with, and even embraced for the purpose of psychic growth and freedom. Such a person will eventually learn how to personify his shadow, to objectify it, to fight merger with it. To work with the shadow always remains difficult, no matter how long one has been doing it. But one improves one's fluency with horror over time.

For the shadow comes to one through an overwhelming horror of inferior feelings. The only way to survive this flood is to learn a process by which one identifies and names shadow feelings—one by one—over and over again for the purpose of purification and differentiation. This is a new gay myth for the future. "There is my worthless, shitty feeling." "There is my victim kid feeling." "There is my 'I need to merge' feeling." "This is my 'if I don't suck that dick feeling, I'll die from emptiness' feeling." Learning how to name inferior needs and feelings of the gay self offers a new theory and a practice of gay inwardness. Differentiating the shadow reconciles the separate worlds of science (naming and classifying) and religion (uniting feeling with thinking). The ability to do this work qualifies a person as an empathic, feeling person. A gay person who develops an inward-feeling attitude can be said to individuate a Gay Anima, a spiritual sister, a friend who helps and soothes and allows for receptivity.[36]

This is why extroverted demonstrations of freedom or anger can never offer full-fledged liberation, sexual or otherwise. One cannot liberate oneself from homophobic internalizations just by chanting slogans and wearing leather; or, to extrapolate further, solely by changing homo- and erotophobia in society, which is what most gay liberationists saw as responsible for all our pain and troubles. Like all people, we gay men and lesbians must also look inside, especially if one secretly loves one's own father but defends against that knowledge through distortions of memory, through negations that say, "I hate my father, but I love the Marlboro Man." A focus on public sex, without a corresponding inquiry into one's object world (or father complex), led many gays in Kramer's time not to freedom or liberation at all, but a *repetition compulsion* at places like: "Keller's, Ty's, Cell Block, Ramrod, Stud, International, Peter Rabbit, Bunkhouse, Rawhide, Badlands, Tulips, Boots and Saddle, Cynthia's, Tubie's, Mine Shaft, Glory Hole, Pits, Anvil, Cock Ring" and the newest one, the Toilet Bowl.[37] People go to such places looking for father-symbols, someone who'll make their heart skip by either treating them like shit or, for a time, allowing them to forget their shitty feelings.

□ □ □

One should not gloss over Kramer's frequent mention of toilet sex as him being simply rude or satirical. Such mentions operate on both a real and a symbolic level. Despite the seeming health that comes with physical muscle and social panache, the focus on extroversion can be read as a sick defense against introversion, a resistance to looking inside, which is to say, a hesitation in facing one's own personal shit, or, more accurately, a refusal to own the fact that one might see oneself as no better than a piece of shit. ("... when will I be able to shit where and when I want to?, what terrors am I so internalizing?"). The focus on the outer object (the perceived) keeps it away from the subject (the inner perceiver). This is a scam, a hidden agenda, especially if the perceiver secretly fears being overwhelmed by his own shitty feelings.[38]

But, like everything psychic, this denial of the unconscious inner life through neurotic gay extroversion can only last so long and, in fact, contaminates the very thing it's trying to scam: public life. The public sexual world of *Faggots* allows for little feeling, because the feeling is shitty, but the gay sex scene of the 1970s (as Kramer sees it) allows for a lot of toilet sex, which is really a displacement of shitty feeling onto something literal. "Who would want me?" one character says, revealing rather honestly the extent of his own self-hatred. "I want to play house, too. I'm hungry, possessive, insecure, successful, a dissatisfied bubby. I'd run from me."[39] He is thus overly identified, in an unconsciously merged way, with his inferior function and has not made an encounter with it. Which is to say, he has not yet effected a separation from his inferiority based on empathy for his inferiority.

Analytic psychology says that each and every person is in possession of four psychic functions (thinking, feeling, sensation and intuition), and two modes (extrovert and introvert), with one function and mode generally being superior, with another function and the other mode balancing it as equally inferior.[40] Sometimes historical factors render one mode and function inferior for a whole group. For example, most Westerners, especially most Western men, seem to have a damaged capacity for introvert feeling. Gay men, having additionally faced their father's rejection and withdrawal from the earliest stages of consciousness, often have entirely bombed out inner feeling worlds. In other words, feeling, as a function, is for shit. This means that inferior emotions will arise through one's inferior function—if for no other reason than the function itself is less differentiated than thinking or sensation. This is how it should be. For only through a partnering of one's inferior feelings can the process of wholeness and self-awareness commence. A person choosing to change his life might, as a matter of fact, make his inferior function the foundation on which he now stands. This is a radical way to lead a life for it is also the most human.

The great secret of gay life—in fact, of all life—is that it can be quite liberating to own that one has an inferior function and to begin to live a life of inner containment rather than an acting out of it. By "containment," I don't mean repression; I mean making a container so that the feelings can be felt and yet cooked in a crucible, that crucible being one's heart. At that point, one can ask provocative questions about inferiority that suggest a change of attitude. "I don't know who's shitting on whom," Fred asks his absent lover Dinky, suggesting that questions about shit can bring about transformation. "But I do know we've got to stop and change."[41]

So there is nothing wrong with shit. The medieval alchemists often started their experiments with excrement. They knew there could be no opus, no gold, no God-Image, no integrated personality, without starting out with first things first: *prima materia*. This integration of the shadow, however, cannot take place without a wrestling with one's psychological defenses against feeling bad and owning the ambivalence and even hatred one has for one's parents. Kramer's book reports on the defenses—"no, no, *we're* the evaders"[42]—against owning this gay shadow, and as such it is an early corrective. Gay men, especially those who found freedom in sexual liberation, got offended when his book first came out. They got angry at Kramer's seemingly puritanical attitude. But chances are it is Kramer's evocation of inferior feelings and father–son psychology that really offended people.

Being offended is a signal that something has not yet been integrated inside. A movement defended against its own Achilles' heel can never take off and is, in fact, doomed. For when the shadow is pushed out from both public *and* private view, this *prima materia* simply returns when you least expect it. But this need not be just a tragedy. For sometimes a person can see reality only through an extreme loss of boundaries between himself and his primitive needs and wishes, an over-identification and merging with the shadow. "Yes, we were the quintessential faggots, Dinky," Fred says at the end of *Faggots*. "One cock teaser and one doormat. Afraid of love. Using our bodies as barter instead of our brains as heart."[43] One sees this realization take place nowadays with guys who slam crystal and then engage in unsafe sex only to wake up after they hit rock bottom or become HIV-infected and then decide to take up the shadow.

To my mind, no single term in psychology so confronts one with the terrifying reality of psychic experience itself as one's "shadow" (and from a gay attitude, one's "gay shadow"). The shadow is a metaphor which helps us to grasp the notion of the unconscious itself, which is, quite frankly, a hard concept to get in this ego-centric day and age, which shows the moronic ego trying to dominate a great power. Put another way, the shadow refers to that part of ourselves about which we remain *unnecessarily* blind. And while every school of psychology strives toward wholeness, my own belief is that only by personifying the shadow as a "not-I," yet a "person" within, and thus walking hand-in-hand with it one's entire life, can psychic wholeness be achieved.[44]

□ □ □

Despite my choice of words—"shadow, wholeness"—I myself am not a "Jungian." The association with Jung actually makes me queasy. No school of psychology offers a gay-centered approach to psychology and, as such, each school is flawed and deeply limiting when it comes to understanding gay male psychology. Only gay people willing to face their gay psyches can cultivate a gay-centered process of inner work, a process which is just now underway.

All the same, unless we are abject fools, we have no choice but to use the available tools psychology has come up with. We are well advised to borrow what we can from Freud, who proves to us that consciousness is an exceptional quality of life, and from post-Freudians like Donald Winnicott and Margaret Mahler who show the importance of the mother–baby relationship in providing an adult individual a secure base. Heinz Kohut, the innovator of Self Psychology, tells us that a mother who uses a baby to fill something up inside her empty heart injures the baby's self-esteem, making him, as an adult, compliant and secretly enraged.

No one else besides Jung understood that the unconscious produces symbolism of a deeply impersonal and religious nature; he also understood that like all complexes, the soul tends to become personified and to function as though it were a separate personality, a personality that is projected on a Mr. Right when we fall in love or in lust. For that reason, we are also constrained to look to Jung who, it seemed, often looked to gays of the past (the alchemists must have been gay; certainly Plato was!) to identify archetypes of the collective unconscious.

How can gays avoid talk of religious life? Gay men place such a high value on love—as well as on the phallus—that to *not* ask questions about the true nature and potential of cock worship or homosexual romantic love is to act in an irresponsible way to the pressing facts of everyday gay life. There are rational, upper-middle-class, muscular gay men these days who pay good money to attend "Circuit Parties" in cities across North America where they take Ecstasy and dance for twelve hours so they can lose their minds in flesh, cum and psychedelic reverie. Whether or not these men are channeling their homosexual libidos in ways that promote a change of attitude is beside the point. The psyche attaches a deep symbolic value to an object or to a scene despite our desire not to believe in such values. In *Faggots,* Fred Lemish makes Dinky Adams into his god; Dinky does the same thing with one vanilla trick one day, another leather trick another. We can say nothing about the existence of some abstract entity, but we can prove that all people go to heroic lengths to get close to that which they love. Despite the fact that I borrow from a variety of schools to understand gay life, my main interest is in the phenomenology of gay love and the way some homosexual men sacrifice a great deal to worship each other.

Before one learns how to reach and thus worship the object of one's greatest homosexual love—"the Orphic figure of phanes, The Shining One, the First-Created, the Father of Eros"[45]—one needs to be on familiar terms with the lowest, else it will continually contaminate the individuation process. One feels empty, shitty, worthless on one's own—in a word, psychologically orphaned. "It was as if each were rather hungry from some already precocious deprivation now being at last fulfilled," writes Kramer of this ache that is rooted in childhood and that propels a certain Dunnie and Sammy to merge through sex, "holding on to each other's dickies as if they were holding on to their own." This merger takes place after the two engorge themselves on chocolate brownies. The elicitation of childhood needs and wishes will always summon up the metaphors of food and waste in Kramer's world, metaphors that reference the early stages of child development, the Freudian oral, anal and genital stages. After the scene, Sammy studies "the improbable combination of semen and chocolate" all over himself.[46]

But to get at the root cause of this scatology one must look no further than family life, to issues of early mothering, and in particular the issue of paternal rejection of the gay boy. Fred Lemish has impressive bowel problems, problems he traces to his childhood: "Whatever had gone wrong with his early training, toilet or otherwise, he could for years not consider being out of range of a john." It gets so bad that "he would be reluctant to leave his current home base unless he could pinpoint a clean extra-home toilet somewhere along the way."[47] Borrowing from Freud's classic analysis of anality in "The Wolf Man", one can easily surmise that Lemish had a severely punitive father who shamed him during toilet training. Toilet training generally takes place before the child is about to enter into that romance with one parent, between the ages of three to six, which Freud called the Oedipal stage of development. Children tend to associate childbirth and shitting as coming from the same area—the behind of one's parent—suggesting the close relationship between the Oedipal complex and one's toilet business. It is not for nothing that shit and love are so closely related in the unconscious of gay men, though that's not to say that you won't find similar correlations among straight men.

Richard Isay, arguing that homosexuality is inborn, suggests that the causal event behind the hate some gay men seem to have for their fathers stems from unrequited love. "It has become clear to me from working with these and other gay men that homoerotic fantasies are usually present from at least the ages of four or five years. This period of development is analogous to the Oedipal stage in heterosexual boys, except that the primary sexual object of homosexual boys is their fathers."[48] To woo the father, the boy may identify with the mother and take on some of her traits.

In a patriarchal and homophobic culture one cannot fathom the amount of emotional rejection or withdrawal the boy experiences as he reaches out to his father at this age, a feature that takes place soon after he had been shamed to not shit in his pants. Isay writes that homoerotic fantasies directed at the father make "these children feel different from their peers," and can result in "greater secretiveness than other boys, self-isolation, and excessive emotionality."[49] Fred's inability to shit away from home shows a failure to resolve a crucial stage of childhood development. He has not separated from his childhood psyche where he is still married psychically to an internal punitive father, who shits on him as an act of revenge by filling him up with negative, self-hating kinds of feelings. "Particular to the childhood of homosexual boys," adds Isay, "is that their fathers often become detached or hostile during the child's early years, as a result of the child's homosexuality … This may lead both to the father's withdrawal and to his favoring of an older or younger male sibling who appears to be more sociable, more conventional, more masculine."[50]

Fred begins to walk down the path of psychological health when he wakes up to the fact that his father has pushed him away: "Yes, Lester Lemish, your totally poor record in Fatherhood included an inability to kiss and hug, keep bargains and promises, call and say Hello, inquire after studies and well-being, offer love, do anything but pull the Disappearing Act, with its constant curtain line: 'You Are Unwanted! I Reject You Through and Through!,' delivered unto Fred and truly bringing down the house."[51]

Such venting does more to clarify the relationship between father and son; it also sheds light on the sick connection between son and lover. As Fred lets out his true feelings about his father as he begins to wake up to the fact that he is chasing after a man—Dinky—who, in superficial looks and bearing, resembles nothing about his own father, but who, in action and behavior recreates some (if not all) of the same crucial failures to "keep bargains and promises," and "do anything but pull the Disappearing Act." In this way, Dinky is nothing if he is not a father-symbol.[52]

A reader cannot grasp the true intensity of the shadow world of *Faggots* without paying rapt attention to paternal rejection as it developmentally compounds early and conterminous issues in maternal good-enoughness and the way it can be often acted out in orgy rooms and bedrooms. Isay insists that the withdrawal of the father, which is invariably experienced as a rejection, may be a cause of the poor self-esteem and sense of inadequacy felt by so many gay men. To Walker's mind, "The father usually rejects his gay son's love, but whether he does or not, forever after a gay man seeks a 'representation of his father' in his sexual and romantic striving." Kramer, speaking of frustration, says, "Yes, Lester Lemish, you were the first in the long line of danglers who held out the lollipop but who wouldn't let Fred lick."[53]

But, looking closer at Kramer's book (and gay life) one sees immediately that there is more to gay love than a desire to heal unfinished business with one's father. In fact, there are *two* different ways to understand father, or rather, there are two types of father in the gay mind. Isay will always reduce the gay male attraction to a man to the effect a person's father had on his psychological development. But the gay analytic psychologist, which is to say one concerned with archetypal values, will note Isay's contribution and then as well acknowledge a more supreme dimension to "father."

Here "father" represents the psyche itself, one's "Patrix," what Jung calls "the master of life,"[54] the "hero as a symbolic figure who attracts libido to himself in the form of wonder and adoration," and who predates one's biological father. Yes, this archetype was projected on one's biologic father at an early age, but the archetypal force, as it exerts itself in our lives, has a greater value and potential than the man who reared us. In other words, it is possible to be attracted to men who have fatherly virile qualities, long after one has spent time in therapy working through one's father complex! Any-one who has witnessed a magical S/M scene, where the master ceases to be the man holding the whip but an inner voice in the slave's psyche (as well as the master's), knows something about the archetypal father, his sway in gay life and the effect father–son incest has within a single psyche. Every time the ego merges with its Primal Source, which is to say every time a man has sex, a meaningful type of homosexual incest occurs (mostly unconsciously, of course).

But we should think twice before rhapsodizing over the archetypal dimensions of father–son incest before we face, fairly and squarely, our childhood memories of father and the way we might still defend ourselves against the love and hurt we as four-year-olds might have experienced before we had the tools to put the older man's good or bad behavior in context. Nowadays one hears gay people continue to resist the notion that their early parenting experiences could so profoundly affect their choice of, and reactions to, a lover. (But not choice of a sexual orientation, which is inborn and not subject to parental influence). I believe this skepticism around either the love or the hate (or both) for father is often a measure of people's defensive system around protecting the mental representations they have of their parents. Most gay men have not caught up with the most basic discoveries made by psychologists, in particular those from the school of object relations, that one identifies with and internalizes negative aspects of the parents as a way to control what the baby perceives to be intolerable family life.[55]

In other words, one falls in love with a cold, distant man who rejects one's love—over and over again, either through anonymous sex or brief courtships. This falling in love (over and over again) serves a profound purpose. It provides one with a host of reparative possibilities. The fleeting yet delicious feeling of romantic love can act as a defense against feeling the primal pain of the first great romance and its failures. It can also act as a way to revenge and vent one's unexamined hurt-rage, especially if the romance turns immediately sour.[56]

If the affair develops into a relationship, it can provide a person with an attempt to repair the agonizing abandonment and betrayal of the first failed romance. If there is a fair amount of processing in the crucible of the adult relationship, it can help to make reparation and thus break the circular chain of cause (paternal rejection) and effect (failed romances with Dinkys).

There is a great energy system in this father–son incest and its frustration, but the underlying hurt-rage needs to be engaged by the conscious mind for a change of attitude to be effected. This is nothing short of a great struggle with an inner demon; it is fiery rage, sickening homophobia and shame, inferiority and hurt. One has but to compare comments made about Fred's father to comments made about Dinky to see how the unfinished material around father–son incest gets transferred to a relationship with an alleged peer.

Fred speaks about his father ("Oh, Lester Lemish, with a degree from Harvard and one from Harvard Law School . . . why did you lie down and die, in so doing, almost, *almost*, bringing down your younger son, you idolized your elder, he played ball") in ways that mirror how he speaks about Dinky ("How dare we have treated ourselves and each other so badly?"). Expressing an Atom bomb's worth of belated hurt-rage, Fred sees, once and for all, how the Myth of the Homosexual has played into his unfinished family business around paternal rejection. He is pissed off "For settling for so little." He is angry "For having loved half a person." He is embarrassed for his "cowardice" and for "being Lester's sissy."[57]

Fred engages in a repetition compulsion throughout much of *Faggots* to find his father. He has much in common with Shirley Temple in *The Little Princess*. Like her, he finds his man, but unlike her, he eventually finds it inside, through owning his rage and venting it. But by the time his last diatribe is spoken against Dinky, Fred has gathered up the courage and ego strength to pull away from being just a doormat to his father complex.[58]

□ □ □

So far, we have looked at faggot psychology mostly from a reductive lens, that is, in terms of the causal past. We have shown Kramer wondering why gay men are so dysfunctional in their feeling worlds. We have located Kramer's answer to this complex question in two arenas: the gay boy's dysfunctional family life segueing into his later entrance, as a wounded being, to the homophobic, extroverted world (e.g. the Myth of the Homosexual), whereby being gay is all about action and visibility instead of self-realization or inward feeling.

But if we only pathologize the sexual life of *Faggots* and *reduce* the gay male hunger for a phallus to a causal event stemming from maternal inadequacy, paternal rejection, or adaptation to the Myth of the Homosexual, we do ourselves a disservice. There is another piece to the puzzle Kramer puts together that must at least be addressed: that is the issue of gay soul and its primal yearning, the archetypal dimension to father–son incest. Let us not forget that the child is born gay. Optimal frustration of the incest wish is as advisable for gay boys as it is for straight ones. Sublimation through the incest taboo is the motor of all subsequent transformations of libido.

We see such transformation in *Faggots*. Despite the fact that the universe of *Faggots* appears soulless, it is actually steaming with hunger, need, yearning, hoping, dreaming, fantasizing, and cumming—for treasures and ecstasies, for the profoundest possibilities. Kramer delights in rhetorical displays in the manner of Philip Roth to satirize gay life, so his descriptions of ritual are more ridiculous than sublime. Nevertheless, they are legion, as in the case where the Winston Man, who likes to get walked on, fucks a beautiful teenager in public: "Winnie fucks this virgin chicken ... feeling his own love grow as he comes closer and closer, no, hold it back, make this time last ... wanting to cry out: I love you, you little fucker ... Jesus God it never has felt like this, his little ass is squirming for more, wriggling about wanting me to fuck it, look, no don't look, at the drops of blood on Garfield's Bill Blass sheets . . ."[59]

The garden of everlasting love does reveal itself now and again, despite the immense amount of greed and shame characterizing *Faggots*. Men do get a taste of what they have been hunting for, union with a great archetypal mystery: "And they held each other tightly, and each began, unseen by the other, to cry. If this was love, this was wonderful, and the moment must last forever, and each tried to memorize the feeling and what their senses were doing so that, forever, they would be able to remember, to summon up at will."[60]

For there is another object or presence in the gay unconscious besides the gay shadow. Walker identifies this figure as the "Homosexual Soul-Complex." He reviews the literature of Jung's notion of the soul figure for a heterosexual man—the anima—for the purpose of making an analogy between heterosexual romance and homosexual romance. There is a necessary frustration of the incestuous longing a child feels for his parent at the Oedipal state that canalizes libido inward and, according to Jung, "constellates a spiritual and immortal figure within," a "ghostlike presence which has objective reality." This figure is felt as the *very source* of life itself, and as the doorway to ultimate values and meaning, to creative and spiritual truth, to mystical union.[61]

From a homosexual viewpoint, Walker suggests, formation of the soul complex would be entirely different from but analogous to that of a heterosexual man. Such a soul figure would not be a figure of the opposite sex, but one of the same sex: for a gay man, a masculine double.

Quoting Jung, Walker sees the soul figure as a "clearly demarcated functional complex" that functions as a peer, as a special partner, as a personality of the greatest magnetic allure. According to Walker, a gay man feels this soul personality whenever he is in the presence of a man or a fantasy he loves or wants. He feels it when he opens up a porn magazine and gets turned on. He feels it when he masturbates and forms a crush. One generally attributes the cause of the biggest turn-on to a certain Mr. Right. But according to Walker (and Jung) that thinking is backward. Mr. Right has merely provoked a sleeping personality in one's own unconscious, the felt "source of life." But most people do not own their feelings; nor do they treat them as inner realities that can be personified and related to. They give the object so much more credit than their own subjectivity.[62]

Part of the problem is that this experience of the gay soul figure cannot be seen by anyone on the outside; it is not observable by anyone but the perceiver and can thus only be understood as a powerful feeling that overtakes one from the inside. No wonder that, in a culture that only values "objective reality" and the thinking function, inner feeling is so deeply suspect.[63]

But inner reality will not be discounted! Romance is compelled: subjective, private, lush, and, when it comes to archetypal forces, all-consuming, all about the inward experience, and complexes, of the person in love. Eros (whether of a romantic or sexual nature) grabs our attention, seizes us, and becomes the pivot around which life spins. As Jung puts it, libido is the "creative force which man knows only by subjective experience." It is nothing less than God.[64]

The focus here is not on nineteenth-century classifications or extroverted ways of observing reality, but on an evaluative inquiry into things that take place inside. This approach is no different from how most religions try to view the soul. Jung refers to mythological attempts to name this personification as "The Shining One, the First-Created, The Father of Eros."[65] This approach to try and name the soul is not new. What is new here is its gay-centeredness. What is new is the ability of gay psychology to objectify the homosexual soul. Bringing together these two strands—gayness and psychology—offers the making of a gay-centered depth psychology with an attendant technique of great potential and seriousness.

To gay readers trained to look at the world from a heterosexual (and thus breeding) world view, efforts to name inner objects may seem off-putting. I can imagine certain readers diminishing the description of these powerful inner states as "Jungian," or "West Coast" (or most erroneous of all, "New Age"). This is inaccurate at best, defensive at worst. Every school of depth psychology talks about the "inner object world" and how a "mother object" or a "father object" unconsciously exerts control over each and every person. Our description of the "gay soul complex" takes object relations one step further. It helps to name the powerful feelings that overtake one in homosexual romantic love. It gives scientific language to what every ballad names as a truth: that Romantic Love is the greatest energy system, the Glory from on High, that will redeem our despairing lives.

Analytic psychology suggests that there is a natural tendency in all gay people to visualize this creative force of homosexual libido—to regard the homosexual soul figure as an entity who guides and directs one's erotic libido during life. Generally most gay men experience this "erotic being" in a lover or a crush. This is called projection. It is a natural and unconscious process that leads us into relatedness with others. One thinks one is meeting one's Mr. Right during romance, but nothing could be further from the truth. One is meeting up with a split-off part of one's own personality. This explains the numinous experience called "falling in love." Confusing one's lover with one's soul figure, which, in truth, is hard to avoid, has the effect, nonetheless, of erasing the actual identity of the other man with whom one has fallen in love. No one notices the erasure, of course, because romance feels so wonderful—for as long as it lasts. It is only with a Mr. Right revealing his human side that a certain amount of ugliness, and even a sense of betrayal, can ensue.[66]

This is the "make it or break it" moment of every relationship, during which the return of the repressed makes its showing. If this moment seems harder in gay relationships than in heterosexual ones, this factor may result from a slew of obstacles: societal homophobia, the Myth of the Homosexual, one's inferior feeling world, not to mention one's father complex, and early parenting in general. The return of the repressed is a great challenge, but also holds the greatest possibilities, so it must be faced.

If that ugliness can be borne out on the part of the lover—for it is nothing but a confrontation with his own shadow—then a wonderful marriage of opposites can take place in the inner world (within a single individual) and, of course, in the outer world (between the lover and the beloved). There are at least three objects that must be related to when one falls in love with another person: one's gay soul figure, one's shadow, and then, of course, the flesh-and-bones individual with whom one has allegedly fallen in love (with his soul and shadow). Almost no one separates this all out in a lifetime. It is an ever deepening process more than a single-minded goal.[67]

However, the failure to at least try to separate one's shadow from one's inner and outer objects, is a failure of humanity and a failure of feeling like a decent human being. The fact is that most gay men suffer a good deal around unrequited or requited love, more so, arguably, than heterosexuals. Relationships last a day or two, in some cases, a few months. Or a longer relationship loses its heat and becomes a domestic compromise. The soul figure evaporates: gone. Life grows arid; suburban. This is how gay marriages can resemble the static environment in which so many of us were raised—straight marriages too, for that matter.

A world view that emphasizes the gay soul figure as a living inner reality, to be differentiated from our outward pursuit of an appropriate partner, not only provides one with a mystical union on one's own throughout one's life, but can help achieve a more human connection with a gay mate. Practically speaking, it is almost unbearable for a Mr. Right (Dinky) to shoulder the burden a beloved (Fred) lays on him. Fred might have a better chance of cultivating a Dinky—or someone a bit more human than Dinky—as a dating partner if Fred owned his nuclear soul projections and contained them in the crucible of his heart through inner work while he continued to relate to them through Dinky. If Fred shows the capacity to know his needy, grabby, demanding shadow-kid and if he develops the capacity to soothe this needy shadow-kid through a relationship with it and the gay soul figure (an inner relating that is called "containment"), Fred will then have a relationship with three distinct objects: his shadow, his gay soul complex and Dinky. At this more differentiated point, chances are that Fred will become quite attractive to someone, maybe even Dinky, but probably someone more appropriate and a touch less distant.

Every now and then, the men who people *Faggots* get a fleeting taste of their dreamed-for soul figure, their own inner "creative force." Kramer understands that such a profound inner epiphany might depend on the presence of another person, but ultimately even Kramer sees that love is nothing if it's not a private psychic affair: "And they held each other tightly, and each began, unseen by the other, to cry. If this was life, this was wonderful, and the moment must last forever, and each tried to memorize the feeling and what their senses were doing so that, forever, they would be able to remember, to summon up at will."[68]

Here we see an effort to reach and integrate the gay soul figure, the symbol of all promise, to try and objectify it. Working with and through the partnership with the gay soul complex individuates the ego-Self axis and Self-realization with the Spirit and the boundless possibilities within human nature. But because the feeling exists as a projection—as something split off from the person's conscious attitude of himself—it is also the treasure hard to attain. It cannot be instantly seen or integrated, surrounded as it is by layers of defense and repression. Only by working slowly in from one's shadow feelings—one's need, one's hurt, one's ugliness—can one begin to withdraw the romantic, godlike projections, recollect them, and own a real relationship to the power and the wholeness that being with a Mr. Right (or his more human equivalent) provokes. Being with a lover can thus be profoundly whole-making. For at this point, one engages in projections not for their own sake, but in an effort to recollect them, only to project them yet again. Engaging in this circular process of projection and recollection results in an ever deepening process of expanding consciousness by which a gay man differentiates what has previously been unconscious. Ideally, one engages in this gay-centered myth of meaning with another who is struggling to own his soul projections and thus become a more differentiated individual. Through owning one's shadow—and one's gay soul figure—one brings powerful opposites together (one's inner monstrosity; one's inner lover) for the purpose of psychological transformation and individuation of self.[69]

Leaving the madness of gay extroversion, and looking inside, represents, for Kramer, the next stage of gay liberation. By working through one's own father rage ("Anger's a prelude to courage?") and waking up to the archetypal parents one had before one was poisoned by the biologic one ("Be my own Mom and Pop"), Fred can free up the mind to leave the extroverted gay world of *Faggots*, which is to say the beaches of Fire Island. He walks along the ocean's edge to see that "The sun is coming up. Blessing the new day." Fred's new day signals the creation of an indigenous sense of "being gay" with a revolutionary new sense of depth and power, a coming out the like of which none of us has yet seen, for it comes from the inside, whereby one no longer feels so alone in one's own heart and soul but, walking hand-in-hand with one's shadow, one is afforded glimpses at first (through dreams) and then more fleshed out presences later on (through active imagination) of one's own inner relations and one's very own gay soul figure. But first you have to leave that which you know, the streets: "Yes, all my friends are here.

It's hard to leave you. All this beauty. Such narcotic beauty. Yes, it's hard to leave." But leave Fred does. "What I want is better though!"[70]

Introverting libido is Fred's new myth. Through turning one's attention inside, and working with the gay shadow *vis-à-vis* the gay soul figure, an indigenous gay culture and gay inwardness can emerge as living realities. Blocks toward psychic growth and fulfillment of deeper potentials can be identified, struggled against, and thus dislodged. While such transformations have profound political implications for the entire society, they are not based on group-think or the streets or even celebratory ritual sex, but on the courage a given gay individual brings to encountering his own terrifying shadow world and engaging in that lifelong process to become a new and differentiated Gay Individual and not just a faggot.

Notes

1. For more information about this tenet of transpersonal psychology, that a person's resistance to interior feeling must be overcome before personal or social transformation can take place, or genuine love can occur, see *Awakening the Heart: East/West Approaches to Psychotherapy and the Healing Relationship*, ed. John Welwood (Boston: Shambhala, 1983). Also see Robert Johnson's *We: Understanding the Psychology of Romantic Love* (New York: Harper Collins, 1983), p. 4: "The appearance of romantic love in the West began a momentous chapter in this cosmic drama of evolution. Romantic love is the mask behind which a powerful array of new possibilities hides, waiting to be integrated into consciousness. But what has begun as a huge collective surge of psychic energy must be perfected at the *individual* level."

2. For a discussion of repression and its consequences, see Melanie Klein and Joan Riviere, *Love, Hate and Reparation*, (New York: Norton, 1964).

3. See Jacob Needleman, "Psychiatry and the Sacred," in *Awakening the Heart*, p. 11: "But the modern psychiatrist faces a tremendously difficult task as a surrogate parent ... for there may be something far deeper, subtler, and more intensely human, something that echoes of a 'cosmic dimension,' hidden behind the difficulties and therapeutic opportunities of the classical psychoanalytic transference situation."

4. C. G. Jung, *Collected Works 9*, trans. R. F. C. Hull, (Princeton, New Jersey: Princeton University Press, 1956) par. 17. For a more accessible description of shadow, see M. Esther Harding, *The I and the Not I: A Study in the Development of Consciousness* (Princeton, New Jersey: Princeton University Press, 1965).

5. C. G. Jung, *Collected Works 5*, par. 198. Jung speaks of libido as a creative force within the unconscious that has a will of its own and can be personified: "This view leads to a conception of libido which expands into a conception of *intentionality* in general" (par. 197).

6. Larry Kramer, *Faggots* (New York: Plume, 1978), p. 102. For the reader who comes to this essay eager for information on gay social history, see George Chauncey, *Gay New York: Gender, Urban Culture and the Making of the Gay Male World, 1890–1940* (New York: Basic Books, 1994); John D'Emilio, *Sexual Politics, Sexual Communities: The Making of a Homosexual Minority in the United States, 1940–1970* (Chicago: University of Chicago Press, 1983); Allan Berube, *Coming Out Under Fire: The History of Gay Men and Women in World War Two* (New York: Free Press, 1990);

John D'Emilio and Estelle B. Freedman, *Intimate Matters: A History of Sexuality in America* (New York: Harper & Row, 1988); Martin Bauml Duberman, Maretha Vicinus and George Chauncey, Jr. (eds), *Hidden From History: Reclaiming the Gay and Lesbian Past* (New York: New American Library, 1989); Lawrence D. Mass, *Dialogues of the Sexual Revolution*, 2 vols (New York: Harrington Park Press, 1990); Arnie Kantrowitz, *Under the Rainbow* (New York: St. Martin's, 1996). Also see my *Sex Between Men: An Intimate History of the Sex Lives of Gay Men, Postwar to Present* (San Francisco: HarperCollins, 1996).

7. The term "holding environment" refers to how psychologists in the school of object relations raise and heal developmental problems stemming from lack of maternal good-enoughness during the first several years of life. See Donald W. Winnicott, "From Dependence to Independence in the Development of the Individual," in *The Maturational Processes and the Facilitating Environment* (New York: International Universities Press, 1963), pp. 83–99. Also see Jung, *Collected Works 5*, par. 276: "We might also mention the intimate connection between excrement and gold: the lowest value allies itself to the highest."

8. See Robert Johnson, *Owning Your Own Shadow* (New York: HarperCollins, 1991). Also see C. G. Jung, *Collected Works 9*, par. 17.

9. For a thorough discussion of the ego-self axis, see Edward F. Edinger, *Ego and Archetype* (Boston: Shambhala, 1972). For social constructionist writers who come at identity from a different perspective, namely that the "self" is a fiction, see Domna C. Stanton (ed.), *Discourses of Sexuality: From Aristotle to AIDS* (Ann Arbor: University of Michigan Press, 1992) for analyses that deconstruct the notion that sex is the natural, unchanging, essential core of self; see also Jeffrey Weeks, "Against Nature," in *Homosexuality, Which Homosexuality?*, ed. Dennis Altman, Carole Vance, Martha Vicinus, Jeffrey Weeks and others (London: GMP Publishers, 1987), p. 207; 17. Judith Butler, "Imitation and Gender Insubordination," in *Inside/Outside: Lesbian Theories, Gay Theories*, ed. Diana Fuss (New York: Routledge, 1991), p. 17; Michael Warner, *Fear of a Queer Planet*, p. xv; Judith Butler, *Bodies that Matter: On the Discursive Limits of Sex* (London: Routledge, 1993), p. 10.

10. Kramer, *Faggots*, pp. 99 and 82.

11. Also see Jung, *Collected Works, 5*.

12. Kramer, *Faggots*, p. 43. See also Needleman, "Psychiatry and the Sacred," p. 9: "what we feel to be the best of ourselves as human beings is only part of a total structure containing layers of mind, feeling and sensation far more active, subtle, and unifying than we have settled for as our best. These layers are incredibly numerous and need to be peeled back, as it were, one by one along the path of inner growth...until one touches in oneself the fundamental intelligent force in the cosmos."

13. C. G. Jung, *Man and His Symbols*, ed. C. G. Jung (New York: Anchor Books, 1964), p. 24.

14. Kramer, *Faggots*, p. 21.

15. C. G. Jung, *Collected Works 9*, par. 16: "Although, with insight and good will, the shadow can to some extent be assimilated into the conscious personality, experience shows that there are certain features which offer the most obstinate resistance.... These resistances are usually bound up with projections, which are not recognized as such....While some traits peculiar to the shadow can be recognized without too much difficulty as one's own personal qualities, in this case both insight and good will are unavailing because the cause of the emotion appears to lie, beyond all possibility of a doubt, in the *other person*.

16. Kramer, *Faggots*, p. 191.

17. *Ibid.*, p. 80.

18. Richard Isay, *Being Homosexual: Gay Men and Their Development* (New York, Avon, 1989).

19. Mitch Walker, "Father–Son Incest and the Oedipal Stage in Gay Men: A Reconceptualization," 1989. In manuscript, p. 1.

20. Isay, *Being Homosexual*, p. 4.

21. Walker, "Father–Son," p. 12.

22. Isay, *Being Homosexual*, p. 20.

23. Walker, "Father–Son," p. 2.

24. This definition of individuation suggests that the new gay myth for the future would show an individual gay man making a conscious encounter with his own unconscious to find a unique and personal meaning for himself, as well as a taste of immortality.

25. Robert H. Hopcke, *Jung, Jungians and Homosexuality* (Boston: Shambhala, 1989), p. 106.

26. Mitch Walker, "The Double: An Archetypal Configuration," in *Spring*, 1976, pp. 165–75. Jungian Studies, published by the Analytical Psychology Club of London, 1976, pp. 165–75.

27. Mark Thompson, *Gay Spirit: Myth and Meaning* (New York: St. Martin's Press, 1987). Mark Thompson, *Gay Soul* (San Francisco: Harper San Francisco, 1994).

28. See Howard S. Baker, M.D. and Margaret N. Baker, PhD, "Heinz Kohut's Self Psychology: An Overview," in the *American Journal of Psychiatry* 144 (January 1987). Also see Michael St. Clair, *Object Relations and Self Psychology* (New York: Brooks/Cole Publishing, 1996) for a basic description of splitting and the Kleinian "good breast" and "bad breast." Also see Harry Guntrip, *Psychoanalytic Theory, Therapy and the Self* (New York: Harper Collins, 1971), pp. 45–67 for another analysis of Klein's contribution in turning psychoanalysis from drive theory to a theory of relatedness with others (object relations) and how those relations become internalized.

29. Kramer, *Faggots*, p. 61.

30. *Ibid*, pp. 172–3.

31. Jung, *Collected Works 5*, par. 456.

32. Kramer, *Faggots*, p. 92.

33. Ian Young, *The Stonewall Experiment* (New York: Cassell, 1996), pp. 11–14. Also see Gayle Rubin, "Thinking Sex: Notes for a Radical Theory of the Politics of Sexuality", in *Pleasure and Danger: Exploring Female Sexuality,* ed. Carole S. Vance (Boston: Routledge & Kegan Paul, 1984); Pat Califia, *The Culture of Radical Sex* (San Francisco: Cleis Press, 1994), for the most trenchant defense of public sex to date, especially the essay, "Public Sex," pp. 71–94; Jeffrey Weeks, *Sexuality* (London: Tavistock Publications, 1986).

34. Kramer, *Faggots*, p. 76.

35. For a practical account of differentiation, see Robert Johnson, *Inner Work* (New York: Harper Collins). See Julia Kristeva, *Desire in Language: A Semiotic Approach to Literature and Art* (New York: Columbia University Press 1980), p. 39, for a cogent discussion of how the symbol was weakened by the sign from the thirteenth to fifteenth century.

36. I do not have the space to go into the individuation of the Gay Anima in this essay. The reader interested in the powerful role the feminine plays in gay individuation is directed toward Walker, "Jung and Homophobia," p. 66. For the reconciliation of logos with eros, see Edward F. Edinger, *The Creation of Consciousness: Jung's Myth for Modern Man* (Toronto, Canada: Inner City Books, 1984):

"Religion is based on Eros, science on Logos, Religion sought linkage with God, science sought knowledge. The age now dawning seeks *linked knowledge*."

37. Kramer, *Faggots*, p. 82.

38. *Ibid.*, p. 122

39. *Ibid.*, p. 23.

40. Jung, *Psychological Types*, *Collected Works 4*. Also see Marie Louise Von Franz, "The Inferior Function," in *Psychotherapy* (Boston: Shambhala, 1993).

41. Kramer, *Faggots*, p. 380.

42. *Ibid.*, p. 23. Also see Jung, *Collected Works 5*.

43. Kramer, *Faggots*, p. 381.

44. Marie Louise von Franz, *Shadow and Evil in Faerie Tales* (Boston: Shambhala, 1974).

45. Jung, *Collected Works 5*, par. 198.

46. Kramer, *Faggots*, p. 87.

47. *Ibid.*, p. 119.

48. Isay, *Being Homosexual*, p. 29.

49. *Ibid.*, pp. 29–30.

50. *Ibid.*, p. 34.

51. Kramer, *Faggots*, p. 70.

52. The person who "works" as an object for projecting the father-symbol may *not* correspond superficially in looks or demeanor to one's actual father. He may be tall, dark and handsome—as opposed to your father who, let's say, is short and heavy-set. But I'm not talking about actual correspondences. I'm talking about a symbol and a feeling: "He hastened after Mr. Perfect. Where was he?...Fred gulped. Not bad, though perhaps a bit too stern. And, as occasionally happened when Possibility reared its impossible head, Fred became a slightly helpless, slightly speechless, bordering on the ditzy, futile wreck" (Kramer, *Faggots*, p. 177). Now we can see what's going on. This stranger is being made into a father-symbol. In other words, the man on whom you have a crush may provoke in you the same hope for acceptance and the same fear of betrayal as your father did. The desire to be held may be primal, archaic, numinous and mysterious, even if the man is your junior or you superficially take a top role; it may magically carry with it all the hope of redemption and all the pain of its opposite. This is merely one way of understanding a father-symbol.

53. Kramer, *Faggots*, pp. 23, 70.

54. Jung, *Collected Works 5*, par. 477.

55. St. Clair, *Object Relations*, p. 34. Also see M. Esther Harding, *Psychic Energy: Its Source and its Transformation* (Princeton, New Jersey: Princeton University Press, 1947). Also see Jay R. Greenberg and Stephan A. Mitchell, *Object Relations in Psychoanalytic Theory* (Cambridge, Massachusetts: Harvard University Press, 1983).

56. No wonder it is easier, in Kramer's universe, to meet up with a father-symbol in a bathhouse rather than in a series of dates that could amount to a courtship. The way toward intimacy is thus blocked by circumstances. Yet the anonymity of the bathhouse also allows for a full and rich fantasy life: "And then he saw one! A perfect specimen of what he'd best start looking for again if Dinky was going to play Nervous: early thirties, blond and handsome, an obviously intelligent face, yes, a definite possibility to take his mind off his present Dinkylessness" (Kramer, *Faggots*, p. 177). A rejection by a stranger is easier to handle than from someone of whom you have grown fond, and so is rejecting, in turn. Defenses keep one from experiencing intolerable pain, but they also keep one from experiencing full relationships. Writes Isay, "The withdrawal of the father ... is

also an important reason why some gay men have difficulty forming loving and trusting rather than angry and spiteful relationships" (Isay, *Being Homosexual*, p. 34).

57. Kramer, *Faggots*, p. 379.

58. People live life in secret alliance with their defenses, unconsciously merged, rather than in a conscious partnership with the psyche. Writes Isay: "Important to and ubiquitous in the love life of adult gay men is the persistence of an early erotic attachment to the father and a need to defend against these feelings" (Isay, *Being Homosexual*, p. 35). A person may defend against the pain of paternal rejection through the self-medicating principle of sex acts that soon enough end while—at the same time—using that sex act as an effort to redeem and reclaim one's masculinity, if even just for that one safe moment before the need to control such dangerous symbolism soon leads to termination of the scene. Such a person may be left feeling depressed and enraged: "What two lovers? What love? Where's love? Tomorrow! Always tomorrow! What's going on here today? Why is he doing these things? To himself! To me! I'm a fucking towerful power of rage!" (Kramer, *Faggots*, p. 264). A person engaging in this new kind of alchemical gay science will soon see that any kind of "fix" cannot satisfy him for very long if the hidden agenda—one's ancient hurt and yearning—isn't felt and differentiated over and over again (especially during any kind of sexual intimacy). One acts out from painful yearning but does not heal its web of associations through the sex act. This is what is meant by living life unconsciously through one's shadow, unknowingly merged with it. (Shadow is another word for undifferentiated feeling). The day will soon come when two men will not fuck numbly, but will bring introverted "thinking," "feeling," and "intuition," into their cocksucking.

59. Kramer, *Faggots*, p. 151.

60. *Ibid.*, p. 152.

61. Walker, "Father–Son," p. 32.

62. Walker, "Father–Son," p. 15. Also see Henri Corbin, *Creative Imagination in the Sufism of Ibn 'Arabi*, trans. R. Manheim (Princeton: Princeton University Press, 1969). Also see James Hillman, *The Myth of Analysis: Three Essays in Archetypal Psychology* (New York: Harper and Row, 1972).

63. Edinger, *Ego and Archetype*, p. 108: "Since the decline of religion, we have had no adequate collective sanction for the introverted, subjective life. All trends are in the opposite direction...Whether the goal be the state, the corporate organization, the good material life, or the acquisition of objective scientific knowledge, in each case human meaning is being sought where it does not exist—in externals, in objectivity. The unique, particular, not-to-be duplicated subjectivity of the individual which is the real source of human meanings and which is not susceptible to an objective, statistical approach is the despised stone rejected by the builders of our contemporary world view."

64. Jung, *Collected Works 5*, par. 198.

65. *Ibid.*

66. Walker, "Father–Son," pp. 26–34.

67. *Ibid.*

68. Kramer, *Faggots*, p. 316.

69. Walker, "Father–Son," p. 40.

70. Kramer, *Faggots*, pp. 381–2.

The Normal Heart Condition According to Auden

Alfred Corn

A LMOST BY ACCIDENT Larry Kramer found titles for his plays *The Normal Heart* and *The Furniture of Home* (which was the first working title for what became *The Destiny of Me*) in "September 1, 1939," a well-known poem by W.H. Auden. While at work on the first of these plays, he remembered William Maxwell's novel *The Folded Leaf* and wondered if its title were drawn from a poem. He was staying in a friend's house in Virginia, a rustic setting where there were almost no books. It occurred to him that he might ask his friend Richard Howard for the source of the phrase and promptly made a telephone call to him. Howard suspected that the origin of Maxwell's title might be the phrase "the folded lie" from the lines "All I have is a voice / To undo the folded lie, / The romantic lie in the brain / Of the sensual man-in-the-street / And the lie of Authority . . ."[1] In fact, Richard Howard read the entire poem (by long-distance) to Kramer, whose imagination fastened on another phrase from several lines in the poem's sixth stanza:

> What mad Nijinsky wrote
> About Diaghilev
> Is true of the normal heart;
> For the error bred in the bone
> Of each woman and each man
> Craves what it cannot have,
> Not universal love
> But to be loved alone.

When Kramer wrote his second play, he returned to the poem and found *its* title in the following lines:

Faces along the bar
Cling to their average day:
The lights must never go out,
The music must always play,
All the conventions conspire
To make this fort assume
The furniture of home;
Lest we should see where we are,
Lost in a haunted wood,
Children afraid of the night
Who have never been happy or good.

If this poem engaged Larry Kramer so much that he chose to title two of his dramatic works with phrases drawn from it, we can also note that he is not alone in his admiration. It is one of the few Auden poems that "the common reader" (that endangered species) can be counted on to recognize, and its apologists include Joseph Brodsky, who has written persuasively about its meaning and importance. The famous line from stanza eight, "We must love one another or die," has become proverbial, often quoted by people who have no idea where it comes from. A strange irony is that Auden himself, within a few years after the poem's composition, came to dislike it. In his first *Collected Poems*, published in 1944, he reprinted "September 1, 1939" minus the eighth stanza, which must have disappointed readers who were looking for what they regarded as its profoundest line. In later collections of his poetry, Auden dropped the whole poem and always refused permission for its inclusion in new anthologies; it was not reprinted until after his death. Auden decided that the famous line about love and death was untruthful; he remarked, in public and in private, that we are all destined to die, whether or not we love each other.

It takes only a moment's reflection to recognize this as a misinterpretation of the line's actual meaning. In a poem whose point of departure is the date on which Nazi Germany invaded Poland and set into motion the Second World War, we are clearly meant to understand that the opposite of love is killing; that, if we fail to love, inevitably we will perform acts of violence. Auden could have revised the line and made its real meaning more explicit by saying, "We must either love or kill each other," but that revision wouldn't fit the iambic trimeter in which the poem was written, nor would it rhyme with any other line in the stanza. No doubt Auden could have found some other workable solution, but he didn't attempt to do so (apart from simply excising the stanza in its first reprinting).

I suspect that he found other things in the poem objectionable, above and beyond the inclusion of a potentially misleading line: its public tone, its claim for poetry's capacity to influence political events ("to undo the folded lie ... of Authority"), and just possibly its "confessional" dimension. After having attempted to write effective political poems during the "low, dishonest decade" of the Marxist 1930s, Auden came to believe that political poetry was a contradiction in terms, and that "Poetry makes nothing happen," as he put it in another famous poem, "In Memory of W.B. Yeats." What we see in "September 1, 1939" is an intermediate step in his transition from the poetry of political engagement to the more detached position he later adopted.

As for the confessional dimension, the "dive" mentioned in the poem's opening lines was in fact a gay bar on what was known as the strip (along Fifty-second Street in Manhattan), the location of many cabarets and jazz clubs, where Billie Holiday, among others, performed. When Auden returned in late August 1939 from what he described as a "honeymoon" out in New Mexico with Chester Kallman, the latter's friend Harold Norse recommended the bar (called Dizzy's) to Auden as the latest gay hangout. Auden didn't long delay his first visit. The poem presents him as being alone, and no biographer seems to have been able to discover why Kallman didn't accompany him on his first foray to the bar. It's true that strains in their relationship had surfaced already during the possibly misdescribed "honeymoon," and their first serious quarrel may well have been brewing even at this early date. Two summers later Kallman revealed that he had been for some time involved with another man and no longer wished to continue a physical intimacy with Auden. In Humphrey Carpenter's biography, Auden's reaction to the news is recounted as follows: " 'I was forced to know', he afterwards wrote of the days that followed his discovery of Chester's unfaithfulness, 'what it is like to feel oneself the prey of demonic powers, in both the Greek and the Christian sense, stripped of self-control and self-respect, behaving like a ham actor in a Strindberg play.' "[2] He admitted, moreover, that he even considered killing Kallman, but reason or love fortunately prevailed and that particular demon went unsatisfied.

Circumstances coming quite some time after the poem's composition nevertheless confirm the human potential for violence, both at the private and the public level. When, two years after, Auden felt betrayed in his love, he was almost ready to kill; and the years 1939–45 saw the unleashing of demonic forces of international (indeed, genocidal) hatred and destruction on a scale never before witnessed in human history. The poem wants to establish a connection between the two realms, which are regarded as mirroring each other. If we consent to murderous rage at home, we are also tacitly consenting to warfare. If we consent to warfare, we are also authorizing domestic violence. The public is not discontinuous from the private.

> Waves of anger and fear
> Circulate over the bright
> And darkened lands of the earth,
> Obsessing our private lives;

> The unmentionable odour of death
> Offends the September night.

And further on:

> I and the public know
> What all schoolchildren learn,
> Those to whom evil is done
> Do evil in return.

It is what might be called the universal economy of violence that Auden opposes in the poem—which he then goes on to account for at greater length in the lines about "the normal heart." The "error bred in the bone" is really another phrase for the theological category of Original Sin: Ever since Adam and Eve's Fall, human beings are born with a propensity to do wrong and to commit violent acts, as part of their inescapable inheritance. These lines show that Auden had abandoned the Rousseau-like faith in human goodness of his earlier phase, during which he regarded society and oppressive social institutions like capitalism as the source of all human misery and wrongdoing. In the later perspective, he acknowledges that it is innately human to be selfish and to desire "to be loved alone." When that desire is thwarted, violence of some sort will almost certainly result, and the process of retribution will be set in motion. For the descendants of Adam and Eve, the normal condition of the heart is selfishness and a propensity to harm others.

I don't know whether Larry Kramer, who is Jewish, would agree with a view of humanity that derives from Christian theology. After all, according to Genesis's creation narrative, God saw all of what he had made as *tov*, Hebrew for "good", "fitting," "suitable." In any case, Kramer feels no obligation to agree with Auden on every point, certainly not with the view that imaginative writers have no business turning politics into art. Kramer is, as an artist, a moralist; and political activity is simply the application of ethics to the public realm. It is the ethical content, no doubt, of "September 1, 1939" that appealed to Kramer. We can speculate, too, that the poem's setting may have intrigued him as well. These monumental reflections on human nature and destiny take place not on Capitol Hill or in a cathedral, but at a corner table in a "dive," a gay bar. Moreover, the lines about the normal heart's propensity toward self-love at the expense of others are introduced as echoing observations that Nijinsky made concerning Diaghilev, the dance impresario who both launched Nijinsky and took sexual advantage of him. Just how much Auden saw the Nijinsky–Diaghilev relationship as a paradigm for his own with Kallman remains unclear, but the reference to them in this context at least establishes that Auden did not consider gay citizens as exempt in some special way from the propensity to wrongdoing—a view that Kramer himself shares.

What is effective in Kramer's use of the phrase "the normal heart" as a title is a hidden irony lent to it by the moral content of the lines where it appears. "Normal" has traditionally been a term of praise, which, by a reciprocal implication, makes anything "abnormal" reprehensible. But here "situation normal" is Original Sin, selfishness, and violence. The irony gains extra point from one of the oppressive applications of the normal/abnormal antinomy: heterosexuality has in the past been regarded as "normal," just as the other orientation was "abnormal." To label a person "abnormal" who is simply living according to his or her own nature is, needless to say, oppressive. This contradiction stands behind the dispute between the character Ned and his brother in *The Normal Heart*, where it soon emerges that the brother cannot regard homosexuality as "normal." He would reserve the term for heterosexuality, viewed as the "right" sexual orientation, as opposed to Ned's, which isn't good. Meanwhile, Auden's poem *reverses* expectations by applying "normal" to the universal tendency to harm others, a tendency traceable to Original Sin. In Auden's perspective, abnormality would be immeasurably better than normality; if we could find some way of eluding the "error bred in the bone," we would then become good, abnormally good. Going back to the conventional use of these terms, we can see that people in categories traditionally viewed as "other" or "abnormal"—women ("abnormal" because they are not men), Jews, people of color, lesbians, and gay men—may well have special insight as to why normality (as it was formerly defined) is oppressive, indeed, an instance of Original Sin.

Given that oppression, even when mild, is a form of violence, those who consent to the oppression of gay people (if we follow the logic outlined in Auden's poem) are really authorizing a condition of universal warfare and may expect violent retribution in return—though not, at least in theory, from Kramer. He would maintain that not even an oppressed minority is entitled to physical violence, which only perpetuates the cycle of retribution running through most of human experience. *Writing* about oppression and violence, condemning them in blistering terms, is, on the other hand, entirely permissible because strong denunciations of violence or injustice are not the same thing as killing or harming other people. Writing, indeed, is Kramer's way of responding to the summons pronounced in the conclusion of Auden's poem:

> May I, composed like them
> Of Eros and of dust
> Beleaguered by the same
> Negation and despair
> Show an affirming flame.

The affirming flame for both Auden and Kramer is their imaginative writing. To Auden's antinomy between love and killing, Kramer would no doubt add another, encapsulated in the motto of ACT UP, the AIDS organization that he helped to found. "SILENCE = DEATH," in decompressed form, really means, "If we don't speak out, they'll kill us or, short of that, do nothing, and just let hundreds of thousands of us die of AIDS. Those who won't speak out, on some level, are dead already. But maybe they can be brought back to life by 'an affirming flame.'"

Notes

1. *The English Auden: Poems, Essays and Dramatic Writings*, 1927–1939, ed. Edward Mendelson (London: Faber and Faber, 1977), pp. 245–7.
2. Humphrey Carpenter, *W. H. Auden: A Biography* (Boston: Houghton Mifflin, 1981), p. 311.

A Mouthful of Air

Michael Denneny

> They have spoken against you everywhere,
> But weigh this song with the great and their
> pride;
> I made it out of a mouthful of air,
> Their children's children shall say they have lied.
>
> W. B. Yeats, "He Thinks of Those Who Have Spoken Ill of His Beloved"

LARRY KRAMER presents an interesting case to anyone curious about the interaction between writing and politics, two realms whose relations have been strained ever since Plato banished poets from his ideal Republic. No one today would deny that Kramer has been one of the major political players in the AIDS epidemic, as one of the founders of GMHC, the first and now the largest AIDS support organization in the world, as the man who called ACT UP into existence and tried to guide it through its early years, as the tireless agitator whose thundering diatribes and denunciations have shaped the attitudes and politics of more than one generation of gay men. Few writers in our day have plunged into the political arena as deeply and as energetically, and even fewer have made their impact as widely felt as Kramer, "whose pronouncements, ultimatums, vilifications, lampoons, and dramatizations seemed ubiquitous in the early years of the epidemic."[1]

What is interesting about Kramer as a political actor is the means he employed. After all, Larry Kramer represented no one; he had no constituency, no political following and no organization to back him up; indeed, he was more or less thrown out of GMHC and, in its later years, attacked by various factions and individuals in ACT UP. In fact, after his first purely political statement, a 1978 op-ed piece for the *New York Times* called "Gay Power Here" which he wrote at the suggestion of the Random House publicity department to garner attention for his first novel, *Faggots*, he "received a number of phone calls and letters, all saying, more or less, 'Who the fuck are you and what right do you have publicly mouthing off?' Indeed, I was criticizing an entire community and its leadership that I hardly knew and that certainly didn't know me. 'Where have you been all these years, while we've been working our asses off fighting for the gay rights bill?' was screamed at me by not a few."[2] Three years later when he began to write about AIDS, he was still not a popular figure, to say the least, in the gay community; he had alienated many people with *Faggots* and its satirical portrait of a gay world delirious in its pursuit of sex. Having taken what was widely viewed as an anti-sex stand in that novel, Kramer was not a person most gay men were willing to listen to easily. In the years ahead we found he was never easy to listen to, but listen we did. And the fact that we did listen is remarkable and worth looking into.

For Kramer had nothing but his mouth. It was only his stunning ability to use language, to speak in public and to write in fury, that gave him any political position at all. This strikes me as remarkable. Not since Emile Zola's *J'accuse*, has the sheer power inherent in the written word been as effectively deployed for political ends. Who would have thought that one man raising his voice—loudly and repeatedly, then more loudly and repeatedly, then, when you thought he couldn't, *still* more loudly and repeatedly—that one man could mobilize a whole community, could force the media and the politicians to pay attention, could bring into existence the major activist organization of the 1980s with a speech at one public meeting? We have seen many instances of grass roots political initiatives, of clever media campaigns, of relentless lobbying, but nothing quite like this in a very long while. Kramer presents us with a remarkable example of the political power that can be generated by language alone—one man raising his voice—and this, it seems to me, should be of intense interest to anyone concerned with language and its uses.

Many people, trying to define Kramer's role in the gay community during the great catastrophe of AIDS, have used the word "prophet" and referred back to the Old Testament, and it is not an inappropriate comparison. A prophet is a person who becomes a hero to the community—at least in the retrospective view of history—by speaking out and telling people what they don't want, but need, to hear, which was certainly the case with Kramer. Furthermore, it is generally true of prophets that they get no respect in their own country or their own time. From the beginning—from the first piece of writing he ever did about AIDS, which provoked a blistering response from the playwright Robert Chesley: "Read anything by Kramer closely, I think you'll find the subtext is always: the wages of gay sin are death."[3]—not only was his message rejected, but his motives were called into question; he's saying these awful things because he's fanatically anti-sex, because he's on a demented ego trip, because he hates gay people.

In retrospect it is startling how little credit this man was given for the now quite obvious concern for the gay community that animates everything he ever wrote. Unlike John Preston or Paul Monette, writers also mobilized by AIDS but whose dedication to the community was acknowledged and appreciated, Kramer was viewed as a divisive and destructive force. His trenchant satire of the gay world of the 1970s like all satire, was the work of a moralist, a man committed to strengthening, to reforming, the gay community. If he attacked the extreme value placed on sex, it was to make room for love and friendship; but few readers saw this at the time. As a prophet, Kramer got precious little respect, but he was right. At each and every point, Larry Kramer was right. What appeared to most to be wildly exaggerated scenarios of doom turned out to be accurate, sometimes even conservative, predictions, utterly borne out by events. Kramer outraged people by public speeches in which he asked the right half of the audience to stand up and then bluntly told them they'd be dead, half the room would be dead, in ten years. Of course, in New York City the number turned out to be more like 75 percent—three quarters of the room *was* dead after ten years—but who could have believed that at the time?

And here the figure of the Old Testament prophet gives way to the image of Cassandra—"I wanted to be Moses but I could only be Cassandra," says Ned Weeks in *The Destiny Of Me*[4]—Cassandra who saw so clearly the terrible vision of the destruction of her beloved city, who tried to warn her fellow citizens of their impending doom, but whose prophesies failed to avert the destruction of Troy. Cassandra was right, but it didn't matter, Troy still fell. Like Cassandra, Kramer failed. Larry Kramer failed to stop the AIDS epidemic. A point not often stated for obvious reasons, but worth pausing over for a moment. Kramer failed, just as the movement against the war in Vietnam failed to halt that bloody conflict, a fact—an essential fact one would think—that tends to be overlooked when memory turns to the anti-war movement of the 1960s.

Whatever the retrospective view of Kramer as a political figure may eventually be, that central point—the bitter knowledge that all his efforts, judged against their original purpose, ended in failure—is starkly clear to Kramer himself. He records it, repeatedly, in *Reports from the holocaust*. Gay Mens Health Crisis, founded to alert the gay community to the clear and present danger and mobilize the nation's political and health establishments to come to our aid, became a social welfare organization that helped people with AIDS die, alleviating the pressure that otherwise would have been felt by the federal, state and city authorities. ACT UP had perhaps its greatest success in twice forcing the pharmaceutical companies to reduce the price of AZT; only in retrospect would many come to believe that tens of thousands of people had died not from AIDS but from AZT. When Kramer wrote his first piece on AIDS there were 120 cases in the United States; with more than 500,000 cases in America today and estimates of more than 20 million worldwide, the point should not need driving home, but it does: however heroic, the effort to stop the AIDS epidemic was an utter failure. We lost the battle against AIDS, no matter how noble that battle was, and this failure began to be apparent even in the heyday of ACT UP. What is impressive about Kramer is that he began to recognize this, in public and private conversations, even then, although it didn't stop him for years and years.

You're probably objecting that this is too harsh a judgment, that it is utterly unreasonable to think that any one individual could have stopped this disastrous epidemic. Yet I am only giving due respect to the motives that compelled Kramer into action in the first place. It is utterly clear that he had one overriding purpose in all his writing during the 1980s and that was to stop the epidemic before it wiped out the entire gay male community. As he testified at the time, "I don't consider myself an artist. I consider myself a very opinionated man who uses words as fighting tools."[5] The point was not to produce writing—"I am no longer interested in plays and movies and books"[6]—but to have an effect in the world. But Kramer was caught in the same irony that Randy Shilts laid out with such bitter clarity in his essay, "Talking AIDS To Death,"[7] which described the enormous success of *And the Band Played On* and his own total failure: he had set out to change the world, to end the epidemic, but he only produced a bestseller.

Of course, in the political realm, success or failure is not the final word in judging any action or actor. Since the Greeks, since Herodotus announced he would relate the great deeds of the Greeks *and* the Persians alike, and Thucydides decided to tell the story of the Athenians and their enemies equally, the victors *and* the vanquished, we have realized that in the political realm success cannot be the sole standard of judgment. When it comes to action what is important, what is worthy of praise and memory, is not the outcome of the act but some inherent quality that shines forth and is illuminating and inspiring to future generations. As Hannah Arendt taught us, action can reveal a certain kind of greatness that is quite independent of success or failure. For the sobering truth is that almost all the great acts of history, almost all the great historical actors, were, in their own terms, failures. What makes them still worthy of memory is that which shines through the act, that greatness of spirit which can inspire future generations by its example.

My hunch is that future generations will find this kind of greatness in Larry Kramer's mighty but ultimately futile efforts to stem the tide of this epidemic; that Kramer will be judged a true hero in a time when catastrophe threatened to destroy a gay community that had barely emerged into the light of history. And, although the battle to prevent the AIDS epidemic from overwhelming us was indeed lost, the fight to resolve it, to find a cure, remained fully engaged and was doggedly led by Kramer, when so many others considered talk of a cure to be wildly optimistic. And now, in no small measure because of his efforts and his vision, that goal may be truly in sight for the first time. Kramer's insistence that the focus be kept on finding a cure struck many as reckless, and there *is* a quality of sheer recklessness in

Kramer, in both his writing and his actions—in setting himself against this epidemic—which combined with a nearly unbelievable relentlessness has made him a hero, one of the founding fathers of the community and the culture, the major voice of resistance during its darkest hour.

But what about the writing? After all, what is unique about this case is that Kramer's political impact was the result of his writing and speaking, his use of language, and, when all is said and done and suffered through and the AIDS epidemic has become another episode in the nightmare of history, what will be left are the words on paper.

How do we judge Kramer's writings?

Oddly enough, though many people willingly give him credit for much in the political arena, when it comes to the man's writings, considered solely as writing, the enthusiasm diminishes. Although most of my friends and acquaintances have eventually come to have great respect, and even affection, for him, they seem to shy away from discussing his work and would be taken aback were one to claim that Kramer is one of the most important *writers* of our time. Perhaps this is because we are so used to thinking of politically motivated writing as the realm of the second-rate; after all, books like *Uncle Tom's Cabin* or *What Is To Be Done?* seldom head our lists of favorite literary works. Such books are honored in the canon, but more for their extra-literary merit than for their intrinsic worth as writing. In the western tradition, the vast majority of those considered to be great writers tend, when not being totally apolitical, to be conventional and conservative in their politics, if not downright reactionary or simply loony; while the writers admired for their politics, their commitment to a cause or a community, tend to be distressingly mediocre.

If this is indeed the case, the prospects for Kramer's literary reputation do not look bright, for all the writing he has produced is intensely political, more so, in fact, than any other contemporary American writer I can think of. Consider each of his works:

Faggots may have shocked his contemporaries into apoplectic fits of fury, but it is pure, if savage, social satire in the tradition of Jonathan Swift. One critic, describing it as "a phantasmagoria of rape, incest, drug addiction, coprophilia, pedophilia, and torture," confessed to having "difficulty imagining how Kramer expected readers to find the mordant comedy he intended."[8] Of course, the Irish readers of Swift's "A Modest Proposal," and perhaps even the English, might have experienced the same difficulty. Successful satire is not nice, and never polite; it aims to draw blood. With *Faggots*, Kramer clearly intended to jolt his readers into reconsidering the lives they were leading.

The Normal Heart is, arguably, one of the most successful pieces of agit-prop theater ever produced; unabashedly a propaganda play, it set out to instruct and arouse its audience to political passion and political action, and it worked remarkably well, much better than most such attempts. "When I wrote *The Normal Heart*," the author states, "I knew exactly what I wanted to achieve: to hear my words screamed out in a theater, and to hope I'd change the world."[9]

Reports from the holocaust: The Story of an AIDS Activist is a book crafted from Kramer's political writings and speeches, pieces mostly written to have an immediate practical impact, which even the author originally doubted had any lasting literary merit. Indeed, it took several months to convince him to run them out of his computer so they could be read together to see if they would make a valid book. The resulting work still has the capacity to rouse the activist instincts of any reader not clinically dead and is intensely admired by young black students who gather after Kramer's college lectures to discuss with him how to write in outrage and anger without being consumed by those emotions.[10]

With *Just Say No: A Play About a Farce*, Kramer used the form of the classic French bedroom comedy to skewer the Reagan administration's hypocrisy and deceit, while lambasting their indifference and neglect of the major public health threat facing the country. "The style is classic farce," wrote one reviewer, "with roots in Swift ... and Restoration comedy. *Just Say No* does not merely drop names. It flings them, usually into the mud."[11] And another critic applauded "Kramer's lonely frontline commitment to theater as a political instrument."[12]

In *The Destiny of Me*, the author puts onto the stage the public and highly politicized figures of Larry Kramer and Tony Fauci, head of the National Institute of Allergy and Infectious Diseases, to act out the complex tragedy of gay men in the AIDS epidemic. A classic family play, yet it is enmeshed in the politics of the moment.

And in his currently uncompleted epic, a historical novel called *The American People*, Kramer seeks the roots of the disease of homophobia, tracing the growth of this sickness through the course of American history.

It is hard to imagine a more intensely political oeuvre, and impossible to find a comparably political writer among contemporary gay authors, or anybody else for that matter. Yet what saves this work from being consigned to the dustbin of agit-prop theater and second-rate propaganda work—the famous man meets tractor, man falls in love with tractor, man marries tractor school of socially motivated writing—is the paradoxical fact that it is, simultaneously, intensely personal. *Faggots* is the story of Kramer's own unhappy love affair, a revenge novel to be sure, but virtually every fact, character, incident and institution is taken directly from life, and with much less exaggeration dolloped in than anyone who didn't live through the gay scene in New York in the 1970s could imagine.[13] In *The Normal Heart* and *The Destiny of Me*, Kramer put chunks of his intimate personal life on stage to capture the great tragedy his generation of gay men was living through. In *Reports*, Kramer's anger and outrage are so personal and particular, especially his obsession with Mayor Koch and the *New York Times* and the huge and ever increasing list of his dead friends, that some readers thought he was on an ego trip of monumental proportions. And finally, the sheer venom and stinging bitchiness of *Just Say No* are about as personal as the slanderous assaults of political theater have been since Aristophanes.

In the realm of literature, the political is hardly ever personal—think of *Uncle Tom's Cabin*, think of *What Is To Be Done?*—and, contrary to popular wisdom, the personal is seldom political. But in this case, at any rate, the personal and the political have been smashed together to the point of fusion. If Kramer is the most political of all contemporary gay writers, he is also the most immediately and unguardedly personal. And it is this remarkable fusion, I believe, that will allow Kramer's writing to escape the dreary literary fate of so much politically inspired art.

Rereading Kramer's various works, what is striking is how remarkably *alive* his writing remains. His three plays possess a taut immediacy and dramatic urgency that not only hasn't diminished but seems to have clarified and concentrated over time, convincing me at least that his position in the history of American theater is secure. The three plays cohere so remarkably it is almost as if Kramer had intended to write a trilogy, two tragedies followed by a satyr play, in a modern update of the ancient Greek tradition.

Faggots is as outrageously funny as a Marx Brothers movie dreamt by a queer Philip Roth, a linguistic farrago barreling ahead at an unsafe speed. With his very first book Kramer placed himself in the mainstream of postwar Jewish American humor, in the tradition of Philip Roth and Woody Allen as well as the great television comedy writers of the 1950s. *Faggots* is written in a classic New York yiddishe, faegele voice that is utterly hysterical when read aloud—when the reader really *hears* it as voice. The narrator is a stand-up comic in the Borscht Belt tradition, a sort of Jack Benny afflicted with logomania, as his torrent of words cascades over the reader with the relentlessness of Niagara Falls. From its opening page the author lets us know that he is addressing grand themes and addressing them with a writerly amplitude that sometimes threatens to drown the reader: "There are 2,556,596 faggots in the New York City Area," the first line announces sweepingly, going on to break down the numbers by borough and suburban area before continuing, "There are now more faggots in the New York City area than Jews. There are now more faggots in the entire United States than all the yids and kikes put together. (This is subsidiary data, not overtly relevant, but ipso facto nevertheless.) The straight and narow, so beloved of our founding fathers and all fathers thereafter, is now obviously and irrevocably bent. What is God trying to tell us . . . ?" Like a latter-day Sid Caesar, armed with patter, dropping asides left and right, the narrator stands stage left and introduces the narrative. The voice is grandiloquent, even operatic at times, gliding easily from stagy declamation to whispered asides to muttering meditations to sweeping arias, and this narrative voice vibrates with sympathy, sympathy even for the furniture of the world, the buildings—the sexual haunt of the piers off Christopher Street gets a direct address worthy of Whitman[14]—and sympathy for the characters it evokes with clouds of words before directing our attention to the often vaudevillian scenes about to take place on the page before us. Kramer's language is simply extraordinary; and while its voluminousness at first seems excessive, a closer look shows how much information and atmosphere is conveyed in a style that might be described as loquaciously concise. Just try to unpack the information conveyed in that ode to the piers, for instance, as the narrative voice slides seamlessly into the consciousness of the main character, and see if you don't end up with many more words than Kramer used. So much for the temptation to say, "Too many notes, Mr Mozart."

But perhaps most surprising is how alive the language remains in *Reports from the holocaust*, essays and speeches written on the spot for specific occasions and specific effect which years later retain their impact. The voice—which is again operatic, as critic David Bergman has noticed[15]—is urgent, personal, demanding, exasperated, loud and absolutely unrelenting. The presence of the author haranguing you is almost physically palpable; indeed, Kramer seems to have a patent on what might be called the Ancient Mariner ploy: you feel like you have to break free of his hold every time you put the book down. Which might have made for an uncomfortable read if Kramer had not added the second, more meditative, occasionally rueful voice that appears in the interstitial material which introduces and frames each piece, giving its occasion and commenting on its impact, as he rounds out a story which takes us from sheer activism to the philosophical questions of evil and personal responsibility in our time.

It is precisely these qualities of his language—the fact that it *is* so personal, urgent, extreme, unrelenting and intimate—that accounts for both the immediate political impact it had and the tendency of some to dismiss it as not serious "literature".[16] This is not strong emotion recollected in tranquillity, it is strong emotion being thrown in your face. Kramer is not interested in the making of well wrought urns, he wants to hurl well aimed bombs into your consciousness. And this, I think, gets us to the root of the problem. It is Kramer's apparent disregard for form, for the classic forms of literature, that inclines people not to consider him as a serious, literary writer, and to dismiss his work as "rhetoric."

Of course, such critics are, oddly, forgetting that for two thousand years rhetoric was considered not only legitimate but one of the highest forms of literary art. Some of the most respected authors of western literature—Cicero, for instance—were revered precisely because they were masters of rhetoric. Today, on the contrary, rhetoric carries the overtone of *merely* rhetoric or *empty* rhetoric. In an age when the private and the intimate seem the only guarantee of authenticity and sincerity, rhetoric seems bogus almost by definition. The more public the speech, the less we trust it; only what is intimate is true and sincere. But Kramer, with a brilliant stroke, has abolished this dichotomy. By smashing together the private and the intimate with the public and the political, he has found a way to bring rhetoric back to life as a legitimate, indeed inspired, capacity of language. His startling use of the personal insult and abusive street language so shattered the general conventions of the day that the protective shield most of us have against public and political speech disappeared. And this, in turn, allows him to employ many of the classic tropes of rhetoric to great effect. Kramer's use of repetition, for instance, or of the simple list are astonishingly effective in piece after piece. And who would have thought that the thundering rhetorical question—"DO YOU WANT TO DIE???!!!"—could actually viscerally enrage audiences today? It would be interesting to see a scholarly analysis of all the classic tropes of rhetoric Kramer uses, for it might go some way toward showing there is more literary structure there, a curiously organic structure, than might be first apparent.

Be that as it may, it is nonetheless true that form is not Kramer's strong point. His aim, when he puts pen to paper, is not to construct a perfect object, but to release energy into the world through his readers. It is not form but voice that is the touchstone, providing the unity and aesthetic coherence in his various writings. Here Kramer joins a tradition that stretches through Allen Ginsberg all the way back to Walt Whitman—also criticized for his neglect of form, for his long-windedness, for putting himself so viscerally into his poetry. What Whitman said of his work—"Who touches this book, touches me."—applies to Kramer with a vengeance. And, as in the case of Whitman, the voice is the secret of the vitality, the aliveness of the writing. Kramer is an absolute master at the use of voice, and it is his brilliant fusion of the public voice with the personal voice that makes him one of the most remarkable writers at work today.

This voice was called forth by the great catastrophe that overtook the gay community at the beginning of the 1980s: Larry Kramer raised his voice in response to the onslaught of the epidemic. (Of course, *Faggots* was written four years before AIDS emerged; but in an uncanny way that novel now seems to anticipate the crisis—the wages of gay sin are death, indeed.) For gay writers or writers with AIDS, the personal and social catastrophe of this epidemic forced on the mind radical questions about the act of writing, its nature and purpose and the standards by which we judge its inherent quality, at the same time offering the opportunity to look afresh at the deepest roots of this cultural act. When you are facing death, when all your friends are dying, why do you write? So posterity might have a few more well wrought urns? I don't think so.

Kramer responded to the harsh challenge history presented him with using the only tool at his disposal, language. In the midst of such a total disaster for the gay community and this particular gay man, silence did indeed equal death. In such circumstances what is required is speaking out, talking back, not finally because such action will solve the crisis—as we know, nothing stopped this epidemic—but because if speech does not equal life, it does equal dignity. Answer back the hammer blows of Fortune with great souled words, chants the last chorus in Sophocles' *Antigone*, *this* is the only defense of human dignity in the midst of true tragedy. As Mark Doty says in his magnificent memoir of the devastation AIDS wrought on his life, "The deepening of the heart, the work of soul-making, goes on, I think, as the world hammers us, as we forge ourselves in response to its heats and powers."[17] To speak out is to declare oneself present; to answer back is to resist what one is presented with; together, speaking out and answering back mean bearing witness, and to bear witness is perhaps the most elemental as well as the most powerful use of language.

This is why I believe that Larry Kramer is one of the most important writers of our time. His work has borne witness to the despair, death and destruction that almost swept away the gay male community. His example makes clear to us that language is an act. It is how we declare ourselves present and how we insert ourselves into the world. At root, the act of language is the act of witnessing. Through his spirit and his language, Kramer has crafted a testimony that runs alongside the disastrous reality his words are responding to. And I believe that this voice and this catastrophe will be yoked together for as long as people remember these dark days and as long as people value the power of language to keep our spirit alive through the tragedies of history.

Notes

1. David Bergman, "Larry Kramer and The Rhetoric of AIDS," in *Gaity Transformed: Gay Self-Representation in American Literature* (Madison: University of Wisconsin Press, 1991), p. 123.
2. Larry Kramer, *Reports from the holocaust: The Story of an AIDS Activist* (New York: Stonewall Inn Editions, St. Martin's Press, 1994), p. 6.
3. *Ibid.*, p. 10.
4. Larry Kramer, *The Destiny of Me* (New York: Plume, Penguin Books), p. 87.
5. Kramer, *Reports*, p. 145.
6. *Ibid.*, p. 145–6.
7. Randy Shilts, "Talking AIDS To Death," *Esquire*, Vol. 111, No. 3 (March 1989), pp. 123–135.
8. Bergman, "Larry Kramer and The Rhetoric of AIDS," p. 126.
9. Kramer, Introduction to *The Destiny of Me*, p. 2.
10. Personal communication from Larry Kramer.
11. Linda Winer, *Newsday*, quoted on the back cover of the paperback edition of *Just Say No: A Play about a Farce* (New York: Stonewall Inn Editions, St. Martin's Press, 1989).
12. Gordon Rogoff, *Village Voice*, quoted on the back cover of *Just Say No*.
13. Kramer himself has written: "Some readers tell me my novel, *Faggots* is about as surreal a portrayal of the gay world as could be, but it was all the real McCoy to me," in the Introduction to *The Destiny of Me*, p. 3.

14. See *Faggots, a Novel* by Larry Kramer (New York: Random House, 1978), p. 102: "Ah home away from home, ah black hole of Calcutta . . . . *Play, Guts, Ball!*".

15. Bergman, "Larry Kramer and The Rhetoric of AIDS," p. 128: "The voices of the family float up . . ."

16. Critic David Bergman is a perfect example of both these reactions: "Kramer's habit of responding to political events as personal affronts, of transforming impersonal bureaucracies into individual bogeymen, of subsuming all conflicts into a version of the Freudian family romance is the source of both the power of his political polemics and of the problems with them" (*ibid.*, p. 128). While I agree with Bergman about the "source," for the life of me I can't see the "problem". The "political event" Kramer is talking about is AIDS, and the man is HIV-positive and, until recently at any rate, expected to die of it relatively soon—if that's not as personal an affront as fate can hand one, I don't know what is. Nor can I see what's wrong, in this situation, with "transforming impersonal bureaucracies into individual bogeymen" (though bogeymen is unnecessarily loaded)—I'm pretty sure it's what Hannah Arendt would have advised, but if Bergman has a better political strategy for dealing with such a situation, which one might call genocide by bureaucratic indifference, incompetence and folly, I'm open to hearing it. And as for "the Freudian Family romance"—"Kramer's tendency to place the gay community within the bosom of the heterosexual family"—that, it seems to me, is precisely where the gay community is situated, as the catastrophe of AIDS made abundantly clear to us. The illusion that the gay world was totally separate from the straight world, the fantasy of the ghetto, was only the wishful thinking of the 1970s and was hardly tenable then, since we all come from straight families. In any event, it was totally demolished with the advent of the AIDS epidemic in which we realized that we were inseparably (intimately and sexually) connected to the rest of the world, and that we needed the rest of the world (and its social and scientific resources) to survive as individuals and thus as a community.

17. Mark Doty, *Heaven's Coast: A Memoir* (New York: HarperCollins Publishers, 1996), p. 157.

PART FOUR

Voices, Audiences and the Theater

Three Screeds from Key West:

For Larry Kramer

Tony Kushner

E DITORIAL NOTE: The piece which follows was presented at the fifteenth annual Key West Literary Seminar, devoted to "Literature in the Age of AIDS," in January 1997, and subsequently published in the Spring 1997 issue of the *Harvard Gay and Lesbian Review*. In their commentary, "The Order of Ideas at Key West," in that issue of the quarterly, *HGLR* editor-in-chief Richard Schneider Jr. and co-author Peter Marcus noted that "To live and write in the age of AIDS is to grieve the lives that have been lost and to search for continued meaning in life through writing." They concluded with a quotation from "The Idea of Order at Key West" by Wallace Stevens:

> Words of the fragrant portals, dimly-
>   starred,
> And of ourselves and of our origins,
> In ghostlier demarcations, keener sounds.

For Larry Kramer

These are prefatory remarks written for the three panels upon which I sat at the recent Key West Seminar on "Literature in the Age of AIDS." I wrote each one about an hour before the panel; Larry Kramer called them "screeds" and that sounded right so I've used his title. The titles of each section are simply the titles somebody else assigned to the panels. I think everything I write sounds like a dramatic monologue, which isn't surprising; these monologues were written by and for the almost-entirely fictional character Tony Kushner, a playwright, who, as he said in the last of the three panels, spent the weekend feeling like the bastard child of Neville Chamberlain and Attila the Hun. There's a reference in the second screed to a struggle Sarah Schulman and I had over several instances of thoughtless exercising of privilege and exclusion. Better, I said, borrowing a lesson I've learned from my collaborator friend Kimberly Flynn, to be awkward in admitting a mistake than to be a totally irresponsible fuck-up; and this I think is in a sense the point of all that follows.

The Theater and AIDS

I can't image I'm the only one here—I certainly hope I'm not—who feels odd that she or he has benefited, even profited from the epidemic. This is an ugly statement and I hesitate to write it or utter it, but I've been haunted all weekend, and was anticipatorily haunted before coming here, and even considered *not* coming, up till the last moment, because of strong feelings of unworthiness, inadequacy, and fraudulence. I've acquired a habit now of confession to these feelings before crowds of people, and I probably should have stayed at home and sought out the appropriate 12-step program, Playwrights' Anonymous, instead of mortifying myself before artists and activists I admire so much—whose presence, I suspect, made the promise of suffering a really intense abjection entirely too tempting to pass up.

I didn't set out to write a play about AIDS, I set out to write a play about what it was like to be a gay, Jewish, Leftist man in New York City in mid-80s Reagan America. I really think I set out to write about Reagan. I'd seen a few plays and TV films "about" AIDS, and with one single exception they were all terrible, in my opinion, disease-of-the-week weepies addressing something manifestly monumentally of another order—an order, I felt, like the Holocaust, the scale of which was incommensurable with representation on the tacky-tawdry-showbizzy stage. The one (and without attacking other playwrights and screenwriters I'd like to stress this one) towering exception was *The Normal Heart*, of course, which galvanized its audiences like no play any of us—any of my generation of theater artists, certainly—had ever seen; and which—and I'm certain this was the least of its author's intentions, if indeed it figured at all—awoke in theater people a long-dormant ambition to make popular theater that enters full-bloodedly into civil life, into immediacy, crisis, and public debate.

The Normal Heart, scene for scene, is a great American play. People have an annoying tendency to call it a polemic, but "1,112 and Counting" is a polemic—a historically significant polemic, that rare thing, a sermon that works; *The Normal Heart* is a great play. It has depth, complexity, symbolic and political and psychological and musical strata, strains which proceed, unerringly orchestrated with the gripping, terrifying narrative until all the pennies drop at just the right moment to move a large, impatient, distracted house full of people to terror, pity, empathy, reflection and outrage.

But the play set an impossibly high standard and we suspected, and we were not wrong in this, that its urgency and phosphorous brilliance were not exclusively the effects of its author's talents and technical skills, but also of his activist engagement with AIDS. As we have demonstrated with AIDS and every other human and political calamity, and with our passive acquiescence to the destruction of the National Endowment for the Arts, among theater folk the activist impulse is forever devoured, or rather eviscerated, by our fatal attraction to its inherent drama. We love the flash and thunderclap and are too impatient to do the work of constructing the bomb. We could not, and I think we have not, followed Larry's lead.

(In a way, this is just a 90s version of what grand old theater queens used to say to excuse appalling, inexcusable sloth or misbehavior, quoting Duke Theseus, usually in a tremulous voice when accepting your award at the Sarah Siddons Society dinner: The best in these are but shadows, the worst no worse, blah blah blah.)

We all know that there's been a lot of theater about AIDS, a lot of dramatic literature, and some of it is very good, even if it is only "dramatic literature" and hence a thing of indifference outside of annoyed envy at the size of dramatic royalty checks to many novelists and poets and scholars and book reviewers and (dare I say it? and I say it with the greatest respect) Keynote Speakers.

We all know that the form, the public forum, the instant community of actor and audience, collective attendance, catharsis, can in the right hands suit any subject of a vast shared grief and rage. We know that theater originates in the sacred, but we should also remember that the Church banished actors, once full-throttle mimesis, representation and narrative had insinuated themselves into the Mass; not because of a good actor's power to inspire idolatry but rather because the whole business started to smell of something dangerously cheap, risible, carnal; the ecclesiastical rapidly became the dialectical opposite of its Sacred subject. The proximity of the Divine and the Preposterous, the Infinitely Grave and the Infinitely Embarrassing, made the theatrical bits more exciting than the sacramental ritual and hence the theatrical became, ripe for, and deserving of, anathema.

We come to the theater—and to literary conferences, which are also affairs of voices and bodies and flashes of excitement and lingering doubts and disappointments, mean and bruising and cruisy and fun—to be mortified, and to delight in the mortification of others, to suffer with those we see (and cause to) suffer and pay money to see suffer. Theater is always self-evidently political because it is always dialectical and always dialectical because this paradox, Inspiration Flashing and Modesty Blushing, simultaneously, is at its heart; it's what makes the engine go. All theater is a waste of time, which reminds us that our best and dearest dream for ourselves and for our fellow humans ought to be oceans of time to waste in a cozy seat in which you have (and here we see the difference between the theatrical and the literary) very little work to do to receive the best kind of pleasure: free of consequence.

I think what I'm trying to say is that it is theater's inappropriateness that makes it a likely place for the staging of scenes from a pandemic. To borrow an image used by Herbert Blau, Shakespeare, and Beckett, where else but the theater can we go to mourn, and mourn deeply, over a corpse, noting all the while that the corpse over which we grieve, oh beautiful, impossible sight! is *breathing*.

I did not set out opportunistically to write about AIDS because it's such *great material*: but it is, isn't it? And so am I not opportunistic? Am I not, as I have been accused of being, an AIDS profiteer?

Perhaps I haven't heard this said because I haven't been at the panels where it's been said, or perhaps it's too despicable or vulgar or in some sense unnecessary to say, or perhaps survivor guilt is a sufficient rubric, but something has compelled me to make this declaration to the conference. I know my play has helped people and helped the cause. It has also made me comfortable. And there's something unbearable about that. Which, maybe, I ought to keep to myself, but, playwright, theater worker that I am, I am too much in love with the drama of declaration and mortification.

We've talked about a fear of using AIDS metaphorically, about comparing AIDS to the Holocaust, and this dilemma I think speaks to my theme: *Using* AIDS. Using AIDS to make art, to make a political point, to achieve a desirable goal. Of course we're squeamish. But I have always thought that the only point in remembering and then organizing memory into an event and then naming that event "the Holocaust" or "the AIDS epidemic" is to provide ourselves and the future with a standard by which comparison can be made. Otherwise, *forget*, for God's sake; do us all a favor.

But in this standard-construction business is implicit the notion that the Holocaust and the epidemic are *for* something, are utilitarian, can be turned into phenomena by which we might profit—morally, spiritually, and yes, materially. We must approach this dialectically, I suppose is my point: to use human suffering, whether it originates in viral infection or from malignant human agency or from a blending of the two—is necessary *and* appalling, neither more one than the other, always unbearable, always unavoidable, a terrible mandate, always both.

"Seeking the Truth, a Matter of Life and Death," Part One

I struggle a lot with what I've come increasingly to describe to myself as a divide between Wisdom with a capital W, which I am reasonably certain I do not possess, and the something that I do possess—opinions? In my opinion, my opinions are the correct opinions to have, but having the correct opinions is not the same as knowing the truth, having Wisdom; some people have that, but I don't know where they got it any more than I know, really, why I'm gay. But I'm reasonably sure I'm gay and I'm reasonably sure my opinions are at least 65% right 70% of the time, which makes me cleverer than all of the Republican Party and 90% of the Democratic Party and a whole lot of others besides, and that really is all I know of truth and how to get it.

My favorite writer Melville loved those pearl divers, he wrote in a letter to his boyfriend, Hawthorne, who go deep down seeking the truth, rising to the surface again with bloodshot eyes, their pressurized, lachrymal stigmata indicating how hard a struggle it is to seek Wisdom. Some dark nights I can guess at what Melville meant, but I'm too afraid of the bends to try it myself; and why should I, really, when Wisdom doesn't work as well in the theater as having the correct opinions, and I can always get Wisdom seated in my armchair, reading novels?

Truth is a matter of life and death and nothing proves that more than this plague; lies, as often as silences, equal death. Wisdom will save you, reliably, that's how you know it's Wisdom, or at least if it can't save you it will help you make sense of your demise. And it lasts: truth is the daughter of time. But I have been bewildered since 1981. Opinions work in the moment, if you're voluble enough, but they can betray you. Here are some of my false truths, opinions that betrayed me: In 1981 I thought AIDS was a distraction from the real struggle, which was for a lesbian and gay rights bill in New York City. In 1983 and 1984 I refused to be tested and encouraged others not to, certain that it was a mistake, a hysterical over-reaction, cooperation with an oppressive medical/political homophobic establishment—and maybe back then it was, who knows? I have held the opinion that AIDS was legionnaire's disease, swine flu, a monkey virus, and practically become a maintenance illness (on several occasions, which is why protease inhibitors make me feel glad but very cautious).

The illnesses, sufferings, nightmares, struggles, heroism, and deaths of friends and idols, such involvement in the movement as I can claim, reading, writing *Angels*—my opinions get corrected, but there's still so much I don't know and am afraid to know, and some of it may be life-and-death. Is it okay to suck cock without a condom? Should I or shouldn't I say that I do, sometimes? My bemusement is a luxury, which Amiri Baraka has defined as living in ignorance, comfortably. But it's also genuine un-knowing in the face of mysteries, and so I seek out my multicultural fallible rabbinate, for exegesis, for rescue. My chiefest wisdom, I think, is knowing myself to be unwise. I don't mean this to sound as bromidic as it does, it's not *universally* true, thank God. And it goes without saying you can probably hear it, that may greatest danger is my complacency. For agnostics, both of the secular and of the sacred order, complacency is the most venal sin. That, and having the wrong opinions. Lots of people have the wrong opinions and *know* them to be wrong and still act in accordance with their error, and every morning I thank God I'm not one of those.

I have a few truths, which I believe to be truths and not opinion, because I don't understand them fully or even partially after thinking about them for a long time, and in that quality of unfathomableness these truths resemble God as I intuit God to be; if God is anything at all, one thing S/He is, is unknowable. I know three truths: Democracy, because I can't imagine justice without it, nor can I imagine anything better; Socialism, because capitalism sucks; and Internationalism, or Solidarity if you will, because we'll never have the first nor the second without this third. It is almost always for a lack of solidarity that democracy and socialism (or whatever you choose to call a more sane and just way of organizing human economic affairs in the global community) fail.

It is very easy to say this and it makes me feel good to say it, but solidarity is immensely difficult, especially for the privileged—my friend Kimberly Flynn gave me a quote once from Gayatri Spivak about 'the slow unlearning of privilege" being the necessary work of the privileged interested in participating in justice. Slow because painful. Sarah Schulman taught me a painful lesson in that unlearning today; learning hurts; I'm going to try to learn. I don't want my opinions to fossilize in the honey-colored amber of my ignorance, or cowardice. I don't want to start defending ignorance, which is always indefensible.

I think the cure for AIDS is Democratic Socialist Internationalism, or Internationalist Democratic Socialism, or Socialist Internationalist Democracy—help me out here. This may be opinion rather than Wisdom; but if it's Wisdom to despair, I'd rather be opinionated; if, as Larry Kramer seems to write in the program, it's a choice between opinion and artistry, I'd rather be opinionated. Activism and art about AIDS have run up against the wall of Economics; so has race, gender, homosexual rights, disability rights, immigrant rights—the whole rainbow of progressive causes has hit the Milton Friedman Memorial Firewall barricade, and balkanized. All await a decent answer to the pitiless capital-logic of the Balanced Budget; we must make this barricade bulge. This is why I so thoroughly despise gay conservatism. They don't believe in regulation, they want to cut the capital gains tax, and cutting the capital gains tax is homophobic, preserving the capital gains tax a lesbian and gay rights issue. Cutting taxes is racist, sexist, homophobic: if it is any one of these it is all three. That's *my* opinion.

We people have two hedgehog questions, it seems to me: How much trouble are we in? And can we do anything about it? If the answer to the first question is "a lot!" and if the answer to the second question is "no," then it would be a kindness to die, the only decent thing, really. And if that's Wisdom, who wants it? If the answer to the second question is "yes," then a third question inevitably follows, my favorite: "What is to be done?"

"Seeking the Truth, a Matter of Life and Death," Part Two

Theodore Adorno wrote a really great essay called "On Commitment," which I think reaches the wrong conclusions but lays out pretty much the same dialectic we struggled with last night, and I think we've struggled with it through much of this conference, at least the parts I've attended. Adorno, as I recall (and I didn't have the essay here in Key West to refer to, so if I misconstrue, and anyone here knows better, don't bust me), writes of art which moves in its urgency right up to its audience, or at least towards it; and art which almost seems to retreat from its audience—"reticent" art, to borrow an apt word Robert Dawidoff used on Friday—but for all its reticence, still committed, still purposeful, art which persists in indulgence in a grand and necessary luxury, the hope and faith in human beings that whatever it was that compelled them to pick up a book, a poem, to see a play— that this same impulse will get them moving when they cease to be consumers and spectators of culture and return to the social world and its demands for action, for agency.

Of these two aesthetic stratagems, one which addresses you aggressively and one which demands of you exertion by virtue of its flight from you (we might choose to call one political and the other literary, or accessible and difficult), Adorno prefers the reticent, the literary, and the difficult, while recognizing that each contains elements of the other, and both seek different means to engage in public, political struggle. But this doesn't mean his essay is a kind of "I'm OK you're OK, I say potato you say rutabaga" affair. He writes: "One is better than the other." He reaches a conclusion about committed art many of us have reached: that the faith in one's audience or reader to perform empathic leaps (empathy perhaps being art's most sublime gift and function) must be matched by the artist's embracing a rigorous discipline of non-partisan (to the extent that it is possible) observation, self-investigation, eschewing of pretentiousness and metaphysical, rhetorical posturing—to become the constantly-retreating horizon point upon which the wayfarer, the reader, expects to find redemption, wisdom, peace, succor, epiphany—the future.

Adorno, because he thinks dialectically, and does not feel the need we Americans seem to feel to pretend that we don't struggle, or to pretend that the struggling, the wriggling, isn't Life, and isn't Infinite as long as there is a species and unceasing unto our deaths and, who knows? perhaps beyond. Adorno, inarguably an elegant writer, a great stylist, is comfortable with difficulty; indeed he revels in it, even in the scars difficulty can leave. He doesn't do something I think a lot us do. He doesn't announce his mastery by clobbering the dialectic, he doesn't get sere, or vatic; he doesn't say, "I personally know how to do this impossibly difficult thing, and so I no longer struggle." He says, "I know what is best" but he leaves open the possibility, dangerous to him, that in 1997 a gay 40-year old Jew facing four more years of Speaker Gingrich and Bill "Bipartisan Compromise" Clinton, young friends and family with AIDS and breast cancer because the world is poisoned and the whole endless catalogue of it, who is *frightened* by the whole endless catalogue of it, the greed and the bigotry and the terrible death, because last year one of his secular rabbis from whom he has come to expect hope and marching orders told him in a confidence he now compulsively betrays by sharing it, that in one hundred years he is certain that there will be *no life on earth*—Adorno's fidelity to dialectics forces him to forsake the burnished flow the "the solution" and offer up the very tools with which this frightened queer American Jew in 1997 might conclude that Adorno is a very great thinker who finally—Brecht was right about him—finally was in some regards a compromised paid state intellectual talking out of his hat.

I guess what I'm saying is that truth is dialectical, which does not mean that it politely nods to the opposition, which nods and winks back signaling brandy and cigars in the back room after the rubes have been fooled by witnessing a sham fight. A live model for this sort of false opposition might be the House Republicans and Democrats, and now the Ethics committee's Primate Parody of justice in calling the tax thief Gingrich to an utterly zipless account.

Dialectics should be the opposite of polite, or reassuringly relativist. Neville Chamberlain was not a dialectician. Dialectics is messy. A dialectically-shaped truth is a heated argument and it should be three things: first, outrageously funny, because puzzles are fun and because, faced with the improbability and impossibility life's contradictions present us with, what else is there to do but laugh; secondly, absolutely agonizing, because faced with the above, what else is there to do but feel terrible pain, fear, pity?, because a proper dialectics will make us face something most us can't, namely the probable truth that suffering, as E. H. Carr writes, is indigenous to history, and that's *horrible*; and thirdly, a dialectic should move forward. Don't, in other words, lose sight of the fact that you are probably almost as wrong as you are right but *knowing*, if it is given to you to know, requires the courage to combine your contemplation with your action and act—*Praxis*, in other words, *movement*, because we are, after all, bodies on this earth and it is as much a chalkboard and a laboratory as it is a temple, and always remember what Robert Duncan once said in an interview: Symmetry is what life resists arriving at; symmetry is stasis; symmetry equals death.

Kramer vs. Kramer, Ben and Alexander:

Larry Kramer's Voices and His Audiences

John M. Clum

But gay truths are different from straight truths.

—Introduction to *Just Say No*

L IKE EUGENE O'NEILL, America's most overrated playwright, but still a force those few of us who still love drama have to contend with, Larry Kramer's theatrical voice is powerful in its clumsy commitment to talking, sometimes screaming, its auditors into submission. As in O'Neill's plays, Kramer's dysfunctional family becomes an *idée fixe*, a self-justification, and the post-Freudian version of fate. Yet unlike his more canonical and prolific dramatic predecessor, Kramer writes out of a political commitment that to some extent justifies the urgency and stridency of his voice.

Why begin an essay on Larry Kramer with Eugene O'Neill, who was hardly "gay" in any sense of the word? Because for me Kramer's similarity to O'Neill crystallizes what is bothersome about his work. However contemporary Kramer tries to be, and he does want to be the voice of the contemporary gay man, whatever Brechtian and postmodern theatrical devices he employs, he, like O'Neill, is an old-fashioned realistic/naturalistic playwright whose commitment to the family as causality, to the very psychoanalytical principles he attacks, work against his activism and his contemporaneity.

Kramer is tied to the narratives and families of straight, domestic American drama. His presentation of his family in *The Destiny of Me* is a monstrous version of a Eugene O'Neill/Arthur Miller family: failure father, desperate mother, and two sons trying to be successes despite what they learned at home. The traps of desire and guilt that his characters inhabit are out of O'Neill. So is his obsession with his brother. O'Neill devoted two plays to his self-destructive brother, for him a figure of the Dionysian (in the Nietzschean sense) principle that fascinated him.[1] Kramer's brother, who appears as a central figure in the two Ned Weeks plays, is the opposite: the straight ideal whose love and approval Kramer's alter ego craves, but never believes he has.

Yet Larry Kramer is a force to be reckoned with—I wouldn't bother writing about him if his work weren't powerful and haunting—and both the critic and the playwright in me find it necessary to figure out why, when asked to write about Kramer's place in American drama, particularly gay drama, I am compelled to place him with straight playwrights like O'Neill rather than with contemporary gay colleagues like Tony Kushner and Terrence McNally. The answer to this, I am convinced, can be found by focusing on Kramer's conflicted sense of a relationship to his gay and straight audiences. To and for whom is he writing? How does the audience for his plays differ from the audience for his essays? Who does he see "out there in the dark," as Norma Desmond would say? And, perhaps most important, what does his brother have to do with his audience?

Oh, My People

I wanted to be Moses but I could only be Cassandra.

—Ned in *The Destiny of Me*

Though he had written one unsuccessful play before the AIDS epidemic, Kramer was best known for the homoerotic wrestling match between Oliver Reed and Alan Bates in the crazy-overwrought film version of *Women in Love,* and the satiric novel, *Faggots.* Critics then gave Ken Russell most of the credit for the film (*auteurism* was all the rage), but one can as easily detect Kramer's voice and vision. His novel, a dark, grotesquely comic version of gay life that offered a counter to the Gatsby-like romance of Andrew Holleran's *The Dancer from the Dance,* showed that Kramer had the makings of a gay Ben Jonson who could see the grotesqueness and vanity of his milieu without placing himself at an Olympian distance from it. He was there too and, therefore, also a target of the satire.

Then AIDS came. For all intents and purposes, AIDS gave Larry Kramer a calling and a voice. The horror of this terrible disease and its initial appearance in urban gay men, the cautious response to AIDS on the part of politicians, the fact the doctors could not and cannot find a cure, the new, violent expressions of homophobia AIDS inspired—all these were and are grist for the mill of an intelligent, articulate man with a propensity for paranoia and a gift for inflammatory rhetoric. The logical media for Kramer were those best suited to diatribes: polemical essays, speeches, and plays.

Kramer's theatrical writings are as polemical as his essays. His major plays, *The Normal Heart* and *The Destiny of Me*, are filled with angry diatribes, often reaching a pitch more hysterical than any other "major" American playwright (however problematic Kramer's works are, they are major), and not much different in tone from the verbal brickbats he threw in his essays for and letters to the *New York Native*. I want to argue that the difference between the diatribes to the gay community and the dramatic tirades lies in Kramer's conception of his audiences. Kramer has two audiences and different voices for each of them. His voice to his gay audience is that of an Old Testament patriarch. To the straight audience he is the representative gay man, the good fairy who will speak for what being gay should mean. To both he's a victim, raging at the causes of his frustration and hurt, but never moving fully beyond a language of victimization.

From the beginning of the AIDS epidemic in New York City, Kramer aspired to be Moses, bringing the Law from the mountain top to his gay people who had been worshipping the false god Priapus. Lacking divinely written Law, he armed himself with statistics. Numbers and lists were his authority. His first major diatribe, "1,112 and Counting," is filled with both:

> There are now 1,112 cases of serious Acquired Immune Deficiency Syndrome. When we first became worried, there were only 41. In only twenty-eight days, from January 13th to February 9th [1983], there were 164 new cases—and 73 more dead. The total death tally is now 418. Twenty percent of all cases were registered this January alone. There have been 195 dead in New York City from among 526 victims. Of all serious AIDS cases, 47.3 percent are in the New York metropolitan area.
>
> We grasped at the straws of possible cause: promiscuity, poppers, back rooms, the baths, rimming, fisting, anal intercourse, urine, semen, shit, saliva, blood, blacks, a single virus, a new virus, repeated exposure to a virus, amoebas carrying a virus, drugs, Haiti, voodoo, Flagyl, constant bouts of amebiasis, hepatitis A and B, syphilis, gonorrhea. (*New York Native*, March 1983; reprinted in *Reports*, p. 34)

The numbers reinforced Kramer's authority as an expert in "the facts" of AIDS, as the list presented him as an expert in gay life. He was one of the gay men, but also the leader who knew the facts and would set the terms of the discourse, which he did in a series of paragraphs which begin "Let's talk about ...":

Let's talk about which gay men get AIDS . . .
   Let's talk about surveillance . . .
   Let's talk about various forms of treatment . . .
   Let's talk about what gay tax dollars are buying for gay men.

   (*New York Native*, March 1983; reprinted in *Reports*, pp. 35–7)

The villains here are the medical profession, particularly the tax-supported
National Institutes of Health, and the Mayor of New York City, Ed Koch.
Throughout his essays, Kramer marshals his forces against these two enemies. The NIH soon becomes personalized in its leader, Anthony Fauci, the
representative of the government's AIDS policy who alternates in Kramer's
writings between villainous toady and "incompetent idiot" (*Village Voice*,
May 1988: quoted in *Holocaust*, p. 194). Koch remains the evil closet queen
who lets gay men die rather than set up a humane city AIDS policy which
might make some homophobes think he's gay. Kramer does to Fauci and
Koch what George Bush did to Saddam Hussein; he demonizes an individual rather than present the complex political picture and underlying attitudes that cause a problem. It's effective, if simplistic, rhetoric, though for
Kramer it's more than that. Rage must have an identifiable human target. *Ad
hominem* arguments are his forte.
   Having united his gay readers by defining the common enemies, establishing his position of "one of you, but your chosen leader," Kramer excori-
ates his gay readers with a list of targets of his wrath, each paragraph
beginning "I am sick of . . ."

   I am sick of gay men who won't support gay charities . . .
   I am sick of closeted gays . . .
   I am sick of everyone in this community who tells me to stop creating
a panic . . .
   I am sick of guys who can only think with their cocks.

   (*New York Native*, March 1983; reprinted in *Reports*, pp. 43–6.

The voice here is that of angry parent or schoolteacher, not a peer; hardly a
voice to win the hearts and minds of grown men.
   After attacking straight political and medical leaders, and sexually active
and closeted gay men, Kramer presents his goal, which is finding a group of
3,000 men who will follow him in acts of civil disobedience.[2]
   Essays like "1,112, and Counting" are fascinating in their mixed message
and their lack of political savvy. Kramer screams at the very people he wants
to lead. The urgency of the epidemic demonstated by his statistics justifies a
jeremiad, but Kramer was bound to alienate as many people as he won over.
Only those as angry as he would make it to the call to arms at the end of the
essay.

Kramer had only his own rage to fuel him. Unlike Moses, he didn't have any tangible assistance from the wrath of Jehovah: no stone tablets, no thunderbolts. Yet the voice was insistent, its audience growing. Later his essays reached the mixed readership of the *Village Voice* and, eventually, the predominately straight *New York Times*. It is clear from his editorial commentary in *Reports from the holocaust* that he understood the difference in his two audiences. Kramer wrote of his 1988 "Open Letter to Dr. Anthony Fauci": "The separation between gay readers of this diatribe, for whom it reads with the utmost sane clarity, and straight readers, who think I've now gone round the bend, increases" (*Reports*, p. 199).

Kramer's characterization of his gay reader's response to his writing may be a bit too sanguine. He could hardly believe that everyone in the New York gay community associated him with terms like "utmost sane clarity." He was aware that he had, as he put it, a "fundamental problem" with the gay community he wanted to lead, "how to inspire you without punishing you" (*Reports*, p. 186). "Punish" is an interesting choice of verb. Kramer saw himself not merely as offending some of his readers, but actually in the patriarchal position of punishing them. In the same speech, he finds his new voice, no longer Jeremiah, but now Isaiah; not wrathful patriarch but loving one: "Oh, my people, I beg you to listen to me. I say all of this because I love you and don't want to leave you or lose you" (*Reports*, p. 191). This form of address crystallizes Kramer's role before a gay audience. Gay men are not his brothers, his equals: we are his "people," his flock, to whom he preaches, rails, gives and withholds approval.

Out There in the Dark

I want to tell you what it's like to be gay (Did you want to hear that one?).

—Introduction to *Just Say No*

Kramer's plays came from those moments when he felt he lost his gay audience, when he felt separated from or betrayed by the groups he founded: after his "snub" by the board of Gay Men's Health Crisis, which led to the writing of *The Normal Heart*; and his sense of distance from the young activists in ACT UP, which is an integral part of *The Destiny of Me*. *The Normal Heart* chronicles Kramer's founding of and alienation from Gay Men's Health Crisis. At the end, his alter ego, Ned Weeks, is isolated from the men he wanted to lead out of the wilderness of closetedness, promiscuity, and political impotence. At the beginning of *The Destiny of Me*, Ned has lost his essential fuel, anger, and feels separated from the activists raging outside the National Institutes of Health, where he is a patient. At the play's conclusion, Ned is still isolated, but he has regained his anger and is, like the AIDS activists, spraying the walls with infected blood.

This sense of isolation from the gay community is central to Kramer's two major plays, for which he envisioned a different audience from his diatribes.

The introductory essays to his plays attest to the fact that Larry Kramer envisioned a straight audience and readership for his plays. His central statement of his position as playwright is contained in the introductory essay to his farce, *Just Say No*, "The Farce In Just Saying No." There Kramer allies himself with the major canonical playwrights—Aeschylus, Sophocles, Shakespeare, Shaw, and Williams—who saw theater as a forum of ideas, "of opinion and anger," for assertion of morals, and for heightened language. None of this is particularly new or revolutionary, of course, and one can only praise Kramer for his ambition, but Kramer's relationship to gay theater is problematic. Kramer states that his primary goal is to "tell you what it's like to be gay" (p. x). The "you" is obviously the straight audience member for whom Kramer writes. Yet, paradoxically, Kramer believes that "most of the straight world does not want to hear gay truths" (p. 24).

There are enormous problems involved in Kramer's ambition here. Is there an essential gay position? Can one gay writer define gay experience? Kramer sees that impossible task as his mission, but believes that straights will inevitably victimize and misunderstand him, just as his gay followers did. If Kramer is an Old Testament prophet or patriarch to his gay audience, his favorite rhetorical position before a straight audience is that of Cassandra, the visionary doomed to be ignored and vilified:

The opinionated play published herein is *about* something. About something that may murder millions of people, that is murdering tens of thousands of my fellow gay men, and that is possibly set to murder me. I was not surprised when a number of New York critics slaughtered me. I'm accustomed to that by now. By now I have learned that I rarely get good reviews, and that theater critics don't review what Larry Kramer writes or says, they review what Larry Kramer is, which is a homosexual. And they review what they think of homosexuality—they don't like it— or what they think homosexuality should be—they don't like it the way it is— and they aren't very interested in hearing what I, or any other gay writer, has to say about it. (p. xiv)

Kramer's critics do not criticize his plays, they "slaughter" *him*! This violence is perpetrated out of homophobia, which leaves Kramer inevitably frustrated at achieving his goal of explaining homosexuality. This slaughter makes it impossible for Kramer to fulfill his artistic promise: "I would have been a more productive artist if I didn't have to withstand all the diatribes hurled at me because few critics, and the publications they write for, have empathy or interest in homosexuality and what it's like to be gay in this world" (p. xv). Clearly no criticism of Kramer from a straight critic can be fair or directed solely at his work. It must be directed at gayness itself. When *The Normal Heart* received an ambivalent review from *Times* critic Frank Rich, Kramer notes that Rich couldn't have panned the play because, "Even he wasn't that cruel as to totally crucify a play about dying young men" (p. xxi). Even if a play about AIDS was poorly written, it cannot be criticized because of its subject matter. Content is everything! (The *Times* review of *Just Say No* was by Mel Gussow.)

Kramer weakens his argument by offering a list of gay writers, many of whom have been highly praised by gay and straight critics; but his point is to question how many of these gay writers his straight audience has read and challenge them to read gay writers. In offering this list, Kramer is authorizing a canon of contemporary gay writing. However, a number of these writers have succeeded precisely because they haven't worried about what straight readers or audiences will think.

By the end of his essay, Kramer has made it impossible for his straight reader to criticize the text of *Just Say No* that follows without drawing the charge of homophobe or sadist. Yet this gay critic can state that *Just Say No* is an incoherent mess of a play, not because it outs closeted conservatives or Ron Reagan, Jr., or Ed Koch (gay men have heard all this before), or suggests that Nancy Reagan is a bitch and her husband incompetent (a lot of folks, gay and straight, figured that out), but because it's all too strident and over-the-top and not really very funny. The control of tone that made *Faggots* a successful satire is missing here. Compare the flailing of *Just Say No* with Tony Kushner's controlled, sustained satiric vision of Reaganism in part one of *Angels in America*. Compare the desperation of the farce here with the hilarity of Terrence McNally's *The Ritz*. Kramer won't— shouldn't—be remembered for this play, but I'm not the audience he targets in his introduction. I'm not straight.

Kramer wants his straight audience to understand and accept his version of gayness. While he is virulent in his criticism of certain aspects of gay life, he does not want to be criticized for depicting and defining gay life.

Why is it so important for Kramer that straight critics and audiences know and accept his work? Why not be content with reaching a predominantly gay audience? Throughout his plays Kramer's alter ego Ned Weeks is in a conflicted dialogue with straight authority figures, personified by his brother, Ben, who is the straight persona with whom Ned Weeks and his creator must battle and find a rapprochement. While Ned doesn't seem to find an effective way of leading, or even joining his gay brothers, he does move to an embrace of his brother. Both *The Normal Heart* and *The Destiny of Me* chronicle Ned Weeks's violent separation from and reconciliation with his principal straight antagonist, his brother Ben, a not-too-veiled version of Larry Kramer's brother, Arthur Bennett Kramer, to whom the latter play is dedicated. Much of both plays is devoted to Ned's justifying himself to his beloved brother and ultimately resolving their differences.

Like a Brother, Like a Lover

I can't give you the courage to stand up and say to me that you don't give a good healthy fuck what I think.

—Ben to Ned in *The Destiny of Me*

While Kramer repeatedly presents his parents as monsters in *Faggots* and the Ned Weeks plays, his brother is the person whom he loves most and whose love he most seeks. His dedication to *The Destiny of Me* is the sort of sentimental appreciation usually reserved for a spouse or lover:

For my brother,
Arthur Bennett Kramer.
"I guess you could have lived without me.
I never could have lived without you."
Thank you.
I love you.

Even here there is insecurity about where he stands in his brother's life, but the happy dimension of the ending of both plays is contained in the reassurance of his brother's love and approval.

Ben Weeks is a straight Jewish hero. In the heyday of Hollywood, he would have been played by Gregory Peck. Accepted into West Point in the 1940s when few Jewish men had that honor, Ben fought the false charges brought against him by anti-Semitic officers and won. He left West Point to become a scholarship student at Yale, went on to law school and became a successful lawyer. He married, had children, and proceeded to make all of his family, including Ned, rich: "That's what he wanted to do— indeed I believe that has been his mission in life—to give all of us what he and I never had as children—and he's accomplished it" (*Destiny*, p. 110). Above all, Ben is a man of principle: "Can't you see I don't mind being the only one on my side?" (*Destiny*, p. 42).

For Alexander, the young, pre-therapy version of Ned in Kramer's autobiographical drama *The Destiny of Me*, Ben is a role model, a protector, an authority figure, and an object of desire. All this is crystallized at the end of the second act of *The Destiny of Me* when Ned narrates how Ben saved his life:

> That night ... when Benjamin stopped Poppa from beating me up, he put me on his shoulders and carried me down to the shore. We swam and played and ducked under each other's arms and legs. We lay on the big raft, way out on the Sound, side by side, not saying a word, looking at the stars. I held his hand. He said, Come dive with me. I dived in after he did and I got caught under the raft and I couldn't get out from under. I thrashed desperately this way and that and I had no more breath. . . . When I thought I would surely die, he rescued me and saved me, Benjamin did. He got me to the shore and laid me out on the sand and he pressed my stomach so the poison came out and he kissed me on the lips so I might breathe again. (*Destiny*, p. 98)

Alexander/Ned is eighteen years old when this scene takes place. What might have been sexually innocent in the life of a child is now inescapably erotic. This is the last primal scene in which Ben plays an unambiguous role as his younger brother's protector and the last scene in which Alexander/Ned can see Ben unabashedly as an erotic object. Ben saves his brother from the vicious homophobic hatred of their father and offers the affection his father finds it impossible to give. When Ned almost drowns, Ben brings his brother back to life, something the doctors at the National Institutes of Health cannot manage with older, HIV-infected Ned. Raising Ned from the dead is accomplished with a press on the stomach and a kiss on the lips. Kramer pushes the comparison between this loving healing and medical treatment for AIDS by referring to the water that fills his lungs as "poison." Indeed, one of the interesting dimensions of *The Destiny of Me* is that Ned treats Anthony Della Vida, the AIDS clinician, the way he treats his brother: eroticizing their relationship, making personal demands, judging constantly any compromise with Ned's pure morality.

Ned constantly accuses Ben of refusing to accept his brother's homosexuality, though what we see is that Ben, a dutiful, loving brother, accepts it within the language of their time. When Ned first tells Ben, in the 1940s, Ben responds as an enlightened person of the time would respond: "It's unhealthy, it's caused by something unhealthy, it'll do nothing but make you unhappy" (*Destiny*, p. 83). Ben encourages Ned to begin the psychotherapy that could only do harm to him and countless other gay men: "I'll always fight for you and defend you and protect you. All I ask is that you try. The talking cure, it's called" (*Destiny*, p. 86). But my judgment—and Kramer's—is one of hindsight. In the play, immediately after this moment, Ned confesses his sense of failure as a leader of young gay men: "They look to me for leadership and I don't know how to guide them" (*Destiny*, p. 87). Ned wants to be to gay men what Ben has been to him: protector, leader, big brother.

He fails as his brother failed him.

The Destiny of Me ends with Ned's affirmation of his brother's courage and the brothers' declaration of their love for one another. Before the final curtain, Ned, as he throws the blood bags against the wall, says: "My straight friends ask me over and over again: Why is it so hard for you to find love? Ah, that is the question answered, I hope, for you tonight (*Destiny*, p. 122). Though one can question why Kramer cares so much what straights think, one part of the answer to his question is that Ned has found his perfect man in Ben. This is made even clearer in Ned and Ben's turbulent relationship in *The Normal Heart*.

The Normal Heart ends with the deathbed marriage of Ned and his lover Felix, witnessed by Ben who, unbeknownst to Ned, has become friends with Felix. Throughout the play, Ned feuds with Ben because he does not feel Ben has given his unconditional support for Ned's homosexuality. What Ben keeps—rightfully—telling Ned is that Ned shouldn't care what Ben thinks. Ned's response is intriguingly problematic:

> I'm beginning to think that you and your straight world are our enemy. I am furious with you, and with myself and with every goddamned doctor who ever told me I'm sick and interfered with my loving a man. . . . You still think I'm sick, and I simply cannot allow that any longer. I will not speak to you again until you accept me as your equal. Your healthy equal. Your brother! (*The Normal Heart*, p. 71).

Why is it *Ben's* straight world? In what sense does he possess it? Except that the straight world is Ben for Ned and his creator. Anthony Della Vida, the version of Anthony Fauci in *The Destiny of Me*, is a version of Ben. Della Vida's wife is a form of Ben. Why in his fury toward Ben and homophobic psychiatrists, does Kramer include himself? He's neither straight nor an outside adversary. If Ned is "sick," and incapable of establishing a loving relationship with another man, it is not because he's homosexual but because he still has a problem with his sexuality and makes irrational demands on those close to him. Why, for instance, should his brother's law firm support his political projects? Where in this play does Ben say his brother's homosexuality is unhealthy? What he says repeatedly is that what he thinks shouldn't matter so much to his brother. Ned projects the disapproval onto his brother.

Ben does make peace with his demanding brother because of Ned's lover, Felix, and the marriage Felix represents. Through Felix, Ned has found a way to bridge homosexuality and heterosexuality and place his homosexuality within a paradigm that straight Ben understands. He may not support all his brother's political alliances but he will support his marriage. Herein lies the subtext of *The Normal Heart*: the paradigm of marriage validates homosexuality. However, alas, Ned seems more content with the role of widower than with the role of spouse.

The thesis of *The Destiny of Me* is that Ned is a product of his monstrous, dysfunctional (except for Ben) family—is there a play more filled with images of castration than this one?—and the psychiatrists Ben told him to see: "Over and over and over again they will pound into your consciousness through constant repetition: you're sick, you're sick, you're sick. So your heart is going to lie alone" (*Destiny*, p. 84). But the only healing force in Ned's life is Ben. If he can't ever totally believe in Ben's love and approval, he can at least continue to fight for them through the straight audience which, for Kramer, represents the Bens of this world. As Ned demands that Ben understand and accept his homosexuality, so Kramer demands that his straight audience understand and accept "the most important defining characteristic of my life" (*Destiny*, p. 3), his homosexuality. But how does homosexuality define Kramer? What does his homosexuality mean to him? He doesn't approve of the sexual promiscuity thought by many to be a defining factor of gay culture, but will not allow his dramatic persona another loving relationship. What is homosexuality but an oppositional stance to the majority that makes one a victim of hatred, loneliness, unhappiness, misunderstanding, slaughter by homophobic critics, disease, medical incompetence. Homosexuality may define Kramer, but not in a positive way.

Joining Alexander's Band

I was learning—not originally by choice—that necessary lesson for anyone who insists on speaking his mind: how to become a loner.

—*(Reports, p. 7)*

Judging a playwright personally is usually irrelevant, but Larry Kramer demands that we deal with him personally. His work is so clearly, insistently autobiographical. Moreover, he demands from his readers and his audiences not only attention but behavior modification and is quick to attack anyone who does not fall into line. He demands that his plays be judged for what they say, not how they say it, and the greatest strength of his plays is their nakedness, their insistence on placing his id and libido in our faces. How can we separate Larry Kramer from the work?

In late twentieth-century America, where likability and cosmetic perfection are the primary criteria for credibility, Kramer's nakedness and stridency are particularly welcome. Who says artists have to be normal and nice? O'Neill and Williams devoted much of their writing to people who would never fit in, never lead. The paradox of Kramer is that he wants to be the loner, the outsider valorized in our literature, but also wants to be understood, accepted, and followed. In being the loner, the angry railer at his gay brothers, he is in danger of fitting the stereotype of the pre-Stonewall, self-loathing queen, a middle-aged version of one of Mart Crowley's characters.

We see Ned's forced isolation in his inability to conceive of having another lover after "Felix." Why settle for the lifetime role of widower. Was Felix the only man in the world? "I was in love for five minutes with someone who was dying. I guess that's all I get" (*Destiny*, p. 47). Who says?

The answer is contained in *Reports from the holocaust*, and, yes, Kramer does assume that his audience knows all of his work. There Kramer recounts the agony he goes through with a new lover because of fear of HIV infection:

> What it amounts to is that I cannot stand the torture that each coupling brings to our lovemaking, and the nightmares that come into my dreams and the walking dialogue that plagues me every time I think of it. It constantly jams itself into my thoughts: You must be crazy, you must be out of your mind, you are gambling with your life. (*Reports*, p. 272)

The horror of AIDS is not only that it kills, but that it poisons the possibility of love by turning sex into an exchange of poisons. Kramer's response is characteristically extreme: "Another hour later, I vomit." I can understand Kramer's response: AIDS or the fear of AIDS has infected the lives of every gay man who isn't in a dangerous state of denial. I have felt this too. But Kramer has assumed the role of the voice of AIDS precisely because he obsesses on this sort of self-torture and finds the role of victim attractive.

Kramer's dramatic work, like his essays, is filled with rage, and much of that rage is directed at gays closeted or uncloseted. He may rail at brother Ben, but Ben always comes through in the end, and the anger toward Ben never seems fully justified—it is only a noisy plea for an unconditional love he has already received. Ned's relationship to the dramatic version of the villainous, incompetent, Anthony Fauci, is as ambivalent as his love for his brother. He hates politicians, but, hey, who doesn't these days except members of the Christian Coalition and listeners to Rush Limbaugh? His stance toward straights in his prefaces to his plays is, for Kramer, almost placating.

Is the rage at other gays a sign that Kramer still has not fully resolved his own internalized homophobia? In the preface to *The Destiny of Me*, Kramer states: "I think the lives many gay men have been forced to lead, with AIDS awaiting them after the decades-long journey from self-hate is the stuff of tragedy" (*Destiny*, p. 4). This view hardly allows for much sunlight.

What does Kramer want of gay men? He wants them to be angry activists like himself who see that straights are out to get them, like the Nazis got the Jews, and that AIDS is our gas oven. History has shown that he at least partially got his way. AIDS did lead to greater courage on the part of gay men. More of us are loudly and proudly out. More are fighting the resistance on the part of homophobes and their minions in government. To some extent, we have Larry Kramer the indefatigable activist to thank for that. But many of us also see that we have to continue to fight any narrative that makes us victims and they are central to Kramer's dark version.

Is there any possibility of happiness in Kramer's vision? Can Kramer envision a joyful gay life? A potential but unrealized answer comes in *The Destiny of Me*, in Ned Weeks's restored relationship with Alexander, the young, courageous queen he might have become had he not submitted to psychoanalysis. Alexander was able to defy the viciousness levelled at him by his father. He could engage in sex without guilt and was capable of love. Truly connecting with courageous Alexander might make way for a positive image of homosexuality and a transcendence over the impulse to settle for the role of passive victim. However, Kramer keeps Alexander in the past, soon to suffer the same fate as Ned:

> NED: You're going to go to eleven shrinks. You won't fall in love for forty years. And when a nice man finally comes along and tries to teach you to love him and love yourself, he dies from a plague. Which is waiting to kill you, too.

Ned looks back on his past and sees no alternative to the lonely, unhappy life he had. There is hope of happiness for the young queen he once was. In this sad conclusion, one finds the crux of my problem in dealing with Kramer as a gay playwright. Kramer cannot really find in the language of theater or the possibilities of gayness a liberation from the canards of straight American drama. To offer a Kramer-like list, he is not a gay playwright in the sense that Tennessee Williams, Robert Patrick, Doric Wilson, Robert Chesley, Harvey Fierstein, Tony Kushner, Victor Bumbalo, Martin Sherman, Terrence McNally, Nicky Silver, Chay Yew, Christopher Durang are gay playwrights. He can offer a call to action, but he cannot offer liberation from heterosexist conceptions of gayness or the restrictive narratives of canonical straight, realistic, domestic, American drama.

Gay American drama, at its best, seeks ways to disentangle homosexuality from homophobia by avoiding or treating ironically narratives that problematize homosexuality. Much of this is accomplished by using the languages gay men have mastered over the decades: irony, overt, flamboyant theatricality; camp. The primary function of gay drama is liberation from oppressive norms and heterosexist narratives. Above all, gay drama speaks uncompromisingly its own voice to a gay audience.

Straights are welcome, but they will have to listen to us as we have for centuries listened to them.[3]

There is one liberating, gay moment in *The Destiny of Me*, when, at the end of the first act, Alexander's father, in a moment of Freudian high drama beyond O'Neill's wildest dreams, rips off his teenage son's dress (a costume for a play Alexander has written and in which he has been assigned the female lead) and grabs for his son's penis. Alexander's response is to sing "I'm Gonna Wash That Man Right Out Of My Hair," which is oddly appropriate since, in a fit of pubescent self-consiousness, he has removed his pubic hair. Railing at his sissy son, the monster father then tears the boy's beloved theater posters from the wall crying, "This is what we do to sissies" (p. 58). Alexander puts his drag back on and exits yelling "Trick or Treat!" The defiant gay voice has the last, ironic word. The theater posters may be gone, but Alexander's sense of theater prevails. But that's Act One. However much Ned Weeks embraces Alexander, he can't let him win. The urge to be victim is too overpowering.

After Ned tells Alexander what his life will be like, Alexander responds:

ALEXANDER: I'm sorry I asked. Do I learn anything?
NED: Does it make any sense, a life?
(*The Destiny of Me*, p. 122)

It is interesting that Ned begs Alexander's very important, final question. What does Ned learn? If Ned could see that it is Alexander, the gayness in himself, that he should love, should speak to; if he could see Alexander, his young, brave gay self, as a present option—perhaps he could see gay men as his brothers, his family. Then, too, Kramer the playwright could escape the traps of tragedy, finally rid himself of the ghost of O'Neill, and write a truly gay, in all senses of the word, play.

Works Cited

Larry Kramer, *The Destiny of Me*. New York: Plume, 1993.
Larry Kramer, *Just Say No*. New York: St. Martin's, 1989.
Larry Kramer, *The Normal Heart*. New York: Plume, 1985.
Larry Kramer, *Reports from the holocaust: The Making of an AIDS Activist*. New York: St. Martin's, 1989.

Notes

1. O'Neill's dramatic version of his relationship with his brother is explored in *Long Day's Journey into Night*, a play with which *The Destiny of Me* has more than a passing resemblance. "Jamie Tyrone," O'Neill's fictional version of his brother James, is also the central character in *A Moon for the Misbegotten*.
2. The history of Kramer's involvement with and leadership of activist groups is another story, but a crucial chapter of his history. He was instrumental in the founding of Gay Men's Health Crisis and, later, of ACT UP. The angry

demonstrations of the latter were more to his liking than the bourgeois caution of the former.

3. This is a very brief distillation of an argument I develop at length in my book, *Acting Gay: Male Homosexuality in Modern Drama* (New York: Columbia, 1994) and, more concisely, in my preface to *Out On Stage: An Anthology of Contemporary Gay Male Drama* (Boulder, Colo.: Westview HarperCollins, 1996). I also offer another, quite different discussion of Kramer's plays in the former volume.

The Abnormal Talent:

Larry Kramer's Electro-Shock Treatment for the World Theater

David Willinger

LARRY KRAMER was catapulted to fame as a playwright with his successful *The Normal Heart*, one of the pioneering AIDS plays. Up to that point, Kramer was known primarily as the screenwriter for the landmark film *Women in Love*, as the author of the very controversial novel *Faggots*, and then as a political activist who spent his time feverishly stumping for funding for AIDS research, education, and loosening up legal restrictions on experimental treatments. It was easy to consider his single play more an outgrowth of his muckraking for AIDS than the fruits of a vocation as a playwright.[1]

Furthermore, according to the sexual and ethnic ghettoization of artists which has flowed incontinent since the postmodern tyranny was installed, Larry Kramer is conveniently cubby-holed as a "two-fer," a gay and a Jew! The ghetto playwright has a conveniently ready-made ghetto audience of folk of like persuasion.[2] Of course the author's noisily avowed identity is not the only criterion for the categorization which determines who his audience will be and how the critics will treat his products (kindly or harshly according to the political climate, and only secondarily based on the inherent strength of the drama); the plays' subject matter too contributes to these judgments. And, indeed, three out of four of Kramer's plays are in some sense AIDS plays; for now there *are* four.[3] The three are *The Normal Heart*, a hilarious political farce, *Just Say No* (written after *The Normal Heart*, but less well known), and the capstone to a thus far short but varied career, the seething domestic drama, *The Destiny of Me*.[4]

But, in concert with Kramer's own lament, "there is no writer who can accept relegation to a ghetto happily. Like any other writer, we want to be universally heard,"[5] it is our aim here to explore not only what is obviously gay or AIDS-centered in Kramer's *oeuvre*, but what is American, what is universal, what is illuminating, stirring, revelatory for the world at large.

□   □   □

Curiously, his fourth play, *Sissies' Scrapbook* (later retitled and substantially recrafted as *Four Friends*) was the first play written, and it preceded *The Normal Heart* and the AIDS crisis by many years. In this forgotten and unpublished work, there are two gay characters, who are far outnumbered by the straight ones. This play bears special consideration, for it clues us into the fact that the destiny of Kramer as a playwright neither begins nor ends with *The Normal Heart*, the AIDS crisis, or even with homosexuality (or Jewishness), while all of these have latterly become central dramatic material in his work.[6]

Sissies' Scrapbook is a sprawling play in which a few actors are meant to double three and four times and into which Kramer crams four interweaving plots and a complex set intended to be supplemented with a plethora of slides. A Narrator fills in the blank spots in undramatized time and starts the action off by introducing the characters and announcing the several destinies lying in wait for the four main characters. The action proper then begins with a reunion of those four friends who have remained close long after their college days, who themselves speculate on their probable futures; some of their predictions for each other and themselves hit the nail on the head, tallying with the omniscient Narrator's version, and others are wildly wrong.

We then see the destinies fulfilled, as predicted. John is about to get married; he does. While abroad in Egypt he becomes convinced that his new wife doesn't love him and promptly goes totally catatonic. His wife brings him back to America where he undergoes a series of electro-shock treatments which are ultimately successful. However, he does not survive long after his "cure," but languishes and dies. Barry is a sadist, who goes through one woman after another, mistreating them; some like it and pursue him until the moment he goes too intolerably far, and others walk out on him before it gets to that level of cruelty. He even tries to get his friend John's father to engage in S/M play with him, switching to the masochistic role, but the father's interest is purely intellectual. Dick is a therapist who plays God, but has no answers, and can't make a go of it in his own relationships. He ultimately degenerates entirely and drops out of society and into drug addiction. And Ron is a closet gay, who conceals his proclivities even from his closest friends. An advertising executive, he goes from one trick to the next, but forms a more lasting relationship with a model he hires for his agency. Even though the latter is prepared to commit to him, Ron self-destructively manages to sabotage that relationship as well, and winds up alone with all his accumulated, unsatisfying riches.

Interwoven are fascinating secondary characters, such as John's cold wife,

Jennifer; Laura, a masochist infatuated with Barry; and all the men's fathers, of whom the most explored is John's. John's father is an Englishman, an urbane, wealthy and successful writer of pulp fiction. His detachment is as monumental as his success, but he continues to seek some experience which will bring him back to life; he is a fascinating and unique creation in the Kramer canon. The commanding image of the play resides in the unbearably painful attempts to snap John out of his catatonia through electroshock. These treatments, of which there are six, are thrust raw at the audience with excessive blatancy. John, seated downstage center in his torture contraption, is on six unremitting occasions set jangling like an hysterical marionette. While this theatrical strategy is monotonous and unnecessary (and ultimately eliminated in the rewritten version, *Four Friends*), the electro-shock idea does epitomize the vibrant feeling of aliveness which all the characters are in search of or running from. *Sissies' Scrapbook* is, finally, a theme and variation on the notion of numbness and the quest for the sensation of being alive.

Whether it is Laura, who is willing to submit to Barry's emotional cruelty, rejections, and physical assaults; or Jennifer, who longs to feel something resembling love for her catatonic husband, especially since he has let it be known that without her love he refuses to live; or John's father, who conjures up the most vivid adventures in his books, but is incapable of any compelling human interaction; or Barry, who is trying to get a rise out of his lovers and get them to reciprocate the pain he inflicts on them, and so feel *something*; or Ron, who can't trust that anyone could love him, and so pushes love away entirely—Kramer paints a panorama of the seamy side of desire, the earnest quest for pain and loathing, illuminating the underestimated significance of hate, as opposed to love, as a motive force in relationships.

These quests engender scenes of great dramatic power, with gigantic denunciations and confessions—in short the stuff of high drama—which is undercut somewhat by a tendency to structural sprawl and occasional theatrical indulgence. *Sissies' Scrapbook*, which was produced in an Off-Off-Broadway production at the Clark Center in 1974, needed some trimming and modulating to make it absolutely stageworthy. What it got was a total reworking, with the result that *Four Friends*, while more appropriately titled, is a greatly diminished play. It is easy to see why a producer with his eye on the bottom line agreed to produce the latter but found the former unacceptable. *Four Friends*, not *Sissies' Scrapbook*, was chosen as the best new play of the year by the theater division of the Ford Foundation and was consequently produced at the then Theatre De Lys (now the Lucille Lortel where *The Destiny of Me* later had its run). The life of *Four Friends* was nipped in the bud by an excessively harsh review in the *New York Times* by Clive Barnes, one of those reviews in which the critic marshals the familiar harsh invective calculated to nip an incipient dramatic career in the bud.

Four Friends has a much more regulated, almost mathematical structure than *Sissies' Scrapbook*. The pools of light, thousands of sets, and slides are gone. There are only the four friends, each with one single amorous partner. All the other characters have been jettisoned, including John's fascinating father. The many loose ends and extravagant theatrical paraphernalia are gone, but so is the play's intrinsic power. This is a case of dramaturgitis. It is a sad allegory of our contemporary theater wherein the playwright, so eager to get his work on a stage, any stage, will make any compromise on his play, even to eviscerating it. Even now, Kramer would do well to go back and have a look at *Sissies' Scrapbook*, and see if a bit of tender-hearted editing might not yield a high-power and complex (but not undisciplined) piece of theater.

As a first play, *Sissies' Scrapbook* contains too much plot and too many characters for its dramatic scale. It is as though Kramer has tried to write all the drama of which he was then capable, and was then thrown up on an impasse. It was the AIDS crisis which ultimately catalyzed him out of the impasse and back to playwriting. Larry Kramer's reputation as a polemicist and gadfly could blind one—as indeed *New York Times* critic Mel Gussow appears to have been blinded in his review of *Just Say No*—to the fact that playwright Kramer never subordinates dramatic values to his political beefs.[7] Nowhere in his dramaturgy, not even in his most explicitly polemical play, *The Normal Heart*, does Kramer batter the audience with his opinions or put a character who espouses a viewpoint divergent from his own at a dramatic disadvantage.[8] Each character holds the stage long enough and with enough eloquence to hold up his end of the *agon*. Not only is each character invested with their own measure of sympathy, but those characters who are presumably surrogates for Kramer himself each have their own self-mocking and ludicrous dimensions, and are revealed in their full humanity, warts and all.

□   □   □

In the case of *Just Say No*, which has the content of a social comedy of 1980s politics and mores grafted onto the structure of a farce à la Plautus, the several "messages" embedded in the action are so artfully delivered, so cleverly cloaked, that the audience might just walk out having bust a gut without ever realizing they were supposed to alter their way of thinking.[9] As Joseph C. Koenen sums it up, "*Just Say No* argues that the indifference continues while the country's political powers hide their own sexual indulgences behind a facade of impropriety."[10]

Just Say No accomplishes this by contriving a collision between the two power figures who most nearly epitomize the politics of the 1980s, Ronald Reagan (who never actually appears onstage) and Ed Koch. Their respective agendas, particularly but not exclusively relating to homosexuality and AIDS, are unmasked and held up for ridicule. According to the logic of the play, both teflon public figures have a political Achilles' heel, and it is the same for both: homosexuality. In the case of Reagan ("Mr. Potentate" or

"Daddy"), it is his son, "Junior," who, defiant of his father's order that he stay deep in the macho closet, aspires to life as a mediocre ballet dancer in that artistic and sexual mecca "Appleberg" (code for NYC) and a consummated existence as an announced and expressed gay man; in the case of Koch (or "Mayor"), it is his former meticulously concealed lover, Gilbert Perch, a functionary who, when Mayor's ardor cooled and when Perch threatened to go public with the enormity of a certain growing health crisis, was drummed out of the "Department of Sex and Germs" by none other than his sugar daddy.

The deliciously topical *Just Say No* has, regrettably, become dated in an astonishingly short period of time. Both Reagan and Koch have been demoted to a lower drawer, although their legacy remains. So while a revival of this brilliant farce is probably not imminent, still we can appreciate its craftsmanship and mastery of the genre and chortle at its nonstop quips, lightning reversals and complications.

The play takes place in the sumptuous duplex of Foppy Schwartz, an insatiable maven of the upper realms of society, whose entrée to this rarified world is certified by playing confidant to its most powerful goddesses. The curtain's rise finds him hard at work kibitzing socialites over a vast number of juggled telephone receivers:

> Cynthia, of course a woman can have a best male friend just as a man can have a best male friend. But a woman cannot have a best woman friend because a best woman friend will do her in. Whereas I won't. Stay away from Carolina. She is evil. (Picking up a ringing phone) *Momentito, cara.* Carolina, I am just telling Cynthia you are evil. Yes, you are.

The social butterfly, Foppy, maintains his privileged position through the prestigious patronage of none other than "Mommy," otherwise known as "Mrs. Potentate," alias Nancy Reagan, whom he assists in couturier consultations and by providing a pad for her numerous assignations with younger men. She requires this servicing, since her husband, in addition to being totally addled in the head, is not the most randy thing going.

> The latest problem is he mixes up his movies with real life. He plays with footballs in his bathtub and wakes up in the middle of the night to see if his leg is still there. His leg! The hardest thing I've had to deal with over 30 years of marriage is his leg!

Foppy also performs the same service for Mayor, providing secret pad, beefcake, and ample victuals (Mayor: "Eustacia, here comes your favorite hozer. Piggy, piggy, piggy!"), which results in an eventual collision between the two whoremasters. Everyone comes to Foppy's. Mayor and Mommy come to get laid. Gilbert Perch comes seeking refuge from Mayor, who is literally out to kill him, since he is living proof of Mayor's gayness; Junior comes seeking encouragement to live an "out" gay lifestyle. And it is against Foppy's interests for any of them to meet any other.

The play's ignition gets switched on when a certain Herman Harrod, one of Daddy's pugnacious, formerly loyal subalterns (based on the real-life figure Alfred Bloomingdale) becomes a political liability and is shunted to one side. Herman then teams up with a certain well-known call girl in "New Columbia" (read Washington DC), Trudi Tunick, to make a sex video of an orgy featuring a large number of Daddy's intimates besporting themselves in thoroughly un-Republican fashion. Herman and Trudi turn up at Foppy's (who has already received phone instructions from Mommy to confiscate the video should it ever cross his, Foppy's path), bringing with them the video which then becomes the hot power potato that gets inadvertantly passed from character to character, is repeatedly lost, appropriated, secreted in Mayor's codpiece, and found throughout the course of two acts, until it ultimately winds up back with Mommy, who uses the video to whip all the others back into line.

The characters, even as they are thinly veiled well-known figures from once-current events, are also the stock characters right out of classic Roman comedy descending directly from Plautus's *The Twin Menaechmae*,[11] better known through the Sondheim musical *A Funny Thing Happened on the Way to the Forum*. Foppy, the procurer and host, reminiscent of Pseudolus, provides the fulcrum of the play, as it devolves on him to keep his incompatible guests far apart. Mayor is a combination of Miles Gloriosus, the braggart soldier, and Senex, the lustful old man out for one last fling. Mommy is the old lady, in this case a female senex, equally lustful; Gilbert the young juvenile; Junior, in a twist, the ingenue; Eustacia Vye, Foppy's African-American maid, is the clever servant ("What does it look like I am? A Nubian princess down on her luck?") who sees through all the guests and calls them on their hypocrisy.

Aside from the sex video, which gets passed from hand to hand and pocket to pocket, the Plautus farce (not to mention the Feydeau farce) requires a plethora of doors—doors to secrete people behind, shove people into, out of which the wrong person creeps at just the wrong moment *almost* to be confronted by just the person they *mustn't* meet—and Foppy's apartment/bordello fills the bill.[12] He has multiple doors to chambers named after the most illustrious gays in literary history: the Jean Genet Suite, the Oscar Wilde room (as Foppy shoves Junior into the latter, he exclaims, "Go into Oscar Wilde!"), and the Marcel Proust.

Kramer's portraits of Koch and Nancy Reagan are both savage and irresistably hilarious. Mayor can't be pinned down to anything for which he holds ultimate responsibility. "When will I learn. Never trust old friends. They get indicted." His monologues are modules of catchphrases which can be reordered in bright non sequiturs and fired off at will:

I am not technically responsible. [...] You got anything to eat? I only diet in Appleberg. I'm here to pig out. Where is he? I know he's here! How'm I doing? My streets are clean. I just got a lot of people like to sleep outdoors. I got no disease. I got no epidemic ...

And Mrs. Potentate's tirades bring out all the fun in history:

Lady Bird planted her pansies on the highways. Eleanor Roosevelt was a lesbian with bad teeth. Mamie was a lush. Betty Ford was such a mess she opened her own cure. Roslynn was Attila the Hun. Pat Nixon pleaded a bad heart and she certainly had one. Who even remembers Bess Truman? I'm better than all of them. Mrs. Wilson ran the country, so can I! Why don't I get as good press as Jackie? I dress better and my husband is faithful.

Where the farce climbs practically to the level of Brechtian *lehrstücke* (and so anticipates *The Normal Heart*) is in Foppy's uncharacteristic conversion to political consciousness and then political action. Foppy just wants to lead a blissfully apolitical life smack dab in the heart of the political capital of the world. He feels he can rub elbows with kings and queens of reaction without ever committing himself to any point of view or having any of his political patrons' policies rub off on him. The young lovers, Gilbert Perch and Junior (who unwittingly, and over Foppy's dead body) meet and immediately drown in a sea of mutual lubricity in "Oscar Wilde"), become the instruments of Foppy's conversion. An imaginary *deus ex machina* from the world of judicial politics intrudes on the idyll: The fate of gay freedoms and safety are in peril, as a "Supreme Tribunal" decision proclaiming gays "null and void" is about to be handed down and as both Mayor and Daddy have swept the growing AIDS epidemic under the carpet, refusing to act out of homophobia (all the worse since Mayor is patently gay. "I'm not gay," is one of his oft-repeated lines in the play, second only to "How'm I doing?"). Potential possession of the sex tape together with knowing the intimate dope on both Mayor and Mommy puts Foppy in a uniquely powerful position to blackmail Mayor and Mommy into reversing their positions on gay rights and AIDS and changing the face of America. Foppy, who has seen so many of his closest friends sicken and die, ultimately becomes galvanized, and the uninvolved socialite instantaneously transforms into a gay Ralph Nader.

Maybe Junior's right. Something's got to be done. Someone's got to do something. Where is that tape? Why am I pimping for all these pimps? What have they ever done for me?

The serious dimension of *Just Say No* is epitomized by Foppy's transformation from socialite *entremetteur* into political activist, from a gay man who lives for pleasure to one committed to changing society so that his brothers may live and prosper. In this way, he is akin to Shaw's Saint Joan in the play of the same name or Brecht's Saint Joan in *Saint Joan of the Stockyards*. The latter, like other Brechtian heroes, such as the Young Comrade in *The Measures Taken*, come to a deeper understanding of their social responsibility once they are vividly confronted with social ills and made to see that political activism is the only moral choice available. In the sense that Kramer's dramatic writing on political subjects is corollary to a life of political activism, he is following in the footsteps of Shaw, Brecht, and, during his Group Theatre period, America's Clifford Odets. None of them was content to spin yarns in ivory towers, but followed an inner moral imperative to get their hands dirty in the political movements of their day. Kramer, who was one of the first to attempt to awaken the gay community to political activism in response to the AIDS crisis, himself underwent a conversion analogous to Foppy's and dramatized it in the more explicitly serious framework of *The Normal Heart* as well as in *Just Say No*.

□ □ □

If *Just Say No* is Kramer's Plautus play (with the serious overtones we have noted above), *The Normal Heart* is his Ibsen play. As Joseph Papp says in his Foreword, "Larry Kramer is a first cousin to nineteenth-century Ibsen," presumably the Ibsen of *Enemy of the People*. *The Normal Heart* is also Kramer's Schiller or Victor Hugo play. For at the heart of *The Normal Heart* is an impossible love. As with the heroes of *Don Carlos* or *Hernani*, Kramer's heroes fall in love absolutely but ephemerally, as they are in short order torn irreversibly from each others' arms. In the Romantic playwright's world, it is cruel fate which parts the lovers; in Kramer's it is cruel fate in the guise of an epidemic.[13]

Like Daniel Defoe's *Journal of the Plague Year*, *The Normal Heart* begins at a fever pitch of panic—like iron claws around the audience's heart. What could be more tense than a doctor's waiting room full of people who know in their guts that they've got the same mysterious incurable illness which seems to be attacking all their friends? Written relatively early in the AIDS crisis, it is about the period of time even earlier when the disease was just a rumor on the horizon, before the press and official institutions would allow word of it to spread to the general public, and so is meant, like the *lehrstücke*, to shock the audience into action.

As in *Just Say No*, there is a conversion which is dramatized, in this case a conversion by Dr. Emma Brookner, AIDS doctor and researcher, of Ned, the Kramer surrogate character. The conversions enacted in *Just Say No* and *The Normal Heart* are akin to the electro-shocks administered in *Sissies' Scrapbook*. Nor are they so different from the provocations little Alexander (the boy-name for the adult Ned) directs at his family to elicit direct emotional contact and response in *The Destiny of Me*. If there is one thread running through all of Kramer's work, it is a clarion call against numbness and passivity and for direct, expressed passion and action.

Ned, living habitually on the fence like Foppy Schwartz, is reluctant to get involved, but dives into activism upon his conversion by Dr. Brookner, who convinces him to take to the political field and rally the gay masses, while she tries to save patients and invent cures. Then it is *he* who attempts to convert everyone around him to regard the illness in the same way he does and to employ the same blunderbuss tactics as he to combat it.

The Normal Heart, whose plot is too well known to require detailed recounting here, chronicles the early days of political response to the growing health crisis. Ned's own line of action cuts through the center of both that evolving movement and the play as well. After years of barren, anonymous encounters, he enjoys a meteorically passionate and equally brief relationship, one that is nipped in the bud when his lover Felix brings Act I to its climax with the admission that he has a purple lesion which won't go away. Act II ends with a deathbed marriage ceremony between Felix and Ned, officiated over by Dr. Brookner in Felix's hospital room.

In between, Kramer alternates scenes of Dr. Brookner's struggle to get funding for her research; scenes of the internecine struggle within the gay community for power and over which tactical approach to use; scenes about Ned and Felix's simultaneously developing and crumbling relationship; and scenes of Felix and his brother Ben. Kramer knows how to write encounters of unbearable, soul-baring intensity. And he succeeds in doing so time and time again in *The Normal Heart*. From Bruce, the manicured and anal retentive president of the health organization, comes an excruciating narrative of his taking his latest lover, Albert, on an airplane trip to Phoenix, Arizona. Albert, both losing his mind and suffering from severe incontinence due to AIDS, dies gruesomely before Bruce gets him to the hospital in Phoenix.

> The . . . hospital doctors refused to examine him to put a cause of death on the death certificate, and without a death certificate the undertakers wouldn't take him away, and neither would the police. Finally, some orderly comes in and stuffs Albert in a heavy-duty Glad Bag and motions us with his finger to follow and he puts him out in the back alley with the garbage.

And the intolerant and impatient Ned is continually challenged to maintain his loving stance toward his own Felix as he feverishly endeavors to stuff healthy food down his throat and keep him off of the AZT he considers so dangerous to Felix' well-being. When Felix can't summon the strength or will to follow Ned's stoic, ideal regimen, Ned rages in relationship-destroying tones:

> You can't eat the food? Don't eat the food. Take your poison. I don't care. You can't get up off the floor—fine, stay there. I don't care. Fish—fish is good for you; we don't want any of that, do we? (Item by item, he throws

the food on the floor.) No green salad. No broccoli; we don't want any of that, no, sir. No bread with seven grains. Who would ever want any milk? You might get some calcium in your bones. (The carton of milk explodes when it hits the floor.) You want to die, Felix? Die! (Ned retreats to a far corner. After a moment, Felix crawls through the milk, takes an item of food, which he pulls along with his hand, and with extreme effort makes his way across to Ned. They fall into each other's arms.) Felix, please don't leave me.

How many speeches in the modern canon are more moving? It is not the raw power of the words alone, but the theatrical image of the sustaining nourishment getting slammed on the floor, finishing up with the exploding container of milk, the icon of life-sustaining nourishment itself. And how many contemporary playwrights dare introduce such vulnerability on stage?

Again, Kramer sidesteps the opportunity to berate the audience with his own preferred opinion, giving other characters plenty of opportunity to competently articulate opposing viewpoints. Many of the members of the gay health organization, for example, advocate more moderate, less offensive tactics for gaining their cause; and they make sense. When they at first exclude Ned from meeting with the mayor and later blackball him from the leadership of the organization he was instrumental in founding, the pain and injustice of his rejection is evenly counterbalanced by the fact that the audience has seen how his deliberately obnoxious and confrontational demeanor has dearly cost the organization internal unity and credibility with government officials. There is justice on both sides, and Kramer is rigorous in giving the opposing one its clear voice.

A very strong fulcrum of drama in *The Normal Heart* is Ned's relationship with his straight brother Ben, as strong a connection in its way as that with his lover Felix. At the play's temporal center is a big scene with his brother. Therein Ned rakes up their past when Ben succeeded in getting Ned to seek psychiatric care to rid himself of his homosexuality; now Ben accepts Ned to a degree, but not to the degree Ned wishes him to; namely he is trying to extract from his brother an avowal that they are the *same*, sexual preference notwithstanding. This admission Ben refuses to make, grasping at this last shred of homophobia. But despite their differences, the final image in *The Normal Heart* is not the *pietà* of Ned holding his dead lover, but that of the two brothers embracing, suggesting that Ned's connection with Ben is in fact *the* great (if non-sexual) love affair of his life.

□ □ □

This pivotal relationship between the gay and straight brothers turns up again in Kramer's recent masterpiece, *The Destiny of Me*, a play which should guarantee Kramer's stature as one of the major American playwrights of our time. Kramer intended *The Destiny of Me* to be "a companion play to The

Normal Heart and perhaps the second in an eventual trilogy—the third to be 'the deathbed play.' " He goes on to write: "There is only one *Long Day's Journey into Night*. There is only one *Death of a Salesman*," thus betraying his own ambition in writing "one of those 'family' slash 'memory' plays,"[14] as well as false (?) modesty in assuming that *The Destiny of Me* couldn't possibly aspire to the same stature as the classics he invokes.[15] But following Tolstoy's oft-quoted dictum about unhappy families, we have an appetite for yet another classically unforgettable play about a dysfunctional family–which is what Kramer has given us.

We have the same Ned as in *The Normal Heart*, only later on when he himself has contracted HIV, *and* before, in his parents' house, when he goes by his boyhood name of Alexander. Older brother Ben is the same character; and the preeminence of the brother relationship is again reinforced, when in the play's penultimate scene they are lying in parallel beds that hearken back to Biff and Happy Loman. One of the structural links which we follow throughout the play, and thus one of the most important leitmotifs in *The Destiny of Me*, is the oft-postponed attempt by Ned to confide his gayness to Ben. And Ben is ultimately the one person in Ned's life who has cared enough about him not only to see that Ned has a financially secure existence, but who never abandons him and stays with him nights at the hospital. And it is Ben who awards him a serious enough position in his own life that he is eternally struggling toward ever greater acceptance of his younger brother, *exactly as he is*.

Is it an accident that Kramer cites *Long Day's Journey into Night* and *Death of a Salesman* as antecedents to his own masterpiece?[16] What these plays have in common, in addition to their apparent lasting greatness as modern classics, is a leitmotif of brothers in conflict, as do Kramer's *Normal Heart* and *The Destiny of Me*. Foregrounding this particular relationship puts Kramer foursquare in the central tradition of modern American drama which, according to Bernard Dukore, officially got off the ground when O'Neill's first hit, *Beyond the Horizon*, opened on Broadway on February 4, 1920.[17] Tracing the treatment of American brothers from the milestone *Beyond the Horizon* through to *The Destiny of Me* exposes the ways in which Kramer violates traditions laid down by his acknowledged forebears; just as importantly it reveals how his writing is an extension of that tradition.

Who remembers *Beyond the Horizon*? And yet it contains the seeds for much of O'Neill's (whom Eric Bentley and others consider "the national playwright"[18]) future dramaturgy and, apparently, that of many other important American writers; and it arguably contains, in and of itself, much greatness. It is not, however, our task at present to argue for O'Neill's greatness (rather, Kramer's greatness and "mainstreamness"), but to examine how he develops the leitmotif of two brothers in order to better appreciate the tradition to which Kramer belongs. In the Mayo family there are two brothers—Robert, a "sensitive," poetic young man with a hankering after the world "beyond the horizon" of his family's rocky New England homestead and Andrew, a robust figure rooted in the land. Although not exactly a poet or possessor of any accomplishment at all, Robert dreams of other worlds, a propensity which fails to earn him many points when it comes to running a farm. "His features," the stage directions tell us, "are delicate and refined, leaning to weakness in the mouth and chin." And he is sickly.

The erudite reader will doubtless have already recognized the prototype of Edmund Tyrone from *Long Day's Journey* in this prodigal dreamer, but is it so many steps from him to Biff Loman in *Death of a Salesmen* who dreamed of a romantic life cattle rustling? And is it so far a leap from these straight *ratés* to the gay version: Ned in *The Destiny of Me*? For even though it goes without saying that these earlier dramatic figures are heterosexual, in every other way they share with Kramer's Ned a plethora of characteristics. They are: aesthetic if not downright artistic, thwarted and involuted in love and ambition, mama's boys, and ... they are ill, at least Robert Mayo and Edmund Tyrone are. They are sick with the unstoppable plague of their time: consumption (or lung affection or tuberculosis), a disease which was fatal in something like nine out of ten cases.

"It's just Beauty that's calling me, the beauty of the far off and unknown ..." So confides Robert Mayo to his pragmatic brother, whose earth-bound response is, "I should say you were nutty." Is this beckoning of Beauty in Robert so different from the longings experienced by Alexander in *The Destiny of Me*? Why else does he take refuge in the Andrews Sisters, in dressing up, in play-acting and in his frank, disarming bouts of humor? He is stretching out to great, if unformed dreams, dreams which raise him above the grim domestic prison; his is a nature which cannot be contained in the workaday family. In that event, it perishes. Robert Mayo's spirit and body both do indeed perish when they are so contained. And they are contained, overlooked, sneered at by the other male family members simply because such longings are foreign to their natures. Robert is his mother's son; his refinement, once again according to the stage direction, "may be traced to her." Andrew is the spitting image of his father—robust, pragmatic, and concealing a fundamental vulnerability. He becomes a successful man of business (although he ultimately loses all he gains), and makes up for want of imagination with steadfastness, a deep-seated wish to help and save everyone, especially his brother, together with all manner of practical skills. Andrew is again the forerunner to Jamie Tyrone, that inveterate ladies' man who, with such ambivalence, tries to save brother Edmund from the ravages of consumption and the bad treatment he is about to receive. In *Beyond the Horizon* the born farmer Andrew, whom circumstances have wrenched from the farm and sent to far corners of the earth, rushes back, medical specialist in tow, to save his dying brother. The fact that it is too late does not diminish his heroism, unique in the family, whose virtue is to attempt *something* concrete and decisive to save his brother's life.

In Andrew we not only see Jamie Tyrone, but brother Ben from *The Normal Heart* and *The Destiny of Me*. Ben, who has an unshakeable block against totally accepting his brother's gayness (sensitivity, dreaminess, whatever), nonetheless, to the utmost extent of his financial, emotional, and pragmatic means, is the most effective ally his brother has in combatting his disease. And Ben is the most important man in Ned's life.

The grappling to understand despite a fundamental failure of empathy, a wish to reach out to each other over the gulf of misunderstanding and messy past interactions, pervade the relationships of both sets of brothers. We see variations on this archetypal lineage wherever we cast our eye in the modern American dramatic tradition. Whether it be Biff the failed dreamer and Happy the troubled ladies' man from *Death of a Salesman*; or the anal retentive screenwriter Austin juxtaposed to his extroverted, outlaw–misfit brother Lee (who exchange identities in the course of the action, in a modernist twist on the leitmotif) of Sam Shepard's *True West*; or the closet-gay Brick in *Cat on a Hot Tin Roof* whose sensitivity and pain are in high contrast to his doofus, impervious brother, Gooper (a cartoon version of his prototype, who tries to undermine his troubled brother, not save him); when brothers appear, they seem to reassume analogous and enduring identities in relation to each other. Kramer's is the latest.

Like the characters in *Long Day's Journey* and *Death of a Salesman*, the members of the Weeks family both inflict unpardonable and ineradicable hurts on each other, and are exempt from outside judgment, since the hurts which have been inflicted on them in the past are so vast and consuming that, like furious waters bursting the bounds of a dam, they simply overflow and rush up against anyone in the vicinity, mowing down the unwitting victims in their path. All the characters are steeling their psychological immune systems against their father Richard, and that patriarch's contagious psychological eunuch-hood. His own father was a *mohel* (the man who performs the obligatory circumcision on Jewish male babies) whose own life was destroyed when he cut too much foreskin on one occasion. Richard, the father, ultimately tells Ned on his deathbed that he "didn't have a father either," thus confessing to his own failure to rise to the occasion. Struggling against castration, which seems to menace from all sides, Richard creeps through life, trying to salvage whatever vestige of his manhood he can, though scarred from early life in his most private associations. This is a central image also in Kramer's novel-in-progress, *The American People*.

Rena, the mother, is maniacally striving to conduct a significant life, one that rises above the domestic squalor which surrounds her. Ignoring his father's objections, older brother Ben insists on conducting an appeal against an army courtmartial which is being perpetrated against him through an anti-Semitic strategem. And Alexander's nonconformism, his blatant flying in the face of propriety, are all ways he devises simply to feel existence and a modicum of power in a family which can't look beyond their own pain to acknowledge that he has either power or existence. His younger son's perkiness, vivacity, and freedom from inhibition are a thorn in Richard's side. And when that son tries to provoke his father out of his quotidian grayness (with "What's a penis?" and "I don't believe in God," as well as by spouting a medley of Rodgers and Hammerstein hits followed by one of the Andrews Sisters'), it only serves as an intolerable reminder of the inner life Richard has long since sacrificed. Again we see the Kramer thread woven through: the struggle against numbness and for vivid experience.

The family drama of the past is interwoven with the horrifying present of AIDS hospital care. Ned checks into an experimental treatment program run by his arch-nemesis, Dr. Della Vida, the czar of national AIDS research, who has developed a method of purifying the virus-contaminated blood and replenishing the patient with newly enriched blood. So, swallowing his rancor at this public figure he holds personally responsible for the slowness of government response to the epidemic, the HIV-positive Ned, whose T-cell count is dangerously low, pins his hopes on the competence of the very man he has been stridently denouncing on every available soapbox.

Dr. Della Vida, embodiment of the doctor/bureaucrat, head of the AIDS research establishment, is modeled after Anthony Fauci and Robert Gallo. He intends to use Ned as a willing guinea pig in an experiment he hopes could prove a miracle, an expectation which is dissappointed in the play's penultimate scene, when Ned pulls all the tubes out of his body and dashes the bags of blood against the wall in an image which palpitates both symbolically and concretely. Here Ned joins the line of characters in recent American drama who throw, slam, and dash objects, as in Sam Shepard's *Buried Child*, where Vince throws beer bottles, or his *True West*, where it's Lee smashing typewriters, or Kramer's own above-mentioned *The Normal Heart*, where Ned throws the milk carton. First milk, then blood.

Ned is destined, apparently unto death, to encounter raging, impotent father figures, face them down, and be disappointed. As a patient he must yet again put his destiny in the hands of the man whom he suspects wishes his death in reciprocity. That man again has the power either to hasten his demise or at least fail to prolong his life.

The two time-frames alternate and interpenetrate most skillfully, which is best seen from the construction of the play's climaxes. For example, the climax of Act I, when Richard starts beating his son, pummeling him with the term "sissy" as well as with his fists, coincides with that of Ned's Nurse (who is also Della Vida's wife) rushing into the hospital room spattered with blood, pitched at her by ACT UP-like demonstrators who have besieged the hospital.

Later, Rena, in the most cathartic scene from the past, tries to break away from her marriage, and Richard in utter frustration and helplessness, lays into Alexander more savagely than before, while in the dramatic present tense, Ned's treatment is receiving a setback. As the enriched blood is being pumped into him, he suffers a side-effect of convulsions, causing the staff members to once again pour into the room in a concerted emergency response. And at the end of Act II, when Ned's brother Ben saves Ned from drowning, as he did in their youth, Dr. Della Vida arrives exalted with the news that the cure might actually be working! The formal coincidence of the parallel actions, past and present, reinforces a causal relationship between the two, adding to our suspicion that Ned's present predicament is somehow propelled by his past, and that the present hospital scene is a spiraling repetition of identical past dramas in fresh disguise.

While the relationships between Ned and Dr. Della Vida, his dead lover Felix, and most important, his brother Ben are vital, Ned ultimately moves beyond the embrace with his brother to finish off the play with his own younger self, Alexander, whom he is learning to accept, appreciate, and incorporate into his present self. The young and mature Ned wind up by singing a duet of "Make Believe" from *Showboat*. It is on himself now that he is pinning his hopes.

The Destiny of Me is a big play, taut to bursting with pyrotechnic scenes and speeches, its energy pulsating, its pathos continually shot through with heart-rending humor. It contains at least two unforgettable characters: Ned and his mother, Rena. The latter must go down in the pantheon of great American heroines along with Blanche Dubois, Linda Loman, and Amanda from *The Glass Menagerie*. Rena tries gallantly to rise above the lackluster domestic arrangement, to substitute philanthropy for love and romance. Her tough Jewish wit is on a par with Amanda's southern belle charm; and her refusal to face reality is no less than Amanda's either. When a playwright is able to weave such a successfully complex structure and create a virtual human redolent of such originality and inner contradiction, is he not himself now, already and at last, to be enthroned in the pantheon?

Parenthetically, is it not curious that Kramer, who couldn't be more "out," has created such a memorable female character? This achievement belies the cliché, which passes for a rule, that gay writers' successes at creating great female characters are ascribable to a process of mutation; instead of putting taboo gay men onstage, they create women as surrogates! And yet, what a lineage: O'Neill, a straight playwright who created fabulous women characters; Williams, a gay playwright who could only indirectly dramatize gay issues, but who created equally fabulous women characters; and Kramer, an "out" gay playwright who wrote fabulous women characters both before *and* after he was out! Who can deny the compelling originality of Rena and Mrs. Della Vida in *The Destiny of Me*, of Dr. Brookner in *The Normal Heart*, of Mrs. Potentate in *Just Say No*, of Jennifer and Laura in *Sissies' Scrapbook/Four Friends*? A male playwright's ability to create valid female characters may have more to do with fertile imagination, empathic potential, and dramatic talent than with sexuality or society's norms.

The Destiny of Me is a drama of disappointment. It has become the easy byword of critics to speak of the *rage* in Larry Kramer's plays. Not that rage isn't there in truckloads. But are the critics' acquaintance with the play-wright-as-public-figure blinding them to how Kramer's plays run the emotional gamut and back again?[19] And perhaps they have missed the essential emotional link in the chain of rage, namely disappointment. Is it not first the fear of disappointment, and then disappointment realized which fuel Ned's rage at Dr. Della Vida, the super-physician treating him for AIDS?

Is it not Richard, Ned's father's disappointment in life, marriage and himself which precipitates his violent reactions? And so on down the line. This disappointment includes the rage Ned feels at the premature loss of his one true lover, a rage that can only be directed at the Cosmos. The rage is also counterbalanced by a whole gamut of other consequences of repeated disappointment including both hopefulness and even reconciliation. This emotional range is another element in Kramer's dramaturgy which, when coupled with intellectual content and technical cunning, elevate him to the level of the masters.

□ □ □

Looking at Larry Kramer's kinship with Brecht, Shaw, O'Neill, and Miller is not merely an exercise in lionization, although I truly believe that his significance has been gravely underrated. It is an attempt to re-envision someone who has been, perhaps more than any other, assumed to be only, always, and exclusively a "Gay Playwright."

When we hasten to label Larry Kramer a Gay Playwright (or, for that matter, August Wilson an African-American Playwright or Maria Irene Fornes an Hispanic Woman Playwright) we are responding to many causes and bringing about many consequences at once, some laudatory and some not. We are justifiably claiming gayness as a legitimate identity for a playwright (which was apparently impossible in the past) and sympathetic gay characters and concerns as legitimate material for the drama. Also, because Kramer is a master of his craft, we are further consolidating the respectability of Gay Playwrights by adding the brilliant Kramer to its already undeniably impressive pantheon.[20]

On the other hand, are we not, at the same time, limiting and diminishing Kramer, in that the very distinction which lends his sexual persuasion dignity concomitantly robs it of the broadest recognition it merits (Is *The Importance of Being Earnest* a "gay play?" Is it better or worse for having been written by a homo- or bisexual? Is it not first and foremost a great English nineteenth-century play?), depriving it of the very same stature which O'Neill, Miller, and, yes, Williams enjoyed? It is a great advance that today's playwright may today proclaim loud and clear that he identifies as gay or that he or she may explore gay characters and issues to their heart's content in their creations. But why must that perforce limit the context of the audience or a priori demarcate the discourse which will elucidate their works? Why can they not join the national and world landscape along with other writers of the most disparate persuasions and be enjoyed by a general audience and elucidated for the artistic qualities of their works?

Is there not a risk that a degree of the richness and complexity of the play be overlooked or reduced when peered at through the filter of Gay Theatre and Gay Playwright as primary categories? I am certainly not here joining Arlene Croce's pernicious point of view as expressed in *New York* magazine, wherein she stigmatizes and dismisses all of what she deems "victim art," Bill T. Jones's dances being the specific victim of her own merciless barbs.[21] My polemic arises from, and is animated by another concern entirely. How can we strike a balance between, let us say, a gay playwright such as Larry Kramer writing from and about his condition honestly and forthrightly and known for his elucidation of that special world, yet who wants and deserves "to be universally heard". It cannot have failed to strike us that the entire world is presently a-swim in a tidal wave of renascent tribalism, a splitting off of autonomous peoples, each proclaiming its distinctness (and some-times superiority), with a logical next step of implicit or explicit antagonism to other peoples. This tendency is quite unlike Ned and Ben's relationship in *The Destiny of Me*, as they retain a base line caring and respect for each other even as they recognize certain unbridgeable differences.

Some may see it as farfetched to discern any connection between the tragic events in the former Yugoslavia and Soviet Union, or even those between white working poor and minority welfare mothers and the post-modernist categories of discourse which are so current and so all-pervasive. In each of the above instances, whether it is a matter of Serbs, Croats, Chechians, Armenians, American women, or gays, there is undeniable merit in proclaiming the righteousness of the particular cause. The consequences which then ensue, however, are too often questionable and destructive to world peace.

My own strong feeling is that postmodern categories (of which Gay Playwright is one) are simply one more manifestation of a present-day universal and damaging tendency toward claiming distinctness from as opposed to the undeniable interpenetration between and commonality that exists amongst peoples. It is this point of view which is behind the present polemic, second only to an authentic, awed admiration for Larry Kramer's artistry and craftsmanship.

Notes

1. Kramer's own career ambivalence has compounded the widespread underesti-mation of him as a professional playwright. He openly admits to this difficulty. "I seem to be good at getting things going and not so good at keeping them going. Also, I've been writing and you can't write in a vacuum. Activism is very seductive in a way." Joseph C. Koenen, "A Play for Our Times," *Newsday* (October 12, 1988).

2. Postmodern gender studies critic, John M. Clum, says of those who venture forth from the ghetto that "the playwrights who have achieved the greatest exposure, through both stage production and publication are those who ... write for the commercial mainstream theater, and who, as a result, must mediate between gay and straight members of their audience." The implication is that this mediation brings in its wake moral equivocation and artistic diffuseness. Ergo: ghetto is better. *Acting Gay* (New York: Columbia University Press, 1984), pp. xvi–xvii.

3. Kramer's work has been performed on yet another occasion. Edward Hunt and Jeff Stoker, who run the Man Bites Dog Theater in Raleigh-Durham, N.C., used some of Kramer's essay "Report from the holocaust" (from *Reports from the holocaust*) verbatim as one-half of an evening, the other half being called "Unnatural Acts," which used, verbatim, the words and writings of Jesse Helms, both halves brought together under the title of *Indecent Materials*.

4. Even *The Destiny of Me* is not universally regarded as "a gay play" or "an AIDS play." Lucille Lortel, whose theater housed it, described it as "the story of a Jewish family. . . . And it's a family play, a touching play," which is, perhaps, to wear opaque blinders. But why can't one also see *The Destiny of Me* in this light? Isn't it all of the above and more? "All in the Viewpoint," *New York Times* (January 1, 1993).

5. From Kramer's introduction to *Just Say No* titled "The Farce in Just Saying No" (New York: St. Martin's Press, 1989), p. xvi. In the Introduction, incidentally, Kramer lambastes Clive Barnes for his uncomprehending and insensitive attitude toward *Just Say No*.

6. This *oeuvre de jeunesse*, since it is written by a gay playwright but is not predominantly about gay subjects, would be grouped by John M. Clum along with most of William Inge and Tennessee Williams as a "closet drama," which is driven by "the playwrights' negative feelings about their own homosexuality." *Acting Gay*, p. xvii. I would aver that this play, like Inge and Williams's masterpieces, is rather driven by a vast apprehension of the human spirit.

7. John M. Clum seems unhappy about Kramer's evenhandedness, since it doesn't make for smug morals and clear propaganda. As a result, he disparages *Just Say No* as a "chaotic farce." He goes on to say that "Kramer's introduction to the published version of *Just Say No* is far clearer than the play itself, showing that during the AIDS crisis, Kramer grew as an essayist, while his ability to form a coherent drama dwindled." *Acting Gay*, p. 80. I would challenge any reader to discern what is dramatically or comedically incoherent about this eminently clear play. Perhaps he is alluding to the frenzied rhythm of the play, which is essential to its genre. Cf. Albert Bermel, *Farce* (New York: Touchstone Books, 1982), pp. 27–48. If the ideas cannot be readily extracted from the play as they can from an essay, that only goes to show that Kramer knows the difference between the two forms of writing and is true to his craft as a dramatist—whose function is *not* to concoct dramatized lectures, but human situations. How often do critics, trained as they are in expository writing, require that playwrights misapply the skills proper to criticism in their dramaturgy?

8. Kramer doesn't even realize that this evenhandedness is a strength in his playwriting. "I'm not about to give Nancy Reagan her day in court," he crowed, unaware that she stands up for herself perfectly well in his play. Gerard Raymond, "Multi-Media Voice of the Gays," *West Side Spirit* (October 31, 1988).

9. On this subject, Kramer is quoted as saying, "People are always accusing me of

being 'a message queen.' But this time, I wanted to get the message out with humor." Donna Maychick, "On the Town," *New York Post* (October 19, 1988).

10. Koenan, "A Play for Our Times."

11. Kramer himself avers that *Just Say No* is in the tradition of Restoration comedy, due to its reliance on scabrous verbal wit. Joseph Lanza, "Stranger Than Fiction: Larry Kramer on His New Farce, *Just Say No*," *New York Native* (October 10, 1988).

12. Critic Albert Bermel eloquently takes up the importance of doors in farce in the chapter titled "In and Out" in his seminal book, *Farce*, pp. 33–4.

13. John M. Clum points out that all AIDS plays grow out of the tradition of Camille, the heroine of the well-made nineteenth-century melodrama, *La dame aux camélias* by Dumas *fils*, who died of consumption. He remarks that "Kramer gives a death scene that Dumas or Giuseppe Verdi would have admired." *Acting Gay*, p. 76. See below, my discussion of O'Neill and consumption.

14. Larry Kramer, "A Man's Life and the Path to Acceptance," *New York Times* (October 4, 1992). This article later became the introduction to the published version of *The Destiny of Me*.

15. Kramer is nothing if not up front about his aspirations to write in the long tradition of issue-oriented classical playwrights from Sophocles to Odets, and his native fervor is oriented toward reviving what he considers as a neglected and persecuted brand of drama. In his essay "The Farce in Just Saying No" he elaborates greatly on this mission and on the ways in which he feels the critical establishment has discouraged playwrights from writing significant plays with a point of view. In any case, Kramer does not consider being grouped along with Williams, Miller, and Odets an insult, even if two of them are straight.

16. John H. Clum also concedes the favorable comparison between *The Destiny of Me* and Odets, O'Neill, and Miller. "Yet," he follows up, "for a student of gay drama, it is Kramer's alliance to this dramatic tradition that causes the play's infuriating flaws." *Acting Gay*, p. 293. These are flaws when judged beneath the Stalinistic searchlight of prescriptive postmodern gender criticism, not when esteemed as high drama. Does *Beyond the Horizon* fail by American Family Standards because it presents a negative portrait of *heterosexual* relations? It seems to me that what Clum is actually prescribing is a gay version of *Father Knows Best* and *The Donna Reed Show*, a cozy, sanitized, and always rosy version of gay life; unfortunately this version, while it may present a glorified image of gay life, is antithetical to great drama, which is by nature complex and paradoxical.

17. Bernard Dukore, *American Dramatists*, 1918–1945 (New York: Grove Press, 1985), p. 2.

18. Eric Bentley, *In Search of Theatre* (New York: Vintage Books, 1954), p. 220.

19. Kramer himself has compounded the situation by repeatedly referring to the rage in his own work when interviewed, to cite just two examples, "I write out of anger," Stephen Holden, "Larry Kramer's Update on the War at Home," *New York Times*, (October 9, 1988), and "This is an angry play," Douglas Brin, "Backstage with Larry Kramer," *New York Daily News* (April 14, 1985). John C. Clum, taking all this reductive talk about Kramer's rage on face value, dismisses this rich play: "Anger isn't enough." *Acting Gay*, p. 7.

20. Even though many gay critics and commentators have, in a sense, disowned Kramer as a spokesperson for "the gay cause," finding him just critical enough of gay behavior to justify homophobia in straights. Such an anti-Kramer polemic is Richard Goldstein, "Kramer's Complaint," *Village Voice* (July 2, 1985). But Kramer counters such arguments, claiming he does indeed echo the voices of

the gay community, just not those of the gay press, which is a minority view. Lanza, "Stranger Than Fiction." My own view is that the gay world is not monolithic, and the gay artist is in no way obligated to reflect any prescriptive version of it.

21. Arlene Croce, "Discussing the Undiscussable," *New Yorker* (December 26, 1994– January 2, 1995).

Larry Kramer and Gay Theater

Michael Paller

I N 1984, the first full-length play about the effect of AIDS on New York's gay community was produced in New York City. A year later, two more plays reflecting the growing crisis premiered in major theaters in New York. After that, the floodgates opened. By the end of 1994, over sixty plays had opened in New York that either took people with AIDS as their principal subject or in which some aspect of the AIDS epidemic played an important thematic part.[1] No doubt many of these, to say nothing of the dozens of others that were produced elsewhere during the decade 1985–94 would have been written whether or not the incendiary bomb of *The Normal Heart* had been thrown onto the stage of the New York Public Theater in the spring of 1985. It is equally likely, however, that many young playwrights were encouraged, not only by *The Normal Heart*'s brash theatrical power but by its success, to follow Larry Kramer's example and recast the emotions that threatened to overwhelm them into dramatic form. Certainly, it would be difficult to imagine an *Angels in America* had there not been *The Normal Heart*. Kramer, who believes that the purpose of gay theater ought to be to encourage gay playwrights to write about their experiences, might well be pleased.[2]

So thick did the proliferation of plays written in response to the epidemic become that in time it would be difficult for audiences to view contemporary gay plays that didn't reflect any of the various aspects of AIDS and not wonder in what century, or on what planet, the author was living. No less eminent a critic and playwright than Eric Bentley was confronted with this new theatrical world by the fate of his play *Round Two*. A gay adaptation of Schnitzler's *La Ronde* updated to the New York of the 1970s, Bentley found few theaters interested in producing his paean to the days of frenetically casual sex. Times, indeed, had changed.[3]

By 1992, *The Normal Heart* had been produced over 600 times.[4] *Torch Song Trilogy*, with its Broadway production and subsequent film, could not compare to this highly visible success; nor would the Terrence McNally plays peopled with gay characters—*The Lisbon Traviata, Andre's Mother, A Perfect Ganesh, Love! Valour! Compassion!*—which would follow. The only comparable achievement has been Kushner's *Angels in America*, which won the Pulitzer Prize and brought its author the sort of national recognition that includes interviews in national magazines and on network news programs such as *Nightline* (such recognition is not automatic to previously little-known writers who win the Pulitzer Prize for drama—as Robert Schenkkan, who won it in 1992 for *The Kentucky Cycle*, can attest). Of these playwrights, only Kramer has achieved his success writing plays that deal so single-mindedly with the lives—and the deaths—of gay people. Still, for someone who would have such influence on gay playwrights, and so on gay theater, Larry Kramer is a playwright who has had strikingly little to do with gay theaters over the course of his career. His work for films, novels and plays had been entirely mainstream. In Kramer's own estimation, very few of *The Normal Heart*'s 600 productions have occurred in gay theaters.

In fact, Kramer's influence on gay playwrights, and on the allowable content of the plays they were writing, happened precisely *because* of his distance from the gay theaters. Gay playwrights could follow Kramer's lead only because they saw it, and they saw it because *The Normal Heart* (as well as William M. Hoffman's *As Is*, which opened at the Circle Repertory Company six weeks prior to *The Normal Heart*) was produced not at a gay theater with a minuscule budget, fickle audience and little chance of receiving major reviews, but at a prestigious venue in New York City, and received a positive, if not glowing, review in the *New York Times*, and was published by Samuel French, Inc., the country's largest publisher of plays. "Minority" playwrights will always need the mainstream theaters with their access to the wider media, to inform the rest of the country of their existence. How it was that Larry Kramer, who would so influence a generation of young playwrights and cause new images of gay men to appear in drama, came to have so little involvement with gay theater has something to do with the history of gay theater in New York, including the degree to which it was supported by the gay community, Kramer's personal history and his relationship with the city's gay community. The story also involves the differences between gay theater's purposes and Kramer's intentions as a playwright.

□ □ □

These are many definitions of "gay plays," from Robert Patrick's often-quoted remark that a gay play is a play that sleeps with other plays of the same sex, to his more prosaic, "A gay play is a play about gay people," to Victor Bumbalo's, "A gay play is the exploration of gay life by the people who live it." No absolute definition can be arrived at, but for the purposes of this essay, a gay play is defined rather narrowly, as one written by a gay playwright centering upon the lives of gay characters. A gay theater is defined as a producing entity that produces gay plays for a largely gay and lesbian audience. As for gay sensibility, one can do no better than repeat journalist Jeff Weinstein's often-quoted remark, "No, there is no such thing as a gay sensibility and yes, it has an enormous impact on our culture."[5]

The playwrights who began writing gay material in the early 1960s grew alongside of and developed with the gay theater movement, which in turn evolved because of the writers who faithfully furnished it with plays. The early days of gay theater in New York, from the Caffe Cino beginning in 1958 and the development of Off-Off Broadway, to the days of gay liberation, were heady ones. At the Caffe Cino, young people found an atmosphere in which they were able "to express what they had never been allowed to before."[6] Plays at the Cino, while not exclusively gay, were very often about the lives of gay men or, if having little specifically gay content, were soaked in the campy, witty, arch, highly theatrical and self-aware style recognizable as examples of "gay sensibility." Robert Patrick, Doric Wilson, William M. Hoffman, Claris Nelson, Lanford Wilson, Jeff Weiss, H.M. Koutoukas, Tom Eyen and others found their voices and their subject matter there. During the same period, gay playwrights were at work at the Judson Poets' Theatre, John Vaccaro's Playhouse of the Ridiculous and a little later, at its offspring, Charles Ludlam's Ridiculous Theatrical Company.

The majority of the Cino playwrights wrote in response to an inner urge for authentic expression, and a need to reorder the chaotic events of life in ways that were coherent and satisfying. They wrote, in other words, for the same reason that most writers do. Most didn't view their work as overtly political, nor did they usually write from a political agenda. Nevertheless, from this explosion of creative work the identity of a community was beginning to emerge.

These playwrights would be joined by others at the theaters that flowered as expressions of the gay liberation movement in the wake of the Stonewall riots (which, as William M. Hoffman pointed out, were themselves significant examples of gay theater); TOSOS, The Glines, Medusa's Revenge, the Shandol, Women Write Theatre, the Paris Project, A Piece of the World, More Fire Productions, the Meridian, the Stonewall Rep and others. In the decade that followed Stonewall, Magaly Alabau, Arch Brown, Victor Bumbalo, Jane Chambers, Robert Chesley, Clare Cost, Richard Hall, Jordie Mark, Susan Miller, Terry Miller, Deborah Sherman, Sarah Schulman, Peggy Shaw, Ana Maria Simo, Edwina Lee Tyler, Lois Weaver, and others began writing for a network of theaters that produced gay and lesbian plays for gay and lesbian audiences.[7] In the newly politicized atmosphere of liberation in which it was hard to separate the sex from the politics, their plays differed from those of the Caffe Cino era in that they were, irrespective of their subject matter, political. No matter how apolitical a gay or lesbian playwright might personally have felt, the plays produced in gay theaters between 1969 and 1981 were political acts. They reflected back to the gay community its history, images and current conditions, and in so doing, continued the work of affirmation, community- and identity-building in a culture that denied gay men and lesbians all of these things, as well as their civil rights.

Except perhaps as an occasional audience member, Larry Kramer was not a part of this world. He came to theater not by way of Off-Off Broadway, where shoestring budgets and a cheerful informality shaped the aesthetic, but from the movies. He began his career at Columbia as a young man running a teletype machine, became a producer and writer and spent the early years of gay liberation in London. When, in the mid-1970s, he felt the need to write about his homosexuality, he discovered that this was subject matter in which the movies had no interest. Still, being an Academy Award-nominated screenwriter and successful producer had its uses: along with the stature attached to his executive positions at Columbia and United Artists came many contacts in mainstream media. In 1973, he wrote a gay play called *Sissies' Scrapbook*, which he was able to get produced at Playwrights Horizons, one of the new rising stars in New York theater (and for a long time, New York's leading unofficial, non-self-identified gay theater). Revised the following year as *Four Friends*, the play was produced as a commercial venture at the Theatre de Lys, smack in the middle of Christopher Street (and closed after one performance, following a brutal review in the *New York Times* by Clive Barnes).

Given the different worlds that New York gay theater and Larry Kramer occupied in 1974—one was, in relation to the mainstream, marginal and invisible, making up in energy, devotion and ingenuity what it lacked in recognition and money; one was an Academy Award nominee—it would have been surprising indeed if Kramer had sought out a gay theater to produce his first play. As he began his playwriting career, Kramer was a gay playwright who didn't need a gay theater to get his gay play produced.[8]

□   □   □

In their initial stages, the years between 1958 and 1981, one might say that New York's gay theaters had at least three purposes: to affirm the existence of a community by telling gay stories by gay artists to gay audiences; to help define that community's identity by telling stories that underline shared experiences, common feelings or history; and to provide public places for gay men and lesbians to assemble and identify with others around them in the making of cultural artifacts that reflected their lives. Since the performance of a play cannot take place without an audience, the men and women who gathered to see gay plays were active participants in the creation of their own culture. All of these purposes were inherently political, as were the plays that a gay theater might produce, regardless of subject matter. In the decade after Stonewall, the plays produced by a gay theater might be light romances (as indeed a vast number of them were), exercises in wish-fulfillment indistinguishable from straight romances except for the lovers' gender—but that distinction changed the nature of the play and of the event that was its presentation. If identification with the play's gay characters led an audience member to a new or renewed acceptance of his or her sexual nature, or helped forge a bond between one audience member and another, then the public performance of such a play, no matter how personal or trivial its content, constituted a political act. Attending it, and holding a lover's hand during it, became political acts as well.[9]

But these were political acts of a very specific character. They did not allow for significant dissent. Identity-building, community-building, and dissent, if the dissent comes from within, are not always compatible. An oppressed community that is forging the images on which it can base an identity can tolerate only a limited amount of disagreement; by the end of the day one set of images and the values they represent are likely to predominate. Since the difference between gays and straights has been proposed, more often than not, by the culture as a sexual one, gay liberation in the 1970s and the early 1980s meant, to a great many men and women, sexual liberation; therefore, gay identity would be built primarily on gay sex. As identity-building enterprises eager to satisfy their audiences' demand for liberating images, gay theaters would of course produce plays in which the principal concern was almost always the getting of sex. Love would enter into it, too, in formulaic ways, but it would almost always be the sort of love that was expressed with a hot kiss. Very occasionally, a playwright would criticize the central, frenetic role sex played in the lives of many gay men— and gay culture. Such was the case with Jonathan Katz's 1972 play, *Coming Out*. Most of the play was a celebration of gay life and history, but one powerful speech was an indictment of gay men's sexual habits and appetites. He was roundly attacked by some for what they considered an assault on sexual liberation.[10] Even in a play meant to affirm all aspects of gay identity, the notion that too much sex might be a bad thing was unwelcome in, and largely absent from, gay theater. Happily ever after was expected, liberation was what was celebrated, and gay sex was in the air.

□ □ □

It was also in the discos, the baths, the tearooms, the back rooms and the Ramble in Central Park. At the height of this sexual fever, Larry Kramer published *Faggots*. In his cover blurb, Edward Albee hoped that the book wouldn't cause gays to lose their sense of humor. Many didn't, but many did. The novel provoked not only debate but rage within the community it depicted as living almost entirely by the dictates of its penis. Kramer may have considered his novel a moral statement, but given the tenor of the times for gay men, it could not escape being taken by many as a political one. In the minds of those who hated the book, Kramer, by suggesting that a life obsessed with sex and physical appearance was a hollow life in which any kind of meaningful love or accomplishment was impossible, was attacking the very center of gay identity. At best, Kramer was a puritan, a frustrated party-pooper who couldn't get laid; at worst, he was a sex-hating, self-loathing homosexual. On the other hand, where some smelled a Quisling, others sensed a Swift. The message of *Faggots* was either "Sexual liberation is evil," or "Put aside destructive pursuits and seek love."

Those who didn't keep their sense of humor about *Faggots* would prove to have lone memories. Even as late as 1988, an acquaintance of mine would refer to it, with the intensity borne of a grievance long-nursed and unexamined, as "pure Evil." When Kramer began writing in the *New York Native* of his alarm at the mysterious cancer and pneumonia that were suddenly killing gay men, more than a few in the gay community heard only his same old self-loathing song.

"It's easy to become frightened," he wrote in the *Native* of August 24–September 6, 1981, "that one of the many things we've done or taken over the past years may be all that it takes for a cancer to grow from a tiny something-or-other that got in there who knows when from doing who knows what." This sentence, in an appeal for research funds so brief it could scarcely be called an article, and which contained none of *Faggots'* sarcasm or anger, was all it took to unleash the still-simmering resentments toward the "anti-sex" message of *Faggots* and its finger-pointing author.

The first angry public response would come, ironically, from a gay playwright in a letter the *Native* published two weeks later. Since the age of ten, Robert Chesley had been having gay sexual fantasies that shamed and frightened him deeply. At twenty-two and a virgin, he married, and all that he and his wife, also a virgin, knew about socially sanctioned sex was what they had read in a 1930s sex manual they found in his grandmother's attic. In 1975, at thirty-two and on the verge of suicide, he came out. Gay liberation, he would come to say, saved him. By broadening the area of allowable sex and eroticism, liberation gave people like himself a real alternative to despair and suicide. "One of the things that gay people were about in the seventies," he said later, "was exploring [sexual] territory and making it allowable for other people."[11]

Chesley began writing gay plays in 1980. Suffused with the sexual giddiness and freedom of the era, they celebrated men loving men. His plays were not the coming out stories that some other playwrights were writing; they took the naturalness of gay sex as a given and went from there. The world of Chesley's plays was not Eden; he knew as well as Larry Kramer did that people could be cruel, selfish and superficial. But it was a world in which gay men stood a chance of being happy, a chance made possible only because gay men could have gay sex. Having gay sex without fear or guilt was what the men of Chesley's plays did. The popularity of his plays in gay theaters around the country indicated that a great many gay men agreed with him, and wanted to see their lives portrayed that way in their own theaters.

Chesley had not liked *Faggots*. Nor did he care for Kramer's appeal in the *Native*. The full text of his response as published in the *Native* is more balanced than the excerpt Kramer included in *Reports from the holocaust* might suggest (Chesley begins by saying he is glad that Kramer is raising funds for research on "the gay cancer" and is sending him a check). Still, it is clear that in Kramer's appeal Chesley detected "gay homophobia and anti-eroticism." In the person of Robert Chesley, the New York gay theater was telling Larry Kramer to take his message of self-loathing and "gay homophobia and anti-eroticism" elsewhere.[12]

What followed—Kramer's involvement in the founding of the Gay Men's Health Crisis, his disputes with some of his co-founders and members of the Board of Trustees and his continued writing in the *Native* that exacerbated these disputes—was a replay of the controversy over *Faggots*. Now not only was Kramer a self-loathing homosexual, he was a loud-mouthed, bullying, self-loathing homosexual. By the time he wrote *The Normal Heart*, it would have been difficult to find a gay theater in New York willing to produce it.

□ □ □

Of course, by then it would have been hard to find a gay theater in New York at all. They certainly existed, but by 1984 they had become more marginal, more invisible, than they had been a decade earlier. There was the Stonewall Rep, the Glines, the Meridian Gay Theater and a few others, but one read about them only in the *Native* or the *Village Voice* (and the Glines was about to join forces with the mainstream Circle Repertory Company to co-produce *As Is*). The first generation of playwrights who had written so loyally for gay theaters had been repaid with invisibility. As long as they remained committed to writing plays that celebrated gay men as sexual beings, their work would be produced only in gay theaters. Meanwhile, mainstream theaters and commercial producers began producing plays by gay playwrights that played down liberation's sexual aspects. Perhaps because the second and third parts of Harvey Fierstein's *Torch Song Trilogy* suggested that gay men wanted nuclear families just like straight people's, his portrait of gay life seemed less threatening to a mainstream audience than might Victor Bumbalo's *Kitchen Duty*. Likewise, the first installments of William Finn's musical trilogy, *The March of the Falsettos* and *In Trousers*, proposed that gay men were not really so different from straight men. Not only were these images acceptable to straight audiences, they seemed to satisfy a growing number of gay men, as well. It seemed that many gay men were more comfortable going to the Helen Hayes Theater on Broadway or to Playwrights' Horizons (where there were always plenty of gay men in the audience) to see images of themselves than they were going to the Meridian, the Glines, or any other self-identifying gay theater.[13] Another alternative for gay audiences seeking something more "respectable" than what the gay theaters were offering was work that was clearly gay in sensibility if not in content: the work of Charles Ludlam at his Ridiculous Theatrical Company and later, Charles Busch's Theatre-in-Limbo. Loaded with double entendre, accessible on one level to a gay audience and on another to a mainstream one, such theater developed parallel to the more gay content-oriented theater, but it achieved a "respectability" that the gay theater hadn't, because its gayness was subtextual. By the mid-1980s, the work of Ludlam and Busch was being reviewed in the mainstream press with increasing frequency and prominence. No doubt the gay theater in New York had always been a minority theater even within its own community. But by 1985, what a decade earlier had been a vibrant theater, connected to its community's concerns, was in large measure being deserted by even that element of the community that considered itself its supporters.

There were other reasons why the gay theater in New York had become increasingly ghettoized and invisible, reasons more or less particular to New York. Like every other small theater in the city, the gay theaters were hobbled by rising rental costs, making production more costly and less regular. Added to that were the possibilities of more profitable and visible employment in the mainstream theater—many more than could be found in other cities at that time. Mainstream theaters producing "safe" gay plays; the shrinking number of gay men willing to go to self-identified gay theaters; increasingly threadbare production values due to rising costs; low—or no— salaries for artists: all of these circumstances produced an environment in which no gay theater has survived more than a few years in the city with America's largest gay population. By 1985, the audience at New York's gay theaters was drying up. And in that year, what Larry Kramer wanted above all was an audience.

The advent of AIDS slowed whatever impetus toward community- and identity-building was left in New York's gay theater. A hunkering down began; fissures within the community (which, in any case and like every "community," was always an amalgam of many communities) became more pronounced. The gay theater in New York found itself in something of a time-warp, doing the kind of plays it had been doing all along, for a dwindling audience. If it seemed a bit paralyzed in this regard, at least it was reflecting an aspect of the gay community.

Robert Chesley began documenting these fissures in *Stray Dog Story*, produced by the Meridian Gay Theatre early in 1983. Although it had been over eighteen months since "the gay cancer" and pneumocystis had made their deadly appearances and began moving through the gay community with terrifying swiftness, there was no mention of AIDS in this queer, *Candide*-like fairy tale about a dog turned into a gay man by his Fairy Dog Mother, only to experience cruelty after cruelty in the big city. There was, however, a Leatherman Activist preaching to a Demonstrator at a Sheridan Square candlelight vigil. The play is a cartoon, and Chesley's Leatherman is a tongue-in-cheek portrait, but in the Leatherman's upbraiding, one can clearly see Chesley's targets: Larry Kramer and other early AIDS activists.

LEATHERMAN ACTIVIST: I'll tell you where the movement people went wrong. I can tell you *exactly* where. They alienated the bar community. It's almost as if they deliberately tried to make enemies of the bar community. Their approach was pure hostility, and what did they expect? Well, they got what they were asking for, by marching through the bars like Danny's shouting, "Out of the bars and into the streets!" The bar community won't have a *thing* to do with the movement people. You don't see them at demonstrations, and that's the reason why. That's just not the way to get people to join you, by shouting at them.

DEMONSTRATOR: Uh-huh.

LEATHERMAN ACTIVIST: And I'll tell you something more. I could've told the movement people that it was going to happen. They *ought* to have known in the first place, but it's typical that they turned their anger against their own people. The irony of which is that they attacked the very people they claimed to represent. But it was like the way they alienated the lesbians. It was the same thing, really. What the *fuck* did they *expect*? *Anyone* could see it coming. It's almost like they did it deliberately. Their approach was pure hostility. The irony of which is that they got *exactly* what they were asking for.

DEMONSTRATOR: Uh-huh.[14]

The Leather Activist and the Demonstrator move off to consummate what turns out to be a pickup, ignoring the vigil memorializing an openly gay city councilman slain by a gunman. Chesley is ambivalent: he criticizes both characters for choosing sex over participation in the political event occurring in front of them. However, his attitude is also clear regarding what he saw as the futility, if not the stupidity, of berating one's own people when what was needed was unity. Larry Kramer may have been well outside New York's gay theater, but he was providing it with new, if for the moment unflattering, images.

In the spring of 1984, Chesley's *Night Sweat* was produced at the Meridian Gay Theater. It was the first full-length play produced in New York to deal directly with AIDS. Saturated in sex, *Night Sweat* is clearly in the gay idiom. Sex is viewed as more than two bodies coupling; it is an expression of personal authenticity. Even in the play's bizarre circumstances, men devote a single-minded energy to their sexual fantasies.

Written from projections of fear and, in part, as Chesley admitted in notes accompanying the published text, from his own self-hatred, *Night Sweat* (subtitled "A Romantic Comedy") takes place in the Coup de Grâce Club, "sometime in the near future." The Coup de Grâce is a suicide sex club where HIV-positive men pay exorbitant prices to commit suicide during the sexual fantasy of their choice, rather than die a lingering, painful death from AIDS. One character ends his life with an auto-erotic hanging; another indulges a super-hero fantasy complete with tights and capes. A third, dressed in the white of the Old West good guy, is shot down in a gunfight by a bad guy in black whose gun is loaded with real bullets.

Received later with equanimity in San Francisco, the play caused an uproar in its New York production not unlike the one caused by *Faggots* though on a smaller scale. But because the play was produced at a gay theater, it received little attention from the mainstream press. Otherwise, *Night Sweat* probably would have received the same sort of reviews that inflamed the *Faggots* controversy, in which conservative critics used the opportunity to praise Kramer for chastising the "lifestyle" of people they clearly hated. In 1984, these critics would have had a field day with *Night Sweat*.

Controversial as it was among those who saw it, the version of *Night Sweat* produced in New York was tamer than Chesley's rehearsal text. The original first act curtain called for the appearance of the New York Gay Men's Chorus singing "The Hankie Anthem," which detailed all the colors and codes of the handkerchiefs gay men wore at the height of liberation. At the conclusion of the anthem, Chesley called for the entire chorus to be gassed to death. The director, Nicholas Deutsch, had to plead with Chesley to cut this musical finale, fearing that the audience wouldn't return to the theater for the second act. Even toned down, the play was not a popular success. Gay men, it seemed, did not want to go to gay theaters to see plays about AIDS any more than many wanted to read Kramer's articles about it in the *Native*.[15]

□ □ □

The message of *Faggots* had been either "Sexual liberation is evil" or "Put aside destructive pursuits and seek love." *Either way, it was the message that mattered.* From the beginning of his writing career, Kramer has been a "Message Queen": a term aimed at him derisively but which he considers a compliment. Unlike other gay playwrights whose work might be seen as political after the fact, and which generally fit Wordsworth's definition of poetry as emotion recollected in tranquillity, Kramer's writing has always been (at least until *The Destiny of Me*) white-hot, of the moment, a record of emotions and experiences recorded virtually at the time they occur. It has the virtues and flaws of work created by a highly opinionated, passionate man possessing dramatic craft: raw, direct, uncompromising and, in the moment of performance, emotionally overwhelming. The material can also seem inadequately digested, unfair, overweening, impatient of other points of view, Manichaean and, in time, dated. Beginning with *Faggots*, Kramer's writing has been activist writing. Its primary purpose is to send a message; words, for him, are fighting tools.

Kramer only occasionally refers to himself as an artist. "I'm a writer who writes," he has said. "I feel useful when I'm used properly, and I enjoy using whatever gift I have for a useful purpose. What always gets my juices started is a perceived wrong and the question of how do you tell the world what the perceived wrong is. . . . Certainly, the writers who mean something to me— Dickens, Dostoyevsky, Tolstoy, Swift, Waugh, Balzac, Proust—all presented a very specific point of view concerning how they saw the world, what was wrong with it, and how to make it better."[16]

In April 1983, Kramer resigned under pressure from the Board of GMHC and found himself without a forum. The message he had been trying to convey—that gay men and women must organize and fight—had not been sufficiently heard. And now that he was speaking only for himself and not on behalf of an organization, he feared that people would be even less inclined to listen than before.

He turned again to writing. He tried putting the message into a novel called *City of Death*, but the form proved too removed, too distant for the message's urgency. Film was out of the question: he knew from his years at Columbia and United Artists that no major company would make a film about AIDS. By the summer, he had begun thinking of the material in dramatic terms. In June, he visited London and saw how many plays on political subjects were being produced—and how visceral an impact such plays could have. Performed live before an audience gathered in a public place, a play that aroused an audience's passions about a controversial issue was far more galvanic than a novel read by one individual at a time in the privacy of a living room. He was especially impressed by David Hare's *A Map of the World*, a disputatious play about self-delusion and pretension at a UN conference on poverty. Hare's reasons for the choice of subject matter could have been written by Kramer. "I deliberately chose a subject to which there was such in-built resistance and determined to make it live in the theatre."[17] Hare's example convinced Kramer that drama was the proper form in which to relate the experiences of the previous two years; he forged ahead. Next, he visited Germany, and at Dachau, his attitude toward the material came into focus. He came home and on Martha's Vineyard completed the first draft by the end of August.[18]

Given his history with elements of the gay community, his contact with mainstream media, the gay theater's lack of an effective forum and, above all, his desire for the largest, broadest audience possible, it's not surprising that, play in hand, Kramer looked for a mainstream producer. After several attempts (the mainstream theater proved almost as uninterested in a play about angry gay men and AIDS as the film companies were), he found one in Joseph Papp's Public Theater. For the Public and for Kramer, the choice turned out to be a wise one. *The Normal Heart* became the longest-running play in the Public's history, and Kramer got the visible forum he so badly wanted.

The mainstream success of *The Normal Heart* didn't endear Kramer to his enemies in the gay community. The problem with being a message queen is that people often confuse their feelings about the messenger with the validity of the message, and some of those who still hadn't forgiven him for *Faggots* indulged in what seemed to be a willful misunderstanding of *The Normal Heart*. In a harsh article published in the issue of July 2, 1985, Richard Goldstein, the gay editor of the *Village Voice*, took the play and its author to task on several counts: Kramer was a narcissist; Kramer's depiction of the events surrounding the founding of GMHC was brutal; Kramer always cast himself as the hero; Kramer always got the last word; Kramer wanted to paralyze gay men with shame; Kramer had a profound contempt for sex; Kramer was a figure of scorn in the gay community. Clearly, there was no end to Kramer's perfidy. Goldstein quoted gay critics who disliked the play and cited some of the more inflammatory mainstream reviews of *Faggots* to bolster his case ("*Faggots* is the *Uncle Tom's Cabin* for homosexual men whose worst oppression is their lack of courage to change the way they live," from the *Library Journal*, was one). And the praise for *The Normal Heart* from *New York* magazine's theater critic John Simon, widely regarded as homophobic, equaled, as it were, death. Goldstein concluded by aligning Kramer with the right-wing Christian evangelist Jerry Falwell, who was urging the federal government to identify and quarantine all HIV-positive people. Kramer, Goldstein wrote, "brings the message that homosexuals are guilty until proven innocent. And that is the crucible of self-hate."[19]

Unable to separate his dislike of Kramer from the play itself (which he barely mentions, except to quote Dr. Brookner's speeches which urge gay men to stop having sex until the cause of the disease is known), Goldstein also speculated about the reasons Kramer was getting all the attention from the mainstream press instead of William M. Hoffman, whose own play in response to AIDS had also opened that spring. The answer, Goldstein decided, was that Hoffman insisted that gay men be taken *As Is*—without criticism. The straight press wasn't about to embrace that notion, especially when it had the self-hating *Normal Heart* to throw its arms around. *The Normal Heart*'s crime was not only that it criticized gay men but that it attacked what many gay men still regarded as the crucial aspect of their identity. Now Kramer was not only a moralizing killjoy and a pill, he was a full-blown self-hating moralizing killjoy and a pill whose play was liked by the *New York Times* and cried over by John Simon.

Goldstein's other thesis was that straight audiences liked *The Normal Heart* more than gay audiences did. It seems more likely, though, that the crucial distinction between approving and disapproving audience members was whether or not they had previous knowledge of Larry Kramer or of *Faggots*. Those who knew nothing about Kramer's controversial history within the New York gay community did not necessarily see the play's central character, Ned Weeks, as Goldstein did: namely, as Kramer's self-aggrandizing image of himself. They were more likely to see Weeks as an obnoxious man who, though courageous, more often made things worse by yelling. They might even have considered him something of a failure. However they viewed Weeks, nothing came between these audience members and the play's ferocious call for action.

David Drake came to a performance of *The Normal Heart* without ever having read *Faggots*. An apolitical actor, he had only a vague notion of who Larry Kramer was. He left the theater so affected by the play's urgency that he turned himself into what he called an "actor-vist." His response, *The Night Larry Kramer Kissed Me*, went on to have a successful Off-Off Broadway run and subsequently several tours.[20] Later, Drake became editor-in-chief of *Poz*, a magazine for people with AIDS. (Less prominent was my own response. Staying in my seat for several minutes after the performance ended, drained by what I had seen and heard, I noticed that I wasn't the only one so affected: others were also unable or unwilling to leave. A short time later, I became involved in gay politics, joining the board of a gay political action committee. Only then did I learn that the playwright was roundly hated in some quarters for his past sins and that *The Normal Heart* was merely one more excuse to inflict another round of self-hatred on the gay community while the mainstream press looked on in approval.) *The Normal Heart*'s enormous success outside New York was doubtless due in part to the ability of gay and straight audiences to view the work without the distorting filter of Kramer vs. his New York gay critics.

□ □ □

Still, Goldstein must be given his due. The mainstream's response to *The Normal Heart* was as significant a factor in the play's success as its prestigious performance venue. It also ensured that gay playwrights around the country would hear about the play and consider its implications as they contemplated new directions for their own work in response to the health crisis that the mainstream culture was ignoring. By contrast, Kramer's next play, *Just Say No*, was first produced by the mainstream but less prestigious WPA Theatre, to generally negative reviews. The *Times* panned it. As a result, it was not published by the ubiquitous Samuel French, Inc., but by the smaller Broadway Play Publishing Company and received only a handful of productions. Unhappy with this lack of exposure, Kramer took the publishing rights back and assigned them to French. Still, by early 1996, almost eight years following its premiere, *Just Say No* had received only about four productions.[21] By and large, in order for a play to be seen in theaters across America, it still must receive a critically and financially successful production in New York.

While Kramer's example may well have encouraged playwrights to write about gay men and lesbians who are militant, angry or sorrowful in the face of AIDS, even the success of *The Normal Heart* has not helped most of them achieve productions in mainstream theaters outside of New York. The reason is not hard to understand. Where once the purpose of the regional theaters was to provide an alternative to New York mainstream commercial theater, now nothing succeeds in them so much as a play that has succeeded already. The regional theaters long have suffered from a serious loss of nerve, and audiences across the country have seen productions of gay plays that are stamped with the imprimatur of a New York mainstream success— *The Normal Heart, As Is, The Baltimore Waltz, Falsettos*—and few other gay plays by gay playwrights. Of these most-often produced gay plays, it is also worth noting that only *The Normal Heart* features gay men who are angry about dying and demand that the larger society confront its implication in their deaths. Gay characters in the other plays are either undemanding of society, or polite to a fault. In the regional theaters, apparently one *Normal Heart* is enough. We can forget about seeing lesbian plays by lesbian playwrights until one is produced in New York by a leading theater and acclaimed by the mainstream press.

It is still left to gay theaters to actually produce the gay work of most gay playwrights. Those who work in gay theater will continue to debate whether their ultimate purpose is to go out of business by making productions of gay and lesbian plays so common that they will begin happening with regularity in mainstream theaters. History suggests that this will not happen any time soon. History also suggests that the audience for gay and lesbian theater will always be limited. Mainstream society has little enough interest in theater about itself, let alone in theater by and about gays and lesbians. That being the case, perhaps those who work in gay theater ought to reaffirm their purpose of using drama to assert new identities for gay men and lesbians.[22]

□   □   □

If they do, then it's possible that Kramer's plays may yet find a home in gay theaters. What kept a play like *The Normal Heart* out of the New York gay theater besides its author's strained relationships with members of the gay community and his ability to be produced in the mainstream, was the undeniable difference between the play's message and the gay theater's primary purpose: identity-building. With good reason, most of the gay plays produced in New York between Stonewall and the onset of AIDS reinforced the notion that gay identity was predominantly a sexual one, and within that context, and given the reception of *Faggots, The Normal Heart* and its author were accused of being anti-erotic. But with the distance of more than a decade, the play can be viewed differently. A play that once could be viewed as identity-denying can now be seen as identity-building. Within the continuum of identities that gay men and women construct for themselves, *The Normal Heart* signaled the construction of a new identity: gay men and women as angry, fierce, implacable activists who could be as visible and vocal as necessary in order to save their own lives; unafraid of controversy or criticism, accepting nothing as the necessary status quo. This ferocity has been a party of gay identity since at least Stonewall, but with such exceptions as Jonathan Katz's *Coming Out* and Doric Wilson's 1982 *Street Theater*, rarely had it been reflected in gay theater prior to *The Normal Heart*. Under the influence of *The Normal Heart*, yet another image of gays and lesbians emerged in gay theater. Plays began depicting gay men and lesbians as caregivers when the body is no longer an object of desire. In *Falsettoland* (the third part of Finn's *Falsetto* trilogy, Marvin, Dr. Charlotte and Cordelia ("the lesbians next door") care for the dying Whizzer. Both Victor Bumbalo's *Adam and the Experts* and Ed Cachianes' *Everybody Knows Your Name* include "AIDS buddies" from organizations like GMHC among their portraits of gay men. Even John Glines' *Men of Manhattan* depicts an AIDS activist who passes up a demonstration he has organized to be with his dying brother. This last portrait is a trivial one, to be sure, but the fact that the image of an AIDS activist found its way into a play that in every other way was a throwback to the plays that depicted gay men as little more than roving penises, suggests how inescapable that image had become. Where AIDS activists begin appearing as characters in plays, one sees Kramer's influence on gay playwrights as twofold: As a co-founder of GMHC and ACT UP he provided writers with new materials and images; as a playwright, he demonstrated the powerful way in which these images could affect theater audiences. Although it never mentions AIDS by name, *The Normal Heart* is so closely tied to the events it depicts that some consider the play a period piece—but is also a record of a moment in time when what it meant to be a gay man or lesbian was undergoing a profound change.

Robert Chesley's *Night Sweat* has also been changed by the years since it was first produced. In his letter to the *Native*, Chesley wrote that if one examined Kramer's writing closely one would find that the subtext is always that the wages of gay sin are death. In *Night Sweat*, that message is not subtextual. With its depiction of gay men choosing suicide over fighting, and its sorrowful, unequivocal equation of sex equals death, the play seems more dated today than *The Normal Heart* in its depiction of gay men as passive victims. Certainly, Chesley's original first act ending is more anti-erotic than anything found in *The Normal Heart*. The conflict in *The Normal Heart* is over how a community should be organized and how a callous system should be fought: either quietly, from the closet, or publicly, and if necessary, in the streets. Either way, the characters have chosen to fight. In *Night Sweat*, the characters choose to retreat into a world of fantasy and death. The fantasies are undeniably gay and their characters own them. But it has become hard not to view the retreat into the Coup de Grâce Club as a surrender.

Controversial even in its day, Chesley depicts the same community at the same point in time seen in *The Normal Heart*, and in terms more graphic and theatrical. Next to the growing anger and demands for fighting back that Kramer portrayed, fear, denial and paralysis gripped many gay men. Chesley was not advocating surrender or suicide, but he witnessed them as two reactions among the gay men he knew, and he sensed the potential for either one in himself. It was a tragic moment for a man who had once been saved from suicide by the possibilities of gay liberation. *Night Sweat* is a period piece, too, and a more disturbing one than *The Normal Heart*: it captures a moment when, for many men, their hard-won identity as sexual beings turned on them. Kramer wrote in white-hot anger and an almost unbearable sadness; Chesley in horror. The two plays would make an interesting contrast performed today by a gay theater in repertory.

□   □   □

Robert Chesley would have more to say about Larry Kramer and much more to say about AIDS before he died of it in 1990. In the unpublished and unproduced *Pigman*, Chesley included a character who, according to Nicholas Deutsch, "believed you could change things by screaming at people." The play also contained several references to lines from *The Normal Heart*.[23]

Chesley was not the only gay playwright who had responded to what he found objectionable in Kramer's work. The same week that Chesley's response to Kramer appeared in the *Native*, the Glines opened *Pines '79* by Terry Miller. *Pines '79* is an unabashedly gay romantic comedy that takes place over a summer in the Pines on Fire Island, following five love- or sex-hungry housemates on their cheerful rounds of sex laced with the latest drugs. Curt and Hank, the house's one couple, develop serious relationship problems but after working them out, are likely to live happily ever after. Young, naive Jeff falls in love with Larry in June, only to be devastated in August when Larry is transferred to San Francisco. But Larry finds a job for Jeff in his firm and, relocated to the Castro, they are bound to live even more happily ever after than Curt and Hank. The single Brace continues his life of joyful, creatively costumed one-night stands, while John, the drug dealer and Joan Blondell of the group, will remain, less happily and more wise-crackingly, single (as of course Joan Blondell must). Miller called *Pines '79* a romantic comedy. Many who saw it no doubt considered it faithful to the culture it depicts and appreciated the cheerful non-judgmental stance it took toward its characters' actions: no one is harmed by the lives they lead and in the end, everything either works out for the best or at least is no worse than it was at the start. However, *Pines '79* was not merely a romantic comedy. It was a gay romantic comedy with an agenda. In his Notes which follow the text, Miller wrote:

> One of our more prestigious publishers recently gave us an alleged satire of contemporary gay life, which instantly became a subject of heated discussion among gay men. Almost everybody had an opinion. This was somewhat surprising, as almost nobody actually read it (which itself was not surprising, as the book is virtually unreadable). Yet the book existed,

thus raising a curious question: How did we go from silly stereotypes to self-vivisection without nurturing our lives with positive, healthy romantic fantasies?

Romantic comedy has long been a valid form of fantasy for the heterosexual masses. Although homosexuals are, either by choice or by force, often outside the stream of society's currents, this does not mean we are prohibited from Loving. Indeed, Loving has long been one of the causes championed by homosexuals, as it is the nature of our Loving that defines us, individually and collectively. We are entitled to such Romances as we choose, perhaps even with happy endings, but we cannot rely on misanthropes . . . to provide them.

Pines '79 appropriates the form of standard (i.e., hetero) Romantic Comedy, as well as certain theatrical conventions. In other matters, the play is cheerfully, straightforwardly gay. It may well be that the use of familiar theatre patterns allow straight audiences to experience something of our lives as they could not in an experimental piece, while providing gays with a well-deserved romantic fantasy. In this way, Gay Romantic Comedy may become our most subversive form of theatre.[24]

Miller hoped that gay romantic comedies would move into mainstream theaters and from there launch their subversive message that gay love is as good as straight love. This hasn't happened. That the regional theaters aren't interested in trying out a gay romantic comedy on their presumably straight audiences is one reason; another is that Americans consider culture in general and theater in particular too marginal to be subversive.

Which leads not to the question of whether Larry Kramer's plays belong in the gay theater but whether Larry Kramer belongs in the theater at all. The theater's advantage is that it is live and direct, its impact on an audience more immediate and visceral than television or film. Its disadvantage is that it reaches such a small number of people. To send a message, one is smarter to use television, magazines, the op-ed page and, increasingly, the tools of cyberspace. Gay characters—and some with AIDS—are even turning up in mainstream films.

On occasion, a play can arouse an audience to take immediate political action (one audience at Jonathan Katz's *Coming Out* marched to a nearby bar and demanded that the management remove an anti-gay sign[25]). But a play's effect is more likely to be cathartic. Indeed, since the advent of gay plays, public catharsis for grieving gay men and women has become one of the gay theater's most important functions. In its sad but necessary way, this has become another affirmation of community and identity. Some academics have said that plays about AIDS have run their useful course. This demonstrates not how much they know about "AIDS plays" but how little they understand what happens in the course of a theatrical event.[26]

Kramer himself has experienced the theater's ameliorating effects on audiences of *The Normal Heart*, and it has not made him happy. "The play doesn't seem to make people into fighters. I want them to go out there and throw bombs," he said. "It doesn't make people want to stop the wrong; it seems to make them want to *manage* the wrong."[27] It certainly didn't stir any governmental body, from the city of New York to the National Institutes of Health, to any significant action. It is simply not in the theater's nature, or in any art's, to cause swift social change. The theater has the power to change one person at a time, but Kramer is too impatient to wait for society to advance at such a glacial pace.

The question of whether theater can provoke social change is a controversial one, and so it deserves elaboration. A Larry Kramer writes *The Normal Heart* and *Just Say No* because he sees a social problem and wants society to wake up and fix it tomorrow—although today would be better. At the beginning of his career, Bernard Shaw expected the audience to rush from performances of his plays and demand—and effect—the social and economic reforms he himself demanded. Fifty years later, he had to admit that very little outside the theater had changed as a result of all his work—even after the advent of the Labour Party, which he helped to create, and the introduction of a partly socialist state. Audiences had laughed at his jokes but refused to take his prescriptions.

It is true that many regimes in many countries have feared the theater (and literature and art in general) and have suppressed it. They have done so, as Eric Bentley points out in *Thinking About the Playwright*, with good reason: A theatrical presentation is a particularly potent form of writing because it is enacted before a live audience and the things enacted take on a powerful appearance of reality, and thus may stir an audience to action. People in a crowd have the potential to act with more force and bravery (also with more cowardice) than they would were they alone. But what causes repressive regimes to fear the theater is not the image of an audience, riled by a playwright, streaming *en masse* from the auditorium to storm the seat of power, but *the circulation of ideas*, the saturation of the intellectual air with suggestions, if not proofs, that the regime is wrong, is lying, is criminal. In Eastern Europe, communist regimes were largely able to control the theater (although they could not always keep people from gathering in apartments for private performances of proscribed plays, or from scrutinizing productions of classics for hidden, contemporary meanings), but they could not as easily suppress the *samizdats* which kept free thought circulating. Such regimes could search history and find very few examples of drama that created rapid social change. The myth that the French Revolution was "caused" by Beaumarchais' *Marriage of Figaro* is just that. The mobs that liberated the Bastille or cheered as the royal family passed by in tumbrils on their way to the guillotine were not patrons of the court theater; nor were their leaders. It's unlikely that they had ever heard of Figaro.

In America, where it is difficult to know whether the public cares less about art or politics, the case is even clearer. The Congress closed down the Federal Theatre Project in 1939 not because they feared it was the vanguard of the revolution but because productions such as *One-Third of a Nation* showed certain members for the bigots that they were by quoting verbatim from *The Congressional Record*. That the American government, whomever happens to constitute it, has little to fear from the power of the arts is proved, alas, by the collective shrug the country has given as the Congress slowly kills the National Endowments for the Arts and the Humanities.

The most famous first night in American theatrical history also proves the point. Clifford Odets wrote *Waiting for Lefty* as a benefit for striking taxi drivers. The play took place at a taxi drivers' union meeting; debates over whether or not to strike alternated with scenes from the hackers' difficult lives. The story has been recounted many times about how, on that January night in 1935, when the characters took their vote at the play's climax ("Well, what's the answer?"), the audience rose, in the orchestra and balcony, and with arms thrust in the air, shouted with the characters onstage, "Strike! Strike! Strike!" They had been electrified from the first moment by the play's reflections of their own fears, frustrations and hopes. The sun rose the next morning, however, and there was no general strike. Life went on as it had before *Waiting for Lefty*.

This does not mean that lives of individuals who were in that audience were not changed. Perhaps some joined a union, or started one, volunteered for a relief agency or voted for Norman Thomas at the next election. The point is that if theater changes anything, it changes one individual at a time. That is why, as Bentley also points out, the fact that political plays do not cause social change with the speed and thoroughness that a Shaw or a Kramer desires is no reason for playwrights not to write them. There is always the hope that someone, somewhere, someday will get the message. Art works on society by the evolutionary Fabian process of permeation— ironically for Bernard Shaw.

Kramer himself has realized the futility of being a message queen in the theater. He wrote two plays after 1985: the angry farce *Just Say No*, which faltered precisely because it contains too much information and polemic for a farce to bear, and *The Destiny of Me*, which is in several respects the play *The Normal Heart* started out to be before Kramer removed his family history from it. In subsequent years, he has written scores of speeches and articles, and made several television appearances—any one of which was probably seen by more Americans than have seen the 600 productions of *The Normal Heart*.

"The experience of *Just Say No* has made me question whether or not I should be writing plays," he said, shortly after its brief New York run. "I want to get the message to the biggest possible audience, and the theatre just isn't time-, energy- or money-efficient. Especially if the *New York Times* doesn't want you to get the message out."[28]

The title *The Normal Heart* comes from W. H. Auden's "September 1, 1939," and in the published text of the play, Kramer requests that two stanzas from the poem be published in the programs of all productions. Not long after he wrote "September 1, 1939," Auden, alarmed by the temptation that his position as a famous young poet gave him to make political pronouncements, added two lines in an earlier poem, "In Memory of W. B. Yeats." The lines stated a revised belief about the power of poetry:

> For poetry makes nothing happen: it survives
> In the valley of its saying.[29]

A message, perhaps, from one (former) dedicated message queen to another.

Notes

1. This figure was arrived at by examining issues of the *New York Native* and *Out-Week* between 1985 and 1994 for reviews of plays having to do with AIDS. An exact figure would be difficult, if not impossible to come by, but both papers were particularly good about covering "AIDS plays."
2. Larry Kramer to Michael Paller, interview, November 22, 1988.
3. Eric Bentley to MP, interview, October 17, 1988.
4. David Friedman, "Larry Kramer's New Cool," *New York Newsday*, October 20, 1992.
5. Vito Russo, *The Celluloid Closet* (New York: Harper & Row, 1987), p. 326.
6. William M. Hoffman (ed.), *Gay Plays: The First Collection* (New York, 1979), p. xxiv. Hoffman's introduction provides an excellent summary of the development of gay theater in New York.
7. It may be more accurate to say in this context "gay *or* lesbian plays" since the two were and in New York largely still are, very separate enterprises. There is little documentation concerning lesbian theater in New York. My thanks to Sarah Schulman for helping me compile this partial list.
8. Indeed, he consciously avoided them. "Many of us stayed away," he later said, "because in those days a lot of gay theater appeared to be vaguely soft-core porn of saccharine soap operas with some good looking numbers." Larry Kramer to MP, interview, November 22, 1988.
9. This isn't to suggest that there were no overtly political plays in gay theaters in the 1970s. There were. Two of them were Jonathan Katz's *Coming Out* (1972) and Ron Tavel's *The Ovens of Anita Orangejuice* (1978).
10. Jonathan Ned Katz to MP, phone interview, June 6, 1996.
11. Mark I. Chester, "Robert Chesley," *Taste of Latex*, Issue 5, 1991, p. 12.
12. Robert Chesley, "A Hidden Message?", *New York Native*, October 5–18, 1981, p. 4.
13. Terry Helbing, the co-founder of the Gay Theatre Alliance, the Meridian Gay Theatre, the founder of JH Press, the co-founder of Gay Presses of New York and for thirteen years the theater editor of the *New York Native*—and thus as responsible for the production of gay theater in New York as anybody in those days—used to say that gay theater without gay sex was only sanitized gay theater. Terry Helbing, interview with MP, October 5, 1988.

14. Robert Chesley, *Night Sweat*, in *Hard Plays, Stiff Parts* (San Francisco: Alamo Square Press, 1990), pp. 73–4. Chesley's other plays about men dealing with AIDS are *Jerker* (1986), *Pigman* (see below), *The Dog Plays* (1990) and *Private Theatricals* (1990).

15. Nicholas Deutsch to MP, telephone interview, April 12, 1996. Deutsch, like Terry Helbing, has been a major contributor to gay theater, in New York and elsewhere. He directed the first productions of many of Robert Chesley's plays, as well as the 1973 Boston production of Katz's *Coming Out*, and the American premier of Noel Greig's *Poppies* at San Francisco's Theatre Rhinoceros. He also co-founded New York's Three Dollar Bill Theater (now the Molly House Theatre).

16. Michael Paller, " 'Dangerous, Unpopular and Controversial': An Encounter With Larry Kramer," *TheaterWeek*, October 17–23, 1988, pp. 8–17. See also *Reports from the holocaust* (New York: St. Martin's Press, 1989), pp. 145–8.

17. David Hare, *The Asian Plays* (London: Faber & Faber, 1986), p. xiii.

18. Patrick Merla, "Love and Death at the Public Theater: Larry Kramer Talks about *The Normal Heart*," *New York Native*, April 8–April 21, 1985; Larry Kramer to MP; telephone interview, May 9, 1996.

19. Richard Goldstein, "Kramer's Complaint," July 2, 1985, pp. 20, 22.

20. David Drake to MP, telephone interview, April 18, 1996.

21. Larry Kramer to MP, telephone interview, March 29, 1996; Linda Kerland to MP, April 10, 1995. Publication by Samuel French, or by the somewhat smaller Dramatists Play Service, is crucial to the future life of a play and to its influence on writers and producers across the country. French's catalogue is found on the shelf of virtually every American theater, from high schools to community theaters to the largest regionals. It provides exposure that a small company like the intrepid JH Press, which for many years was the leading publisher of American gay plays, could only dream of achieving.

22. See also the example of black theater in America since the early 1960s, which has followed a course similar to that of gay theaters. Begun as part of the Black Arts movement which itself was an expression of Black Liberation, the black theater has seen only a few of its artists move into the mainstream, and it has lost much of its impetus and audience.

23. Nicholas Deutsch to MP, telephone interview, April 12, 1996. Deutsch directed a staged reading of *Pigman* in December 1985.

24. Terry Miller, *Pines '79* (New York: JH Press, 1982), endnotes on unnumbered pages.

25. Hoffman, *Gay Plays*, p. xxxi.

26. See, for example, *Acting Gay* by John Clum (New York: Columbia University Press, 1992).

27. Paller, " 'Dangerous, Unpopular and Controversial'," p. 17.

28. Larry Kramer to MP, interview November 22, 1988.

29. W. H. Auden, "In Memory of W. B. Yeats," in *W. H. Auden: Selected Poems*, ed. Edward Mendelson (New York: Vintage Books, 1979), p. 80.

Larry Kramer at the Public Theater

Gail Merrifield Papp

WRITTEN WITH NOBLE FIRE in a time of cruel silence about AIDS, Larry Kramer's *The Normal Heart* showed us the human dimension of political struggle, a subject that is never out of date. This essay, recalling the play's history and its author, is indebted to my husband Joseph Papp, who produced *The Normal Heart* at the Public Theater in 1985. I have drawn on my recollections as head of the Play Department at that time, on personal papers, and on the lively, sensitive and honest reminiscences of three theater colleagues who worked on the production. For these I am deeply grateful to Emmett Foster, Bill Hart, and Rosemarie Tichler.

□ □ □

In the mid-1980s, Larry Kramer and Joseph Papp were outspoken public figures whose paths had never crossed. Both men had volatile personalities not likely to mix well in the same room. A short biographical account will set the stage for them.

Larry Kramer graduated from Yale, worked in film production, and had written a screenplay, a stage play, and a first novel about gay life in the 1970s, *Faggots,* when, in 1981, he read an article in the *New York Times* titled "Rare Cancer Found in 41 Homosexuals." He investigated the report and began to sound an alert in the gay community about the AIDS epidemic. In January 1982, he co-founded the Gay Men's Health Crisis (GMHC) to address the urgent need for medical information, services, and government action.

Larry's confrontational tactics and emphasis on a political agenda for the organization brought him into sharp disagreement with GMHC's Board. After months of feuding, Larry exploded in a now-famous call to arms titled "1,112 and Counting" in the *New York Native*. It was a howl of rage against the silence of the federal government, the Mayor, the *New York Times*, the gay community itself. It came tumbling out in a slugfest of words: "If this article doesn't scare the shit out of you we're in real trouble. If this article doesn't rouse you to anger, fury, rage and action, gay men may have no future on this earth."[1] He added that his views were not to be attributed to the Gay Men's Health Crisis. Soon after, Larry was dismissed by the GMHC Board in a bitter rupture with the organization he had helped to create.

He went abroad. He visited the Dachau concentration camp near Munich. In London he saw David Hare's *A Map of the World,* which excited him with its fusion of theater and politics. When he returned to the States, he was fired up by the idea of writing a play about his experiences with GMHC and the AIDS crisis. He rented a shack in Cape Cod and poured out the first draft, then borrowed a friend's cabin in Virginia and finished the second draft. He called the play *The Normal Heart,* from W. H. Auden's poem, "September 1, 1939."

He sent the script around in search of a production, but the response was disappointing. It was rejected by directors, producers, regional theaters, and fourteen play agents. He turned for help to Emmett Foster, a GMHC volunteer who was an Administrative Assistant to Joseph Papp, the celebrated Founder-Producer of the New York Shakespeare Festival/Public Theater. Emmett Foster recalls Larry Kramer's siege of the Public Theater:

> I'd met Larry a couple of times. He wanted to know how to get this play to Joe. I didn't know about his personality and tactics at that point. If I did, I probably would have said "All right, whatever you want, just spare me the years of aggravation." So I told him I thought he should go about it the proper way, and to give the play to Gail and the Play Department and to have it read. But he wanted Joe Papp to read his play and do his play and he really didn't want to go through the usual circuits.[2]

Emmett, who is a writer-performer,[3] read *The Normal Heart* and gave it to the Play Department. "Then Larry was at me and calling me and asking me questions. I've blocked it out like a really bad dream, but I remember him trying to manipulate me into things that I didn't really want to do."

Not having heard from Joe Papp, Larry dashed off an especially "nasty" letter to him and asked Emmett to put it on his desk. "That was Larry going into Plan B," Emmett says:

> He goes on the attack, and wrote Joe something like "Your own son is gay and you don't want to do this play because you're homophobic." I remember *exactly* what I said to Larry. I said, "I will be *happy* to give this letter to Joe from you. I will be more than happy to take it in there and put it on his desk. But I just want to tell you, if Joe reads this letter, you will not have your play produced at this theater. Joe doesn't go for that kind of tactic. But I'll be *real* happy to go in there right now and put it on his desk." So he came to his senses and said "All right, don't."

I didn't know how to tell Larry that I didn't think it was a well-written play. Of course, when I was reading all these facts, they're very dramatic and very effective, and if you're a gay man in the middle of the AIDS crisis, yes, it's got some resonance. But it was hard for me to tell Larry things. He came to the theater once, and was right outside of Joe's office, and was saying to me "Well, what the *fuck*, he's doing that *Cinders* thing up there in that hall" and I said, "Larry, *Cinders* is a well-*written* play."

This was the thing that I thought would snap our relationship. What I didn't know about Larry then was, don't be shy and bashful and co-dependent because nothing you could say is gonna hurt *his* feelings.

Joseph Papp was born Yussel Papirofsky, the son of Jewish immigrants from Eastern Europe. He graduated from high school in Brooklyn during the Depression, served in the Navy during the war, and studied theater on the G.I. Bill. Redbaited during the McCarthy era, he was fired from his job as a television stage manager at CBS. He became a public figure during a David-and-Goliath dispute with Parks czar Robert Moses, which brought attention to his free productions of Shakespeare in Central Park and to the New York Shakespeare Festival, which he founded in 1954.

In 1966 Joe acquired an abandoned building in downtown Manhattan where he launched the Public Theater, a five-theater complex devoted to new American plays. The building became *the* place for new writers in the era of the civil rights movement and the Vietnam War. At the Public Theater Joe produced a broad range of socially driven work from David Rabe's Vietnam plays to Ntozake Shange's choreopoems, from *Hair* to *A Chorus Line*.

In the early 1980s, Joe pondered on the fact that this era was over. "The theater reflects the world, and the mood is very conservative now. There's no question the country has seen a diminution of the kind of energy a place like this draws on."[4]

Unhappy about the lack of American plays with social content, he turned to British playwrights David Hare and Caryl Churchill, and redirected his prodigious energies to political causes— including several AIDS organizations that his son Tony, who was a volunteer at GMHC, put him in touch with.

"When GMHC had its first fundraiser, they *sold out* Madison Square Garden. It was the circus," Emmett recalls:

It was the largest fundraising event that ever happened at Madison Square Garden. Mayor Koch was there, and Leonard Bernstein conducted; there were stars and politicians. And, you know, anytime Koch went out of his *apartment*, it was always in the paper. But there was not *one mention* of this event in the papers. You'd at least expect to see the stars on the gossip page.

I was driving in the car with Joe, and I was really upset, and I said,

"Something horrible has happened. Last night GMHC had its first fundraiser and no one followed up." I told him the whole story. Joe said "This is not right. Something has to be done. When I get back to the office, I'll call the papers and ask them why it wasn't covered." I started crying in the car because I was so moved that he had so much power and would use it. Everybody else was like "What happened?" They didn't know what to do, whereas Joe picked up the phone.

With this as prologue, Larry Kramer is about to make his official entrance.

Bill Hart, the Public Theater's Literary Manager,[5] put a very thick script on my desk one day and said "I think you should read this. It's a play about AIDS. The text is *interminable*, but there are all these little veins of interest—a little bit of gold here and there—in all the sludge. I think it has possibilities."[6]

Reading *The Normal Heart* was tough sledding. The mammoth script seemed like two plays vying to occupy the same space. One was a family drama about a gay brother and a straight brother. The other was an angry political drama about the gay community's response to the AIDS crisis. The script was clumsy. Characters spouted pages of medical facts that were unactable. It had no shape. When I finished it, however, I was moved. Somehow it had taken me on a tumultuous, if confusing and awkward, journey, and I was interested in talking to the author.

After reading such an angry play, I was surprised that Larry Kramer was a warm and genial personality. He brought his little dog with him. He liked the homey atmosphere of my office and settled right in. His dog went to sleep under a table. Larry chuckled and laughed and seemed almost jovial. He was like a Jewish Santa Claus, I thought, but grey and grizzled.

I told him what I liked in the script, then asked a question about something that I didn't understand. To my amazement, he took out a large notebook and began writing furiously. The following week he came back clutching rewrites, eager to do more. I was fortunate in being entirely ignorant of his recent expulsion from GMHC. I couldn't "read" it into the play. So, I inadvertently brought his attention to many elements he thought were present, but, which, in fact, weren't there. He liked the methodology of questions because when he tried to explain something to me, things became clearer in his own mind. He loved to rewrite and was very fast and smart at it.

He thus began a process that I remember with much admiration and affection. For several weeks Larry would drop by frequently. I looked forward to seeing him and became excited as a powerful play began to emerge from its disorderly matrix.

The play's anger was huge, biblical, upsetting. Ned Weeks, the Jewish protagonist who is Larry's alter ego, says:

Do you know that when Hitler's Final Solution to eliminate the Polish Jews was first mentioned in the *Times* it was on page twenty-eight. And on page six of the *Washington Post*. And the *Times* and the *Post* were owned by Jews. What causes silence like that?[7]

Bill Hart followed Larry's work on the script with keen interest, wanting to be involved. "I realized that we were in a situation where something *drastic* was going on—and that nobody *cared*," Bill says. "Now here was a play about it. This is unusual, that a play was about an emergency taking place *right now*, and it affected my own community."

Emmett remembers being struck by the fact that "There was the real drama of the play, and the real situation of people dying all around and nobody noticing. The play was in the middle of the whole thing. Larry's anger needed to be there to be the engine to get something done. On the other hand, it is out of control sometimes and is *the* thing that will keep any progress from being made. It's a really interesting problem in life and in the play."

Larry worked hard, without any guarantee of a production or an option, and was impatient for Joe to read the script. He told me that the number of AIDS cases was increasing at an alarming rate every week, the government was doing nothing, the media was silent, and his play had to be done immediately so people would know that an emergency existed. I learned that he was sending the script to other theaters. I thought about what I should do.

Early on, Joe and I discovered that we had very similar tastes in plays. This was surprising because we had such different backgrounds. I was a child of the Depression, like him, but had been raised in Berkeley, California by parents who were writers of the lyrical left. I had composed music and worked in publishing and theater before coming to the Festival in 1965, when Joe gave me the task of finding new American plays.

I knew he read a play quickly and formed an opinion in a few pages. He could seldom be induced to read further if he didn't like it. He often held the messenger accountable to his displeasure, but he trusted my judgment. What good would it do, I thought, to give him the script now? It was still impossibly long—I figured it would take five hours to perform and it suffered from split focus. Joe would certainly turn it down.

One day Larry told me cheerfully that he had cut all the stuff he loved the best. He had taken out *all* the flashback scenes between the two brothers. He would make another play of them!

"Okay," I told Larry, "I'll give the script to Joe."

In this new version, the main line of the story could be seen clearly. It takes place in New York City from July 1981 to May 1984. Ned Weeks, a journalist, writes blistering indictments against the government and the media for ignoring the AIDS crisis. He is estranged from a straight brother.

As his lover Felix dies from the disease, his partners in a gay health organization repudiate his confrontational tactics and oust him.

I had learned that there was never a good time to ask Joe to read a play and that it usually spoiled his mood. I took the bull by the horns at home. Joe describes the scene:

> Gail told me that she had found an interesting play about AIDS. She says it's a monster, it's huge but she thinks it has great possibilities. I said "Gail, I don't want to read a play about AIDS. I hate to do plays about cancer. I hate to do plays about illness. I have no time to read it." So she left it for a few days. Came back, says "Would you just try to read it?" I said "Gail, I don't want to read this play. It'll only depress me to read about it." So after about a week or so, she finally said "Just begin it." So I said "All right, but I'll tell you right now, I'm not gonna like it."
>
> So I pick it up and I read the first twenty pages and I put it down and say "Gail, I can't get through this play. It's overwritten, it's overblown." She didn't say a word, so I pick it up again a day or so later and I *plow* and *plow* my way through the play, and at each point I put it down, I say, "I can't get any further with this. There's a moment here and there, but some of the stuff is so poor, and so outrageous." Finally I get through the whole thing and say, "This is one of the worst things I've ever read"—*and I'm crying.* I was crying! Could you believe that? I was so moved, because there was so much feeling in the play. The heart of *The Normal Heart* was beating there.[8]

Larry was jittery about meeting Joe. He'd heard about his temper and was afraid they'd have a fight. Joe also had been prepped for a clash. "Everybody told me about Larry. They said, 'He's an impossible man. He threatens, cajoles, wheedles. He does anything to get you. Beware of him, he's a bad number.' However what struck me as so beautiful in his play was that he was very honest about himself."

Joe greeted Larry in his office, a small room lined with colorful posters of award-winning productions. He told him he'd produce *The Normal Heart* but expected him to do more work on the script. To Larry this meant further delay. He badgered Joe: "But it's a *wonderful* play. Why aren't you doing it *now?*"

After he left, Joe called Literary Manager Bill Hart into his office. "Someone has to get control of the structure," he said confidentially. "Meet with him. See what you can do."

□ □ □

"The combination of people surrounding Larry was amazing," Bill Hart remembers:

> You had this very powerful and intelligent producer, Joseph Papp. A real tough guy, but he was our tough guy. He was on the side of the angels.

Then you have Gail who is also a formidable person, but Gail, you see, is not frightening or intimidating. You had a director, Michael Lindsay-Hogg, who was a real gentleman, always empathetic to trauma in his past work, no ego flying around at all. He listened to everybody, and immediately absorbed me as somebody to help him.

Then you had something very unusual—the writer himself, Larry Kramer, who's a homosexual moralist—outspoken, righteous, dealing with right and wrong and what has to be done—in a culture of *playboys*, which has a whole list of laws like "Leave us alone to our vices, we've barely had a chance to enjoy them." It's unusual to have a person saying *I accuse*. This is not what we're used to, except against the right wing. The homosexual is generally not in this position to be the moral rebel, let alone turn on his own community, and not be a pompous bore or goody-goody.

It was so interesting to have a different type of homosexual writer. This was a writer who wasn't relying on inversions. This is not Genet or Cocteau. This was not a writer invested in deviousness. Quite the contrary, he was invested in being *truthful*. In a sense, in being straight. There's a robustness, a vigor, a directness in the writing, rather than cleverness and charm. Here's a guy who in all his fury is coming right at you. Well, I thought, this is actually refreshing!

For me, the play's turmoil suggested a whole history of overwhelming prejudice and aversion—of things that had been denied by other people to the characters—and to us. And of things that had not been faced by the gay people themselves—all this deviousness and role-playing. This is interesting, and I think it's a key element in the play.

Take the lover of Ned Weeks—Felix. He's a glamorous but rather familiar archetype of the homosexual world. He's in fashion and style and he's quite clever. But he wouldn't mind eventually saying that Dostoevsky was *his* favorite writer too. Meaning that it is all right to be *substantial* as well as charming, that you don't always *have* to be this very sardonic, hip sort of guy. It's okay to be different from that. It's all right to take things "seriously."

Larry was a most attentive person, objective, pleasant, so invested. No temperament. We never had an argument. Some things he would ignore when we talked and other things he would go with. When I said something that puzzled him, the look on his face was like a cross-eyed bird or a pelican that had been hit on the head by a rock.

While working on the script, Larry was needed at auditions and technical meetings. "By the time *The Normal Heart* got its production," Emmett says, "I'd heard around the theater that people had *had* it with Larry. I heard the casting office didn't want him in there. Andy wouldn't let him in the production office. I heard that he threw a pair of costume shoes—'These are *ugly*!'—out a third-floor window. I don't know if that's true. But I had *had* it with him."

Rosemarie Tichler, the Casting Director, now Artistic Producer of the Joseph Papp Public Theater, recalls her struggles with Larry during the casting process.

> He had a critical edgy stance always. He would joke about his dog, and other things, but there wasn't a real sense that we were in this together. He didn't trust anyone to do their job professionally and he maneuvered in outrageous ways. If Larry in any way felt attacked, you would be dead.
>
> I remember when I first came to the Festival in the 70s, Joe went to the City Council to try and get a Gay Rights Bill passed. His sense of justice was always that people should be treated fairly. I believed in *The Normal Heart*. There was a perception that this play was gay-friendly, and I was proud that Joe was doing it. Once the production appeared, on my side I fully realized how effective and powerful the play was, and he realized he had a superb cast, and we both came out of the work with a great deal of respect for each other. He wrote it to me and I felt it for him.[9]

In person Joe found Larry to be "very warm and generous," as I had, and never troublesome, despite his hectoring him about doing the play sooner. "I wouldn't want to have him for an enemy," Joe said, "but fortunately he's a friend."[10]

□ □ □

Larry *was* an enemy of New York City's Mayor, Edward Koch, and of the *New York Times*, with whom Joe had important relationships that could affect the survival of his theater. The play is peppered with Larry's animosity toward them. Ned Weeks flings down the gauntlet:

> It is no secret that I consider the Mayor to be, along with the *Times*, the biggest enemy gay men and women must contend with in New York. Until the day I die I will never forgive this newspaper and this Mayor for ignoring this epidemic that is killing so many of my friends.[11]

Joe decided to call the Mayor and the *Times*.

Mayor Koch was Joe's landlord—the City owned the Public Theater and the Delacorte Theater in Central Park. Joe had campaigned for him, but their cordial relationship cooled when Koch slashed the City's arts budget in 1980. Joe had fired off an angry open letter to him addressed "Et Tu, Brute?"

Matters got worse in 1982, when Joe mounted a highly visible campaign opposing the destruction of Broadway's best dramatic theaters to make way for a hotel, a plan endorsed by the Mayor. Joe led hundreds of people in a two-week protest in the Broadway district, yelling "Shame on Koch!" through a bullhorn on national television. The Mayor was so furious at him that it was rumored he was trying to cut the budget for Shakespeare in the Park by 85 percent.

Joe "does" his phone call to Ed Koch:

I said "Mister Mayor, I have a play here about AIDS. I'm going to put it on. The playwright criticizes you and the administration. Whether it's true or not, he wrote it. He says it's true. I'm not going to be a censor, and I just wanted to let you know." He says "Fine, Joe, thank you for telling me." Very pleased.

Two days later, the *New York Post* comes out saying something to the effect that the Mayor had called me and said "Don't do this play." I get a call. I'm just about getting up. It's eight o'clock in the morning—the phone rings.

"Hello?"

"This is Ed."

"Ed who?"

It was the Mayor. He says "Listen, did I call you and tell you not to do this play?"

I said "No, you didn't."

He says "Well, it says in the paper you said—"

I said "I never said that. I'll call them and tell them that's not true."[12]

Joe was friendly with *New York Times* editors Abe Rosenthal and Arthur Gelb. He had known them for many years, and they enjoyed each other's company. Gelb had written the first review of the Festival in 1957, and ever since then, despite Joe's feuds with its theater critics, the *Times* had been supportive of him and kept his theatrical institution before the public eye. To damage this unique relationship would be suicidal.

Larry's grievance against the *Times* had to do with its meager coverage in the first year-and-a-half of the AIDS epidemic compared to its extensive coverage of a scare about poisoned Tylenol. Ned Weeks says:

Have you been following the Tylenol scare? In three months there have been seven deaths, and the *Times* has written fifty-four articles. The month of October alone they ran one article every single day. Four of them were on the front page. For us—in seventeen months they've written seven puny articles. And we have a thousand cases![13]

After checking the accuracy of the facts, Joe called his friend Arthur Gelb.

I said, "Artie, listen, I'm doing a play here, and it's critical of the *Times*."

He says "What do you mean! We were the first ones to put that thing in the paper! Didn't we have it on June 27th? We had the story on this thing. How can you say that?"

"No," I said, "it was not June 27th. It was August. Mind you, Artie, I didn't write the play. I'm putting on the play because it's an important theme and subject. If you think he's wrong, sue him."[14]

"I was in the office," Bill Hart says, "when he picked up the telephone and called Koch personally, and called the big boys at the *Times*, all of whom, of course, he knew personally, and said 'I have a play that is going to severely criticize your institution—and you personally, Ed—and I'm going to go ahead with it. I can't censor my writer.' To me it was an example of Joe Papp's grasp of what is important and what is not important. In other words, what's the worth of theater if we can't tell the *truth*?"

□ □ □

Larry and Bill worked well together. The script changed significantly. Two hours were cut. An important new scene went in. As the press opening of *The Normal Heart* approached, the play was in good shape. It was raw, a little crass, but, as Joe said, a little crassness is good, because the theater is a very earthy kind of institution. Larry's terror of Joe had long since disappeared, and he had come to regard him with enthusiastic affection as a kind of big Daddy.

The Normal Heart opened on April 21, 1985. Emmett says:

I was there with Raymond Jacobs and a whole bunch of people, and people were sitting around us who were the characters in the play, who had started GMHC. And something had happened with the play, because from the very beginning of it—I'm beginning to feel it right now—I was so moved, I was crying through the whole thing.

And I was in the middle of these people who were *not* crying, who were sitting there with their arms folded, who thought Larry was deifying himself. But he wasn't deifying himself because he showed in the play how obnoxious he was, and he realized how these people came to the conclusion "We have to cut him loose if we're going to go ahead."

After the play I went up to Larry. I hadn't talked to him for *weeks* before this. I was still crying, and I said "Larry, it was so powerful. What an incredible piece of theater. Please don't misunderstand these tears; I still think that you're a big asshole, but the play was so incredibly moving..." And he laughed. Once again, I'd learned you could say anything to him.

Bill remembers watching the play and thinking that "The very style of it, the momentum of it, the heat, was like the AIDS crisis itself—the craziness, the contradictory information, one kind of truth compounded with another kind of revelaton—so that the audience was basically just knocked all over the place, or driven crazy, or terribly moved."

By an unexpected twist of fate, a second play about AIDS opened off-Broadway just a few days before *The Normal Heart*.[15] It received excellent reviews, and we heard that it was moving to Broadway. To Emmett, "It was

sort of a Neil Simon version of an AIDS play compared to *The Normal Heart.*"
Larry was worried because, he said, the critics would not give good reviews
to two plays about AIDS opening the same week.

At the opening night party, Joe read the *Times* review out loud to Larry,
the director, the cast, and others who hovered around him. When he finished, it was clear that the favorable notice had gone to the other show.
Disappointment hung in the air.

Later that year Joe wrote his own evaluation of the play in his Foreword
to the published book:

> Larry Kramer's *The Normal Heart*, is a play in the great tradition of Wes-
> tern drama. In taking a burning social issue and holding it up to public
> and private scrutiny so that it reverberates with the social and personal
> implications of that issue, *The Normal Heart* reveals its origins in the
> theater of Sophocles, Euripides and Shakespeare. In his moralistic fervor,
> Larry Kramer is a first cousin to nineteenth-century Ibsen and twenti-
> eth-century Odets and other radical writers of the 1930s. Yet, at the heart
> of *The Normal Heart*, the element that gives this powerful political play its
> essence, is love—love holding firm under fire, put to the ultimate test,
> facing and overcoming our greatest fear: death.
>
> I love the ardor of this play, its howling, its terror and its kindness. It
> makes me very proud to be its producer and caretaker.[16]

Bill Hart:
There was something about this ritual going on downtown night after
night after night in the theater. There was a kind of testifying going on, a
kind of witnessing. It affected people and it definitely did *change* things.
Maybe Rock Hudson died and changed things too. But I'll tell you
something: What the play had to do with AIDS is one thing. What it had
to do with homosexual consciousness is quite another. *That* is what it
really changed."

It had to do with being able to be free people, and to be reflective
people, and to be as gentle as they wish, and as open and sexy as they like
to be at the same time. You don't have to be obsessed with that if you don't
want to be. Who cares? The point is you can sit down at the table with the
other characters in the play, all of whom are flawed and maybe nutty too,
but they're just the rest of *mankind.* They're not *specially* fucked up.

Joseph Papp:
Every night, at the end of *The Normal Heart*, ten, twelve or fifteen young
men would sit there and be unable to move, absolutely stunned. Sit in
their chairs, not leave. What would happen is, several other people in the
audience, mostly men, would go over and sit with that person. Downstairs, another play called *Tracers* was running—a moving portrayal of

young men dying in Vietnam. Exactly the same thing. All the Vietnam veterans would come over to a veteran, sit there and put an arm around him. You could have duplicated those two scenes. They both dealt with the same thing—buddies under fire, under threat of death.[17]

All kinds of people came to see the play. Sometimes there was a stretch limo parked in front of the Public Theater waiting for its celebrated passenger. "Leonard Bernstein came to see *The Normal Heart*," Bill recalls. "He was really quite impressed, and was interested in the list that Ned Weeks recites in the play of all these famous artists, writers, and respected thinkers in history who were homosexual. And he said 'Oh, this is great! Am I going to be on there next?' So even somebody like him was taken aback."

NED WEEKS: I belong to a culture that includes Proust, Henry James, Tchaikovsky, Cole Porter, Plato, Socrates, Aristotle, Alexander the Great, Michelangelo, Leonardo da Vinci, Christopher Marlowe, Walt Whitman, Herman Melville, Tennessee Williams, Byron, E. M. Forster, Lorca, Auden, Francis Bacon, James Baldwin, Harry Stack Sullivan, John Maynard Keynes, Dag Hammarskjold . . . These are not invisible men. . . . The only way we'll have real pride is when we demand recognition of a culture that isn't just sexual. It's all there—all through history we've been there; but we have to claim it, and identify who was in it, and articulate what's in our minds and hearts and all our creative contributions to this earth.[18]

Joe couldn't bear to close the show. It was important to have it there, he said. He kept it going even when audiences were small. When he finally closed it on January 5, 1986, it had run longer than any other play at the Public Theater. That was not the end, however. It opened in 1986 at the Royal Court and Albery Theatres in London, where it was named Best Play of the Year. By the end of the 1980s, Larry Kramer's howl in the wilderness had had six hundred productions in eighteen countries.

Notes

1. Larry Kramer, "1,112 and Counting," *New York Native*, Issue 9, March 14–27, 1983.
2. Emmett Foster, conversation with Gail Papp, 1995.
3. *Emmett: A One-Mormon Show.*
4. David Richard, "The Passionate Pace of Joseph Papp. American Theater's Dedicated Whirlwind," *New York Times*, March 21, 1982.
5. Subsequently, Bill Hart was the director of *Cuba and His Teddy Bear* on Broadway and of other plays at the Public Theater.
6. Bill Hart, conversation with Gail Papp, 1995.
7. Larry Kramer, *The Normal Heart* (New York: Plume, NAL Penguin Books, 1985), p. 50.
8. Joseph Papp, "Oral History of the New York Shakespeare Festival," Estate of Joseph Papp/New York Shakespeare Festival, unpublished material, 1987.

9. Rosemarie Tichler, conversation with Gail Papp, 1995.
10. Papp, "Oral History."
11. Kramer, *The Normal Heart* p. 73.
12. Papp, "Oral History."
13. Kramer, *The Normal Heart* p. 82.
14. Papp, "Oral History."
15. *As Is* by William Hoffman.
16. Kramer, *The Normal Heart* p. 23.
17. Papp, "Oral History."
18. Kramer, *The Normal Heart* p. 114.

PART FIVE

Personal and Political

We Must Love One Another Or Die:

Larry Kramer, AIDS Activism and Monumental Social Change

Rodger McFarlane

W HERE WERE YOU the first time you heard Larry Kramer scream-ing? Did you cringe watching George Bush shouted down at the international AIDS conference in San Francisco, or Ronald Reagan booed at Liz Taylor's first big Washington gala? What did you think the country had come to when ACT UP infiltrators shut down the New York Stock Exchange?

Those are the images most Americans conjure up when you mention AIDS activism. It's not unlike that creeping sense of embarrassment felt by some gay rights advocates when confronted with drag queens or bull dykes on public occasions, or some highly accomplished women in the presence of a shrill, ideological colleague wearing no makeup and a bad suit. We say we cherish free expression, but most people just can't stand a scene.

It's ironic how we cling to these extreme archetypes, remembering our social discomfort far more acutely than the substance of the struggle or the outcomes. Avoiding conflict is a survival instinct we picked up as children, but—as history has repeatedly taught us—it is a dangerous impulse in grown-ups who influence public policy. Much as the modern gay civil rights movement owes to the transvestites who went toe-to-toe with the cops at Stonewall, the same way a generation of feminists took heart from the literal bra-burners, AIDS activism sowed the seeds of monumental social change benefiting millions of people far beyond this plague.

Long before ACT UP was a twinkle in Larry Kramer's eye, years before a new generation of activists took the fight to the streets, a few good men and women inspired by Kramer were already hard at work. By the time AIDS had a name, Gay Men's Health Crisis co-founder Paul Popham (now dead of AIDS), former National Gay Task Force director and Mario Cuomo-confidante Virginia Apuzzo, and the late (of AIDS) New York State Supreme Court justice Richard Failla, had already talked the governor and New York state legislature into modest appropriations for AIDS research, services and education. Cleve Jones and other San Francisco gay activists had the ear of then-mayor Dianne Feinstein and health commissioner Mervyn Silverman, and set about to establish a system of care and treatment that, like GMHC, still serves as a model today. Mathilde Krim, fresh from the interferon battles in the cancer wars, set up a foundation and began pestering the research establishment.

Soon other beachheads were established. Susan Steinmetz, former chief of staff of the late New York Congressman Ted Weiss, and attorney Jay Lipner (now dead of AIDS), successfully petitioned the commissioner of Social Security in 1983 to add AIDS to the official list of disabling conditions, making people with the syndrome eligible for Medicaid, Medicare and a host of other entitlements, and thus invoking federal civil rights protections for disabled people—revolutionary breakthroughs at the time. At Kramer's and Steinmetz's urging, the first of dozens of Congressional hearings on the federal response to AIDS were conducted by Weiss beginning in the summer of 1983 (a mantle later assumed by Representative Henry Waxman of California and his aide Tim Westmoreland), resulting in appropriations for the Centers for Disease Control to staff its first AIDS office, and prompting seminal reports from the Office of Technology Assessment, the Surgeon General, the Secretary of Health, the National Academy of Sciences, and the Office of Management and Budget—documents that define the AIDS dialectic in government circles to this day, and far more fundamentally so than those latter-day press affairs referred to as Presidential Commissions.

Jay Lipner and I set precedent in 1984 by successfully lobbying the New York Board of Health to prohibit discharge of people with AIDS from the hospital to shelters or the street or alone, which caused health care providers and insurers across America to join the appropriations battles (or at least to get out of our way) because they were suddenly stuck with the patients in house. Legal aces from the Bar Association for Human Rights of Greater New York, Lambda Legal Defense and Education Fund and GMHC (most notably Professor Art Leonard, Abby Rubenfeld, Steve Gittleson, Bill Hibsher, Tim Sweeney and Patricia Maher) were already winning major suits under existing law by 1984, and settling out of court many more legal actions against powerful landlords and giant employers and insurers who used AIDS as a reason for eviction or termination or denial of benefits, setting the stage for passage of the Americans with Disabilities Act and literally hundreds of local laws enacted over the next ten years to protect people with AIDS across America.

By 1985 upwards of $400 million was being leveraged annually from individuals and private foundations, thousands of volunteers were recruited and trained, hundreds of local AIDS service organizations had been built around the country, and these groups had created the AIDS Action Council as their full-time lobby in Washington, DC. It was executives from these ASO's who won legal guarantees for confidentiality and counseling when HIV antibody testing technology was developed, as well as passage of the Ryan White Care Act and its predecessors—not to mention defeating a litany of reactionary initiatives in Congress and state legislatures, ranging from mandatory name reporting to an endless list of line-item budget cuts. By fighting case by case in the face of institutional neglect and abuse of people with AIDS, the community-based organizations set a standard of care unrivaled by any group of patients in medical history. They also seized great moral authority and clinical expertise in the process.

What weighed heavily on us at the time, what forced us to take direct personal action beginning day one, was the lack of leadership and initiative from the medical and public health establishment and our progressive friends who did not perceive themselves to be at risk. The late Linda Laubenstein, a distinguished hematologist at New York University Medical Center and one of the original discoverers of the syndrome (immortalized as Dr. Emma Brookner in Larry Kramer's *The Normal Heart*), provides a friendly example.

Laubenstein's work and her institution depended heavily on large government and corporate research grants and contracts. Consequently, public criticism of priorities dictated at the National Institutes of Health or the pharmaceutical manufacturers, by her or anyone else in her position, was thought to be professionally suicidal. Biomedical research was—and still is—a very exclusive club where breaking rank had transformed others before her into instant pariahs in the competition for funds. If her pleas were ignored in private, she felt that she had little recourse. Linda, like the rest of her colleagues, did not think the fight was worth risking her position over. She at least told Kramer and many of the rest of us what she thought. (In fact, Larry Mass was the first and only physician to speak critically in the American press for nearly three years.)

Similarly, Laubenstein—like many others—believed something transmissible was going around and that gay men should curtail their sex lives until we knew what, but she had no conclusive evidence or official support to advise such a thing publicly at the time. With people literally lying in feces and unfed in our great hospitals, with more cases showing up at the door every day, professional associations, public health officials and government leaders remained mostly silent. For years the only information available to the public and those at risk came from the community groups or from wildly conflicting press reports. We hadn't even managed to get a meeting with the mayor of New York—the epicenter of the epidemic as we knew it at the time—during the first two years.

I mention landing that first obscure meeting with Ed Koch in 1983, because that's where AIDS activism actually was first taken to the streets. AIDS was originally noticed among gay men in the big cities, a group that included some extraordinarily privileged and well-connected people. Many of us had what my dear friend Susan Richardson, a professor of community health at Sophie Davis Medical School in New York and an early AIDS pioneer, calls "a highly developed sense of entitlement." When our friends and lovers got sick, we sought the best medical care, raised money, hired lawyers, alerted the press and cashed in chits with our representatives in government. What success we had enjoyed in life had come from perfecting the role of what writer Andrew Tobias termed "the best little boy in the world." We played by the rules; we usually won by being among the finest in our fields. We were stunned when we ran up against purely political rebuffs in the face of so much suffering and death. Never as white, middle-class men had we experienced such impotence.

While we were working our butts off and people were starting to die by the hundreds in 1981 and 1982, Ed Koch—afraid of appearing too friendly to gays and loath to announce a contagious epidemic in this mecca of commerce and tourism—had all along refused to meet with us to discuss the needs of people with AIDS in New York. After two years of going through appropriate channels, Larry Kramer picketed outside Lenox Hill Hospital where the mayor was speaking one day. It was a slow news day, so Kramer and his rag-tag band, drenched with rain, made the papers and local TV. Koch, facing a tough re-election campaign, was incensed and hastily set about to meet with any one of us working in AIDS *except* Larry. A few of us were beginning to learn about the power of political coercion and the facility of good-cop/bad-cop schemes.

ACT UP was born in 1987 when Larry Kramer substituted at the last minute for writer Nora Ephron in a lecture series at the Lesbian and Gay Community Services Center in New York. By this time the community groups were long since overwhelmed completely, the so-called second epidemic among the very poor was horribly apparent to us, and too many bureaucratic and strictly political barriers to progress in AIDS treatment and research had become plain. People were tired of raising money and caring for the sick only to wake up to more death day after day, year after year. AZT had just been approved for use in AIDS, and—in response to Kramer's impromptu call—we staged our first public demonstration against Burroughs Wellcome's exhorbitant charges for this old "new" drug by shutting down Wall Street during the morning rush hour.

Burroughs Wellcome executives were shocked to see their rising star take a nasty dip in front of investors and the competition, and even more profoundly disturbed at the prospect of defending their corporate practices in the press. The FDA regulators and NIH advisors who had approved the deal were on the defensive, and politicians, public health officials and other drug companies all could see their turns coming. We had created a harsh new political and economic downside to ignoring people with AIDS. Suddenly the government and industry players found themselves negotiating with the street activists, alongside emerging national leaders like Jean McGuire of the AIDS Action Council, Urvashi Vaid of NGLTF and the late (of AIDS) Tom Stoddard of Lambda Legal Defense.

The next few years were marked by tremendous achievement as a direct result of public demonstrations and media manipulation by ACT UP chapters that had sprung up around the globe—tactics that had served other civil rights movements before, but had never been used *en masse* by a disease group. I'll never forget that newly found feeling of power following that first demo. I led the first contingent into lower Broadway to block traffic, was arrested after giving several well-rehearsed sound bites to the waiting press, booked, released, and back at my desk at Sloan-Kettering before 9:00 a.m. The judge who later heard our case dismissed the charges based on our claim that we had acted in moral conscience, having exhausted all our legal remedies. The best little boys and girls in the world *redux*.

For all their perceived excesses, the men and women of ACT UP delivered historic reforms including accelerated approval of investigational new drugs by the FDA, expanded compassionate use of new drugs and new applications of old drugs, statistical alternatives to double-blinded-placebo-controlled studies, community-based research models, ground-breaking science in basic immunology, virology and disease prophylaxis, as well as consumer scrutiny and political oversight of NIH appropriations and FDA regulations—revolutionary changes which were long overdue and which will have a profound impact on the lives of all Americans for years to come. As a direct result, consumers are now regularly involved at all levels of development with many pharmaceutical manufacturers and government agencies in the design and funding of research protocols, regulatory approval applications, and marketing and advertising campaigns—and not just in AIDS. (Witness the sophisticated activism of breast cancer survivors, or Michael Milkin's and Norman Schwartzkopf's advocacy in prostate cancer research.)

ACT UP's halcyon days ended in part because of its very nature. The lack of formal organization and hierarchy gave voice to many talented new activists, and focused public attention and political will on many critical but overlooked issues like housing, addiction treatment, and the needs of women and racial minorities. Too often, unfortunately, it also lead to agendas far too broad for any non-government group to sustain, and an organizational inability to set priorities or specific, attainable goals among such a long list of righteous grievances.

What ultimately caused ACT UP to recede, however, was the harsh reality of a new communicable disease without a cure. In ACT UP's heyday, we all were sustained by a passionately held belief that effective treatment

for AIDS could be found if bureaucratic and political barriers were eliminated. While successes accumulated (and more new barriers cropped up as
they always have and will), the activists began to learn a great deal about
research and the nature of scientific progress. It began to dawn on the
hardest working and best informed among us that definitive treatment
would likely be decades away, that a cure or a vaccine is only theoretically
possible until a mountain of research yet to be started is complete. With
thousands still dying—including many leading activists—and with hope so
delayed, most mere mortals could not sustain the fight at the street level.
The novelty of confrontational theater had worn thin with the press, and
our supporters and the public had tired of the seemingly indiscriminate
indictments. People were finally more put off by the antics than indignant
about the injustices. Clear victories inevitably gave way to modest incremental progress.

In recent years, AIDS activism on the national level has passed into the
hands of a very small group of men who rose to prominence in the late
1980s. These include treatment activists Martin Delaney, founding director
of Project Inform in San Francisco, and stalwarts Peter Staley and Mark
Harrington of the ACT UP spin-off, the Treatment Action Group. They,
along with POZ magazine publisher and PWA Sean Strub, and a few select
others are the faces you routinely see at the various FDA and NIH committee and task force meetings. They are the ones on the phone every day with
the pharmaceutical brass. On the legislative, regulatory, and appropriations
fronts are Michael Isbell and David Barr, seasoned attorneys formerly in
GMHC's public policy and medical information offices, Mark Senak at
AIDS Project Los Angeles, along with Mario Cooper (manager of the
Democratic National Convention that nominated Bill Clinton for President)
and Mark Barnes, former chair and executive director respectively of the
AIDS Action Council in Washington.

These influential activists have a lot in common. Many of them are HIV-
positive, all of them near or under forty years old. They all are gay men, only
one of them black. Most of them began their careers as lawyers or Wall
Street traders, and they each first distinguished themselves through the rank
and file of AIDS activism, public health or Democratic party politics.
(Barnes, Cooper and Isbell, like myself, all hail from Alabama, a trend I
cannot reasonably account for.) Their sustained commitment to the fight is
proven; they each are very smart, accomplished, and media savvy; the
terrible burden they all bear by towing the line for people with AIDS in
the corridors of power weighs heavily on their hearts and minds. These men
know each other well and often disagree strenuously on various strategies,
but there is consensus on how we got here and what the future holds.

First of all, as Gloria Donadello, head of the social welfare graduate
program at Fordham at the time (and Larry Kramer's former analyst),
explicitly warned us in the earliest days of AIDS, social reformers in

America usually end up caring for the needy, instead of effectively attacking the root causes of social problems. The community-based organizations had surged to their natural limits by the mid-1980s, and these contemporary AIDS activists all recognized it. They also recognized during the late 1980s that years of research lay ahead, no matter how well we tried to streamline institutional encumbrances. Once they sat down at the table with the feds and the drug companies, slogans demanding a cure or more money for research had to be replaced by highly specific legislation, regulatory reform, and complex negotiations requiring expert command of scientific data. Staying on top also required either personal financial independence or full-time professional and administrative staff, an office and travel allowance. Continuity in leadership and consistency in objectives became essential to forging working relationships with the officials and corporations.

The current activists are also far more realistic in their expectations than we were during the 1980s. Their principal objectives these days are just keeping science on track (as opposed to demanding a cure), and preventing us from moving backward (as opposed to demanding health care for all Americans right now). Each new drug that comes along must be guided to market safely and quickly, doctors and consumers educated and recruited, data gathered and analyzed. Basic scientific investigation of immunology and pathogenesis must constantly be fostered. Each session of Congress means a new fight just to sustain current appropriations for research, services and education, and to protect the civil rights of people with AIDS.

These are battles that do not lend themselves to sound bites, that require mastery of arcane information and procedures, and which rarely deliver clear victories for people with AIDS, except perhaps in the long run. Our star activists now openly admit what we always feared, that many hundreds of thousands of people, if not millions, are destined to die before their work is done.

AIDS activism is yet another impressive example of the phenomenal power of individuals who step out of socially prescribed roles and accept personal responsibility in the fight for justice. For all that remains to be done, for all the tragedy that lies ahead, it is democracy at its best and worst. Although we once again find the fate of millions in the hands of a very few vested interests, the good news is that contemporary AIDS activists have never been so well prepared for the tasks at hand. The bad news is that they're really only accountable to each other, since the rest of us would be hard pressed to keep up with all the current developments in AIDS science, clinical practice and public policy on a daily basis. An even more frightening prospect is that many of these men may die before their work is finished, and it is not clear who will fill their shoes when the time comes. That is the moral challenge the rest of us, whatever our disciplines, must now take up. Activists are the ones who take action *personally*; those who do not are part of the problem.

□ □ □

At the center and heart of AIDS activism is Larry Kramer, my mentor, ex-lover and best friend. I got a hard-on the first time I heard Kramer call a room full of grown men "a bunch of fucking sissies." (Paul Popham's East 10th Street apartment, August 1981.) I found him refreshingly blunt and socially fearless almost to the point of naiveté. My heart thrilled at the tough guy's passion. He just so manifestly *believed* in what he was saying that I thought together we could fix the world right then.

Several months and many dates later, I found myself telling Larry almost daily that he had seen too many movie musicals as a kid. It turns out that the man is an inveterate romantic. Underneath the human dynamo lurks the person Judy Prince calls Huggy Bear. (See *The Normal Heart*, Act 1, Scene 4.)

Larry's belief in the possibility of lasting love—and the decades he spent pursuing it at great personal cost—struck me as downright sweet, even childlike, and most incongruous in such an apparently sophisticated, accomplished and worldly man. Similarly, his notions of justice and fair play, his sense of simple moral righteousness, and his evident belief that one person could transform the world around him, struck me as sentiments straight out of Rodgers and Hammerstein.

As I came to love him and know him more intimately, I quickly saw how easily he was hurt. I began to fear that my brave friend was destined for epic disappointment. I would scold him in my most sensible down-home manner, telling him that he would be wiser to lower his expectations of others, that he should consider himself fortunate just to have his work, the love of his family (whether he always recognized it or not), and the respect of his peers.

But growing up through the early days of the plague, I began to realize that it was precisely this earnestness which enabled Larry to lead and inspire our generation, particularly when most of us were rapidly losing faith in our nation and in those who professed to love and protect us.

Long before I met Larry, I had been haunted by the loneliness of *Women in Love* and the longing of *Faggots*. When I was stage mother for Joe Papp's original production of *The Normal Heart*, I memorized this verse from W. H. Auden's "September 1, 1939"—the poem from which Larry had taken the play's title:

> The windiest militant trash
> Important Persons shout
> Is not so crude as our wish:
> What mad Nijinsky wrote
> About Diaghilev
> Is true of the normal heart;

For the error bred in the bone
Of each woman and each man
Craves what it cannot have,
Not universal love
But to be loved alone.

Later, as a producer of *The Destiny of Me*, I paced the balcony through every performance, choking each time I heard the line, "What's wrong with wanting more?" Kramer's search for love and the meaning of love has served his art brilliantly, and caused millions of us to ponder seriously why we're here on Earth together.

Likewise, his straightforward expectation that he and the rest of us accept personal responsibility for what goes on in the world—and his utter conviction that we each can make a difference in other people's lives—has made him a great man and an effective agent for monumental social change. He acted like taking care of tens of thousands of sick people, raising hundreds of millions of dollars, and challenging vast institutions were mere administrative details. His singularity of purpose and infectious enthusiasm for the tasks at hand, no matter how fearsome, enabled him to concentrate on the big questions, the overarching debates like courageous leadership and honest science and basic humanity in the face of mounting death.

Existentially speaking, he was also in the right place at the right time. But, as with all overnight sensations, more than coincidence was at work. He had been remarkably well prepared for the occasion.

Kramer was temperamentally suited to leading a charge, but his achievements in the film business and his publishing success (along with his brother Arthur's investment advice), cinched for him a certain amount of financial security by the mid-1970s, as well as legitimacy in the media and a kind of grudging respectability from the tribe of wealthy white men who run this country (many of them, like Larry, Yale alumni). That combination of corporate and artistic experience cultivated in him formidable skill at organizational management, and a real intellectual knack for building popular support around taboo material in an age of images and instant information. He was commercial, and he was a virtuoso with a controversy.

Kramer's rhetoric and actions gained historical resonance beyond AIDS because a number of huge social trends in America were converging just as the plague began. AIDS arrived at a crucial juncture in America's post-1960s funk. Skepticism of government remedies to social problems, the demystification of medicine, and the consumer rights movement were long since in full swing by 1981.

Any notion of integrity in government had pretty much been gutted for most of us baby-boomers after Vietnam and Watergate. Our disillusionment had begun with the nation's bitter reactions to the black civil rights movement, segued into the hopeless erosion of the middle-class dream for most

Americans, and culminated in the blatant failures of the Great Society and the follies of the Cold War. Government entitlement programs, along with the Pentagon, had brought the nation to the brink of bankruptcy and left her in crushing debt. The generation that came to power in business, media and politics in the 1970s and 1980s were hardcore cynics. Liberal or conservative, anti-government sentiment was running high.

This national mistrust of authority, which had enjoyed a popular renaissance during the 1960s and early 1970s, had also breathed fresh life into the civil rights fights by women, African-Americans and gays. Simultaneously, following class actions over product liability and workplace safety, an invigorated consumer rights movement was also in its heyday when AIDS came along.

Medicine was most profoundly influenced by these trends. Beginning as early as the Tuskeegee experiments and the thalidomide debacles, right up through Love Canal and Three Mile Island, common tele-citizens had learned that we could not reasonably rely on medical authorities, government or industry to protect our basic health. In this context and driven by skyrocketing malpractice awards, failed attempts at self regulation, extreme economic pressure from payers, and an explosion of information available to consumers, the doctor-as-god myth crumbled. The man in the white coat telling us everything was under control would never again hold water. A new sense of entitlement was born and bolstered by the very public debates over contraception, abortion rights, the right to die, the so-called war on cancer, and all the extraordinary implications of the graying of America. By the time Larry stepped up to bat in 1981, even most churches and religious leaders had lost whatever vestige of moral authority they once wielded. Only a secular star acting in enlightened self-interest had a chance of being taken seriously in the public forum.

Kramer came along and told the world right from wrong.

He thought that denial among those of us at risk was stupid. He led us to form GMHC, the model from which sprung hundreds of other groups, still the backbone of the nation's response. Larry knew that silence and inaction by public officials was complicity in genocide. By 1983 he was shaming politicians and a vast media machine out of passivity, putting an entire government on track. He taught many of us the practical utility of political coercion. He trained a generation of leaders.

When Larry witnessed the lack of compassion for people with AIDS, he wrote a play to make America cry. When the President was lying, he wrote a play saying the emperor was naked. Larry knew it was evil for those who loved us to go on with business-as-usual while their brothers and sisters and sons and daughters were dropping like flies. He used his art to capture people's attention and to break their hearts.

When Larry realized that we were expending far more effort tending the dying than finding a cure, he took the fight to the streets. Kramer led us once and for all to wrest the exclusive control of biomedical research and clinical practice in America from the medical centers, drug companies and government scientists—and to place standard and experimental treatment choices squarely in the hands of patients. It is this that assures his place in the annals of medicine, and social history.

I know Larry often feels that he's failed us, because there is no cure for AIDS and more people get sick every day. But I say that we're only beginning to reap the fruit of his work. Kramer's most tangible contribution to the public good so far is consumer scrutiny and political overview of NIH appropriations and FDA regulations. The ramifications are vast. Having said that, I believe his most lasting gift to humanity is his prophetic and highly moral voice. While millions of others turned away, Larry spoke the truth as he knew it as dramatically and as compellingly and as often and as well as he could.

The Auden poem ends like this:

> All I have is a voice
> To undo the folded lie,
> The romantic lie in the brain
> Of the sensual man-in-the-street
> And the lie of Authority
> Whose buildings grope the sky:
> There is no such thing as the State
> And no one exists alone;
> Hunger allows no choice
> To the citizen or the police;
> We must love one another or die.

The Mother of Us All

Maxine Wolfe

RECENTLY, I LEARNED that some ACT UP members would affec-
tionately describe Larry Kramer and myself as the "father" and
"mother" of the group, though it wasn't always clear who was who. Though
Larry can lay claim to taking part in ACT UP's birth, I cannot. I never even
heard of Larry Kramer before my first ACT UP meeting in late June 1987,
three months after the group started. Both of us were connected to that
elusive entity called "the community," but our worlds were far apart: Yale vs.
CUNY; the West Village vs. Brooklyn; the *New York Native* vs. *Womanews*; gay
man with no radical history vs. lesbian with lots of it, especially on the left,
in the women's and lesbian feminist movements. I would never have been at
the Community Center the night Larry stood in for Nora Ephron–neither
he nor she would have been a draw for me.

At the first few ACT UP meetings I attended there was no one I knew in
the room. I watched and said nothing (unusual for me) as I tried to figure
out who these people were and whether this was a group for me. I couldn't
help notice the near worshipful reverence reserved for an older man named
Larry every time he spoke. And he seemed to feel free to speak whenever he
wanted, often moving to the front and center of the room. He had no
identifiable political ideology. He wanted to end the AIDS crisis. More than
once he said "drugs into bodies." I did get the message that he was angry. He
had a habit of screaming—about genocide, about incompetent government
officials, about other AIDS organizations selling out. On the other hand,
when people in the group were screaming at each other, he would try to
make peace. Clearly, he wanted the group to survive.

I found out that Larry became positively disposed towards me the first
night I said something at an ACT UP meeting because it was about ACT UP's
survival. It was my third meeting. I realized this was the group for fighting
the AIDS crisis I had been looking for. Passions and tensions were high that
evening. The discussion was particularly acrimonious, with several men
screaming at each other that "people are dying" while we were "wasting time."

The meeting ended with nothing resolved and alarming levels of negativity. Sensing that no one would return the following week and wanting the group to continue, I panicked. As people were breaking up, I suddenly, instinctively stood on my chair and began shouting: "People, People! Can I have your attention for just a moment, please!" "The meeting is over!" I was told in a nasty tone by the facilitator. "I don't care!" I shouted. "I just can't believe that people are going to allow this kind of fighting to break up the group. We should be fighting AIDS, not each other! Please, please come back next week and let's try to discuss the issues without trying to destroy each other." A friend later told me that Larry said, "Who is that woman? She just saved this group." While the last point is highly debatable, Larry and I did share the same ultimate goal, from the beginning and throughout our years together in ACT UP: our belief in the crucial role this organization had to play in fighting AIDS. Along with our age and lack of hesitation in speaking out, this was the germ of truth in the parental analogy.

□ □ □

Generally, Larry and I independently attempted to figure out where ACT UP should go next and how to make that happen. But our ideas about what the group should be and what needed to be done were usually dramatically different. Larry's vision was that ACT UP should be a hierarchical organization—the army was his favorite analogy—with clear lines of authority and a lot of troops following the commander who sometimes would be him and sometimes a person he thought should be the leader. He had no penchant for democracy. In fact, he disdained it, eventually saying that ACT UP was "democratic to a fault." I, on the other hand, supported the anarchistic democractic style of ACT UP and pushed for it to continue that way. Of course, this was only one of many issues we disagreed about. Yet, curiously, we never had a fight. I could—and did—speak against proposals by Larry without incurring his wrath. I recall the first such episode. At that time, I didn't know who he was. After standing up and protesting some claim or strategy he was proposing, there was suddenly all this sucking-in of breath. I couldn't imagine what I'd said that was so horrifying. Of course, it was simply that I'd had the "nerve" to disagree with Larry Kramer. More amazing and revealing, though, was his response: he didn't mind at all. On the contrary, he appreciated and respected assertiveness. In retropsect, I think our passionate, but never personal, disagreements on issues created a positive tension that was productive. Although his patience factor was far lower than mine, we were both willing to listen to good ideas and throw them around until we found the right one.

In fact, it was his impatience that led to the only tension I can recall between us. I was facilitating a meeting when Larry stormed in with a group of people and demanded that everything stop so he could speak. I said we were in the middle of a discussion; when it was over, I would ask the members if he could go next, out of turn on the agenda. He waited impatiently a few more minutes, then demanded we end the meeting and march en masse to Gracie Mansion for a demonstration against the Mayor. After he finished, I asked the membership what they wanted to do. The decision was that the action could wait until the next morning at City Hall since there were other important things on the agenda. Larry was crazed, to put it mildly. He stood on a chair (another commonality!) and began screaming. He called us "a bunch of sissies" (score one for internalized homophobia *and* lesbian invisibility), then launched into one of his diatribes: "Are you going to be like the Jews and let yourselves be led into concentration camps?" (add internalized anti-Semitism). Then he stormed out. At the City Hall demonstration the next day, Larry apologized for disrupting the meeting. "*That*, I just took in my stride," I said, being more concerned about his Holocaust analogies. I told him I thought he betrayed a lot of ignorance about the subject; that Hannah Arendt, his authority, by no means had the last word on the subject; that members of my family died fighting in the Resistance; that I'd appreciate his being more sensitive. He didn't argue and this issue never came between us again.

Larry definitely displayed his ego as well as his id in ACT UP. But unlike some members who had decided that their expertise, strategies and tactics could not be questioned, Larry never believed he had *the* answer to ending the AIDS crisis. He responded best to being treated as a person, rather than as God or the Devil, the two categories most people placed him in. People tend to ascribe to him far more power, positively and negatively, than he ever actually had within ACT UP or the AIDS movement. They've bought the media hype that if Larry says it, it must be so; if Larry wants it to happen, it should or will. So when Larry told AIDS activists, via the media, to "riot" at the International AIDS conference in San Francisco, I got a frantic phone call from an AIDS activist with a long history of political organizing on the left. "Did you hear what Larry said? It's being quoted everywhere! How can he tell people to riot. It's so irresponsible," and so on. He was shocked that I was so calm. "Why do you think people will do what Larry says?" I asked (followed by my own view that a riot might in fact be in order). If he had thought a moment, he might have realized that Larry's frustration with ACT UP, GMHC, and the gay community in general was that despite his screaming and aggressive methods, he could *not* usually get people to do what he wanted. Other than starting groups. So, the "children" of the "father" of AIDS activism became more independent than he would have liked. His notoriety was able to get him meetings with scientists and government officials, but they wouldn't listen to him either. Intuitively, Larry knew that one person alone could not pressure the system to change, try as he might.

Larry was and still is widely if not universally identified as *the* voice of the AIDS movement, as its leader. What he has to say about any AIDS issue is sought after by the media. And he uses that position to put out whatever he thinks will work at the moment, be it provoking fear or sympathy. But it's crucial to see that Larry never claimed that position; on the contrary, he kept looking for leaders, for someone to take the leadership role in actually ending the AIDS crisis rather than fighting it. He was forever bemoaning the lack of leadership, from organizations in the gay community to the absence of an AIDS "czar." At various times, he'd think he had discovered such a person—certain members of ACT UP, a particular scientist, a government official, but they would inevitably disappoint him. Most would reveal too much opportunism, or they would want to do business as usual and not want to rock the boat—the one approach Larry knew with certainty could never end this crisis. When he would see the reality of these individuals, he would turn on them with a vengeance, personal and vicious in his criticism, though what he said was usually on target. He would then proceed to look for the next Messiah.

Since Larry is a draw for the media, many AIDS activists want to use his prominence for their own ends but do not want what comes with the territory. They want him to say what they want, rather than to speak for himself. On more than a few occasions, I have been asked whether I think Larry should be invited to speak at a particular event. Invariably, there is great hestitation because of Larry's reputation as a "loose cannon" who can't be relied on to say "the right thing." My response is always that Larry can't be used to spout what others want him to say, and that is as it should be. I have never wished Larry were someone else. As far as I can tell, he has no consistent political world-view or agenda. He wants to end the AIDS crisis—period. I appreciate what he has accomplished toward that end, even if, like everyone, I still sometimes cringe at what he says or how he expresses himself.

The absence of a consistent political world-view in Larry was likewise the source of his openness to a very broad range of political concepts and strategies. So, when the Women's Caucus of ACT UP conducted a teach-in about women and AIDS, Larry was fascinated. Some of the discussion, about the sexuality of women, about genital anatomy and reproductive functions, included material Larry frankly admitted that he had been ignorant of. He was always supportive of our work. Another example that comes to mind is when many ACT UP members were afraid to take any actions against Mayor Dinkins or his health commissioner, Woody Meyers, because both were African-American. Not Larry. If anyone had bad policies about AIDS, he was against them and was willing to say so publicly. I agreed. The only problem was that Larry had no idea how to be so characteristically up front without alienating ACT UP's African-American members and allies.

Finally, there was the evening I bumped into Larry in the Village. He was very excited about a new book he said was "absolutely fascinating" and that had made him "understand everything. It's class, class. I'd never thought about that," he said, as he immediately escorted me into Dalton's and bought the book for me. The main focus of the book, *Who Will Tell The People: A Breakdown of American Democracy* by William Greider (Simon and Schuster, 1992), using examples of grassroots movements of the 1980s (but leaving out ACT UP), was an analysis of how government officials divide movements by agreeing to meet with the people who are willing to behave in a middle-class way and icing out the rowdy, working-class style street activists who initially forced those officials to take notice. Yale education notwithstanding, Larry could doubtless see his own activist experiences in this context (as when the Clinton administration invited TAG and GMHC members, rather than Larry or others from ACT UP, to be part of various AIDS task forces) and it made sense to him. Again, the salient feature of Larry's activisim was his openness to any idea he thought made sense.

Of course, some ideas took more time than others to sink in. Recently, at a friend's birthday party, Larry and I reconnected. "I hear you've retired," he said. "Are you going to write a book about activism now?" "I'm not sure what I'm going to do now," I answered. "Well, you should," he continued, "because you said one of the smartest things anyone has said about that." "Really," I responded, "and what was that?" "That we have to be in this for the long haul," he sighed, "and you were right." Larry should know. He's been in it for the longest haul of all.

A Legacy of Anger

Michelangelo Signorile

IN THE LATE 1980s, when I began writing angry articles attacking what I saw as the complacency and hypocrisy of various public figures in New York, Washington and Hollywood—many of them lesbian, gay or bisexual, most of them closeted—people sometimes asked me, "Did Larry Kramer teach you how to be angry?" I suppose it was a fair question, given that I'd come of age as a writer and activist within ACT UP in New York at that time, and had worked alongside Larry for a little while. And Larry had been publicly and angrily calling to account closeted public figures and others long before I came on the scene.

Still, I always thought the question rather silly. No one can teach you *how* to be angry, I would answer. That is something that comes from deep inside. And in my case, brought up in a Brooklyn Italian-Catholic family, that kind of passion wasn't hard to come by. What Larry Kramer did do, however, is show me that it was *okay* to be angry. More than that, he dramatically revealed the *power* of anger—how anger, within a culture that demands order, could be of immense value in disrupting the status quo and shifting public debate. His blistering rhetoric and his theatrical style—his face contorting wildly, his veins bulging from his forehead, his piercing eyes focusing on the object of his wrath as the rhythm of his speech increased rapidly—instilled fear in the likes of former New York City Mayor Ed Koch and former New York City Health Commissioner Stephen Joseph. They may have thought he was half-crazy, but they could not dismiss him. Larry established himself and his cause as a force to be reckoned with, and he did that through his anger, backed up—and this is the important part—by reasoned arguments. As long as he showed the logic and basic truths behind his passion, Larry was taken seriously, his anger getting him the foot in the door.

Watching Larry, experiencing his anger in the late 1980s, had a cathartic and inspiring effect on many of us in ACT UP. Larry looked at anger as a *celebration*—not the event or issue he was angry about of course, but rather of the fact that he could finally vent his feelings without limits. Anger, Larry taught us, is liberating, exciting and, yes, even fun. And his anger was our license to go further than we had ever gone. That wasn't always a good thing; sometimes we went too far, inviting scorn and criticism, and seeing our efforts backfire. But that, it seemed, was part of the process: We experienced the double-edged sword of anger. We learned when to push it to the limit, and we learned when to temper it—even if only momentarily.

For me, that experience was most acute while writing for *OutWeek* magazine, from 1989 through 1991, having come off of two years of working in ACT UP. I looked to Larry's writing at the time for strength and guidance, particularly his pointed and often blistering attacks on entrenched bureaucracies as diverse as the Food and Drug Administration, Gay Men's Health Crisis and the *New York Times*. People have often asked me if I was "afraid" when, writing for *OutWeek*, I weekly hurled vicious insults at powerful and well-connected individuals whom I believed were complacent, such as movie moguls David Geffen and Barry Diller (outing them in the process), or pointed to hypocrisy at the highest levels of the Pentagon and the Bush Administration, outing assistant Secretary of Defense Pete Williams. Thinking back, I suppose people were justified in believing I should be afraid. Soon after I had written an article within weeks of Malcolm Forbes's death in 1989 revealing that the multimillionaire was gay and yet had lived a lie for most of his life—published in *OutWeek* at the height of other attacks I had made on various closeted and powerful New York media figures—I was pulled aside on a Manhattan street and warned that "big people" were after me. I also received my share of telephone death threats and letters demanding that I shut up or else.

But in all truthfulness, I never once felt scared. I never once thought I should be more reserved. I never once believed that I needed to stop. And Larry had a lot to do with my feeling that way. No matter how far I had pushed things, Larry was always further out there. He made me feel that I wasn't so extreme after all, that if he could withstand the attacks he was getting then I could certainly withstand the ones I was getting. If he wasn't afraid, I told myself, then I shouldn't be either.

Larry also demonstrated to me the broad range that anger had. Contrary to his reputation, his anger hasn't always been about yelling and screaming. True, Larry's fire and brimstone at its best has been galvanizing and provocative, as when he took to the microphone at the 1993 March on Washington and excoriated the Clinton administration for its indifference to AIDS, and, of course, outed Health and Human Services Secretary Donna Shalala.

But Larry's anger is actually sometimes chillingly subtle and quiet. In December 1993 he spoke at the memorial service for *New York Times* reporter Jeff Schmalz, who died of AIDS. Schmalz had come out as gay and as a person with AIDS several years earlier in a lengthy piece I had written about the *New York Times* for *The Advocate*, and he had described at that time how he had learned he had AIDS after having had a seizure in the middle of the *Times* newsroom. Soon after coming out, Schmalz took up the cause, writing article after article chronicling his illness and covering issues surrounding the epidemic, and he befriended Larry and other AIDS activists. The final article Schmalz had written, printed after his death, was for the *New York Times Magazine*, titled "What Ever Happened to AIDS?" It was a powerful indictment of the government, the media and society in general for losing interest in the AIDS epidemic.

Appropriately for Larry, Jeff Schmalz's memorial service was held in a small theater on the Upper East Side; Larry wore black slacks and a black turtleneck, and stood on a stage before a black backdrop with one dramatic beam of light shining on him. His head and face were all that could be seen, as his silvery gray hair and beard created a glistening, magnetic aura. Only on a couple of occasions did Larry raise his voice, particularly when he made his usual claim that "AIDS IS INTENTIONAL GENOCIDE!" Throughout most of the speech, however, when he in fact launched his most pointed charges, Larry spoke in an almost inaudible tone, slowly and methodically. "The *New York Times* could have saved Jeff. But it didn't," he said. You could hear a pin drop in the room, as all eyes were fixed on Larry's face. "Since this plague began in 1981, it has chosen not to," he continued, at times barely whispering. "Jeff was probably infected about that time. You came here to mourn him. If you cared about Jeff, then you are hypocrites if you continue to do nothing and continue to allow so little to be done and continue to allow the Jeffs of this world to die ... Surely the most noble gesture this paper could make to honor Jeff's memory would be to finally begin responsibly reporting this plague of AIDS. Goodbye Jeff. You will be missed. Perhaps it will take your death to make your employers into responsible human beings."

It was more powerful than if Larry had screamed the same words at the top of his lungs inside the *Times* newsroom. Several *New York Times* editors got up and walked out, appalled. And Larry had once again gotten his message across and created a debate.

Often, the most significant aspect about Larry's anger is not so much its style but rather its recipient. Beyond the larger heterosexual power structure, Larry has boldly taken on many of the sacred cows within the gay community as well. In many respects that has perhaps taken more courage than vilifying even the most powerful and egregious homophobes, its price often being rejection and scorn within his community. As is widely known, soon after the publication of *Faggots* in 1978, a stirring critique of gay male sexual culture and its more destructive aspects, Larry was viciously excoriated by much of the organized gay male activist community of the time. Ridiculed and personally attacked as a prude and a self-loather, Larry was practically banished from Fire Island in those days for underscoring the gay resort's more hedonistic, escapist and self-destructive qualities.

In later years, after the AIDS crisis was upon us and after he helped found Gay Men's Health Crisis, Larry would regularly joust with GMHC and its board over its policies and politics—and would take on other gay and AIDS groups as well—provoking discussion and focussing attention on what he believed the responsibilities of such groups really are.

And yet, though these conflicts have been chronicled, Larry's legacy of anger in this regard, specifically the influence he has had on other activists criticizing the gay community itself, has perhaps been least examined, yet has been no less powerful. Over and over throughout the 1980s Larry pointed to the salient fact that, if we are to end a crisis as devastating as AIDS, we cannot simply demand that society and government make dramatic changes: we must make the necessary changes in our own behaviour as well, and gay and AIDS groups need to lead the way for us rather than coddling us in our self-indulgences. In that way, Larry set an example for other activists to follow. Though for a long time he was often the only voice willing to take a stand—willing to be chastised as a "party pooper"—ten years later there would be many more activists, many of them of the younger generation, taking up his points and speaking out.

In August 1996, for example, New York City's gay and AIDS activist community was embroiled in yet another highly publicized controversy: The annual GMHC fund-raiser known as The Morning Party, an all-day dance party on the beach in Fire Island Pines and an event that had become something of an institution in its fourteen years, became the subject of heated debate because of rampant drug use among attendees.

"Fire Island Fund-Raiser Is Criticized Over Drug Use Linked to Unsafe Sex," went a headline in the *New York Times* on Saturday, August 17, the day before the event. The article, written by openly gay *Times* man David W. Dunlap, reported that it was "widely known that drugs like cocaine, the amphetamine derivative Ecstasy, and ketamine, an anaesthetic often called 'K,' have become an integral part of the Morning Party, not officially sanctioned, of course, but not hard to find, either. And critics are questioning whether the Gay Men's Health Crisis, arguably the most important private AIDS service organization nationwide, is sending a dangerously mixed message. They contend that the agency is turning a blind eye to drug use, which impairs judgment and reduces inhibitions, often leading to the sexual behavior that can result in transmission of the AIDS virus."

Indeed, several important studies had shown that drug and alcohol use greatly increased the prevalence of unsafe sex. And drug use at the Morning Party, unlike at perhaps most other benefits and fund-raising events for AIDS and other causes, was not among only a tiny minority. Begun in 1982 as a small, daytime benefit attended by local people, many of whom were perhaps not well enough to party late in the evening, the Morning Party by 1996 had become a highlight on the international gay party circuit, attracting thousands. In 1996, the vast majority of the 4,500 men who attended were part of a gay fast crowd that traveled the country and the world in search of a good time, taking recreational drugs and dancing their troubles away.

Beginning in 1995, GMHC began handing out brochures at the party, designed to remind people about safer sex and tell them how to do their drugs safely. Many people in the lesbian and gay community, however, felt the group's efforts in this regard were nothing more than damage control intended to offset GMHC's public role as chief sponsor of the event. With the threat looming of a so-called "second wave" of HIV transmission among young gay men reported in the early and mid-1990s, and what appeared to be an overall breakdown in safer sex among gay men of all ages, many people simply felt GMHC should not be sponsoring, promoting and making money off of such a party. The fact that GMHC put some of the money the Morning Party raised to its laudable and successful substance use programs, seemed even more contradictory. It was as if they were exacerbating a problem for the sake of making money, and then just mopping up the mess afterwards.

In the days following the party, more headlines about the party and drug use blared from New York's dailies when it was reported that at least one Morning Party attendee had overdosed on a drug commonly called GHB, an anaesthetic that had become popular on the party scene. The young man had almost died, and had to be airlifted off Fire Island to a Long Island hospital where he lay for several days in a coma. Several other men at the party were treated for drug and alcohol related ailments.

Smack in the middle of this imbroglio was of course Larry Kramer, rightly identified in the *New York Times* as a founder of GMHC, and one who felt "ashamed of GMHC's affiliation" with the Morning Party. "We started the organization to change all that, not perpetuate it," he told the *Times*. And he talked about having gone to the Morning Party two years earlier. "I was pretty shocked," he said. "It was as if AIDS had never happened and I was back in 1974 again." Indeed, Larry had written a blistering critique of the Morning Party in *The Advocate* shortly after that visit in 1994, noting that men were in the portable toilets doing drugs and having sex. The piece raised an important question that no one was asking: while such behavior might not be bad or morally wrong in and of itself, was it appropriate for a "health" organization, a group trying to influence people about safer sex, to host a party at which the vast majority of guests ingest drugs that can be and often are dangerous to their health, and which studies show raise the incidence of unsafe sex?

Larry had at that time, as usual, inspired a heated discussion. What was different about the controversy two years later, however, was that Larry hadn't kicked up the story. It was several other activists, Queer Nation and ACT UP alumni such as advertising executive Andrew Beaver and Troy Masters, publisher of the New York gay weekly LGNY, who were among those at the center of the controversy, pushing the story in the media and also being quoted in the papers. "A party whose point is really drug use has no place benefiting an organization that is fighting for intelligent decisions that lead to safer sex," Adam R. Rose, a real estate executive and former donor to GMHC (who had stopped giving money to the group precisely over this issue) told the *Times*. Jonathan Capehart, a young, openly gay editorial page writer at the *New York Daily News* wrote an editorial for the paper bravely demanding that GMHC pull out of the party. When GMHC wrote a letter to the *News*, recoiling to victimology and accusing the paper of homophobia, Capehart wrote an op-ed piece calling GMHC on its attempts to deflect attention from its irresponsibility. "[C]ritics are blasted [by GMHC] as homophobes and self-hating gays for opposing the party or urging GMHC to reassess it, " he wrote. "That kind of lame, knee-jerk response is nothing short of offensive."

These writers and activists, as well as many lesbians and gay men on Fire Island itself and beyond who spoke out against GMHC's sponsorship of the party, were carrying on Larry's tradition of critically looking at institutions within the community, institutions that might sometimes compromise themselves, and which did not always work in the community's best interests. And, not surprisingly, those of us who spoke up would also receive the kind of nasty criticism and personal attacks that Larry had received years prior.

"You're trying to destroy the agency!" Dr. Howard Grossman, a GMHC board member, angrily charged when, in a telephone call, I voiced my criticism of GMHC's role in the party. Among other ugly insinuations, Grossman accused me and several others of having orchestrated the entire series of events (as if we could even plan the drug overdose too) as a way to bring the agency down, and then he threatened me: "A lot of people are really angry about this—you'd better watch your back!"

I was momentarily jarred upon hanging up the phone. And I was a bit hurt, not at being threatened, but by his assertion that I was trying to destroy the agency, as if my concerns were not genuine. To be sure, the charge was ridiculous, based simply on my own past: I had in fact spent several years ranting at David Geffen to both come out of the closet and to give some of his millions to GMHC—and he eventually did both those things, telling the world he was gay and giving several million dollars to GMHC.

I called Larry, and we both had a chuckle, for these were the same intimidation tactics GMHC officials had used on him in years gone by. "They told me, 'You don't have any friends,' 'nobody likes you anyway,' " Larry recalled. He then read me a letter GMHC had sent him at the height of his criticisms of the group in the 1980s, accusing him of trying to "destroy" the agency, and asserting that they were "trying to combat ... damage" he had done to them. In addition, they played the tiresome sex-negative card: "After years of liberation, you have helped make sex dirty again for us."

"I was always conscious of the fact that they were in a precarious position," he said, underscoring the agency's immense value to the community. "I was *criticizing* them, not destroying them." Larry had rightly believed that, in the role GMHC had taken on as a service organization for people with AIDS and as a group that was dispensing life-saving prevention information to the community, it was perhaps just as important to criticize them as it was to criticize a belligerent government—even if they would call him names and accuse him of trying to destroy them.

For those who would follow in Larry Kramer's footsteps, he is and will always be a testament not only to what they could do to change things but how they could withstand the attacks that come with speaking out. He has taught us all that, in addition to taking on the homo-hating monsters who have kept us down, we must diligently wrestle with our own demons. In that way, he has instilled in many of us a passion for self-awareness and self-criticism that will live on in future queer generations.

Notes on Black and Larry Kramer

Canaan Parker

I SUPPOSE I SHOULD BE FURIOUS at Larry Kramer for his comments about black men in a 1992 interview in *The Advocate*. "I feel great empathy for black women. They are bearing a disproportionate amount of the burden in their community. Black men in too many instances are out to lunch.... Black men weren't there, aren't there for us, to begin with. Black women are."[1] But I'm not especially angry about that. I'll leave it to others to express anger at Kramer's thoughtless overgeneralization. Remove the hyperbole, add a dash of delicacy, and the grain of good sense in Kramer's statement sounds similar to the theme of the Million Man March.

More importantly, I don't want to be distracted from my real enemies. I feel a great need to emphasize this. I refuse to be tricked into seeing Larry Kramer as my enemy. *Larry Kramer is not my enemy!* I have vastly more deadly enemies than Larry Kramer, and most of my enemies are his enemies as well.

At some point, this "he said blah blah" business, even in a sensitive racial context, starts to sound so much like "your mama wears combat boots." My divide and conquer alert went off recently, for example, when I read a newspaper editorial *entirely* devoted to the alleged use of the word "homo" by the Reverend Al Sharpton, who like Larry Kramer is a notorious big-mouth progressive activist. (Sharpton was referring to Archimedes, not to the gay community.) I have never seen an editorial in this particular newspaper protesting the venomous verbal attacks on gays from any number of white conservative leaders. How obvious can it be that this journalist was using the old "he said your mama" tactic that works so well in starting fights in the playground, in an effort to derail a progressive coalition that just might empower both blacks and gays. I see no more importance in Sharpton saying "homo" in an excited flurry of street rhetoric than I do in Kramer's twelve-word explanation of race and gender in American history.

If Kramer and Sharpton sat down to plan a two-front attack on the right wing, would they break down into a fight over "you said homo, you said black men blah blah?" Or would they train their sights on what George Pataki is saying with his budget pen?

Still, I don't feel I can excuse Kramer's careless stereotyping. Some impressionable young black might read and internalize it. Or some unalert white person might read and believe it. Or some "divide and conquer" tactician might quote it during an election to right-wing advantage. But I'll let someone else make a big stink about it. My job is to attack Patrick Buchanan, not Larry Kramer.

Moreover, there is value in Kramer's big mouth. Since he seems incapable of censoring his thoughts, listening to him is like having a listening device at an all-white cocktail party. "Am I saying something everybody doesn't already feel?" he says (*The Advocate*). I can count on Kramer to tell me what goes on among whites when no people of color are present. There is some benefit to that, I think.

And given Kramer's penchant for offending everybody else, I might have felt left out if he had never said anything to offend blacks. It would be more of an insult if Kramer suddenly became a careful, delicate speaker *only* with respect to black men. No one can accuse Larry Kramer of patronizing people of color.

□ □ □

Kramer went on in *The Advocate* interview to explain his public expressive style, why he speaks in outrageous hyperbole, why he irritates people: that's how he gets to be Larry Kramer. It is how he makes an impact; how he gets his name up on a billboard on Greenwich Avenue. Subtleties get lost through a megaphone. Fine points are casualties of war. "Of course I speak in hyperbole. Of course I speak in broad strokes. [I]f I didn't, no one would have heard a thing I have said over all of these years."

It was fascinating to read this, considering that Kramer is a writer and must have spent great energy in his life seeking ways to make a dramatic effect through a given medium, whether it was the written word before AIDS, or the medium of public spectacle after. As a writer, I struggle to keep in mind the subjective experience of reading as I put words down. I'm certain Kramer does the same when he writes, and when he chose to become a public figure, he probably had in mind the subjective experience of those watching him on television, listening to his speeches, or absorbing his persona through nonspecific media. I knew vaguely who Larry Kramer was before I first saw him (at a benefit reading for *In Our Own Write* at the Lesbian and Gay Community Center in New York, sharing a magnificent program with Sapphire and Vito Russo in his last public appearance). I was eagerly curious to see Kramer. When he came to the lectern, he seemed too small and professorial to be who he was. Still, the persona was there, and it seemed that a giant shadow was cast against a curtain wall behind him. Professorial as he was, an enormous rage seemed implicit in him, the way a still pool of gasoline suggests its explosive potential. Did Kramer create this sensation as he read from his unfinished novel, or did he bring the sensation with him that night? Where had I first heard about him? What facts were the foundation for my preconception of him? I vaguely knew that he was my gay champion, the snarling watchdog on my front lawn who would die for me, who would bite off the legs of anyone who tried to hurt me. How had Kramer reached me before I had ever seen him speak, read any of his books, or seen his plays? How do you create a mythology of yourself? And what do you do once you have created it?

Several years ago I met a gay gentleman in the diplomatic field at a Volunteer Night at the Lesbian and Gay Community Center and had an interesting talk about Kramer. As part of his work in diplomacy, the fellow had read a book, *Black and White Styles in Conflict* (Thomas Kochman, University of Chicago Press, 1981) which described the differing communication styles that are respected and celebrated in black versus white cultures. After reading the description of the expressive styles of black people, and recalling his encounters with Larry Kramer, the gentleman marvelously concluded that, pigment notwithstanding, *Larry Kramer was black*! The fellow insisted that Kramer's mode of expression precisely matched the expressive style of black people, as described in the book.

Recalling this conversation, I looked up Kochman's book in the library, and yes! As the diplomatic gentleman suggested, the description of black communication styles was precisely on point with Larry Kramer's, particularly on the most controversial aspects of his style.

Consider, for example, Kramer's tendency to criticize in broad strokes, rather than carefully tailor his accusations. Kochman states about specific versus general accusations:

> Expressed metaphorically, the white perspective holds that the person shooting the arrow is expected to aim carefully and to assume full responsibility for all the targets that are hit, both intended and inadvertent. In the black perspective, the person shooting the arrow is responsible only for its general direction, not for the target the arrow hits, since it is the target that actually guides the arrow home. (p. 90)
>
> As elsewhere within black culture, a defensive protestation of an accusation communicates to others that a vulnerable part of the person's psyche has been touched, with the compelling implication that the accusation therefore must be true, for the culture holds that only the truth hurts. (p. 96)

I.e., the only people who will be hurt by a generalized accusation are the people for whom the charge is accurate. Thus it makes sense to cast a wide net. Kochman's point is remarkably keen. So often I have heard black people speak generally about whites, white racists, honky motherfuckers, and then deny they are being racist. According to the white expressive style, a white person speaking generally about black people is in fact slurring an entire group of people, and, by his intention, making a racist statement. But Larry Kramer does not consider himself a racist when he speaks generally about black men.

When Kochman talks about "fighting words"—differing expressive styles in verbal disputes—again he could as easily be talking particularly about Larry Kramer:

> The different black and white perspectives on whether angry disputes can be contained at the verbal level derive from their different degrees of confidence in their *ability to manage hostile and intense confrontations* without losing self-control.
>
> The confidence of blacks in their *ability to manage anger and hostility at the verbal level* without losing self-control is higher. This is due to the greater freedom of assertion and expression allowed in black culture that also develops their *ability to manage higher levels of heat and affect* without becoming overwhelmed ... the level of intensity reached before the question of self-control arises will be higher for blacks than for whites. [Emphasis added.] (p. 51)

Thus, when a black person is verbally aggressive, it may not indicate genuine hostility. The same words used, in white culture, are intended as an attack; you just wouldn't say such things unless you intended the cessation of friendly relations.

Any cultural generalizations based on race should be offered with care and can have limited accuracy at best. The valid point Kochman makes is that it is necessary to take into account the communication style of a people, or a person, in order to fully understand what is being said. Of course, Larry Kramer isn't really black, but the same principle would apply. Given his expressive style, when Kramer generalizes, it *doesn't mean the same thing* as it might when someone else does. When he is verbally explosive, his communication style must be considered in deciphering his true meaning.

Kramer reminds me of my mother, who is also black. My mother would have made a great boxer. She and Marvin Hagler for the middleweight championship would have been a tough night for Marvelous Marvin. After her ninth round knockout of the champ, she might have met Larry Kramer in The Fight of the Century. She is consciously unreasonable, unfair, head-through-the-wall aggressive. The type of person to take on a gang of gun-packing muggers with a frying pan. Though she is also the type of person who, were she President of the United States, would likely start a nuclear war. (I can see her when the peace talks collapse. "Where's that button?!")

She has never completely respected me as a reasonable, fair-minded wussy, and I've never completely respected her as an egomaniac and a tyrant. But I've come to understand one thing: I would have been slaughtered in her world. A black woman in the 1950s and 1960s with little education? My children would not have survived, and my son would never have grown up to be so judicious, cautious and happily arty and queer. My mother and Larry Kramer would get along famously. They would look in each other's eyes and instantly, mutually recognize the gift of the Furies. They would toast each other as they smiled conspiratorially, like members of an exclusive club. Like Brezhnev and Nixon, except less reasonable.

□ □ □

Kramer went on in *The Advocate* interview to talk about race, class and homophobia.

> You can't use it [homophobia] as an excuse. There is discrimination of all kinds. It's much easier to be a gay person in America than a black person.... [Y]oung black men don't have the advantages of education and income and freedom to walk down the street without people being suspicious of them, which we have.... We are rich, and I'm sure this will provoke any number of letters from lesbians. (p. 43)

I was intrigued by Kramer's statement that it is "much easier to be a gay person in America than a black person." I asked myself, how does he know? It's a curious question, and the greater worth that might come of it is a better understanding of both oppressions, rather than some useless ranking of miseries. On the one hand, I can't imagine a more self-defeating state of mind than chauvinism about one's oppression.

But on the other hand, does this mean that Kramer agrees with the Supreme Court that anti-gay discrimination, being less serious than racism, is not a "suspect classification" (as racial discrimination is), under the Equal Protection Clause of the Fourteenth Amendment? Under present constitutional law, if the State of Utah passed a law requiring separate public bathrooms for gays and straights—if they post signs "No Queers" on public facilities—it would not violate the Federal Constitution, as long as the state showed a rational (i.e. minimal) basis for the policy.[2] When the gay suspect classification test case comes before the Supreme Court, will Justice Antonin Scalia quote Larry Kramer, as Midge Decker quoted *Faggots* in her homophobic critiques of gay people? Given the lack of meaningful constitutional protection against homophobia, Kramer makes a stunning concession.

But I'm willing to consider that Larry Kramer may be more politically astute than I am. Since the same people are oppressing both blacks and gays, an argument over who is more oppressed sounds like the classic divide and conquer mousetrap. Again, Larry Kramer's mouth comes in handy: I often encounter black people who resent any equation between the Civil Rights struggle and gay liberation. Rather than argue, I point out that gay people never said they are *as* oppressed as blacks, and I quote Larry Kramer (identifying him, if necessary, in oversimplified shorthand as the "Gay Malcolm X.")[3] I then point out that right-wing spin doctors, seeking to derail a black–gay political coalition, have *planted* the divisive idea in black people's minds that gays equate homophobia with racism.

So it seems that, strategically, Kramer is right on this point. But I have a niggling concern. Is Kramer really saying, *I may be a faggot but at least I'm not a nigger?* I pray not, and I won't accuse him of something I don't know. Unfortunately, I have met gay men who think this way—I can tell by how vehemently they assert that blacks are much worse off than gays. Their reaction sounds so much like the poor white motivation for Jim Crow. *I may be low on the pole, but a black is lower than me, and I'll prove it.*

I was exasperated by Kramer's statement that "We [meaning gays] are rich." Tell that to the fifteen-year-old living out of a Greyhound station locker, sucking cock for as little as a food stamp in the dead of winter, for whom AIDS has become the lesser of two evils, the greater being hunger, frostbite, and dope sickness *right now.* Tell it to James Baldwin's Giovanni, hiding naked under a bridge from the police. Or to the queer underclass romanticized by Genet in *The Thief's Journal.* Of course, the poverty of the gay underclass isn't passed from parent to child and thereby compounded over generations, as is poverty among blacks—Genet was not trying to support children on a subsistence income. Nevertheless, downward mobility is a theme in the gay experience, though I can only cite anecdotal evidence of this. Consumer surveys, designed specifically for marketing products, tell us nothing about a gay underclass. That some gays with discretionary income can be marketed to *as gays* has no bearing on the number of gays who are unemployed, underemployed or marginally employed, since marketing researchers have no interest in identifying gays with no money.

Kramer is falling back on the clichéd gay defense mechanism of aristocratic fantasy. *I may be a faggot, but I'm rich.* (The person's actual social class seems not to matter. When I first came out, half the gay men I met claimed to have been friends of John F. Kennedy, or to have slept with John F. Kennedy, Jr. It seemed like a mass hallucination.) I'm disappointed that so prominent a gay leader, and so strong a man, relies on a defense mechanism to hold his head high. I don't appreciate defenses against stigma because on the deepest psychological level they don't work. They leave a hole in your strength and somewhere, someone is going to find that hole. Better to invalidate fundamentally the stigma itself. Not a nerve, not a molecule in my body believes for a second the homophobic lies. What need do I have to pretend I slept with Donald Trump?

Besides, it is such bad strategy. Can't you hear the right wing? *Those rich gays with their summer beach houses, what are they complaining about? What are they marching about?*

□ □ □

A final note: I saw *The Normal Heart* in an off-off-off-Broadway production at a tiny side-street theater in Chelsea. At one point during the play, the drama had built to such intensity, the pressure became so unbearable, that I feared I was going to pass out. I do not exaggerate one bit. It was like being in the eighth round of a title bout with Marvelous Marvin Hagler. Scene after scene, left hook, right hook, uppercut. Uppercut, right, left. I nearly had to leave the theater, and I would have if Kramer hadn't had a moment's mercy and let the intensity drop for one brief scene—a love scene, I think it was.

I have never in my life been so overwhelmed by a work of art.

Notes
1. Interview with Victor Zonana, *The Advocate*, December 1, 1992, issue 617, p. 48.
2. HIV statistics alone might meet that minimal basis. Of course, racially segregated bathrooms violate the Fourteenth Amendment because race is a suspect classification. If a form of discrimination qualifies as a suspect classification, the state must show a "compelling" reason for its policy, and not a mere "rational basis." The state would have to prove an actual risk of HIV transmission in public toilets, which it could not.
3. Kramer often appeared at ACT UP meetings wearing a T-shirt with Malcolm X's phrase, "By Any Means Necessary."

Friendship and Antagonism:
The Passionate Tactics of Larry Kramer

Anthony S. Fauci

I HAD HEARD ABOUT LARRY KRAMER some time before we actually met. His reputation according to most of the "establishment" heterosexuals as well as some of my gay friends and associates who had met him, seen him in action, or had heard about him was that he was an "out-of-control wild man" who was set on attacking scientists, public health officials, the Reagan administration, the Congress and just about anyone else who he felt was not responding adequately to the AIDS epidemic. However, according to others of my gay friends and associates, Larry Kramer was somewhat of a prophet, a saint, and a hero. I would find out in time that all of the above to a greater or lesser extent were true. It was this extraordinary dichotomy of opinions that sparked my interest in meeting the man. Furthermore, since I was one of the "establishment," he was already beginning to attack me in my role as an AIDS scientist and public health official. When I did a "background check" on Larry and learned of his extraordinary literary talent and range of accomplishments, from his Academy Award nominated screenplay for the film *Women in Love* to his classic novel *Faggots,* in which he essentially predicted the AIDS epidemic, to his co-founding of Gay Men's Health Crisis, to his founding of ACT UP, it was clear to me that this was no ordinary man. To be sure, he is complex, but I have come to realize that he is one of the most outstanding individuals that I have ever met; unusual, but outstanding. I knew instinctively back then that no matter how precarious it might be to get close to him, it would be interesting to get to know him. I had no idea at the time just how interesting it would turn out to be.

□ □ □

In the early to mid-1980s, I first saw Larry Kramer at a public meeting that was held in a hotel in New York City for the purpose of providing a forum for concerned community constituents to interact with federal and local public health officials. In the middle of an address by someone from the United States Department of Health and Human Services, Larry proceeded to shout obscenities and disrupt the proceedings. Although he seemed terribly angry at the time, I remember observing him from a distance after the meeting was over. I expected him to be bristling with barely controlled rage as he had been during his disruption of the meeting. Instead, he was calm, rational, and extremely articulate as he spoke with a small group of people. This was my first experience with tactics with which in time I would become all too familiar and which he above all others had mastered to an art form: confrontation, outrageous behavior, anger, and insults followed by total rationality, sensitivity, and even humor. I remember thinking to myself that there was something oddly appealing about this person, despite the fact that his behavior was rude and disruptive. I, myself, felt very strongly about AIDS and devoted virtually all of my energy to a scientific attack on the epidemic. If Larry Kramer felt as strongly about AIDS as I did, then we really were not very different, expect for our *modi operandi*. Yet, I was taken aback somewhat by his tactics, which by virtue of my background and even my instincts I felt were not particularly productive. Nonetheless, I could not reject Larry out of hand without understanding better what he was trying to accomplish, for even in the scenario of disruption of a public meeting, Larry showed the characteristics that would elevate him in my estimation far above the level of an "out-of-control" iconoclast. Only later would I fully appreciate that it was pure passion related to his concern for the plight of "his people," the gay community, that drove him to outrageous behavior in order to gain the attention of the government and general public concerning the current and impending disaster of the AIDS epidemic. It is so clear to me in retrospect that despite his unusual behavior, Larry had a pure, simple, and unselfish goal; there were no hidden or personal agendas with Larry. He had a cause and he stuck to it. One could argue about the relative merits or accuracy of his hypotheses: whether the government's AIDS policy was or was not appropriate; whether enough money was being spent on AIDS research; whether the NIH was magnificent or incompetent; whether drugs for HIV infection were being approved too slowly or too quickly. Nonetheless, Larry assumed the worst, for in his eyes the stakes were too high to feel any other way. If he unfairly or unjustly criticized certain people or institutions, no matter; in his mind, all such considerations paled in comparison to the devastation of the AIDS epidemic. Larry was not always correct in his information and in his analyses of statistics and scientific findings. In fact, one could say that he was incorrect as often as he was correct when it came to discussing scientific details; what was important was that his passion was pure and his commitment was unflinching in his attempts to jar people into realization of the seriousness of the AIDS epidemic. In this regard, he was as correct and noble as the most respected scientist and public servant.

The Kramer "rumblings" were heard by me intermittently over the next year or two and indeed, I was the target of several of his attacks. Most of these were related to the fact that George Bush and I had developed a friendship that began when he was Vice President and continued throughout his Presidency. During this period I had the opportunity and the privilege of briefing Mr. Bush on several occasions concerning the AIDS epidemic. Larry felt that because of my relationship with Vice President and later President Bush I should chain myself to the White House fence and, as he put it, embarrass the President into speaking out on AIDS and providing more funding for AIDS research. More on that later.

The first time that I met Larry was in New York City in late 1986. I went there to meet with him and a group of the original ACT UP folks. Soon thereafter in early 1987, I invited him down to the National Institutes of Health in Bethesda, Maryland just outside Washington, DC to visit with me and to see our operation. It was during a period when we were rapidly upscaling our efforts in the Division of AIDS of the National Institute of Allergy and Infectious Diseases (NIAID) of which I was Director. The Reagan Administration and the Congress were pouring money into the AIDS program at NIH and we were scrambling to hire people to administer our rapidly expanding grants and contracts activities and to get the physical plant of offices and units established. I spent several hours explaining to Larry the complexities of such an endeavor so that he could appreciate better what managing such a program entails. In response to a simple question concerning where we were going to put all of these additional people, I mentioned casually that space was a problem since we had not yet opened the new facility that would house the additional people. This was an extremely minor part of the total conversation that day. Within weeks, an article appeared in several gay publications including the *New York Native* sharply criticizing me and the NIH and quoting Larry as saying among other things that "People are dying and the government's AIDS efforts are paralyzed because of lack of office space." I had showed him around in good faith and he used the visit as an opportunity to sharply criticize me and the NIH program publicly. Although I do not believe that he truly meant to embarrass me personally, I felt betrayed. As I began to appreciate later, this is the way Larry is. I should have known better, but I was caught off guard. He just felt the need to attack the government, and I was the government. I promised never to get blindsided like this again.

Time went by and the attacks continued. Perhaps the most flagrant public attack that Larry made on me was in an article he wrote that appeared in the Sunday Magazine section of the *San Francisco Examiner* on June 26, 1988. In that article titled "I call you murderers, An Open Letter to an Incompetent Idiot, Dr. Anthony Fauci," he accused me of being responsible for the deaths of hundreds, if not thousands, of HIV-infected individuals for a variety of reasons, including among others his impression that I had not demanded more resources for AIDS, despite the fact that I requested from the President and the Congress and received the largest increase in resources given to an NIH institute since the famous "war on cancer" in the 1970s. Although by this time I was accustomed to Larry's attacks in the press, this article was particularly vicious. I must say that it did hurt and shock me to be called a murderer publicly in a nationally known newspaper at the same time that I was devoting my entire professional life to fighting the AIDS epidemic. Yet, strange as it may seem, I could not blame Larry completely. I knew that his passion needed an outlet. I happened to be the most visible government figure that was directly associated with the AIDS epidemic. I blame the newspaper for publishing such an article. They did not have Larry's passion; they were merely being irresponsible. In Larry's mind whom was there better to attack? He did not know me well, nor did he seem to wish to know me well; and so he could care less how I felt. In his mind I represented the despicable Federal Government. It seemed that he was borrowing a concept from the movie *The Godfather*. It was "nothing personal, but strictly business."

The "nothing personal, strictly business" approach did get way off track on one occasion. In the same 1987 *New York Native* article referred to above in which he sharply criticized me following his visit to the NIH, Larry went too far. He was writing, somewhat tongue in cheek, that I was really very "cute" and that a lot of gays were attracted to me and that he thought I was probably a closet homosexual. He alerted the readers that I was married, but not to worry since my wife "looks like a lesbian." I had introduced Larry to my wife during that visit to the NIH when I took him on a tour of our clinical wards. My wife, Dr Christine Grady, was and is an AIDS nurse who, when Larry visited the NIH, was involved full-time in caring for AIDS patients at the NIH and implementing protocols aimed at alleviating the symptoms of advanced stage HIV disease such as severe wasting. She later received her doctoral degree in medical ethics related to AIDS research. In one sentence in that article, by "attacking" my wife, Larry managed to directly and indirectly offend virtually everyone, straight and gay, establishment and non-establishment; not an unusual accomplishment for Larry. I am obviously prejudiced; but I can think of no one less deserving of being even indirectly attacked publicly or privately by a person who supposedly cares about AIDS. A co-worker at the NIH showed her the newspaper article and although she did not explicitly say it, she was puzzled and hurt by being the target of outrageous remarks from someone who did not even know her. I mentioned to her that I did not know what Larry meant by "looking like a lesbian"; but whatever he meant, it must be very good because she certainly is a beautiful person, physically and spiritually. In her usual phlegmatic manner, she let it pass. However, I was not finished with Larry. I mentioned *The Godfather* analogy earlier and the unusual codes of warfare in that culture. Well, here was an example of "you do not mess with civilians and especially not with families." I called Larry and told him that it was fine to trash me if he wanted to make a point, but Christine was out-of-bounds. I mentioned to him that he had hurt her feelings. Larry was clearly and genuinely horrified at what he had done. You could feel it over the phone. The last thing that he was trying to do was to deliberately hurt anyone, much less a devoted AIDS nurse. His impulsiveness had just gotten out of hand. We both would return to this episode several years later.

I continued to lead the scientific AIDS efforts at the NIH and Larry continued to criticize the government. Time went by and Larry and I met by chance at the 5th International Conference on AIDS that was held in Montreal in early June, 1989. I was walking back to my hotel after dinner late at night with Dr. James C. Hill (my Deputy Director at the National Institute of Allergy and Infectious Diseases). We ran into Larry who was about to walk his dog Molly. He asked if I would take a walk with him and talk a bit. And so Larry, Jim Hill, Molly and I strolled around the streets of Montreal on that pleasant spring evening and talked and talked. Larry was friendly and warm, and clearly wanted some sort of rapprochement. He admitted begrudgingly that he realized that in my own way I was truly committed to fighting this terrible epidemic. However, he still wanted me to do something outrageous to bring attention to the AIDS epidemic. By outrageous he meant either chaining myself to the White House fence as mentioned above or being quoted in the *New York Times* saying that the Administration was a bunch of murderers. I tried to explain to Larry that I did not think that this was the case. Furthermore, even if I felt that this was the correct approach (which I certainly did not), I would get only one shot at it and then my access to the Administration would cease forever. I explained that I could be more effective by trying to help from the inside rather than by attacking from the outside. He just could not understand my point. Even today, he still is not completely convinced that his way would not have been more effective. We went on to talk about the accessibility of drugs for HIV-infected individuals. He became aware of my sensitivity to and sympathy with this problem. I had been for some time leaning toward the concept of relaxing the restrictions on access to drugs in clinical trails; for example, among HIV-infected individuals who had been denied access because of geographic considerations. I promised him that I would try to help in this regard, to use any influence I had. In fact, because of my strong feeling about the issue, I would soon publicly endorse the concept of "parallel track": of drug accessibility to AIDS patients outside of the confines of a clinical trial when such patients did not meet enrolment criteria. With the encouragement of Martin Delaney, founding Director of Project Inform in San Francisco, and much to the dismay of some government officials, I would declare my support for this concept at a Town Meeting in San Francisco later that year. The meeting and the extended conversation with Larry that evening in Montreal had been enjoyable as well as productive. It was clear that we liked and respected each other and our relationship was beginning to evolve. In fact, soon after I had endorsed the parallel track concept at an open government hearing on the subject, Larry shouted out from the grandstands with the same vigor with which he usually disrupted public hearings: "Tony, I have called you a murderer in the past, but you are now my hero."

As time passed, Larry did not refrain from publicly criticizing me as a symbol of the government's "failed" efforts in AIDS. However, we met privately several times over the next year and spoke often over the phone. We began to get to know, understand, respect and like each other. Indeed, we were becoming good friends. However, Larry was ambivalent about our evolving relationship since, while he rather enjoyed attacking people who symbolized what he felt was wrong and unjust in society, he was uncomfortable with attacking "real" people, people whom he might actually like. As he got to know and like me, he worried that he might compromise his ability to attack a highly visible target and might lose an outlet for his rage. The conflicting nature of our relationship intensified during the transition in his mind and experience of Tony Fauci—from the abstract public figure whom he wanted to dispense with to the real-life friend and confidant. He would later describe our relationship to the press as "extremely complex."

His ambivalence about attacking me publicly was evident on a visit that I made to New York City in December 1990. I was there to receive the Presidential Award of the New York Academy of Sciences for achievements in basic and clinical research on AIDS. Larry decided to use the occasion to protest the government's AIDS policies, even though by this time he knew that the policies in question had nothing to do with me or my responsibilities as an AIDS scientist. Nonetheless, Larry seized the opportunity. However, he did not disrupt the proceedings in the more aggressive manner he was so well-accustomed and skilled in utilizing. Instead, he stood outside the main entrance of the Academy on a freezing night with a light snow falling and handed out leaflets stating his protests. I believe that he modified his tactics because he did not want to ruin the evening of my award.

A couple of years later, after our friendship had fully blossomed, his manner of confrontation assumed a more subtle twist. We had a debate on the Nightline show on ABC and he was relentlessly attacking the government's track record on AIDS. He became angry with me and began shouting at me on the air for my defense of what the NIH had done and was doing. He was in a New York studio and I was in Washington, DC. After the show later that night, we spoke over the phone and he cheerfully commented that it was an excellent exchange and he hoped that I did not think he was too hard on me.

After Larry and I had become trusted friends, we revisited the infamous New York Native article in which he had offended my wife Christine. On the occasion of Larry coming to his home town of Washington, D.C. for a high school reunion in the early 1990s, we arranged to go out to dinner. He requested first to stop off at my house to visit Christine and to see my children, three girls who at the time were six, three, and one-half years old. He wanted to make amends to Christine. He entered my home with a serious look of contrition, not knowing if Christine would even speak to him. However, he turned on the classic Larry Kramer charm and Christine was forgiving. He formally apologized and that was the end of it, though Larry claims that he always regarded the lesbian reference as a compliment and that he had tried to explain that. The dynamics of the rapprochement between Larry and Christine played out even further, in the prize-winning play *The Destiny of Me*. The story of his growing up homosexual, his relationship with his family and his dealing with HIV infection was told in retrospect from his hospital room at the NIH. His physician was obviously Tony Fauci whom he named "Dr. Anthony Della Vida." Tony Della Vida's wife was an AIDS nurse, and Larry had cast an African–American woman in the part. Although Larry does not discuss how or why he chooses characters in his plays, I am convinced that he consciously or subconsciously made Tony Della Vida's wife in the play an African-American so that no one would even remotely associate her with the real Christine Grady. He was not going to even come close to offending her again.

In preparation for *The Destiny of Me*, Larry had asked, and I agreed, to have the actor who played me, Bruce McCarty, visit the NIH and follow me around for the day, to make his portrayal of me more authentic. It was good fun and I even showed Bruce a picture of me in my official United States Public Health Service Commissioned Officer's uniform that I rarely wear. Larry thought that this was terrific and had Tony Della Vida play a scene in the play wearing the exact replica of the uniform.

Larry graciously invited Christine and me to be his guests at the New York opening of the play. We had a delightful time and the play was truly excellent. Although Tony Della Vida was trashed as expected in the play, he emerged as a complex person in a subtly sympathetic light. Before the play began, as we gathered for photographs in the lobby of the theater, Larry was clearly nervous and anxious that I might be offended by what I was about to see. At the end of the play, he rushed toward me and asked tentatively, "are you pissed off at me?" I told him that the play was masterful and that I was not offended at all. His relief was quite visible. It was a happy night for Larry. He had created a magnificent play that would receive rave reviews, would win the 1993 Obie and other awards, and would be runner-up for the Pulitzer Prize. He told a sensitive story about his homosexuality and his life; he blasted the Federal Government, and he did not offend his friends.

Larry is very serious and businesslike when he discusses his HIV infection with me. Although he is cared for by excellent physicians in New York City, he never makes a major decision regarding his general care without calling me first. When it comes to his health, our relationship is completely different: he is philosophical, concerned, realistic, highly rational, and completely non-confrontational. This is an aspect of what he calls the "complexity" of our relationship.

In recent years, Larry has claimed that he can no longer feel the same degree of anger and passion. I do not believe that for one moment. He is disappointed in government, in academia, in the private sector and even in the younger generation of activists; however, his passion is not gone. It is too integral to who he is. You can still feel it when you speak to him. He has found love again and is enjoying his life and his relationship; and he is immersed in his *magnum opus*. Our relationship has evolved and matured. We still intensively discuss AIDS, but there are no more confrontations. We have come to accept each other as we are. I do my science and direct the AIDS program of my institute and Larry writes his book. We are like two old friends who have been through the wars together, old adversaries and allies who have affection and respect for each other, and who check in on each other now and then to make sure that each is all right.

Larry Kramer has had an enormous impact on the way our society views the AIDS epidemic. Implicitly, he warned us about the possibility of such a catastrophe in *Faggots*, and when it came, he shouted and pushed us into action. He single-handedly brought about an unprecedented level of public discussion and debate and created a style of health care activism that was never before experienced in this country or anywhere else, and he spawned a generation of activists who continue the vigilance and debate. Larry sometimes bemoans that he has failed, that all his efforts were for naught, since they have not yet resulted in a solution to the AIDS epidemic. Here, of course, he is incorrect, for he has created a movement that is already abundantly contributing to, and that I am sure will be witness to, lasting solutions. I intend to be there with Larry to point out to him what he has ultimately accomplished. In fact, I look forward to the day when the AIDS epidemic is over and Larry and I can truly reminisce, when we can laugh and cry together as we recall the battles we fought on the same and opposite sides, the personal attacks and rapprochements, and the evolution of our "complex" relationship.

Three Friends

Calvin Trillin

WHEN I WAS ASKED if I could write about some aspect of Larry Kramer's life for this book, I said, "I might be able to write a piece about Kramer as a pain in the ass, but I suppose you have too many of those as it is."

No? Well, then, permit me to continue. I suppose it's fair to say that Kramer and I are college friends—we were in the same class at Yale and we knew a number of the same people—but we didn't get to know each other until our fifteenth reunion, in 1972. Among pre-coeducation classes at places like Yale, the fifteenth reunion normally had about half the attendance of the tenth— partly the result, some think, of the physical deterioration that an American male can suffer in his mid-thirties. It wasn't uncharacteristic for Kramer to have been in New Haven for a reunion not many people attended. At our thirty-fifth reunion, I found myself glancing in his direction now and then, concerned that he might be in a shouting match with one of our more conservative classmates. He would always be chatting amiably with some worthy burgher—the burgher wearing the official reunion hat, Kramer in his ACT UP cap.

At the time of our fifteenth reunion, Kramer happened to be in the process of moving to Greenwich Village, and he has been our neighbor and our friend ever since. I say "our" because he has always been close to our two daughters, Abigail and Sarah, and of course, to my wife, Alice, with whom he was bonded almost instantly during that first reunion conversation by a shared passion for chocolate. Alice can usually be counted on to respond to any suggestion that Kramer is a pain in the ass by saying, "Yes, but he's *our* pain in the ass."

That is what she says in private. In public, she won't even acknowledge that Kramer is a pain the ass. If his name comes up when we're talking with people we don't know well—let's say, just to pull an example out of the air, that the conversation has turned to the subject of public figures who don't always behave with prudence and restraint—Alice immediately says something like

"Larry is a very close friend of ours." I've always assumed that it's her way of staving off attacks on Kramer, or at least making certain we don't have the embarrassing duty of saying "Larry is a very close friend of ours" after listening to some diatribe about what a pity it is that the niceties of the First Amendment have kept him from being locked away in someplace unpleasant.

My way of staving off an attack on Kramer is to tell some relatively harmless story that might turn the conversation toward Kramer as a colorful character rather than Kramer as a menace. I often use the story about Mayor Koch and Molly, the Wheaton terrier Kramer once owned and adored. It's a story that I consider too good to check out for authenticity. What is certainly true is that Edward Koch—who as mayor had been strongly criticized and sometimes shouted at by Kramer for not doing enough to fight the AIDS epidemic—moved into Kramer's apartment building after leaving the mayor's mansion. According to the story, Koch got a peace order prohibiting Larry from talking to him. Kramer was at the mailboxes one day, accompanied by the beloved Molly, when he found himself standing next to the mayor. Gesturing towards Koch, Kramer looked down at his dog and said, "Molly, that's the man who murdered so many of Daddy's friends."

Actually, there probably has not been a time in recent years when Kramer would have been insulted by being called a pain in the ass. In *The Normal Heart*, after all, the character he based on himself is a pain in the ass. Kramer's approach to the struggle over AIDS seemed to be based on the notion that acting with prudence and restraint would have been an insult to those who were dying while others took no action. When, in an interview or a letter or an interruption from the audience, he said things that seemed wildly overstated or embarrassing or terribly unfair or even cruel, part of the message was that whatever was causing this ostensibly civilized and sophisticated man to ignore the rules of normal discourse had to be a desperate emergency. In other words, you could argue that Kramer was a pain in the ass as a matter of policy.

At our house, Alice keeps saying, he has always been a pussycat. For the past twenty years or so, Kramer has been invited to our house every year for Christmas dinner—although I always qualify the invitation by saying, "unless, of course, you get a better offer." Sometimes he does. One year, in the late 1980s, we hadn't heard from him by Christmas, and we figured that he was celebrating in some exotic setting. A few months later, Kramer happened to be in New Haven when the Secretary of Health and Human Services was speaking at Yale. It almost goes without saying that Kramer found this coincidence compelling; he led a group of demonstrators to the speech to protest the absence of government commitment to AIDS research. Apparently, the Secretary was unable to speak above the din, and, since Yale has a strict rule about permitting a legitimately invited speaker to speak, three protesters who had been identified as undergraduates were informed that they faced a hearing on whether or not they should be suspended or otherwise disciplined.

Naturally, Larry sent the President of Yale a seven- or eight-page letter protesting the treatment of the undergraduates and attacking the university for harboring this thug from Health and Human Services in the first place. I happened to be a trustee of Yale at the time—apparently, the only trustee Kramer could think of off hand—and my name was at the bottom of the letter as someone receiving a copy. Alice was reading through it when she came on a passage in which Kramer wrote that he'd been so fed up with his straight friends for not doing more in the AIDS battle that he could no longer face them, and had therefore decided not to go to our house the previous Christmas.

"Odd sort of RSVP," Alice said. "Page five of a drop copy of a letter to a university president three or four months after the event."

Still, it was Alice who got on the extension to make peace when Kramer called me to follow up his letter with a personal harangue. As I remember, he was telling me that if anyone deserved punishment for the demonstration it was him and I was telling him that I couldn't agree more when Alice interrupted and said that we should all just go out to dinner together and try to remember that we're friends. We ate at a new place in the Village—one of those restaurants that's designed with a high noise level to show it's a hot spot. As Alice and I walked home, she said, "Aren't you glad you and Larry made up?"

"I'm not sure we did," I said. "The goddamn restaurant was so noisy that for all I now he was calling me a homophobic fascist the entire time."

"You know very well Larry would never call you names." Alice said.

"Fortunately, the reverse is not true," I said. "Kramer is a pain in the ass."

Christmas Dinner with Uncle Larry

Sarah Trillin

LARRY KRAMER, "America's Angriest AIDS Activist", is my Uncle Larry. Larry Kramer, who throws blood on Saint Patrick's Cathedral, who won't let Forest Sawyer get a word in when he's on Nightline, who founded the militant AIDS activist group, ACT UP, who yells and screams at any chance he gets. That's my Uncle Larry. He's not my real uncle, just a close family friend. I've celebrated almost every Christmas I can remember with Larry. He brought me a big beautiful shell that you can hear the ocean in for my birthday when I was little. He's known me since I was a baby. He's seen our home movies.

Since he's become America's angriest AIDS activist, I've seen him in magazines and on television more often that I've seen him in person. But, in the pages of magazines, he is not the same Larry I know. I open up *The Advocate* and discover that Larry is "the most belligerent man in America." My Larry? The Larry I know has a weakness for anything chocolate, and an almost ridiculous devotion to his dog. But, in the past ten years, my family has had to come to terms with the media version of Larry—the angry, frightening, unforgiving man.

The part of Larry's fame I like much better is that Larry has become a hero among a large group of people. He has a following, mostly made up of people my age. He is like a father to them. They get comfort and strength from Larry. I came home from college once to discover a huge billboard a few blocks away from my house. It was a painting of a handsome, joyful young man—the only character in a new play titled *The Night Larry Kramer Kissed Me*. It is named for the title piece in the show, which is about Kramer looking down on Gay Pride Day a few years ago from his balcony, while the marchers looked up at him and waved. This is the Larry Kramer I like to see.

But this is often not the Larry written about. The newspapers and magazines paint a Larry that is staunch and unmovable, and the press seems baffled when a softer side of Larry shines through. Larry has written a play about AIDS and growing up, called *The Destiny of Me*, a sequel to *The Normal Heart*. The play is angry, but is also forgiving. *The Advocate* tells me that "though the old Kramer is clearly visible in the play, a kinder, gentler Kramer also shines through." This makes no sense to me. The kind, gentle Larry *is* the old Larry, as well as the present Larry.

I don't mean to say that the real Larry is simply a lovely person, and that is it. Larry is what you might call difficult. About five years ago, Larry and another somewhat difficult friend of ours had a fight over whether or not Larry could bring Molly, his dog, to Christmas dinner at our house. Larry saw Molly as part of the family, so naturally she would join us for dinner. Our other friend was afraid of all dogs, and said she wouldn't come if Larry brought the dog. Larry said he would not come without the dog. As Christmas day neared, it was ominously unsettled. Larry arrived at Christmas with his friend Rodger McFarlane. Molly was right behind them. Our dog-hating friend was furious. Larry was furious. My mother, trying to salvage Christmas dinner, suggested that Larry put Molly in the downstairs room and close the door. Instead, Larry took Molly back to his house, a few blocks away. He did not come back. We had Christmas dinner without him. Rodger, incredibly sweet, unbelievably shy, and even more polite, was forced to spend his Christmas dinner with a group of people he had never met before.

The next year Larry came to Christmas dinner without Molly, and everything went smoothly. But, there was one other Christmas, in the past few years, when Larry did not come. Later he told us that he could no longer be around his straight friends. That didn't last for too long. Larry soon let us back into his life. But it's hard to forget that we were banished for a time, no matter how short.

"We've all been estranged for periods, all of us," a friend of Larry's, and one of the producers of his new play said in the *Washington Post*. My family is no stranger to that. Larry wishes we would do more—all of us. Lately he seems to have accepted our choices a little more. "There's only so much you can do," Larry tells me. "I've tried cutting you all off from my life. It hurts too much."

Larry has done a remarkable job of keeping the things that he is more upset about than anything in the world separate from his friendships. I'm not saying he hasn't yelled at my father a few times for not doing what he would have done in certain situations. Sometimes it seems like Larry expects so much more from my father than he does from the rest of the family. Perhaps this is because Larry sees my father as having many more opportunities in his career and his work to contribute to Larry's fight than the rest of us do. More than once, my father has disappointed Larry by not taking a stand where Larry thought he might have. At the same time, Larry is forgiving of my father. "You can't make people be what they're not going to be," Larry tells me. Sometimes I wonder why there is such a strong friendship between my father and Larry. In some ways, they are surprisingly similar people. They are both liberal men who take their politics seriously. At the same time, they are both very conventional. They are men of the 1950s. They both believe in hard work, the importance of families, and telling the truth at all costs. One Christmas, when I was seven years old, my parents decided to finally give in and let my sister and me have cats. They hid them at Larry's the week before Christmas, and on Christmas morning, Larry pretended to just drop by the house to wish us a Merry Christmas. In fact, he and my father smuggled the two Siamese kittens into the basement and then up to the living room, where my sister and I stared speechless at the kittens, wondering if we could be dreaming. We all knew that my father despised cats, but still, he devised an elaborate plan to surprise us with them. If Larry had children, he probably would have done the same thing.

Larry's pre-activist relationship with my family is still intact. "There are just things that make me very angry," Larry says to me, "but they don't exist in our relationship." If anyone has changed, it's been my parents. My mother went to an ACT UP rally with Larry this summer. Larry gave my father an ACT UP baseball cap, which he has been known to actually wear out of the house. Larry makes us think.

And I think we can give something special back to Larry as well. Perhaps some kind of comfort or relief, however small. "I have a special relationship with all of you," Larry says, "and I think one reason why it's special for me is that I can come over there and get away from the rest of the stuff in life which is so sad and make jokes with your father—kind of an escape, a respite from dealing with . . ." Larry pauses. "My world is filled with people who are sick."

Sometimes I feel as if that is the big gap between Larry and us. He is from the world of the sick. We are healthy. "There's no way a healthy person can live with the feelings of those of us who are angrily facing death," Larry angrily told the reporter from *The Advocate*. Larry is right. We cannot understand his fear as well as we would like to. Larry is HIV-positive. Any day he could become very ill. Sometimes I think that is why Larry's bond with my mother seems to have grown stronger in the past few years. Seventeen years ago, my mother was diagnosed with lung cancer. Most people thought she was going to die, but she recovered. She was strong throughout the whole ordeal. "Your mother's just very helpful," Larry tells me. "I respect her judgment a lot. She's a good friend and shit detector. I don't have many whose opinions I respect." Sometimes when my father is out of town, my mother and Larry go to the movies together, two old friends.

For me, seeing *The Destiny of Me*, which is completely autobiographical, brought me some of the understanding I was looking for. I had understood

Larry's anger, but I was not quite prepared to watch Larry's pain performed on stage. In the play, a middle-aged Larry talks with the young version of himself, and watches him grow up. I watched the young Larry being slapped around by his father. I watched the old Larry lie in a hospital bed, sick and frightened. And then there was the final line of the play, a terrified and frustrated Larry pleading, "I want to stay a little longer." I stared throughout the play dumbstruck. When I walked out of the theater, I felt utterly heartbroken.

Watching the life of someone you're close to being performed on a stage is indescribably compelling. The younger Larry danced around on stage, and I couldn't take my eyes off him. He was funny and silly and charming. The older Larry was funny and cynical and so tired that I wanted to reach out to the actor and comfort him, as if he were really Larry. I want to be there for him, but he is on stage, and I am in the audience. There is no way I can cross that line.

"I don't have many straight friends that I still see," Larry tells me. "I guess the reason I don't see them is they do make me very angry." Why has my family been spared, I ask. Why don't we make him so angry?' 'It's probably something you can't see yet," Larry says. "We've all stayed young and curious, and most people as they get older get very stodgy, and boring and frozen in time. They're not open to new ideas or new experiences. People I've stayed friends with are as nosy as I am." I suppose I have an advantage. I really am young, and I was brought up to be curious and nosy. I have asked for an ACT UP baseball cap of my own for Christmas, and will wear it with pride.

Still, we are a separate part of Larry's life, unconnected to most of his world. "My life is very compartmentalized," Larry says. "I feel close to my straight friends, like your parents and my family . . . but everyone's in a special little chapter." We know that we are in the chapter that is quieter and significantly less urgent than the rest of his life. We are the background. But we are glad to be there.

"My younger self was very funny and spunky," Larry wrote in the *New York Times*, "and it is the me of today who . . . has lost a lot of the resilience." Just as Larry separated his younger and older self into two different bodies in his play, he separates them in his mind. To me, they are both still a part of him. The young Larry in the theater who made jokes and made fun of himself was the Larry I know. The young Larry who gleefully ran around the stage singing show tunes was my Larry who always knows all the words to "My Funny Valentine" when we gather around the piano after Christmas dinner. Watching the young Larry on stage made me miss my Larry terribly. He doesn't come around nearly as often as he used to before he began the busy life of America's Angriest AIDS Activist. But my Larry is still there, in his apartment a few blocks away from my house, with his dog. And he's coming to Christmas dinner this year.

PART SIX

Interview

Interview with a Writer

Lawrence D. Mass

> *You must hate yourself so much that only by constant work, striving, passionate attempts to prove your worthiness to yourself through your writing can you survive.*
>
> *Look and study and suck everything you can. Try everything you're emotionally and physically able to try and then push yourself even further than that limit. And study your reaction. Study and dissect it and write it down.*
>
> From *Sissies' Scrapbook,* Act II, 1973

> *If you're any good as an artist, I don't think you do what you do because you necessarily want to do it. You do it because you have to do it.*
>
> —Larry Kramer, from *Paul Monette: The Brink of Summer's End* (documentary film, 1996)

[Editorial note: "Interview with a Writer" unfolded in several sessions, mostly in Larry Kramer's Washington Square home in New York City, and mostly in 1996.]

Mass: Since this interview is especially for this anthology and may be the only or first interview with you to be published in a collection, I want to cover a broad range of subject matter, though there will be an emphasis on your experience as a writer. As with all my interviews (the thirty that are published in my two-volume collection), you'll be able to collaborate to whatever extent you please. That is, you can edit the manuscript. I want to be able to say that Larry Kramer has approved the final text. As I state in the Foreword to *Dialogues of The Sexual Revolution*:

In part because I'm not at my best in spontaneous conversation, my preferred method is to interview others as I myself would prefer to be interviewed: with a greater concern for considered, fact-checked and self-edited opinion than for less but also important values of spontaniety and style. What I've found is that when interviewees are assured that they will be able to edit their responses and share editorial approval, they tend to be *more* open, *more* willing to take chances, generally if not universally, than under more restrictive conditions.

I believe this approach will be most fruitful, even with one of the most characteristically and notoriously spontaneous figures of all time!

Let's start with the title of this collection. If it were up to you, what would you call "the book on Larry Kramer"?

Kramer: I like "The Book on Larry Kramer." (laughter) Let's think about that as we go along. But it's what strikes *you* that's important. It is, after all, your book. I don't want to approve the text beyond biographical errors. You can say what you want.

Mass: The phrase "the normal heart" comes from Auden's poem "September 1, 1939," two stanzas of which introduce the published edition of *The Normal Heart*, as does "the furniture of home," which you had planned to use for the title of what became *The Destiny of Me* . . .

You know, when I reread *Faggots,* even though it was 1994, the title still made me squirm. I mean, even today, when "faggot," like "nigger", has become so vernacular, can you imagine a comparable book about black self-oppression called "*Niggers*"?

Kramer: Actually, there was *Nigger* by Dick Gregory, which I think is mostly autobiography . . . In any case, I don't think "faggot" is as hatefully derogatory as "nigger" was and is. It's interesting that gays, since the book was written, have gone through these periods of calling ourselves names we had originally found very uncomfortable, like "queers," "faggots," whatever. I was amazed that Queer Nation called themselves that, for instance.

Early on in *Faggots*, one of the characters defines what that term means. It's people who don't think well of themselves, and in essence, put themselves down, and don't lead exemplary lives. The book was really about a group of people who I thought should be gay leaders or role models and who, for whatever reasons, weren't. So it was meant to be a critical title. The first editor who saw some pages was Robert Gottlieb, who was then head of Knopf and who encouraged me to write it in the first place. Actually, my shrink encouraged me to write it first, after a very unhappy and unsuccessful sojourn in Hollywood trying to sell a screenplay that never got sold after the failure of my first play *Sissies' Scrapbook*. I was having all these anxiety attacks out there and he encouraged me to come back, and within a year, I did. One day he said, "Have you ever thought of writing a novel about what you think it's like to be gay, what you feel the gay world is like?", and I got excited about the notion. When I had about fifty pages, I showed them to Bob Gottlieb, whose wife, Maria Tucci, had been in *Sissies' Scrapbook* and who was among the very few who had been generous in praise of that play. He got very excited about them and said, "You really ought to call it something like—" I don't remember what the suggestions were, but they were all words or phrases like "faggots," although "faggots" wasn't one of them. Now, I had just been reading about Mary McCarthy, so I was thinking of "The Group." Then, as I wrote it, I thought, it really should be *Faggots*. That just seemed right to me.

Later, I thought, why am I calling it this—all the old ladies who reorder books for the bookstores they work at won't want to reorder it. And the stores won't want to display it. But you know me. Once I want to do something, I plunge ahead, damn the torpedos. Talk about naiveté.

Mass: There are many extraordinary passages in *Faggots*, but there's one I want to ask you about specifically because I found it, in the breadth of its inquiry and character of its concern, to be one of the most probing, revealing and stimulating discourses to emerge from our literatures.

> He did not, as many others did, wear-and-tell all. He scorned the ass kerchiefs and keys, posted and peeking for all the boys to see: navy for fuck and yellow for piss and mustard for big cock and red for fist fucking and robin's egg for 69 and lighter blue for cock sucker and olive for military and green for hustler and brown for shit and orange for Anything and this kerchief or keys on the Left Side meant I Do It To You and on the Right Side means You Do It To Me and on certain streets on certain days at certain times the code might be slightly altered if you knew certain people, and though all of this told all, what did any of it *mean?*

Perhaps I'm reading too much into it, but Fred's question is so grand. It reflects an inquiry into the much bigger picture, bigger even than our communities and times and places. In the much bigger picture of the history and future of sexuality, what *is* all this?! I mean, at some point in the future, anthropologists and historians will look back and write about us the way Margaret Mead does about Samoans: Under such and such conditions of time and place, here's what human primates were doing . . .

Kramer: Oh, God, I think we could talk for hours about this. I started writing the book in 1975, when I was forty years old. In those days, our lives were not only closeted, but so compartmentalized. I wasn't really in the closet, but I certainly wasn't politicized. And the book really was an exploration by its author into the gay world to find out, experience, or at least witness, what was going on. That meant going to these extraordinary bars and clubs and events, from what I call "The Toilet Bowl"—which is based on a real bar that was called, I'm pretty sure, "The Toilet"—to the gay synagogue. I had not been to the gay synagogue either. And this is long before I met the real life Leather Louie, or had my affair with David. I had friends who would see me and make jokes that I was walking around with a notebook: "Here comes the professor again." "Here comes Larry with his notebook." "What are you researching today, Larry?"

By the end, in the writing of the book, what it all *meant* to me, I think, was that we had made sex our be-all and end-all. I guess that would be the best way of putting it. That's all we had, that's what held us together! And not only was that all we were encouraging each other to do, and not only were we doing this willingly, it was what the gay movement was based on.

Now, you and I have talked about this a lot, and I think in the screenplay of *The Normal Heart*, I have had the Arnie [Kantrowitz] character say something that Arnie in fact said to me at some point, and you had at some point said to me, "Well, where the fuck were *you* when we were doing all this and fighting for the right to get married and the right to do all these things?" But basically the movement, as I understood it, as it had come down to me from the '50s and the '60s, was pretty much exclusively or predominantly based on sexual freedom and freedom of sexual expression, and that seemed to be—and this is long before AIDS—and that seemed ... very limiting. At the end of the novel, the Fred character says something to the effect that having so much sex makes finding love impossible. I still believe that, and I never stopped believing that, even as I was in the baths looking for . . .

Mass: Yes, but it seemed to me that the question you were asking was even bigger. I'm talking about a Robert Wilsonian kind of perspective about our time and time itself, which may well be my own projection, but which I find everywhere in the ambience of *Faggots*, something like the sense you get from the Godfrey Reggio/Philip Glass film *Koyaanisqatsi* (Hopi for "time out of balance)." For me, its most spectacular moment comes in the leather bar sequence where the fat cat straight Jewish movie producer, Abe, has inadvertently entered this gay leather bar, a completely alien world he can't begin to comprehend or function in. The sequence, mirrored elsewhere in the novel by the lesbian seduction of his wife, is so "appallingly funny" (as Edward Albee says of *Faggots*) that I think I got a rip in my esophagus. But underneath the humor is this profound questioning, this taking the whole thing out of context, like a scientist, and saying, tweezers in hand and microscope on the table, what *is* all this behavior, all this coding and costuming and ritual? At the simplest level, of course, it's just people, straight as well as gay, trying to connect at the level of shared fetishes and fantasies, but your tone, the atmosphere of *Faggots*, suggests that there's *much* more to know, to understand. What you're asking in literary and artistic terms is what we look to people like John D'Emilio to answer with historical perspective; to *Sexual Politics, Sexual Communities*, and to *Intimate Matters: A History of Sexuality in America* by D'Emilio and Estelle Friedman. What they've pointed out is that a lot of what we might call the commodification of gay male sexuality is explainable by Western economics and its politics; by capitalism.

Kramer: You're getting me excited. This is the kind of questioning I want to do more of in the new book [*The American People*, Kramer's novel in progress]. What do *you* think it all means?

Mass: Well, there can't be any question of the validity of much of what D'Emilio, Freedman and others have pointed out. Certainly capitalism is one of the great, vast trends our sexualities have been shaped by. But in line with their level of inquiry, I think there are even bigger, and certainly other, broad developments and characteristics that haven't yet been articulated; and *Faggots*, like some consciousness-expanding drug, is one of the signs of our times that makes me sense this.

Kramer: Do you think that there's some desire that we have as a group that we haven't recognized? To be part of an army of some kind? Is there some kind of bonding we're prone to that we don't yet understand, that isn't yet understood?

Mass: These are the kinds of questions I find in the background of your art and life. It reminds me a little of Mark Merlis's first impressions of *Faggots*, when what he sensed beneath all the critique and satire, was that these were his people. All the rest was incidental to this overriding reality. Douglas Sadownick is another with this sense of the great, undeconstructed forces at play in *Faggots*. With similar unselfconsciousness and unintentionality, *Faggots*, I believe, reveals a profound malaise and dis-ease about our time, something fundamentally disturbed in the whole picture, in a way no one else has, even though others, such as Andrew Holleran, are dealing with a lot of the same subject matter, and have produced their own rich and enduring takes. In terms of this blunt but so extraordinary question your book actually comes right out and asks, what does it all *mean*? I don't know that anybody has the answer, but *your* art makes us ask this question to an extent I find without peer or precedent in our literatures. It also leads us to believe that it can be answered, and in doing so, literally shepherds us forward, into the future, whatever it may hold.

Kramer: But a lot of what I was dealing with was of the here and now. I've always felt and I think I've always said that we're capable of so much more. I do think that in a lot of ways, gay people are really—I don't want to say better but I do mean—better than straight people. We're more in touch with our feelings. I think we're more perceptive. I know these are stereotypes and generalizations, but I think there's no question that we're more creative and understanding of art and of other people's feelings. I can't tell you how many women have told me that the gay men they've in fact made love with are ten times more attentive and better lovers than the straight lovers they've had. I believe this shows an enormous potential for something that we don't realize. And who knows what this potential is or could be for us as a group. So you can't help but wonder how it all gets so distorted, literally perverted, not in the sense of sickness, but of being turned away, into all of this sexual nonsense. Of course, there isn't anything wrong with healthy pornographic aspects of sex, as in a relationship, but it never seems to get to that. For an awful lot of people it becomes the whole thing. You know, it can be exciting for two minutes in the context of a relationship to do whatever, but then to make that the be- and end-all and parade it around in front of everybody. I don't know what it means, but I don't know that it's exclusively homosexual.

Mass: Of course not. The sexologists have a lot of different names for these behaviors—e.g., polyiterophilia, the repetition of early bonding behaviors in the absence of being able to advance beyond that phase. In the era of *Faggots*, we talked about promiscuity. Today, we talk about sexual compulsivity. Notwithstanding ongoing debate about our sexualities—even in the age of AIDS, we can't really be so naive as to believe that lifetime monogamy is the only way for everybody, or even serial monogamy (which is what Gabriel Rotello envisions as an ideal)—we've stopped putting those words and phrases in quotations.

Kramer: In *The American People*, I guess I'm just beginning to see all that. I'm trying to understand AIDS—in the context of why, where and how—and I find myself going further and further back in time. You can make the case that it started with the Puritans, that same perversion of sexual instincts—attitudes run deep in this country, that turning away from what people say they want, but in effect in no way ever have. I don't know. Maybe it has something to do with the evil in people, a subject I've become very interested in. As you know, I've written an essay about evil that concludes *Reports [from the holocaust]*. And I never thought about it before, or I would have dug into it more in the new edition of *Reports*. It has become ever more fascinating to me—evil in a nonreligious sense, not in contrast to good, but evil in the sense of itself. Why? I don't know that I have an answer, but maybe I will by the time I get to the end of the new book ... Maybe there isn't an answer.

Mass: In your essay, after noting that evil is either ill- or undefined in every major resource (encyclopedias, dictionaries, even theological texts) one could think to look to, you ask, "Why can't anyone define evil in and of itself?" The reason, I think, is that it's invariably, if not always, so relative.

Take, for example, what you'd think would be an absolute bottom-line example of evil—Charles Manson. OK, but as soon as his forehead acquired a swastika tattoo, he and his acts became political. Likewise other such examples: Gilles de Rais, one of history's worst serial killers of children, was apparently embroiled in the politics of his time and region. And if you really believe homosexuality is evil, you might be more sympathetic to the crimes of John Wayne Gacy. If you're a Nazi, Dr. Mengele becomes a patriot.

Kramer: Hitler was supported by his people.

Mass: Precisely. In Iran, America is "the great Satan." There, we are regarded not merely as enemies, but as diabolically evil. *You*, for example. You're a Jew, you're an American, you're queer and you have HIV. My God, you would have been killed sixteen times!

Kramer: But my point is that there isn't even *discussion* of evil any more, except among the religious fanatics. As elusive as it is, and as much as it has been misused and used against us, against innocent people, minorities, and even though fundamentalists are still doing this everywhere, it's even scarier that it has receded so far from *our*—from "civilized"—public consciousness, concern and debate.

Mass: Though I suspect we will no more be able to find any absolute definitions of evil than we will of another aspect of *Faggots* and your other work I want to ask you about—humor.

First, a personal question, which is always a good place to start or proceed with someone in whom the personal is so political and vice versa: Do you laugh much? As much as the next person?

Kramer: I don't know. I don't think that people who are considered funny in their work are ever very funny in their lives. I remember I once met Lucille Ball who was very unfunny. (laughter)

It's just the way she was. She was an actress, and she had to be on stage to do it, I guess. I've rarely heard anyone like Woody Allen or Jack Benny—people who you thought would be funny to talk to—ever actually be so. Usually, people can't just turn it on. And of course, verbal humor is usually humor that you've worked on. Certainly, that's true of *Faggots*, in which, more than anything else I've written, every word is honed. I'd wake up in the middle of the night, or, walking down the street, I'd suddenly think, oh, I want to change that word to this or put it there. It was also oral—how did I *hear* it?

You know, I started out wanting to be a comedy writer. I wrote a movie called *Here We Go 'Round the Mulberry Bush*, which was funny. *Women in Love* wasn't. I happen to think *Just Say No* is very funny, but nobody else thought so ... What makes me laugh isn't necessarily what appeals to others. What does make me laugh? Well, Jerry Lewis *doesn't* make me laugh. (laughter) I don't know who ...

Mass: But you do laugh.

Kramer: But I do laugh? Yes! Of course, there's so precious little you could laugh about these last years, and that's made it hard writing this book, because, in a way, I'd like to make it funny. But I'm not the same person I was when I wrote *Faggots*. My style isn't the same. It's certainly hard to write about AIDS in that way. I can, but it's a much different kind of humor. It's much more morbid.

Mass: It's funny when you think about it, though. I mean, people are going to be looking at you from a lot of different perspectives, and one of them will be, or certainly should be, of this fiery activist who was actually also this humorist. There have been other artist–activists, but has there ever been another humorist–activist? (Ronald Reagan? Dick Gregory comes to mind.) In any event, this is an important perspective, one that is discernible even in the angriest pieces in *Reports*, as well as scattered throughout *The Normal Heart*. It will be a real challenge for some future historian or scholar.

Kramer: I wanted to write for *Saturday Night Live*. Really. I once went up there and had a meeting with Herb Sergeant, who was the chief writer. I see that Lorne Michaels is having a problem with the program now; maybe I should go up there and try again.

Mass: Some people feel that your humor is overwrought—"labored." They've said the same thing about your prose. Earlier, you mentioned your pride in having honed every word of *Faggots*. For me, that really comes across. It is so extraordinarily polished. The strange names, long lists and streams of consciousness keep acting in ways that produce these palpable rhythms and, finally, music. At the level of your bones, you actually become seduced into this fairytale dreamscape of caricatures and extremes you are simultaneously supposed to be observing with such detachment and revulsion. The result is the most powerful tension, and pure literary magic.

Kramer: When *Faggots* was reviewed in the *New York Times Book Review* by John Lahr, one of the things he went on about was how badly written it was. This just broke my heart. I didn't care so much that he didn't agree with me politically, but I really had worked so hard to write well, and I write what I hear, and yes, there were meant to be cadences and music and poetry in *Faggots*, in almost everything I do.

Mass: One of the things I've always wanted to know more about was who/ what got edited out of *Faggots*—e.g., Baron Leon Lambert.

Kramer: Oh, a number of characters got edited out, only because . . . as one hones the novel, one also condenses the plot and the story, and they didn't fit into the stories I was choosing. The first draft, maybe the first two drafts (I think there were four or five total) of *Faggots* took place over a year, and was divided into four sections, one for each season. Slowly it began to get compressed from a year to one weekend. In the original, there was more room for other characters. I remember, for instance, that one section was based on an Islanders cruise that I took to the Caribbean. There were these various comings and goings on the Isle of Bonaire, or something. Anyway, "Lily Lambeau" [based on Lambert] was one of several that got cut out. There was a character based on a famous film producer I'd worked with, Ross Hunter, whom I called "Rust Legend" and on the making of his great musical, which I think I called "Lest We Sleep Alone"; and I had a character based on Roy Cohn, whom I called "Sam Sport," and who may, in fact, make an appearance in *The American People*. It was only with this character, actually, that I felt some danger. In the midst of writing this material, which I hadn't yet shown to anyone, I got two phone calls that scared the shit out of me. To this day, I don't know how they knew. One was a boyfriend of Roy Cohn's, someone I did know, who called me and said "Roy hears that he's a character in your new novel, and he wants you to know that if he is, your life is in danger." And he said "Larry, I don't have to tell you that this is not a joke." It was scary, but by then, I had already cut him out. But I don't think I would have been stopped by this threat. I would have continued if he had been useful as a character.

Mass: But you had met him (Cohn).

Kramer I never met him.

Mass: Did you have other mutual friends?

Kramer: Nope. Just this guy, whom I vaguely knew, only because he'd had an affair with a friend of mine.

Mass: He must have known from somebody that you were working on the novel.

Kramer: The other phone call was in relation to the Bronfman kidnapping, which is the basis of a subplot of *Faggots*. I got a call one day from a woman who had this very cultured accent—I knew I was talking to a lady—and she said *"Monsieur* Kramer, I want you to know that your version of the Bronfman kidnapping is correct, and that you are lucky to be alive." And she hung up the phone. That was just before I was about to go out on tour to promote the book.

Mass: All of which raises the question of an uncut *Faggots*.

Kramer: (laughter). Well, the Lily Lambeau stuff never got very developed, maybe just a few paragraphs. It just didn't take fire in my imagination. I mean, with Leon, all you could do was poke fun at the poor man. There was nothing really redeeming, to make his story worth telling. Roy Cohn was a different story. He was evil, and maybe that's where the problem was. I wasn't really writing about evil then. He belongs much more in the new book, where he probably will be, even though Tony [Kushner] got out there with him first.

Mass: Actually, Marty [Duberman] wrote a play about him ... One of his wonderful history plays (which, collectively, would make a great festival). It was called *Roy*. I don't think it ever got produced or even published.

Kramer: I thought Tony did a brilliant job with Roy Cohn.

Mass: Indeed. I want to ask you about your reactions to Tony and his play, but I do have a few more questions about *Faggots*. Would you be willing to update us on what's happened to some of these characters? For example, Anthony Montano?

Kramer: Well, are we outing everybody here? Outing my characters? Well, Anthony Montano was, had been for a number of years, as we both know, my best friend. He helped me when the book was in progress and actually chose his fictional name. He didn't like the original name I'd chosen. I read him the sections based on him, and he even helped me with a few of the jokes, made them better. He didn't seem to have any real objection to any of it. But then, when the book came out, he suddenly had a great deal of objection to it and we literally didn't speak for many years. We speak now, but it's not the same friendship. I sort of find him sad. I don't know if I want to say this for print, but maybe I do. He's a man who should have been a lot more in life than he has been. He's exceedingly smart, he's got a lot of money, he's handsome, but he's gotten so involved in fighting this lawsuit with an ex-employer who fired him; it's become like something out of *Bleak House*. It just goes on and on and on and on. It's like in that Trollope novel called *He Knew He Was Right*, where the guy just goes to the ends of the world, beyond any kind of possible rational sense, to prove he's right; and that's what this lawsuit is: his life has passed him by while he fights this fucking lawsuit. Even if he wins, he's lost.

Mass: And what about Dinky Adams?

Kramer: Seventeen years later, Dinky Adams has become my lover. His real name is David Webster, and he thinks that I got him all wrong, that I misunderstood him, and our relationship, enormously. He was not happy with the book when it was published, and who's to say he wasn't right—in terms of my take on him? I think it says a great deal about his character that he's back with me, and in a very loving way, and has not held the book against me or the relationship. When the book was written, we were both much younger, and some of what I wrote, in fantasy, in my imagination, probably did make things seem a lot more extreme than perhaps they were in reality. Those were different years. He obviously wasn't ready for a relationship with me, and probably wasn't interested in anyone else either. Since that time, he did have a relationship that lasted about ten or eleven years. He says I made him so fucking mad by telling him he wasn't capable of a relationship that he went out there to prove that I was wrong. And it was a very happy, successful and emotionally fulfilling relationship. Unfortunately, Michael Erickson, who was the lover, died about three years ago from AIDS.

Mass: For many years, you didn't speak—is that correct?

Kramer: For years, I never saw him. Actually, it's a very romantic story, and it shows you that there is hope if you wait long enough. Even though he lives on 25th street and I live on 8th street, I never saw him from 1981 to 1993, though I did try to call . . . I went to our beloved shrink, Norman Levy [Norman J. Levy was also the therapist of Arnie Kantrowitz and, later, Larry Mass and Rodger McFarlane], to get over him in the '80s, and Norman used to always say, "Larry, call up David. Go see him; prove to yourself that he doesn't have this power over you anymore." Because it was extremely powerful, the hold he had on me.

Mass: That's clear in the book. Just as Mark Merlis was able to see the love of community, the tribal bonding belying everything else in *Faggots*, the depth of your love for Dinky is likewise discernible there.

Kramer: I just couldn't get over him. It took me three years of therapy, of going to Norman every day, practically. I was reading Karen Horney all the time [Levy was a Horneyan analyst]. As I say, I did actually call him a few times and usually got a machine. He's an architect with a successful international practice, so he was out of the country a lot. David now says that Michael always checked the machine and didn't give him the messages lots of times because he knew who I was. Not only didn't we make contact, I never even saw him on the street, even though he and Michael had a shop over on University Place. Nor did I ever see him at a party, at the gym, or anywhere else. It's amazing. I figured God was keeping us apart, or fate.

Then, when I started looking for a house, because I wanted to get out of East Hampton and I knew what I wanted, I decided to try again. David has a look to the work that he does that had always been my ideal for comfort. I don't know how to describe it. As a designer as well as an architect, he has a way of making things cozy. I'd felt this in the work he did that I'd seen in magazines and elsewhere. I knew I wanted him to do my house. After all those years, I certainly didn't think I was still in love with him. It was around Christmas. He answered the phone, much to my surprise, and we talked. He said "I'm going to Switzerland. I'll call you in a few months when I'm back." I didn't know that Michael was sick; I did not know that he was even still with Michael. He told me he had a job in Switzerland he was finishing and was going over there, and I didn't know that in essence he was taking Michael back home to die. Perhaps they didn't know he was going to die, but they knew he was very sick. He did call me when he came back in March. Michael had died in February. In April we had our first dinner and it was as if we'd never been apart. We just picked up where we'd left off—our conversation, our friends, the fact that he makes me laugh. You asked about humor, about whether I laugh. Well, to me, David is very funny. I don't know why I should go into all of this, but we actually went to bed that night. I've often thought I should start a play with that because it was probably the most complicated couple of hours in my life. I don't know if you can imagine what it's like going to bed with somebody that you have been so intensely in love with, and it's seventeen years later, and you both have different bodies, and you're particularly conscious of the fat that wasn't there when you had your muscles. And not only are you both physically different—you know, because he is too; he's still a handsome man, but he's not the handsome man he was then—but everybody else is in bed with you too. Everybody who's died. His lover, my lover, all our friends, everybody we knew in common. The other characters in *Faggots*. They were all in bed with us somehow. I just couldn't get all this out of my mind. Also, what the fuck am I doing in bed anyway? I mean, safe sex or no safe sex. It was like . . . it was just a very strange experience, too complicated to be pleasurable; not unpleasureable, but it was certainly fraught. I really felt when I left the apartment that night that I didn't know what would happen. I was terrified I'd fall in love again in that same neurotic way again, that would be so punishing to us both, and I've been relieved and glad to see, at least so far, that I haven't felt that claw-like grip coming over me. "All right," I said to myself, "let's see what happens." So I called my close friend Rodger [McFarlane] and said "You're never going to guess what's happened." David called me later that day and we've been pretty much together ever since. This time, things have proceeded much more slowly, and the fact that he still has had to go back to Switzerland for his work, so there has been a lot of back and forth, which has actually made it easier. I think I've finally learned that lesson of . . . not demanding love. I have a life of my own now, which I guess I didn't then. I always have so many things to do, as does he, so we don't place pressures on the other. Things have developed in a much more natural way. It's been wonderful. It's a couple of years now, and here's hoping. And that's the long history of Dinky Adams.

Mass: In view of all these developments with these characters, is there any possibility of a "Faggots II'?

Kramer: Who was it—Mark Harrington?—who suggested I write "Faggots II—The Nineties"?

Mass: Of course, you've already done that to some extent in some of your other works, in the plays.

Kramer: Well, *The American People* is a very ambitious novel, and there will be a part of it that might be referential to *Faggots;* and I suspect that somehow David's and my love affair could be a part of the novel. But I think it's much more likely that there will be a third play, a trilogy with *The Normal Heart* and *The Destiny of Me* . . . we'll see.

Mass: Just two other characters I want to ask you about—Dordogna del Dongo . . .

Kramer: And?

Mass: Boo Boo Bronstein.

Kramer: Oh, Boo Boo was based on the Bronfman kidnapping. Even though the character was based on the real-life son, the physical characterization was based on our mutual friend Richard Umans, who died from AIDS some years ago. I'd met him through the friend who introduced us, you and me—Tom Holtz. Richard was a writer, or wanted to be a writer. Eventually, he did get a couple of his short stories published. One of them, I think, is in one of the *Men on Men* books ["Speech" is featured in first volume of *Men on Men*, edited by George Stambolian]. He had kept a file on me and, when he died, his lover sent me the file, not knowing what was in it particularly. It was obvious he was keeping a kind of dossier, maybe to get back at me . . .

Dordogna is the one who sleeps with . . . Randy Dildough. I don't know, I guess I'm legally clear now because the book has been in print so many years, but yes, that relationship was based on Barry Diller and Diane von Furstenburg, which I always thought was one of the more bizarre relationships of all time. I do think I got a lot of humor out of it. Barry was certainly not amused, but actually, they have both been rather gentlemanly, if I may use that word. She has always been exceedingly polite, as has Egon, who I think is also in there somewhere. Barry was angry, but we had a sort of touching rapprochement when I asked him if he would help get *The Normal Heart* going as a film. I said I hoped that we could somehow overlook the past, because it was so important to get an AIDS movie out there. Anyway, those were different days.

Mass: (laughter) I'm laughing because I'm just remembering the lesbian seduction sequence with Abe's wife, Ephra, this middle-class, middle-aged, very serious and proper Jewish mother being seduced into this fast-track Fire Island world, seduced into becoming—God should forbid—a lesbian!

Has anyone ever written about the lesbian world and subplots of *Faggots*?

Kramer: Not that I know of.

Mass: One last question for now about *Faggots*. It works so brilliantly as a screenplay, yet it's inconceivable how the sexuality could be worked into something that could be marketed as a mainstream film, even if x-rated. But maybe this is wrong. I think I'm the only person in the world who liked *Myra Breckenridge*, the film, and one of the things I most admired about it was its effort to translate its impossible subject matter into cinematic terms. Anyway, is there a screenplay of *Faggots*, or do you think there ever will be?

Kramer: No. It's a book. I just don't see how you could do it. I mean, it's a story that's really, that's so totally and utterly about fucking. . . . I guess you could do it without a lot of the fucking, but how could you do the orgy?

Mass: It would be fabulous, like a musical or opera, like the orgy sequence in *Moses and Aaron* . . .

Kramer: Speaking of opera and *Faggots*, when Lenny [Leonard Bernstein] was looking for someone to write the book for his opera . . .

Mass: . . . for what became *A Quiet Place* . . .

Kramer: . . . Harry Kraut, Lenny's manager, gave him *Faggots* and Lenny was very shocked. We were friends. We had a loving friendship, and he used to make jokes about it— (gasp) "That book!"

Mass: Well he did do the new opera, *A Quiet Place*, and it has frankly gay material. It has had productions in Vienna and Houston, but it hasn't yet been done in New York. Talk about mysteries. Please call your friend Harry and see if he can solve this one. Some speculate that it's because the opera just isn't good enough, but that's ridiculous.

Kramer: Don't they do them both together [*Trouble in Tahiti* and *A Quiet Place*] as an evening?

Mass: Well, that's the way it was conceived. The lives of the characters in the earlier work are picked up thirty years later.

But you say you're probably not going to write a sequel *per se* to *Faggots*, though there may be some degree of continuity in your new novel, *The American People*. I wasn't there, unfortunately, but Walter Vatter told me that your reading of a chapter, "The Bloods," at A Different Light bookstore was "mesmerizing." He said the place was packed to the rafters but you could hear a pin drop. What can you tell us, at this point, about the new book?

Kramer: Well, it's very long! You'll never have time to read it. I'll never have time to finish it. I don't know. It's like Mount Everest. I don't think I'll ever reach the top. The readings have been very important to me, because I haven't trusted what I've been doing. It's the only time in my life I've ever written anything and been afraid of it . . . and not felt warm toward it. "Warm" is the wrong word . . . Every writer knows you struggle and you struggle and then there comes a point when you say "Aha, I like it," or "I'm getting there," or "I've made a breakthrough." And so you begin to be more accepting of what you're doing and embrace it in a different way. I've been working on this fucking book since I finished *Faggots,* in 1978 or '79, and I have only just begun to feel that way. In other words, I've been working on it with great pain for all these years, pain to such a degree that there have been periods I simply can't work on it. I don't understand where all this stuff is coming from. It's a much more imaginative novel or work than anything I've ever done. And it's been particularly hard because I've spent the last— with the exception of *Just Say No*—I've spent the last ten or fifteen years writing stuff that was biographically very close to the bone, and *The Normal Heart* and *Destiny* are both, as far as I'm concerned, true, and didn't leave much room for imagination. It was almost like writing autobiography. Now, I'm writing stuff that I'm making up and I don't know who, where's it coming from. Who is this character? I haven't trusted it. In fact, I've almost thrown it all away several times. If it weren't for Rodger [McFarlane], I might well have done so. A lot of the writing was done in East Hampton and Sag Harbor, where he was sharing houses with me, and he said "Keep going," "Don't you *dare* throw it away!" He sensed that as crazy as it was, there was something there. So then I had two readings, one at A Different Light, and one at Barnes and Noble a year before, around the time *Destiny* was published. And I read two really weirdo sections, sections that I just . . . I took the most extreme sections I could think of, and both events went like gangbusters. I cannot tell you how much confidence that gave me. Because of that, I'm much more embracing of the work as a whole. Now, I'm much more excited about it and trusting of it.

It's a history of America. It started out to be only about AIDS . . . well, it started out by being about my family; my Proustian novel, I called it. You know, my growing up in Washington, and what that was like, leading up to when AIDS came along. I started writing little bits about that, until I realized that . . . what went wrong with AIDS was what went wrong in Washington. So I'm basically writing it about the same city, and a lot of the same people. It was my blessing that I, in fact, knew Washington, that I grew up there. The more I wrote about it, the more it started going back in time. What existed in the '80s was there for a reason, and the reason did not start in 1981. It started . . . in 1935, which was the year I was born. But then I realized that, well, it didn't start in 1935 either. You've got to go back even further; and before I knew it, I was back to the Indians—I mean the Indians before George Washington! So you can see it's become this enormous thing. It's all over the place. I've got boxes of it over there. It's been an enormous problem technically. How do you keep hold of it all? How do you remember it all? This is the curse of the computer age too—the computer encourages you to be as excessive as you want to be somehow, and then you can't find anything. You print it out in four versions, but you don't remember which version. It's been all those kind of stupid problems, but this aspect of it is also what interests me. You know, I've never done the same thing twice. My two movies are different. My three plays are structurally very different. You know, there's a difference between my prose—between *Faggots* and my essays. I don't like to keep doing the same thing. That's why I stopped writing for *The Advocate*. I just got really bored with writing, in essence, the same column every month. The subject might change, but it's the same tone, the same stance, the same anger, the same length. There are enormously interesting technical problems about writing a long novel that you don't have in a short novel. I think that's what's driven me nuts over these ten or fifteen years that I've been working on it. What makes a reader keep turning the pages over three thousand pages is not the same as what makes a reader turn the pages over a hundred pages. It's the difference between building a little cottage and building, you know, the World Trade Center. There are different principles of physics, of architecture. Finding the right struture has been an overwhelming problem. How do you tell *the* story, especially when you're telling so many smaller stories and there are so many characters. The great fun of *Faggots* was that there are 8 zillion characters in it. I love that. I love having a big cast. One of the reasons I don't enjoy writing for the theater anymore is that you can't write for a big cast— because theater can't afford to put on the play, financially. I hate two-character plays. I hate one-character plays. I hate three-character plays. I want to see a lot of people up there interacting with each other. I must have a cast of a thousand! And how do you help an audience, a reader, keep all those people in line, especially when you're not telling a story that's, in essence, linear? In *War and Peace* you're following several families and a war, one war through, I don't know, thirty years or so. I mean, I'm going for a history of the *world* and all its characters, but what interests me is not following families all the way back so much as the traits, the philosophies, the diseases, if you will, that get passed on, you know, from the beginning of time ... Syphilis, for instance, has been here since the 1400s or something, and probably goes back much further, even though there's no record of it. They have found graves in Illinois that go back to pre-Indian times, in which the bodies have sores that experts think were probably syphilitic. You know that syphilis and leprosy are similar diseases, from the same family of bacteria. Now, they're thinking that some of those who we thought had leprosy—all those legendary leper colonies we've been hearing about throughout history—actually had syphilis. The NIH started out as a hospital that at one time took care of syphilitic patients on Staten Island ... All of this is fodder. In the novel, AIDS is not called AIDS; it's called "the Underlying Condition," "UC," and UC is traced all the way back to the beginning of time ... So it's really a history of the world as reflected through disease, through illness; and that's what gets passed on from generation to generation. AIDS is just this unbelievable flowering manifestation of all of the poison and all the evil that has been here since the beginning of time. That's what it became.

Mass: This is the level of inquiry that I actually sensed in *Faggots*, that had a climax at that moment when Fred asks what it all means. What I see is that, well, just as you see everything going further and further back with roots spreading in every direction, I see that same process in your art. I know you don't consider it anywhere near finished, and that you're not satisfied with myriad aspects of it, but in fact, it sounds like it's pretty far along . . .

Kramer: Well, it is very advanced in characters, in stories, in minutiae, but only certain sections are what I would call well-written, like the section that I read at A Different Light. That's more polished, honed. The rest is what Calvin Trillin refers to as "a vomit out." You know, you just let it out, knowing you'll go back and fix it, but don't want to fix it now because you know it'll change because it's affected by other stuff. So I've got a lot of vomit and very few jewels, but, and I say this jokingly, I think I will be working on it until I die; and then it'll be published, because I won't be able to do any more to it. I am just so blessed and fortunate that my brother has invested for me over the years, so that I am financially able to do this. I mean, I don't have to worry. I mean, if you're talking about patrons to the artists in the Renaissance, my brother has been my patron, and I will just be so eternally grateful to him. This freedom has allowed me to be an activist, to write my *Reports*. I do not have to worry about going out there and making a living and it is such an enormous burden off my shoulders that I can just devote myself to all of this.

Mass: As you know and as you and I have had it out over the years, I was enormously envious and resentful of your freedom to write, which I've so coveted, and which I've always seen as the bottom line of the major depression/burnout I had in the spring of '83. Some of that resentment had to do with the fact that this dilemma of my being a writer and activist who had to work for a living wasn't credited by you in the composite character based on me in *The Normal Heart*. But that's old territory now. Though it still smarts, I've had my say on this elsewhere and won't press you on it further here.

Kramer: I've learned so much from you, Larry—and from your genuine pain from my portrayal of you, which I intended to be a highly—very highly—complimentary one. It's a very difficult matter—writing about real and living people. Dickens might have done it, the Bible is probably a *roman-à-clef*—but that doesn't change the problems. That you were in pain, pained and sensitized me a great deal.

Mass: I take it from your comments about your brother that your relations with your family, whom you've written about a lot, are pretty good.

Kramer: They're fine. They've allowed me to write about them and our interactions, including some particularly painful ones. It has been a growth process for all of us, not only their dealing with my homosexuality, but just dealing with our relationships, and I think everybody in the family is very close and stronger because of all the things we've fought out together, only some of which I've written about.

Mass: I hope we're in that same process in my family right now. If we are, it's still in the early stages. But it's a process, incidentally, that was highly influenced by the original version of *Reports*, which concludes with that excruciatingly awkward and painful moment between you and your sister-in-law, when you expose the little gestures and moments of insensitivity and prejudice that come between you. It's as if the book is saying that a bottom line of change is to open up communication with our straight relatives. Fight the politicians and the system, yes, but how far can any of that go, really, if you can't look your own brother or sister-in-law in the eye?

Kramer: It's tough, but everybody's got to do it.

Mass: Speaking of *Reports* and of opening up to one's family, what ever became of Ron Reagan, Jr.?

Kramer: I don't know. When I began calling him gay publicly—and I don't even remember exactly when or where it was that I first did it, before my play, *Just Say No*—I got a call from Michael Carlisle who was my agent at the time at William Morris and who was also Ron Reagan, Jr.'s agent, and he said (Michael is an exceedingly diplomatic gentleman): "Ron wants to write to you. Do you mind?" And I said: "Of course not." So he wrote me a very long letter, the essence of which was that he said he wasn't gay and was devoted to his wife, that all of this was very hurtful to her, and would I please stop? And I wrote back to him saying, I don't recall exactly what—I don't know if it was one of my more gracious letters—but in essence I was saying that my sources told me he was gay; and indeed I was acquainted with someone who'd been in his class at Yale, who maintained that they had slept together; and there were other stories from other people. I said that if he was prepared to deny these specific allegations I would stop making them. As far as his wife being "hurt," I didn't think there was anything so awful about homosexuality and I was tired of that particular argument. I never got a reply. Over the years, we have not heard anything about his gay life, so perhaps he isn't. I know he's been seen with gay groups at the opera and he made jokes about me and my calling him gay when he had his television program, and so I assume it's no longer such a painful accusation if he's able to make jokes about it.

Mass: In the arts, coincidentally, the only area that is more closeted than classical music and opera is ballet. Apart from a few biographies of the likes of Nureyev, there's next to nothing about the emperors; it's all about their clothes. . . . Do you know if Ron, Jr. saw your play?

Kramer: (laughs) I don't know if *anybody* saw my play! It ran so briefly. When she was working on her wonderful, classic book about Nancy Reagan—one of my favorite books ever—Kitty Kelley and I had several conversations. In the book, she cites my play and my accusations. She also uses some of the information I gave her in her text without crediting me, I'm sorry to say, and she didn't use some of the really good things that I gave her which did get mentioned in my interview with *Playboy*; for example, that she (Nancy) was this big cocksucker. Before they ran the interview in which I called her a cocksucker, *Playboy* asked me for sources, which I gave them. The sources checked out and they said fine. She was known to have serviced not only Benny Thau, who was the Vice-President in charge of production at Metro, but the two stars that he sent her to take care of, Clark Gable and Spencer Tracy. So put that in your mouth and swallow it, Mrs. First Lady who wouldn't pay attention to AIDS!

Mass: And who was really much worse. The portrait you paint of her is very funny, of course, but also chilling. We tend to treat her as an object of satire, but she was really evil . . .

Kramer: Wait 'till *The American People*. Just wait!

Mass: *Just Say No* got trounced by the critics, which is really unfortunate, because it's such a unique work of political theater and history. And most people, even those who are interested in your work and in gay and political theater, don't realize that the published version of the play has, as its preface, the richest and most blistering attack on the American theater of our era.

Kramer: Good! Maybe we'll sell a few copies.

Mass: Is anybody else planning to do it?

Kramer: It's had a few productions. I'm hoping someday it'll come back as a Restoration comedy.

Mass: I've certainly never read anything that so clearly conceptualizes and indicts the American theater of today, though I take it you feel that *Angels in America* was a real exception to the politesse, as you put it, that otherwise characterizes nearly everything we see, as well as we ourselves for our passivity as audiences. Do you think the *Times* is still a major culprit here? And what became of Clive Barnes, who so brutally attacked your first play, *Four Friends*?

Kramer: Clive Barnes is a tragic joke on the history of American criticism and theater criticism. That he is still allowed to review is hateful and that he was allowed to be the man at the *Times* for so many years was even more hateful, and very destructive.

Mass: I don't have that clear a sense about him. Does he have a history, specifically, of homophobia, or is it mostly that he's just a hack? I know that there was widespread unhappiness with him, to the extent that he finally got dumped.

Kramer: He was rumoured to have been an alcoholic. We held the curtain for him for half an hour on *Four Friends*. As for the homophobia, I don't think any of the straight or ostensibly straight critics, with the exception of Linda Winer at *Newsday* and Frank Rich, is comfortable with gay subject matter.

Mass: Why do you think Frank Rich become such a champion of gay issues and perspectives? Now I'm not complaining, but you know me, always looking for subtext.

Kramer: I just think he's an exceptional human being, one of those rare men who isn't threatened by it, who has always had gay friends, probably going back to when he was young, or certainly when he was at Harvard, and who is married now to a woman who also has and has always had a number of very close gay friends. God love them both for that, really.

There's no question that *Angels* would not have been championed around the world to the extent that it has been if it hadn't been for Frank's really extraordinary shepherding of both plays from Los Angeles to New York. And the same for my two plays. Left to any other critic at the *Times*, they would not have had such success. He was a champion of *The Normal Heart*, which was very difficult for him to do because of its criticisms of the *Times*, and he was certainly laudatory of *The Destiny of Me*. Through nobody's fault, he didn't review *Just Say No*. We changed the opening date because we weren't ready, and he wasn't able to come. It was a big mistake on our part because Mel Gussow hated it. If Frank had seen it, I'm sure it would have been better treated.

Mass: Gussow is an old-style homophobe. Like Pauline Kael and Janet Maslin, he mellowed somewhat over the years, but not to the extent of a complete transformation.

Kramer: I don't know about that, but he has a very blinkered sense of what theater is; for instance, his utterly slavish dedication to Samuel Beckett, which, for whatever greatness is inherent in his work, is not everybody's idea of theater, and certainly not the only ideal of what theater can and should be.

Mass: In one sense, Frank Rich is simply being savvy, because, as I'm sure he realizes, he's on the side of history. He senses that he's doing the right thing to really get involved with and excited about gay people and our issues. This *is* our time, and he's one of the few outside observers to really pick up on this. Remember that big piece he wrote for *Esquire*— about gays in the theater? In jumping on the gay bandwagon, I'm sure he realizes he's doing something . . . millennial.

What has become of *Sissies' Scrapbook* and *Four Friends*? Do you think they'll get revived? Published?

Kramer: As you know, they're essentially the same play. *Sissies' Scrapbook* was done at Playwrights' Horizons and *Four Friends* was done Off-Broadway a year later at the Theatre de Lys. It's the same play rewritten, and if I were to publish it, I would have to sort of combine the two because there were certain things that were better in the first that should have stayed in the second. My favorite story here is that Stephen Sondheim saw both productions and was very encouraging of me in my early formative years as a playwright. What he said, in essence, was that *Sissies'* was structurally flawed but very moving. In *Four Friends*, he felt, I'd solved the structural problems but had thrown the baby out with the bath water. At the time, I didn't know how to fix it, I just wasn't skillful enough. Even now, I'm not sure exactly how I could do this—take some from one and put it in the other. I'd like to get it published, and I'd like to get the screenplay for *Women in Love* published, which actually may happen. Plume has offered to publish two of my screenplays together, of *Women in Love* and *The Normal Heart*.

Mass: Larry, in your interview with *DPN* [*Diseased Pariah News*], you said that you don't have AIDS. Were you making the distinction about having HIV infection versus AIDS?

Kramer: You know, some publications try to use that discussion for exploitative reasons—you know, he's got AIDS and he's facing death, blah, blah, blah, blah. Well, I don't have AIDS. I'm HIV-positive and I'm in good shape, and I feel it's cruel and unfair to the people who do have AIDS and who know that I don't want to be presented as someone who does. Does that make sense?

Mass: Of course it does, but when you talked about taking your first dose of AZT in that *Advocate* piece a while back, I assumed your T-cells had dropped into the range that would qualify you for the diagnosis of AIDS by current criteria.

Kramer: No. CDC-defined AIDS is below 200 T-cells, and I think the lowest mine have been is 260. What I'm taking the AZT for is not HIV. It's for my low platelets. I have ITP. Believe me, I'll be the first one to tell the world when I have AIDS.

Mass: Your situation is a bit unusual in that you have a form of chronic active hepatitis, which isn't clearly diagnostic of AIDS.

Kramer: Actually, they say I have a chronic form of hepatitis that is not very contagious. But I still have cirrhosis and low platelets. At one point, my count was down to 28,000. That's when I started the AZT, which has helped. Deciding what I should do involved a lot of opinions. They didn't want me to take interferon for the hepatitis because of some of the side effects. And Jeffrey Green, my doctor at NYU, didn't want me to take AZT, at least not then. But Simon Karpatkin, the ITP specialist, suggested it for the platelets, which had to be dealt with, so we went ahead. But I was also consulting with Donald Kotler because of all my digestive problems. Do you think I was right to go ahead with the AZT?

Mass: If you're getting this kind of relief and improvement? Of course!

Kramer: Well, Joe [Sonnabend] got very upset. He's still so strongly against the use of AZT.

Mass: Now that we know its truly dramatic impact on reducing maternal-fetal transmission of HIV, he can't possibly still be in such uncategorical disagreement with its usage. [In Sarah Schulman's fictional novel, *Rat Bohemia*, the protagonist notes that Sonnabend has even prescribed AZT.]

Kramer: It's basically still the old [Charles] Ortleb position that AZT is nothing but a worthless poison, being put on us only for profit and punishment. [Charles Ortleb was publisher of the *New York Native*, which featured the first coverage of the epidemic, by Mass, and the first appeals for funding and involvement by Kramer. Under Ortleb's increasingly authoritarian and paranoid dictatorship, however, the paper later degenerated into what Kramer called "a worthless piece of shit" (*New York*, February 10, 1997, pp. 22–23). As of January, 1997, under increasingly tough and unanimous criticism and in the absence of advertising revenues and loss of readership, the *Native*, together with *Christopher Street* and *Theater Week*, ceased publication.]

Mass: What I'd say is that to maintain—as the Ortleb/[Michael] Callen/[Peter] Duesberg crowd has—that AZT can never be anything other than a worthless poison is akin to maintaining—as this crowd still does—that the evidence isn't overwhelming that HIV is the primary agent in HIV infection. The questioning of co-factors and of the motivations of individuals like Robert Gallo and of profiteering drug companies is one thing, but the unwillingness to place findings in more balanced perspective has always struck me as fanatical.

Kramer: But it does hurt your bone marrow.

Mass: Yes, there's no question about that. Like the vast majority of anti-cancer, chemotherapeutic agents, and radiation for that matter, there is serious toxicity associated with the use of AZT; the higher the dose, the greater the toxicity. Also, little benefit has been clearly demonstrated for longevity. Leaving out the question of the new combination therapy with the protease inhibitors, it's in individual cases like yours that many reputable researchers and clinicians feel there is benefit. And now, of course, we can say, if only with regard to the qualified circumstance of maternal-fetal transmission, that prior to the advent of the protease inhibitors (with which it's being used in combination), AZT has been far and away the most effective treatment for AIDS. So, as long as your numbers are good . . .

Larry, how do you think you contracted HIV?

Kramer: I'll tell you how I think I got it. I was trying to make David Webster jealous. That's how I think I got it! In 1980, when David and I were at one of our end-points, on the outs, we found ourselves at the same party—a reception for Knoll furniture, which was showing a new collection. There was a guy there named Ron Dowd who was very handsome and who I knew David thought was handsome, so I made a play for Ron Dowd and, lo and behold, much to my surprise, Ron Dowd responded. We had a date, he fucked me, and he was one of the first people to die from AIDS.

Mass: In some recent interviews, you've said that you've all but given up on behavior modification as a means of controlling the epidemic. Doesn't this represent a shift in your position?

Kramer: Let me correct that. I mean, I don't in fact think that behavior modification is going to control the plague, but I haven't given up on it. If you will look back at my writing, as you look back at your own writing, I think you'll see that neither one of us has ever bluntly said to everybody "Stop fucking!" We've said, "Cool it," we've said "Limit your partners," whatever. Maybe characters in the play say we should all just stop fucking, but I don't. Larry Kramer did not tell the world to stop fucking altogether. Larry Kramer said that this was a real problem, that it looks like it's spread by an agent and that we should cool it. But no one said cease and desist all sex completely.

Mass: I do think you wanted us to "just stop having sex," as Ned Weeks says to Dr. Brookner, but that seemed too extreme in view of the limited but certainly suggestive evidence, and we ended up rejecting what was basically a very sane response to the circumstances and very solid advice because of our discomfort with the messenger, and our overall insecurity as a threatened minority. And then there was the placating of the multiple factors crowd, the Ortlebs, Sonnabends and Callens. who were so fanatically opposed to the single-agent hypothesis.

It was complicated. I think you were trying to accommodate us to some degree, as best you could. You felt you needed to be very strong. But basically, you had to keep modifying what you really wanted to say. We were all urging you to be more careful and cautious. I mean, most people don't know that that first appeal for funds from Larry Kramer was edited down by me. The original was considerably angrier and more alarmist. In retrospect, you were right. We were wrong, though we may have been right about the extent of the anger and alarm driving a lot of the people we most wanted and needed to reach further away, at least at that time.

Kramer: I've never given up on behavior modification. It's just that my main interest has always been in treatment and trying to find a cure. The other fights take too much time and energy, and they become such red herrings. We have to fight endlessly with the church, or with the school boards about even using the word "condoms," much less about giving them out. Sometimes I think the right wing makes us spend all our time doing that, so we're not looking at how badly the research is being attended to, or that our most basic questions aren't being answered. So at one point, I just said to myself, I am not going to fight those other fights. I haven't got time, I haven't got the energy. I'm going to devote myself exclusively to trying to untie the knots in research, to go for a cure. Because if there's a cure, we don't have to worry as much about behavior modification.

Mass: Yes, although even if AIDS were to be eradicated from the face of the earth this minute, behavior modification would still be an important priority. Otherwise, we're simply setting ourselves up for other STD epidemics.

Kramer: That's right. I do worry—a lot—about what we're going to do if and when there is a cure. Will everyone go right back to where we left off? Did we fight so hard to end a plague only to welcome with open arms and unprotected assholes the next one? Will we have learned anything? Will we have matured as a community, minority, segment of the population, whatever we're called? Or will all the death and loss we've suffered be in vain? Lately, I sometimes fear this last. We still don't have anything remotely resembling a strong political force in place.

Mass: So where does all this leave us right now with regard to the current resurgence of commercial sex establishments—bathhouses and sex clubs?

Kramer: Oh, I just don't even know! I wouldn't even go to that meeting. Gabriel [Rotello] got mad at me because I wouldn't go and make a speech about all that, but I'm just not going to get involved in all that all over again. I mean, if people want to go to the bath houses . . . at this point, I think, everybody knows what they're doing, certainly in New York City, and if they're going to do it, they're going to do it. I mean, they're going in with a full deck; they know what they're getting involved in. Maybe the odd kid from out of town's going to get in there who doesn't, but mostly, you've got to be living in the wilds of Alaska not to know what's going on. No amount of education's going to change that.

Mass: In the early days of the epidemic, I was so terrified that we were going to hand over the keys to the civil rights we didn't have in the first place to this monolithic right-wing enemy. But even though closing a number of bathhouses and sex clubs didn't have that result, I think people are trying to create the same argument now, especially in New York City, in the face of wholesale closures and crackdowns under Giuliani, which critics are citing as the inevitable result of any efforts at curtailment.

Kramer: I don't know what it is, but I'm never scared by those kinds of arguments. Who was it the other day—Bill Paul (that nincompoop who is head of the NIH's Office of AIDS Research)?—who was saying, how can you criticize the NIH, when Congress is going to close us down. Well, that's not going to stop me from criticizing the NIH! You can't not go forward and say what you think just because of what you fear might or might not happen. It might not happen, and it might not be the worst thing in the world if it did!

Mass: In that sense, I regret a lot my early... I was just too cautious...

Kramer: Larry, I don't want you to regret a thing you did. You were a hero in all of this and we fought, we made history, *all* of us, by fighting out this dialectic.

Mass: We did our best, yes, but the relevance of what you're saying can't be overstated: that you can't be afraid of the truth. If the truth is this extremely important thing that needs to be out there and needs to be discussed and dealt with, you can't say we can't do it because it's inconvenient or dangerous or unpopular. I have this feeling a lot with regard to my efforts to talk about resurgent anti-Semitism. People keep telling me to keep a lower profile, tone it down, or I'll invite backlash. No one seems to like it, certainly not most Jews, even you. And that's where I think this current debate on the bathhouses and sex clubs is. You can't not talk about things that are really serious and concerning—like the escalating rates of HIV infection in younger gay men that are coincident with a new proliferation of commercial sex establishments—and not try to deal with them just because of the possibility of backlash, or of giving fodder to the enemy.

Kramer: Some people never learn that lesson, even when they die.

Mass: Let me ask you another question about AIDS prevention strategies. You've kept a low profile in the current debates about the resurgence of AIDS among younger gay men and the proliferation of commercial sex establishments. Vaccines is another of the big areas of discussion and activity you don't talk much about. Why?

Kramer: I don't understand how vaccines work, but let me put it another way. I don't consider myself a scientist, and I don't consider myself very knowledgeable about all the stuff we're going through, and I get angry at myself when I make too many pronouncements particularly about treatment issues, but when I do come out for something, it's usually because I have talked to an awful lot of people and read a lot of studies, when there are enough people I respect and enough studies that support a certain conclusion; for example, if you take AZT plus 3TC plus a protease inhibitor, you have a good chance of raising your T-cells. Now, I haven't seen anything or been told by anybody whom I respect that any of these vaccines really work. So that's the main reason I don't talk about them.

Whether or not there's a little glimmer of hope with vaccines, they're obviously not doing very well on that front, and nobody knows exactly what to do about it. I was with experts at that vaccine conference in Cold Spring Harbor, and the head of it all, Dr. Watson, was the first one to say that nobody knows what to do or how to go at it. There's a man named Shepherd who runs the Albert Sabin Foundation who was prepared to raise a great deal of money for vaccine research. Even he says that everyone is telling him, why put all this money into a vaccine when nobody knows what to do; let's work on the treatment first, let's spend the money on that kind of research.

Mass: Notwithstanding the current pessimism about vaccines, they are planning to go ahead with these large-scale trials in Africa.

Kramer: It's much easier to get a trial going in Africa because they don't have to deal with a patient population that's knowledgeable, which is a horrible way of saying they have willing guinea pigs.

Mass: You know, I used to wonder why you were always talking about a "cure" when there has never been a cure for any known virus, as opposed to a preventive vaccine. I thought you had your priorities inverted. Yet again you were right. Although we do not have cures *per se* for viruses, and we must still strive for a vaccine, many organisms resist vaccine development, and we do speak of cures with complex and incremental treatments for various cancers; that's the model you were holding up.

In this context, another instance of your vision was your emphasis on the need for an "AIDS czar" and your pursuit of David Baltimore to assume that role, in spite of the allegations against him (recently reversed) of scientific misconduct.

Kramer: I would never recommend anybody for a job like that unless I had the sense that a lot of people felt strongly that this was someone who could do a good job. Of all the scientists I've met, David Baltimore is the one they all seem to respect the most, because they think he's so smart. He did win a Nobel Prize; also, he was the only one who said publicly, during the time we were looking for someone to be an AIDS czar, "I think AIDS can be cured." Actually, he was the first one to talk about finding a cure, which is one of the reasons I was so impressed. So I spent some time with him. That was when I was involved with the Treatment and Data committee at ACT UP, and I took people with me, like Mark Harrington, who's certainly very smart, and everybody was impressed with Baltimore. I have to say that he's a proud man, like Gallo; others would say arrogant. As for the charges against him, they were certainly different from the charges against Gallo, and, I think, really picayune; certainly, they weren't enough that they should put somebody that smart out of commission, and unavailable. All that happened was that David didn't carefully review a paper by a young colleague that had his name as one of the co-authors. You know how they do those things—everybody on the team or in the department gets their name on everybody's paper, and that's exactly and all it was. When the colleague was charged, he felt loyalty and tried to defend her. But it got twisted into a scandal by John Dingle, the hateful Congressman from Michigan who made his name out of crucifying Gallo, and then Baltimore.

I know this is a long answer, but it raises a very interesting question about our times. I mean, this is a country, as I've said in *Reports*, that asked a known Nazi, Werner von Braun, to help us get a man on the moon. Now, neither Gallo nor Baltimore has done anything on that level of meretriciousness, and for those of us who are so desperate to find the answers we need, these two guys are—whatever you can say about their personalities, or their oversights—they are brilliant scientists; that we were being deprived of their knowledge and expertise was just ludicrous, and a great waste.

Mass: In his interview with you for *POZ* [April/May 1995], Andrew Sullivan speaks of your "rhetorical style." In a similar vein, David Bergman wrote an essay called "Larry Kramer and the Rhetoric of AIDS." Any thoughts on being called "rhetorical"?

Kramer: I'd have to look it up in the dictionary. What does it mean?

Mass: I had to look it up the other day myself. I was surprised to learn that it doesn't mean "bad."

Kramer: Pompous?

Mass: No, not necessarily. Let's look it up now.

Kramer: (reads from a dictionary) . . .

Mass: Right. That was also the first definition listed in my dictionary: "the art or science of using words effectively in speaking or writing."

Kramer: I don't know that any writer is all that conscious of style, in the sense of how someone else might label it. One knows when one reaches it, and one knows—until one finds it—that one hasn't got it. But I don't know that one is ever able to define it. I don't even know how you know when your voice is there, when the draft is finally finished and it says what you want it to say. So when and whether all of that is then called "rhetorical" versus "persuasive" or "humorous," or what, it's impossible to predict.

Mass: So you can't really comment further on this accusation, for example, in the Bergman essay.

Kramer: I haven't read it, but I was told it was unkind.

Mass: The problem with it is the problem with the majority of your critics. They allow their subjective impressions/feelings to color what should be greater objectivity—hence the disparity between what some of those who've known and worked with you believe and say versus your impact on the greater public. It's one thing to be critical—and I've been more critical of you than most, more so than David, of whom I'm fond—but to not clearly acknowledge and affirm the achievements, in context and perspective, is, I think, revealing and indicting. Here, a kind of deconstruction is helpful. When you read David's essay, you can read it for what's there on the surface, and what's there does include some valid and challenging observations; but for the bigger picture, which is what David appears to be after, it's more revealing, I think, to read the essay in the context of where *David* is coming from, as the premier chronicler and defender of the gay literary world that shunned you in the early years of your and their writing, and still does so to an extent that bears scrutiny. I mean, to put it bluntly, David's got all these loyalties going with a lot of people who all but took oaths as your literary enemies, people who rejected and renounced you during the period of *Faggots*, and most of whom have never reconsidered their hoary attitudes.

But more on this anon. First, I want to ask some more questions about what we were calling or attempting to talk about as your literary style. We've talked about the accusation that your work is "rhetorical." What about the observation I've often made, not always in affirmation of its literary and artistic value, that your rhetorical style relies on hyperbole? For example, *Faggots* opens as follows: "There are 2,556,596 faggots in the New York City area."

Kramer: Well, I'm often accused of being hyperbolic, but I really don't consider myself hyperbolic. I mean, if we're a sixth of the population or whatever, and more concentrated in cities like New York, is that number of gay people for the greater area really so wildly off the mark? I will grant that *Faggots* is hyperbolic. It's a satire, a comedy; there is a level of . . . heightened exaggeration because it's meant to be bigger than life. But when I write political essays, I don't make up things. I don't lie. I may choose what I select to say. I mean, I will use, for instance, the highest count I have heard about potential infections, like William Haseltine's estimate in the *New York Times* of a billion cases shortly after the turn of the century. When compared to the CDC or World Health Organization estimates, and the other numbers we're using today, a billion sounds hyperbolic, but it's not. It's in fact a figure that has been stated by a very distinguished, reputable scientist. If I call somebody a murderer, which some people—you, for example—have criticized me for, well, I'm sorry, I really do think that person is a murderer. I do think AIDS is intentional genocide. I do think this is being *allowed* to happen. It may seem dramatic to some conservative, nervous nelly somewhere, but that's how I feel.

Mass: OK, but here's another example. In your interview with *The Advocate*, you criticized Edmund White for, as you put it, wasting his time on that biography of Genet, which has subsequently won a number of major literary awards.

Kramer: I apologized for that.

Mass: You're not one who apologizes very often, and I'm surprised that you did so in this instance, especially since it may have been unnecessary. What it took me time to realize about your use of hyperbole, especially with regard to individuals, is that even at its most extreme, there's always some core of serious truth. Difficult as it was for me to swallow, this was the case with regard to your portrayal of me in the composite character of Mickey Marcus in *The Normal Heart*. I think I hated you for all that that character wasn't and didn't say and wasn't credited with, and for the stereotype of the community activist/sex revolutionary he represented, but there was genuine insight there, and truth. Now, in the case of Edmund and *Genet*, could you say something more about what you meant, or thought you meant?

Kramer: Well, I do talk dramatically. I mean, I think Edmund is an exceptionally gifted writer, but I keep waiting for the meat and the heart to break through the polish and facility. He's shown that he can be enormously skillful in . . . just about anything he lends his pen to, be it fiction or essays or short stories, but I'm still waiting for the greatness, I guess, which I think he has in him somewhere. I was saddened when he moved away from New York, from America, because I think he removed himself from the core of the drama of all of our lives. Of course, a writer can write anywhere and experience anywhere, and an expatriate perspective can have real value, and his certainly does, but I think he's put himself too out of touch with a lot of what we're all going through, and especially with our communities here in America, all of which could have been this wellspring for him. A couple of the short stories have actually made me rather angry because they dealt with AIDS in such a facile way. Only his great skill as a stylist allowed them to be as successful as they were. I say this because I know some of the people he was writing about and I knew their circumstances, which were much more fraught than the light treatment they were given would suggest.

Mass: Well, I know some of these same people and had that same reaction. Leaving aside the issue of depth for the moment, it should be noted that the individuals themselves felt that the portrait was affirming. They weren't offended. On the contrary, I think they were touched. But with regard to your failure to find greatness in Edmund's work, I wonder if you aren't onto something. Actually, it was Edmund himself who gave what for me was the sharpest appraisal of Edmund White, the writer. The occasion was his receiving the David Kessler award at CLAGS, for *Genet*. Following introductions by David Bergman, Felice Picano and Sandy McClatchy (and I'm pretty sure I'm not being hyperbolic in noting that their cumulative remarks were considerably longer than Edmund's speech), the first thing Edmund said when he got up to the podium was what he knew at least some of us had to be thinking: Perhaps never has a minor writer been so overpraised. I think the question you raise about Edmund and greatness is entirely legitimate with regard to his fiction and essays. But when we come to *Genet* and your yearning for the bigger picture, assessing Edmund's achievement becomes more challenging. Here is a biography of one of the most influential and discussed literary figures of the twentieth century, and it's the first biography to place this figure in a modern (gay liberation era) understanding and context of homosexuality, and to place that understanding in a greater context of socialist concerns, politics and philosophy. In its trajectory of gay life and consciousness across the broad sweep of our era, it is almost as grand in achievement as it is ambitious. So in what way can this really be called a waste of time?

Kramer: The book wasn't a waste of time *per se*, but it was a diversion of *Edmund's* time—from the mainstream of our lives right now, and he might not have that much more time to write whatever it is he's going to write, that carries on from *A Boy's Own Story* and *The Beautiful Room Is Empty*. I know it's wrong of me to tell him what decisions to make, but . . . I wrote an essay for one of my columns in the *New Yorker*, I mean *The Advocate* (talk about slips, I've had so many rejections from the *New Yorker*, present editors included) about the state of gay fiction, and I'm talking mostly about gay male fiction, as against gay theater. I think we're living through a golden age of gay theater, but we're really in a small time with gay literature because no one is writing about what you and I were talking about earlier—the big picture. Compare any current novel in what it attempts to bite off with the two parts of *Angels in America*, which attempts to encapsulate everything. *That's* what I mean. This is the novelist Edmund could have been. Instead he's given us *Genet*.

I think Chris Bram is another of these enormously gifted writers with unlimited potential who doesn't begin to tap it because the story stays so small, because he limits himself somehow; he doesn't reach for the brass ring, doesn't go for it. I mean, look at any novel by Dickens, Tolstoy, Dostoyevsky. Why aren't we thinking in those terms? Why is it, you know, two guys in bed for four hundred pages? It's so small. Chris wrote a book just now about James Whale. Fabulous idea! But Peter Parnell wrote a play about it which was much more interesting—*Hyde in Hollywood*, I think it was called—because it had a bigger ambition and range. It was less successful as a play, but it attempted to do more. I wanted to say to Chris, why did you just concentrate on that man in the room and this hustler, when you had all of gay Hollywood and all of Hollywood in that era, when you had the whole movie industry? I mean, what an incredible canvas to paint on, and he's got the skills to do it. His previous novel about wartime Washington was this kind of greater work ... I haven't said any of this to him, which I should because he's my friend ...

We have marvelous miniatures, from people who can write lovely small things, like Dale Peck; but I want us to take a bigger chunk of the world, to be talking about what it's all about, about why, as you said, we're sitting here with fucking red and yellow and pink handkerchiefs in our pockets, and doing such small things, when we could be running this world. We're such wonderful people; we have so much to give, so much to offer; we have so much money; we have the Barry Dillers and David Geffens and Dick Jenrettes ... there's so fucking much disposable income in this community!—why isn't it poured into the community? Why are our political organizations so broke? Why are the people who run them so ... puerile and picayune and puny? Well, our literature is puny, too. It may be beautifully wrought; we can wear a gorgeous Armani suit like nobody else, but all that stuff is only window dressing, and I think that Edmund is a prime example of this because he's one of our most respected writers. He's probably our prime example of the Armani suit. Well, I want to know what's *inside* that Armani suit! Look, it's important now that we look at our literature seriously and critically. It's also important to know that we do have a literature, a lot of which was executed in our own lifetimes. I'm in no sense disparaging that achievement. I'm just trying to push the envelope. My nature! Chris Bram, Dale Peck, Mark Merlis, they're all *wonderful* writers. Faulkners don't stand still.

Mass: Well, you will be pleased to learn that Edmund is busy working on the sequel to the autobiographical novels you mentioned; it's to be called *The Farewell Symphony*—inaptly, let's hope. In fact, his immersion in this project, he wrote me, leaves him no free time for others, such as doing a piece for this anthology. In any event, don't you think the Genet biography *is* Edmund's big statement, his equivalent of *Angels*?

Kramer: You may be very right. Maybe Edmund, in writing *Genet*, has written as well as he can write, and has written what was important for him to write, and maybe it is his attempt to give the bigger picture, and maybe it succeeds to an extent in doing so; and we're grateful that we now have a good biography of Genet from a gay viewpoint in the marketplace. But after all is said and done, Genet really was, at best, only a marginal figure in our lives. Why isn't Edmund using these most precious years and energies to write more about what *he's* going through, about the deaths of all his friends; and, if he doesn't want to write about America, about what's happening in Paris? Nobody's really writing about what's going on there which, from what I'm told, is grotesque—many of the backroom bars are in operation again, there has been a major blood-poisoning scandal involving the government—what incredible dramas to write about. I know it's wrong of me to tell him what to write—no writer should ever tell another writer what to write—but I can't help my feelings.

Mass: I don't know that Edmund has been very active in the AIDS or gay movements in Paris (at the center of which is ACT UP Paris), but, again, *Genet* does have that great sweep of history we're talking about. It takes us from a time when homosexuality forced us into being marginal, outsiders, Genet being an extreme example of this, and brings this history right up into the vortex of today's Middle East and world politics. Through this very detailed, personal saga of one individual, it makes a powerful claim for the linkage of gay concerns with some of the great socialist events, initiatives, values and trends of the century.

Kramer: Look, I read it; I grant that it was interesting, but I'd rather have a biography of a greater gay man. Genet is not an uninteresting playwright, but so much of his writing is just too abstruse. Genet may reflect his time, but he was a very strange man; he's not someone I can look up to as a role model.

Mass: It is hard to look up to him as a role model, though I did (Genet's novels provided some of my first glimpses of gay life), not unlike the way Mark Merlis made early discoveries of his community in *Faggots*; and as Edmund points out, Genet was openly homosexual, if never self-affirmingly gay, during times when most other prominent gay writers (like Genet's discoverer Cocteau) weren't. I think one reason Genet's playwriting may be so abstruse, as you put it, is that he used drugs (barbiturates in the later years), a fact Edmund ambivalently documents (at one point he notes that Genet disapproved of drugs) and doesn't know how to weigh. Of course, no one does; this is still unchartered territory for literary criticism and analysis. Eventually, we'll know more about the relationships between drug use and creativity, and it could be a level of revelation that the Angel in *Angels* is talking about when she says that history is about to crack wide open. But what gives me the most pause about *Genet* is the absence of judgment, of a moral position, Of course, biography should be objective. Even so, this is an accusation Edmund has had to confront elsewhere—e.g., when interviewed for the *New York Times*—and which he regards defensively, even contemptuously.

Kramer: Edmund is strangely nonjudgmental when what he's writing about reflects his own life and values. But being nonjudgmental is also a form of approval.

Mass: There's also the issue of inconsistency, of being selectively judgmental. To me, one of the most interesting examples of this phenomenon is this very situation of Genet, in contrast to you. At the level of your both being loners and outsiders who care deeply about social issues but who seem not to be able to get along with people, the similarities are striking. But we're invited to be so understanding, tolerant and nonjudgmental of all the inconsistencies and excesses and extremes in Genet's life and politics and art because of the circumstances of his youth, especially his poverty, because his politics were mostly socialist, and because art is sacrosanct; and because, finally, as Edmund puts it, you can't force a grid onto a complex life. So when Genet is on the one hand actively socialist and on the other a self-proclaimed thief, mugger, cheat and liar who is openly and unabashedly worshipful of Nazism, fascism, terrorism, revolution for the hell of it, and evil, we're sympathetic because we appreciate that underneath all this artistic expression, he's still basically, even singularly, politically correct: he's socialist, anti-bourgeois, and anti-capitalist.

By contrast, your inconsistencies, excesses and extremes—your impulsive, unfettered expressions of emotion, feeling—are considered outrageous, hysterical, offensive, and unacceptable, to say nothing of bad art. Why? Because at some very deep level that no one is articulating, you are very politically incorrect. You're not a real, card-carrying socialist. You won't proclaim that identity. Though you've put yourself on the line for socialist concerns, in some instances (e.g., socialized medicine) far more than Genet (or for that matter Edmund), you're affirming of capitalist systems, potentials and strategies; and you take morality and evil seriously.

Entangled within all this is your so in-your-face ethnicity, even though you're as critical of "Jews" generically and explicitly as Edmund is not all that tacitly, in *Genet* and other writings, of Israel. But you have this very strong Jewish moral, patriarchal, sensibility and character. Translation: You're a loudmouth, pushy Jew—and a screamer to boot. No one would admit that that's what they're really thinking, of course; and you yourself say you've never been confronted by any such accusations; and of course, Edmund's means of dealing with people and things he doesn't care for are the opposite of your means of dealing with people and things that hurt or seem wrong: silence. I mean, apart from the occasional mention, has Edmund ever given you or your work any serious, in-depth consideration? In any event, I think a lot of *this* level of judgment is there, in the silence.

So you get someone like a George Stambolian or a David Bergman or a Felice Picano or anyone else in Edmund's entourage passing judgment on you, implicitly or explicitly, but taking a very different tone or no tone at all *vis-à-vis* Genet, to say nothing of each other. (I don't recall ever reading a single, seriously and substantively critical piece about Edmund anywhere, and certainly not about *Genet*. Such is his hold on the gay and greater literary worlds.) Which also leads one to consider another perspective: of them all as the very bourgeoisie/establishment for which Genet had such contempt. Alternatively, if Genet were around today, he'd probably adore you and loathe them! Though they don't seem to have any inkling of this, what will happen to you eventually is what has happened to Genet: time will hallow our image of you, however warts-and-all, and you will be seen as a saint. [For an updating of the dialectic between Kramer and White, see "The ·Larry Kramer Story," pp. 68–70.]

We'll say more about all this but I don't want to lose our discussion of your being hyperbolic. Here's another example I want to ask you about. I forget where it was—in your interview with Gore Vidal?—but you made a very strongly derogatory remark about the Center for Lesbian and Gay Studies (CLAGS), which has done so much important and wonderful work, which I've been a friend and supporter of since its inception, and in whose programs you yourself have participated. Weren't you being extreme and hyperbolic? I mean, look, why not just admit that a lot of your anger was coming from your old feud with Marty [Duberman]. Why not say that right up front instead of denouncing this whole organization?

Kramer: What did I say?

Mass: You denounced them for being an organization that's telling gay people that gay identity isn't legitimate. And you did this in your interview with Gore Vidal, who couldn't be more in synch with that viewpoint!

Kramer: I still would denounce them for this. It's all this horseshit about homosexuality not existing before the late nineteenth century. How can anybody buy this claptrap, much less deal with it academically? Talk about knifing ourselves in the back!

Early on, there was all this divisiveness between Marty and John Boswell, who was a close friend of mine. What became CLAGS was originally supposed to have been set up at Yale with both of them, but they didn't get along, and some of that had to do with the differences in their beliefs about the legitimacy of gay identity over time. So Marty split off. Now, I've heard different versions of the story and knowing both of them to be as dramatic as they are, I don't know that we'll ever know the real story, the true story, a story that would encompass both sides' versions. And in any case, my own loyalties were with Yale, where I was an undergraduate, and with John; so what I said may have had something to do with that. I don't mind Marty; I bait him almost playfully. But there is a background. Marty's review of *Faggots* was one of the most unkind, ungenerous, hateful reviews that any writer has ever received, that any gay person has ever given to another gay person. And I didn't even know the man then. I'm sure a great deal of my continued baiting of him is attributable to that. I think Marty finds it very difficult to bestow credit on anyone who has come along in the intervening years and sort of made a contribution in territory and turf that he once and perhaps still considers his, where he had been king of the hill. I think the success of ACT UP surprised a lot of the old guard, who were initially scornful of it, and stayed away from it even though they were all invited to be there from day one. It was there for everybody. In the beginning we were very much scoffed at, but then the fact that it was successful made it difficult to denounce. Since then, it's been like Mapp and Lucia. I don't hold any ill will, really, but I don't think we're ever going to be buddies.

Mass: Probably not. Naively, I once recommended to Marty—who, as you know, has been my mentor and close friend (though we've had very little contact since I began working on this book), and to whom I could not be more indebted for all that he's given and taught me—that they consider you for a CLAGS award, like the ones they gave Edmund White and Gore Vidal, and he wasn't as hostile to the idea as you might imagine (not as hostile as he was later said to be over the idea of having a book on you for the Chelsea House series on the lives of famous gay men and lesbians). He even pointed out that you and Eli (Zal, his lover) had once known each other "biblically" (because his work is mostly so scholarly, Marty's droll humor, which really comes through for example in *Midlife Queer*, is seldom commented upon). But the next thing that happened was that you did one of your baitings of him at a gay studies program at Yale, so that was the end of that. Also, I would have to defend Marty and CLAGS here against the charge of delegitimizing gay identity. On the contrary, I believe the social constructionists CLAGS has given such voice have taught us a lot about the complexities and mutabilities of what we've thought of so naively and simplistically as "gay identity." In any case, as a participant in its programs, certainly you acknowledge that CLAGS does good and important work.

Kramer: I have no problem with the CLAGSes of this world. But just as ACT UP was a lot more than Larry Kramer, CLAGS is a lot more than Marty Duberman.

Mass: Since we're talking about inconsistencies, Larry, let me ask you about some of yours. In the area of outing, for example, you've been so brave, often magnificent. And the people you've gone after could not be more appropriate or deserving—e.g., Ed Koch, Donna Shalala, Jac Venza, David Geffen, Dick Jenrette.

Kramer: Did I go after Jac Venza? How could he be in the closet? I mean, all you have to do is look . . .

Mass: But what about the ones you *haven't* gone after, folks who have coincidentally become allies of sorts (people who've endorsed you)—e.g., like Liz Smith, Susan Sontag, and Annie Liebovitz? Isn't this having a double standard?

Kramer: I don't think I have a double standard. I think I have an individual standard, based on each individual person, and I think outing has got to be taken by person, rather than in any kind of sweeping way. I happen to think that Liz does an enormous amount for the gay community and I don't think she's really in the closet. I don't think she sees herself that way. I think nearly everybody is now aware of her sexuality, and I don't know what more her saying she was a lesbian would achieve than what she's already doing. I don't think it would be possible for her to do more for us than what she already does and has done.

Mass: I have to agree with you, even though I believe the problem of celebrities in the closet to be generic and to have a cumulative negative impact that can only be changed by individuals coming out, or being outed. This is a point well made by Sarah Schulman *vis-à-vis* Sontag. But you are right. I can't really feel anger at Liz. It was similarly difficult to be angry with Leonard Bernstein.

Kramer: Donna Shalala is another matter. Our lives are in her hands. As with Koch, we have people who are so petrified of being perceived as gay that they bend over backwards to disassociate themselves from anything that we need. Now, that's a whole other kettle of fish than Liz Smith.

In terms of Annie and Susan . . . I don't know how to say all this. Mostly, the people I've gone after are people who should be fighting a lot harder for our issues, especially and primarily AIDS. Though many lesbians are involved in AIDS, AIDS isn't as much a lesbian issue as it is a gay male issue; so I get angriest at people like Barry Diller who has buried, I believe, two lovers, and who has been the head of film studios and TV networks that still don't put out any kind of movies about AIDS or gay issues. I mean, that's very different from what Annie and Susan do or do not do. So it's a case by case issue. I think Michelangelo [Signorile] deals with this very well in his really fine book [*Queer in America*]. I mean when you're dealing with a United States senator who's molesting boys on his staff and voting against you on the floor, that's a whole other matter.

But Susan's situation is different in another way. Again, I don't know if I'm saying this right, and this may be some kind of projection on my part, but I think Susan is . . . beyond being a lesbian. I know I'm probably saying something very politically incorrect, but, except for the fact that she has affairs with women, she doesn't really fit into that category . . . What she is more than anything else is an Intellectual, with a capital I.

Mass: I think what you mean is that she doesn't want to limit definition of herself in terms of our struggle, and you can't really say, at least in her case, that you have a major problem with that. In this sense, she's like another of those for whom you have great admiration: Gore Vidal.

Kramer: I don't have such great admiration for Gore Vidal across the board, but he has lived with a man for all his adult life.

Mass: Well, isn't *she* living (or cohabiting, I think they have their own apartments) with Annie?

Kramer: OK, but . . . I look upon her as, I don't know, as Venus with Hera, some great goddess that is on Mount Olympus and beyond sexuality, beyond category. She's also written two very good books about illness and AIDS, and so it's not as if one can say she hasn't made a contribution to our fight. And Annie photographs many gay people, often stunningly. Including me!

Mass: But Susan Sontag is one of the most powerful people in the worlds of literature, culture and art. She's so important and influential. What does it say that someone of her stature will not acknowledge her lesbianism, however atypical it may be? Here's an example of what I mean. There's a book called *Great Jewish Women* that was published in 1994 and which includes Sontag. Her bio notes her Jewish roots and details her relationship with Philip Rieff and mentions her son, but nothing is said about her current relationship and circumstances with Liebovitz, who is also featured in the book and whose lesbianism, which wouldn't seem to be as "atypical" as Sontag's, is likewise invisible. At the very least, one just wishes that Sontag somehow felt more passionately about gay struggles. I mean, wouldn't it be great if she put herself on the line for a gay cause the way she did for Bosnia?

Kramer: But she has, with her essays and books on AIDS, with her support of and involvements with gay issues and a lot of individual writers. Look, you simply cannot take on every single prominent gay man and lesbian. Liz, Susan and Annie patently are not the enemy. Ed Koch, Terry Dolan and Roy Cohn were. Surely you see the difference—if only in terms of how much time it takes to deal with only *one* of them.

Mass: Well, that may be more true now, but remember when she was President of PEN, how they did nothing for gay and lesbian writers, or, for that matter, AIDS, and how upset we all were about it?

Kramer: That's when I quit PEN.

I guess there are degrees of complicity here . . . and as with Liz Smith, I just feel we've got bigger fish to fry. Did you see *The Advocate* with John Travolta and Jodie Foster on the cover? It was on this whole subject on how/ whether rumors of homosexuality can hurt a star's career. It used to be that they would never do these kinds of stories because they were too worried about getting sued. I think we've entered a different era now. I think that all our years of fighting are finally paying off. Look at how open the discussion is now about Lenny Bernstein.

Mass: Yes, truth does have a way of eventually coming out, so there's still hope for Susan. Let me go back to something that you mentioned a couple of minutes ago in passing—your experiences with the *New Yorker*. Please elaborate.

Kramer: Tiger! [Larry's terrier] Get down! Good girl. Like many writers, I would like to be published in the *New Yorker*, and over the years I have made many submissions. At least in the old days, you always got a letter back. And I came close a couple of times; a long short story almost made it once. This was when William Shawn was editor.

Mass: Which story was that?

Kramer: It was about my freshman year at Yale, about my relationship with a friend, one of my roommates; and it did have gay content. And in the end, that's why it wasn't published, but I think it came close. When Gottlieb was editor, I submitted a number of pieces, including the long essay in *Reports*. Although he felt it was too strong and "rhetorical," he did make an offer to me to write about AIDS, which I'm sorry I didn't accept, though I don't know if it ever could have worked out.

Then—when Paul Popham died—in the late 1980s, I decided I wanted to write a regular column somewhere in the mainstream press about AIDS, and I wrote three letters—one to Max Frankel at the *New York Times*, one to Gottlieb at the *New Yorker*, and a third to David Laventhol, who was editor of the *L.A. Times* and who was someone I grew up with, went to Yale with and was friends with. I wanted it to be a regular thing, a column. Max Frankel of course, said no, and Gottlieb, to his credit, said he'd be willing to give it a try; he didn't know whether it could be regular, but they were looking for someone to write about AIDS and no one had worked out. But David Laventhol had the best offer, for a column that would be syndicated via the *L.A. Times* and *Washington Post* all over the country and internationally. He said he would put it out over the wire service. I accepted, but it didn't turn out very well. I had to deal with a simply wretched editor who made drastic cuts. The first piece, which is in *Reports*, was put out on the wire service for syndication, and no one picked it up. Three thousand newspapers around the country and no one picked it up, including the *L.A. Times*, which was David's paper! I suppose I should have stuck with it a little longer, tried to continue it on a regular basis because, as I understand it, the more things go out on a wire service, the more you accrue certain papers. This woman who has a syndicated column now out of Detroit—she's got a book coming out; I can't remember her name—told me that you start with one, then you get two or three and it builds from there. As for the *New Yorker* today, I've had nothing but messages from Tina [Brown], saying, through various people (Harold Brodkey, Brendan Lemon, Adam Gopnik), Tina wants you to write for this magazine; please feel free to send things. But every time I've sent things, and I've done it a number of times, they somehow get "lost," including the piece that's there now. After two months of not hearing from them, I called—or Harold [Brodkey] called for me—and I was told they couldn't find it; could I send them another copy? The piece that I read at A Different Light ["The Bloods," from *The American People*] was "lost" three times at the *New Yorker*. Finally it was read, and I got the most incredible letter from the fiction editor saying how wonderful it was. It's the best rejection letter I've ever received. They couldn't publish it, they said, because it was too long.

Mass: But the *New Yorker* does do long pieces.

Kramer: A lot less so now, under the new regime. So I sent a non-fiction piece to them about my extraordinary experience trying to find out what it was like being a Jew in Switzerland during World War II—talking to a lot of people about how you got in, or couldn't get in. There's very little written about all of that. It wasn't very complimentary, although *Condé Nast Traveler*, which commissioned it, urged me to write a hard-hitting piece. But when I did, they wouldn't publish it. So I submitted it to Tina, and again, it was "lost." When I sent them another copy, it was turned down.

Mass: What occurs to me here is something Patrick Merla has observed—that you're a writer whose work often benefits from a fair amount of feedback and editing. I read the Switzerland piece and "The Bloods," which you mentioned earlier. The latter is a grand and polished work of literature. The former is a little raw, but the substance is there. What's disturbing is the unwillingness of these publications to consider working with you, something you've always been willing to do, though perhaps not everybody who gets a piece from you knows that. This, I believe, was a major factor in your feud with George Stambolian, which we'll talk about a little later. In the old days (not so long ago), the problem at the *New Yorker* was sheer homophobia. There were no openly gay folks and no gay content. Today, gay's OK, as long as it's not too controversial; it's substance versus surface. But what would you expect? Though *Vanity Fair* did this nice profile on you under Tina Brown, when she took over at the *New Yorker*, Brendan Lemon became one of her culture editors. Do you remember how badly he trashed *Reports*?

Kramer: Yes, it was in the Sunday *New York Post*. He always maintained it wasn't so negative, but it sure seemed so to me.

There've been two people who have truly surprised me when I read them in print because they had always seemed so supportive of me and my writing in person. One was Brendan and the other was Gregory Kolovakos, who was a good friend. We'd go to lunch like every three weeks or so, and he would tell me, "Larry, I love what you're writing, and I xeroxed this and sent it to this one and that one and to all my friends, and blah, blah, blah," and to "call me." Then, lo and behold, there was a review of *Reports* in *The Nation* in which he was cruel. Now, he died shortly thereafter, and maybe, I don't know, maybe he went through some kind of dementia or something; not that he might not have changed his mind, as people sometimes do. In any case, it was like someone close to me had suddenly turned around and just knifed me. The same was true for his buddy Darrell Yates Rist, who was someone I'd always had a very cordial relationship with. I guess some people surprise more than others. But I guess it's also as Joe [Papp] always said: "If you haven't made somebody angry, you haven't done something right."

I still would like to write a column for a mainstream publication. I wrote to *Time*, *Details*, *New York*, the *New Republic* and others. I was turned down everywhere except, of all places, *Time*. But a lot of this had to do with Bill Henry, who was going to write a biography of me. Unfortunately, he died.

Mass: David Bergman and Ellie Burkett are others who you felt turned on you! But Lar, what about all those who thought *you* were *their* friends, who feel just like you—betrayed? It's the stuff of a novel by Edmund White. Who was Bill Henry?

Kramer: Bill Henry was a senior editor of *Time*. He was also their drama critic, and he reviewed mysteries. He won two Pulitzer Prizes. He's the one who invented the term "outing"; who wrote that first *Time* article on it. And although he was married, he was a lot like Frank Rich in being very comfortable with gay subjects and gay people. He had a contract with Doubleday to do my biography, but then, at age forty, he had a heart attack—he was very, *very* overweight—and died. Anyway, I can't get the new editor to return my phone calls or answer my letters. I keep getting messages from mutual friends that yes, he's still interested, but I can't seem to make any actual connection.

Mass: We were talking about your inconsistencies before. Here's another example, from my friend Scott Tucker, a co-founder of ACT UP Philadelphia, author of the socialist manifesto *Fighting Words*, and a former Mr. International Leather. Scott wrote me that he wonders if you realize, when you keep quoting and praising Hannah Arendt, that Arendt signed a petition, together with Einstein, denouncing the tactics of the Irgun, the Israeli terrorist organization, which you have extolled.

Kramer: Well, I don't bracket Hannah Arendt and the Irgun together, and I always say that I myself could not partake of urban guerilla type activities, although I wish I could. I'm just saying that considering how we've been put upon, I'm surprised there hasn't been more visible outrage. Again, it's the way I talk, but I don't think that what I've *said* is inconsistent.

Mass: I've heard different stories about your use of "holocaust." Why did you use the lower case "h" for *Reports*?

Kramer: In the new edition, it's all upper case on the cover, but still lower case on the title page, the way it was on the original cover. We did it that way because we were so nervous about offending Jews, by using the word "holocaust" at all. In the essay, I talk a great deal about how the Jews don't have any right to own this word. After the book came out, yes, there were a few letters from Jews who objected, but not very many, and invariably, when the book was named anywhere, it was always a capital "H" that was used by the typesetter. So this concession of using the lower case turned out to be a sort of fruitless exercise.

Mass: Though your designation of our holocaust as such comes from a place of identification (of gays with Jews), the accusation that Jews have no special claim to a history of injustice, persecution and suffering is common among anti-Semites. Larry, you once told me that you have never, personally, experienced anti-Semitism. Never even a piece of hate mail?

Kramer: The hate mail that I receive has always been anti-gay. If anti-Semitism was there, too, I don't recall it. It's possible there was something mixed in there with so many other hateful words, but never anything that was primarily or solely anti-Semitic. No. I've often thought about this, especially because of our friendship and my knowledge of your life and experience and what you've written about. But in this regard, I had a blessed childhood and upbringing. Of course, anti-Semitism was present at Yale, to an extent that really affected the lives of my brother and father; but by the time I got there, it wasn't. There were a lot of Jews in my class, and plenty of Jews got into the fraternities and societies. There were no Jews in the Whiffenpoofs. I was in a singing group, and the leader of our group was a Jew, and he was not elected to the Whiffenpoofs when he should have been, and that destroyed his life. But personally, I have to say that I've been very lucky in this regard. And when I went to work in the movie business, it was actually an advantage to be Jewish.

Mass: Was it the movies that endowed you with such an American brand of meliorism?

Kramer: What does that word mean?

Mass: It's the phenomenon of the verb to ameliorate, to make better. It's always been very American to think with almost childlike naiveté that you can solve all problems, make everything better. You know, "the power of positive thinking." At some level, you're really just like Norman Vincent Peale. In his interview with you for POZ, Andrew Sullivan also raises this question of your positivism, your industriousness. This is certainly the stuff of the Hollywood films of your youth. Is it also a characteristic of Jewish upbringing?

Kramer: More than anything else, I think it comes from a lot of therapy. It's hard to say that it doesn't come from a Jewish upbringing or the movies or whatever. Everything contributes. My mother was always saying, "There's nothing in the world my two boys can't do." But my father was a real example of someone who was a failure. It's very interesting that my niece has just been through this terrible experience—she's had to endure an enormous amount of pain—because she was unable to achieve what she felt her parents expected of her. As a child, I certainly went through that. I wanted so badly to write—I didn't really start my writing until I was thirty—but something was preventing me, some neurotic whatever, and those things had to be worked out in therapy. I had to get over the *fear* of writing. So the positivism came about not because of positive influences but from the experience of overcoming the negative ones and all the fears and self-doubt that went with them. One of the reasons Linda [Laubenstein, the model for Dr. Emma Brookner in *The Normal Heart*] moved me so much as a character, someone to write about as a person, was that she allows no self-pity. She was a living example of someone who had totally overcome all her considerable handicaps. As a friend and human being, she was inspirational.

Mass: So a lot of this positive attitude, which we might also call maturity, came about through therapy, which I was so skeptical of. In those days, I think I felt that you were spending all your time in therapy instead of getting involved in the movement. I felt about you and your therapy the way the gay left has tended to regard the recovery movement—with a lot of suspicion, not just because twelve-step programs talk about "God" or a "Higher Power," but because the priority is to get your own act together, rather than just blaming society for everything.

Kramer: I must say I do think therapy worked on me exceedingly well. I was lucky that I had good therapists all along, and I also had a good mix of them. I think my attitude comes from believing that if I can do it, overcome my fears and pain, the abuse of my childhood, and all the self-pity, others can too. I was a mess. I tried to kill myself. I was incredibly shy. I was very frightened. I had a terrible self-image. And I was terrified of writing. It's taken me a long time, and it has not been easy, but I made myself into something that I can accept, that I can live with; and most of the time now, I can write, and I love writing. My voice has given me strength, and I get strength from writing. The lessons you learn are that it takes a long time, and it does take a lot of work; and of course not everybody can afford a lot of therapy. In your case, it was obvious to me that you had a gift, and that you could write, that you could use words, you could make yourself clear in this other way; and that you just had to stop kvetching and apply yourself. Writing is hard. It's all of those things that we say it is, but if you want to do it, you'll do it. As you've found out, it won't happen overnight; I was forty when the first novel was published. A lot of people aren't willing to wait, but if you believe and care enough, you will.

Still, I don't know where it all comes from, this attitude and conviction. My sister-in-law and I talk about this a lot because she's curious about it the same way you are; she agrees that I didn't get it from my parents. She thinks that I literally made myself, which is sort of a nice compliment. This is in contrast to my brother, who has perhaps been more bound to my parents than I was, even though he's the one who left home.

Mass: However you got there, your self-made positivism is very American and was very much the stuff of the movie world that was actually your first professional involvement. That's why I'm curious about that connection.

Kramer: I never really had a love affair with the movies. What happened is that I really wanted to start out in the theater, but got waylaid by these other opportunities.

When I wrote my first screenplay, I was in analysis in London with William Gillespie, a very strict Freudian who helped me become a writer. With each new therapist I worked through a different problem—the writing, being overweight, my father, coming out of the closet—with Sam Klagsbrun. And love, with Norman Levy [to whom *The Normal Heart* is dedicated]. Norman made me ... the first time I ever cried was because Norman taught me how. And also Gloria Donadello, who helped me find a certain kind of tenderness in myself. She was a great therapist, but, also, women have whole other worlds of experience and sensibility. This was such an important relationship for me.

Mass: Actually, several of your closest relationships have been with women. Earlier, we were talking about what an inspiration Linda Laubenstein was for you (speaking of the power of positive thinking, and not indulging self-pity!). I know this is coming out of left field, but I've always been curious: do you think she might have been lesbian?

Kramer: No. She was straight and as horny as they come. I know for a fact that she was having an affair ... with somebody in her building. Also, I can't remember whether any of this got into my screenplay, but early on we were drawn to each other to an extent that there was a physical element, and I ... I ran, literally ... in any case, she was putting out those vibes and I felt them.

I miss her. She was my dear friend. We used to talk at midnight. We'd stay up late on the phone. She had so many stories and she was so funny! There were very few doctors she had anything good to say about. (laughter)

Tiger! Get down!

Mass: Those speakers look like the ones they have at IMAX. Do you listen to music at high volume?

Kramer: No, I don't, and not when I write.

Mass: Then why such huge speakers? Relics from the Saint?

Kramer: No. The ones from the Saint are in the other room! They're the ones David wants to take to the country ... I don't know why I got them.

Mass: What a lovely bracelet. Turquoise, my favorite. Where'd you get it?

Kramer: Oh, now you've exposed my superstitious part! Years ago—sometime in the seventies—a medium, a psychic, gave me a reading; she said I should always wear something turquoise. So I always have, and I'm still here.

Mass: And what can you tell me about that painting [expressionist, gay, erotic, religious and referential to AIDS]?

Kramer: It's by Karen Finley, who—with Tim Miller, the performance artist—was one of the four who lost their NEA grants for using openly sexual stuff. I saw and bought it at a show she was having at a gallery in East Hampton. This was long before I ever met her.

Mass: And the candelabra with the yarmulke on top of it?

Kramer: Joe Papp gave it to me. He thought I was—quite rightly— a bad Jew. I think this was his attempt to make me a better one.

Mass: Why did he think you were a bad Jew?

Kramer: Because I am.

Mass: How so?

Kramer: I don't know. I'm not religious and I haven't believed in God since I was fifteen.

Mass: Every so often you touch on this subject, for example, in your *DPN* interview. And you say different things at different times. Once, during a moment of very deep connectedness between you and me—this was in the '80s—you said to me "Go with God."

Kramer: "Vaya con Dios." I was probably thinking about the song with that phrase. Was it Patti Page? Maybe I'd just heard it.
I know a lot of people who don't believe in God but who believe in some sort of spirituality, and I might have admitted to that years ago, but having been through these last fifteen years, it's pretty hard to believe there's someone—anybody or anything—out there looking out for us.

Mass: Do you think Mr. Papp was being that literal?

Kramer: I don't know… you never knew how serious anything was with Joe. I don't think he was about to make me get bar mitzvahed or anything.

Mass: You never had a bar mitzvah?

Kramer: No, but I was confirmed. We were members of a reformed congregation.
I grew up in a pretty Gentile environment, and, as I told you, I never really had experienced any anti-Semitism. We were, as far as I knew, the only

Jewish family in this suburb of Washington we grew up in, and I went to Sunday school on Saturday, or whatever it was called. And my mother actually taught there for all the rich Jewish kids.

So I had a reformed Jewish upbringing, and having a bar mitzvah is not ... *de rigueur* in reformed Judaism. But I was offered the choice: did I want to be bar mitzvahed? And my answer immediately was no. I didn't want to learn Hebrew. It was a lot of work, and I just didn't feel any strong pull to it. In fact, probably because my mother was a teacher, and I had to go down there and be the teacher's son, I think I probably had less interest than most of the other kids. Even though she was a good teacher and popular, she was my mother, and I tended to play hooky. I'd sneak out and go shopping, explore Washington, whatever. So, if you weren't bar mitzvahed, the other option was to be confirmed, which I was when I was sixteen.

Mass: And that was acceptable to both your parents?

Kramer: There was no protest. My grandparents—this is in *The Destiny of Me*—on my mother's side were orthodox, and both of them would write her letters in Hebrew or Yiddish (I don't remember which). When I was thirteen, a handsome present automatically came from California, where they'd moved, for my bar mitzvah. And my mother made me write them a thank you letter, as if I had been bar mitzvahed, because she was ashamed. But it seemed right at the time. We felt so out of it, in terms of Judaism. I lived in a gentile community all week long; once a week I went to this rich, Jewish temple, where everybody was loaded and we weren't, and where kids were dropped off and picked up in chauffeured Cadillacs. When I was about fourteen, I was invited to join this Jewish fraternity that had all these rich kids. I would go to their houses, where they had two-story recreation rooms and servants. I felt awkward and ashamed because we lived out in Prince George's county, which was really the other side of the tracks. So it was hard to connect with the orthodoxy with its foreign tongues and demands and hard to connect with the wealthy Jews from the temple.

Our rabbi was this guy called Norman Gerstenfeld, who was very famous in rabbinical circles. He'd been to Oxford, and he talked with a plummy English accent you could cut with a knife; he was very grand, and everybody kissed his ring. You wouldn't even think he was Jewish. He was handsome, he had all this silver-gray hair, he always wore a gorgeous suit, and the last year in Sunday school, when we were sixteen, he was our teacher, the one we wrote our confirmation speeches with. He liked me, I guess. He saw that I was a good writer ... and I remember when he was blessing me at the end of my confirmation service—he would do everybody two at a time, one with each hand, but for some reason, I got the one-person version—and saying, "You have gifts," and "Go out there and exploit them and God will do this, and God will do that"; and I remember thinking to myself, I don't believe a word of this shit, about God, I don't believe any of it.

Mostly, what Judaism was to me was all these rich people that made me feel poor.

Mass: Sounds a lot like my own experience, except for the wealth business. I wasn't alienated from Jews because they were wealthy, but because I was surrounded by gentiles and didn't want to be an outsider. Like you, I thought of Jews more as "them"—those religious or ethnic types or rich people, whatever—than "we." As if we could choose not to be Jewish. Also like you, I came to regard my gay identity as my principal identity. Being Jewish was secondary to the point of nonexistence. I had no idea how great a role internalized anti-Semitism was playing in all this.

Kramer: You've put your finger on something very important that applies to both of us. I've always felt like an outsider, whatever or wherever it was, whether it had to do with being or trying to be Jewish or a boy or a man. I never felt I belonged, not at the temple, not at Yale, not at Kaywood Gardens, which was this apartment development we lived in. I always felt very alone, and I think that's part of what being a writer is about. You really do feel you're on the outside, that you're observing, that you're looking in. I don't think I ever felt a part of anything that ever really moved me or involved me until GMHC (and, later, ACT UP), which is why it was so painful to me when the leadership of GMHC came apart. I'd really found this place where I thought I belonged. So the alienation from Judaism isn't really different from the alienation from everything else. On the other hand, however much I've remained the outsider, I did connect with the gay community, with my involvements with GMHC and ACT UP. But I've never done anything like that—like joining the gay temple of some organization of Jews or gay Jews—in conncection with Judaism.

Mass: We're also secular Jews. I participated in the international conference of lesbian and gay Jews they held here, but neither Arnie nor I are members of Congregation Beth Simchat Torah (CBST), and we're not observant Jews, though we participate in some holidays, as occasions for family gatherings. Every so often, I'll take my mother to services on the High Holy Days.

As I say, we're not observant, but there was a little confrontation at last year's seder. We were using these feminist, socialist haggadahs that my sister got from the Unitarian Church she attends in Cambridge. They're lovely, except they're so much about other dispossessed peoples that the basic message of the holiday—the ancient, recurrent history of virulent anti-Semitism, to the extent that the Jews were enslaved, expelled or otherwise persecuted—was relegated to the point of oblivion. In absolutely classic socialist fashion, the holiday became about everyone *except* the Jews and every prejudice *except* anti-Semitism. I registered my concern.

Kramer: But I do feel Jewish, and very good about it. I mean, in the movie business it was like an added bonus. And I'm fascinated by Jewish history, as you know from my writing. Because of my main identity as an outsider, I have a lot of interest in Jewish history and behavior in this context. I mean, the rich Jews of Washington we've been talking about were outsiders, too.

Mass: Precisely. In my own journey, I learned that however true it is that there are rich Jews and that rich Jews are a phenomenon worthy of some analysis, commentary and criticism, the stereotype of "rich Jews" is also a cornerstone of anti-Semitism. I mean, I know, for example, that there are people who think of you that way.

Did you follow that whole business with Michael Jackson?

Kramer: Oh, with the anti-Semitic songs?

Mass: Yes. I mean, in absolutely classic, stereotypical, time-honored fashion, he was banking on anti-Semitism to pull himself out of the abyss.

You'll find this interesting. When I called the Anti-Defamation League to suggest that they organize a demonstration outside SONY, Jackson's distributor, my calls weren't returned. It was just like in *The Normal Heart* when Ned complains that none of his calls to gay organizations are ever returned. Eventually, I did reach a representative, who confided that ADL director Abraham Foxman doesn't believe in public demonstrations because, historically, those are the tactics (e.g., pickets) that have been used by anti-Semites!

Kramer: I'm much more intrigued with how easily Jackson's gotten off from the allegations of being a child molester. There was that very interesting article in *Vanity Fair* about how really tacky and inadequate and cheap that Diane Sawyer interview [on Prime Time] was, and how she let him get away with murder; yet another instance of how money buys you a personality in this country.

Mass: Initially, I felt he was being persecuted by our hypocritical, sexophobic-to-the-point-of-witchhunting society for what may have been relatively harmless, nonvictimizing sexual play. In any event, you can't help but wonder to what extent the whole thing has to do with his being a closet case, a gay man or transgender person who has been twisted into something else.

I want to return to this issue of how you've been perceived by others. In this context, I'm curious to know more about your segregation, intentional or otherwise, from the world of the Violet Quill. Of course, Andrew Holleran, one of the principal stars of this world, has consistently been your colleague, friend and champion.

Kramer: I guess my first connection with them was when I met Edmund, through Lou Miano; it was at a cocktail party at Lou's. This would have been in the early seventies? I don't think I saw him again for years; Andrew

Holleran [his pen name] and I knew each other from the Y. I don't remember exactly how we became friendly but we did, and, as you know, I helped him get *Dancer* published.

Mass: I knew you then, and I remember how that happened. I met the agent, Ron Bernstein, who represented you both.

Kramer: But I didn't know George Whitmore or the Ferro-Grumleys [Robert Ferro and Michael Grumley were lovers], and I didn't know Felice Picano or George Stambolian.

Mass: But Felice knew you. He's got several journal entries from those years that were published in Bergman's book.

Kramer: I haven't read them. Are they unpleasant?

Mass: Well, here, I'll read you one of them [from "Rough Cuts From a Journal," by Felice Picano, from *The Violet Quill Reader* (St. Martin's, 1994), edited by David Bergman, page 31. The entry is dated 9/6/78, Fire Island]: "Everybody hates [*Faggots*]. Not only because it's politically retrograde or repulsive (which it is), not only because it's slanderous, self-hating, homophobic (which it is), but also because it's poorly written ... Evidently Larry hasn't given up, though he grovels in front of all who he wanted to be his peers."

Kramer: Felice said all that? Interesting. Methinks he doth protest too much.

I know *they* all hated *Faggots*. The first of these terrible reviews from the gay community that I saw was in the *Body Politic*. I was in Florence with my brother and sister-in-law for the month of August, and the book wasn't coming out until October. They had jumped the release. The review was by George Whitmore, whom I didn't know, and it was awful, the worst. It literally urged you to tell all your friends not to buy this book. I guess that was my first inkling that it wasn't going to be received as rapturously by one and all as I had hoped! It was sort of funny reading it in Florence, so far away from the real world. I think I was in the middle of reading *Portrait of a Lady* ... And I was still trying to get over David—we'd split up yet again.

Mass: You had your own experience with George Stambolian, one that has become legendary. During the period of the first two volumes of *Men on Men*, George told me that when he rejected a story you had submitted—and he made it clear that it was you who approached him—which he said he'd shown to others (including Andrew Holleran?) and everyone had agreed that it was just impossibly, hopelessly bad, that you sent him one of the angriest, craziest letters of his or your lives. I've heard George's version, and Michael's [Michael Hampton, Stambolian's lover], though I've never actually seen the letter. Let's hear yours.

Kramer: First, let me say that I'm not so certain why so much is made of the Violet Quill. I'm sure there were associations of gay writers before. And the only two who are any good who were in that group are Ed and Andrew. Felice is, you know, just a sort of a pop hack at best. Chris Cox was pleasant, but not a very productive writer. George Whitmore only wrote something sort of decent after he got sick, which was years later. There was a story by Grumley in one of the *Men on Men* volumes that was wonderful, about going with a black guy on a Mississippi River steamer, but he wrote very little. Robert [Ferro, Grumley's lover] was serious but not very imaginative, a competent writer. So why this group has been so elevated into this core circle, and how that elevation has come about (who has been pulling the strings and how), are, I think, legitimate questions to ask. I don't know. I guess we're so desperate to have myths.

Mass: Reminds me of "the sexual revolution," which we thought was this unique development in the history of the universe, but which was only a mirage of moments from much bigger and more complex trends.

Kramer: Chris Cox wrote a travel book about Key West. We are not talking about a major literary movement here, one that defined a moment in time or a culture. In fact, I think it would probably have been detrimental for most budding writers to be thrown in with a bunch like this. Felice, George, Robert Ferro, Edmund, these were big mouths and strong wills, and not particularly generous then.

If Robert and Michael Grumley and Andrew hadn't been friends since their [University of] Iowa Writers Workshop days, the group probably would have eaten poor Andrew, who is a timid soul, alive. As it was, it was years after he finished *Dancer* before he had nerve enough to show or read any of it to anyone. That makes me think the Quill guys either didn't even have any sense of how good it was, or if they did they weren't telling Andrew. They certainly didn't do very much that I know of to help him get it out there. I'm the one who helped him get it published. We used to work out at the 63rd Street Y, and I fixed him up with my agent [Ron Bernstein]. *Dancer* came out a few months ahead of *Faggots* and got all the rave reviews. I had to fight against all my baser instincts not to be jealous and wish I'd never helped him! *As Is* opened a few weeks before *The Normal Heart* and got all the rave reviews, too. I wondered if my timing was always going to be so off! A funny story: *The Normal Heart* would have opened six months earlier if Linda Ronstadt hadn't been performing in *La Bohème* in the next theater at the Public. The music came through the walls into our space, and we didn't know this until we were ready to start casting. Joe Papp didn't have another space, and we had to postpone until Linda closed. Actually, the music would have been very apt as background music for us! In retrospect, I think that *Dancer* and *As Is* each coming before *Faggots* and *Normal Heart* was beneficial to me. They were gentler works than mine and, coming first, I think they made mine easier to accept. If mine had come first, they probably would have evoked brickbats. What am I talking about? They did! Well, they would have evoked bricks.

The story with George is that he had asked me to submit something for *Men on Men*. It was the first volume and he wanted something from all of us, and I thought that was sort of nice that he reached out to me because we certainly hadn't been all that friendly. I had been critical of him before, of some of the interviews that he had done for *Christopher Street*, the ones that got collected and published by Felice.

Mass: Right, the interview with the masochist, the beautiful man, etc.

Kramer: And I had that short story that I had sent to the *New Yorker*. It was called . . . "To Sleep 'Til Monday" or something. It was about the experience I had at Yale with one of my roommates, with whom I had wanted to go to bed but didn't until many years later . . .

Mass: Is that the episode that's alluded to in *The Destiny of Me*?

Kramer: Well, what's alluded to in *The Destiny of Me* is that I tried to kill myself at Yale, and I think that was in the story, too. So I had sent it to the *New Yorker*; this was when Shawn was still the editor. There was an editor there, Fran Kiernan, who was very supportive. She liked the story very much, and was willing to work on it with me, to somehow make it more for the *New Yorker*. I said I was willing. Then George came along and encouraged me to give it to him, which I did. I sent him the story, and he led me to believe he was going to publish it, so I told Fran that I would rather have it published as I'd conceived it and so was planning to give it to George. She was actually a little annoyed. Then George wrote me this really pompous letter saying, on second thought or whatever, he'd changed his mind. He then went on like a high school teacher with all his points and criticisms. You know, those rejection letters where they feel they have to tell you how to rewrite the story? Now, as you know, I'm not at all unwilling to edit my work, which usually goes through a number of drafts. I was in L.A. when I got the letter. I forget what I was working on, and it made me just fucking furious! So I wrote him that letter you're talking about, and it was indeed very angry and nasty. I don't remember everything in it, but I'm sure I told him he was a shit and to go fuck himself in no uncertain terms. And knowing me, I probably sent copies to people. So it became this scandalous thing; also because it apparently arrived at his house the day or right around the time his father died, so he was in mourning. I did lose my temper, and people like Felice made the most of it.

Mass: I've never seen the letter, though I ran into Michael Hampton recently and he said he'd show it to me, that I wouldn't believe how insane and extreme it was. But that was before my response to him, which went something like: now, Michael, are you actually going to stand there with a straight face and look me in the eyes and say to me, in all seriousness, that whatever it was Larry submitted to George was of less potential, less interest, less value, less character, less importance, less *substance*, than whatever it was George ended up publishing by Felice or Brad Gooch (to say nothing of six or so others—a third of the writers in *Men on Men I*—in that collection no one's ever heard of before or since)?

To give them their due, it's important to understand how these people saw/see themselves, as *real* writers—writers of refinement and taste, of style; not ranters, not screamers. And substance? I think that was less important. But perhaps this is all just sour grapes—from you and me, who, together with Bill Hoffman, were all rejected by George for *Men on Men*.

Kramer: I think you're probably right that I wasn't a real writer in their terms. The Ferro-Grumleys really did lead this kind of literary life; you know, they had teas and salons and things. They were so self-important. I mean, Robert would treat having a reading at a bookstore to five people as if he were going to be on the stage of Carnegie Hall.

As for the question of sour grapes, I never asked to be admitted to their group or any other. I didn't even know about it. I don't believe in writers' groups, and I never would have joined them, even if they had asked me.

You know they actually got money for their papers from Yale. I'm curious to know how much and where the money came from. Somebody must have put it up because Yale didn't have any funds for this kind of thing.

Mass: Your papers may go there, of course, but Arnie [Kantrowitz] ultimately decided not to put Vito [Russo]'s papers there [Arnie is literary executor of Vito's estate], despite pressure from George, you and Yale. George and Felice wanted his papers to be at Yale because they wanted them to be linked with those of the Violet Quill. But as we've said, the link with the Violet Quill consisted of one meeting Vito attended. Also, Vito disliked George. Ultimately, Arnie felt, and I certainly agree, Vito's contributions were more sociocultural than "literary," and really belonged in New York. So that's where they've gone, to the New York Public Library. Ours are going there as well.

Of course, you've had these "real writers" issues with a number of former close friends and colleagues outside the world of the Violet Quill, but of the same ilk—for example, Seymour Kleinberg and Sandy Friedman. What's happened to those relationships?

Kramer: Sandy and I say hello when we see each other, but ... he's a difficult person to be friends with. Richard [Howard] says his Beethoven book is very good. As for Seymour, I wasn't unwilling, but it just never seemed to happen. He became exceptionally critical of me.

Mass: I know that you're indebted to Richard Howard as a literary mentor and colleague, and friend. But I also recall a confrontation over a short story you'd written that he was trying to help you place in a Southern academic literary journal. When they rejected it, you hit the ceiling.

Kramer: Why do people keep coming up with all these little ... Look, Richard has always been, as he remains, one of the most important literary people in my life. He is a very noble and great writer and human being, and he was the very first writer whom I respected who took me seriously as a writer. This goes back to *Faggots*, which he loved, before we became friends.

Mass: How did you meet?

Kramer: I think we actually first met at the baths.

Mass: Somehow I thought you knew each other from Yale.

Kramer: No. He went to Columbia. And, you know, he certainly moved in a much more talented circle than the Violet Quill could ever aspire to. He'd received a Pulitzer Prize, became a President of PEN and was friends with many distinguished people. That he thought my work was good meant an enormous amount to me. The incident you're referring to was when I gave him a story to submit to *Shenandoah*, a Southern literary journal. Richard thought the editor would like it. In his poetic way, Richard said something like, "I think he'll look upon it favorably." I was probably thinking, aha, that means he's going to take it. In any event, when I got a rejection letter from this editor, I wrote him a nasty letter back. Richard then called me and said, "Why must you be so naughty?" or something like that, but I don't think it's ever hurt our friendship ... I guess it's starting to sound as if I don't take literary rejection so well. It doesn't bother me now, of course, but it did then, in part because, like you, I didn't start writing until relatively late. I was sort of a grown person who'd achieved in other areas, but I was writing and sending out first stuff at thirty that people like Edmund were sending out at fifteen or sixteen. I think taking rejection is one of the lessons you learn through experience. Now, I don't give a shit if somebody doesn't like my work. If I like it, I'm confident enough to know that that's what's most important and that I can find somebody else to do it. Especially with work like mine, you come to realize and accept that not everybody's going to like it. As Joe Papp always said, if you haven't offended somebody, you haven't done something right ... I learned so much from him ... Of course, being an activist has helped, too.

Mass: The thrust of this interview has been to look at you in what I've always seen as your primary mode and identity: as a writer, even though you're more widely known as an AIDS activist. But within that identity, there are others. When you and Tony [Kushner] did that conversation at the CLAGS symposium on Queer Theater, he said that his primary identity is as a playwright, and you said yours was as a writer. Have I got that straight?

Kramer: People are always trying to categorize me, but I've written in so many modes. So why should I be called a playwright? I've written screenplays, a novel, short stories, essays, journalism; I've written polemics; I've written for television. I really don't like to be categorized. So I'm a writer, but I think it is appropriate to say that Tony is a playwright; he's in love with the theater; it's his mode. I'm not in love with the theater, or with any particular literary form. It seems to me that different material dictates different forms. Some things you could write as a play that you can't write as a screenplay, and you can certainly write different things as a novel that you can't write as either. And I have different things I want to tell. But there's no way that the novel I'm working on could ever be anything but a novel because it's got such a large cast and such a huge canvas and unfolds over so many years. I wrote *The Normal Heart* as a play, as I've said, because that's what worked; I didn't think anybody would make a movie out of it. I'm not *in love* with the theater *per se*, unlike Tony, who loves everything about it.

For me, plays have been the hardest things to write. And I think that probably has something to do with why I say I'm not in love with the theater. I don't know why playwriting has been so tough for me. I've tried to analyze it—a little in that introductory essay to *Just Say No*. In playwriting, there are different tensions and energies to deal with; there are some things that will make a person sit still in a theater that are very different from what will make them sit still while reading a book. And storytelling is different. I mean, you don't really tell a story in a play; you resolve conflicts, make resolutions between characters. So there are all these differences. I would think I'd be a better playwright than I am. I'm always fighting, and drama is all about fighting. And, you know, it's very easy and natural for me to take both sides of a fight, to pit two people against each other, and be really sympathetic to both; but a play has to be more than that.

I've often wanted to teach a course where—I don't know if this has been done—where the kids, the students, would take an idea they had and then write it in three different ways—as a play, as a screenplay, and as a short story—and see what comes out.

I have purposely stayed away from the literary world in general. I always have. That's why I never had any interest in being a member of the Violet Quill. But even when Richard tried to draw me into his literary crowd, I stayed away. I mean, I don't know any of the top editors of the *New Yorker*. I could easily have been very close to Harold Brodkey. We've had a nice friendship, and now that he's got AIDS [from complications of which Brodkey subsequently died], I've managed to be helpful to him, but I've always kept my distance otherwise. I don't want to be sucked into anything. I love Richard because he is so innocent in a way; his literary knowledge is very pure; his respect for writers, for what they're able to accomplish, is genuine. And we agree very often, which is interesting; I think that's where we really enjoy each other; we have the same sensibilities about so many things. And, of course, he's *so* knowledgeable. I can say I'm looking for a model for a book about hopelessness, and he'll give me four suggestions. That's Richard Howard.

But he's also very generous, which most literary people aren't, as we all know ... I think most groups are not pleasant to belong to. Movie people are the worst. And doctors are the worst of the worst! I've never heard people badmouth each other as much as doctors. It's absolutely without parallel in my experience. But of all the groups, I think playwrights are perhaps the most generous to other playwrights, perhaps because they know how hard it is. Of course, they can get pretty bitchy ... It's almost as if people want you to fail somehow. I try to stay away from that kind of negative mentality. So I can honestly say that I've never been very good belonging to groups, including the ones I helped to start! (laughter)

Mass: Yes, Richard *can* be generous. But I still wince whenever I recall that profile of him in the *New York Times Magazine* (September 25, 1988), in which he is described as "devoted" to his pug, Mande (now deceased), but there is no mention of his lover, the artist David Alexander. In the course of that interview with Tony Kushner, some interesting things came out. You were in the Army?

Kramer: Yes, very briefly.

Mass: Did you ever write or talk about that anywhere?

Kramer: Oh, it was hardly the Army. I graduated from Yale in 1957. At that time, by law, everybody had to do six months of military service. There was a program called R.F.A., I'm not even sure what it stood for anymore, but if you were on the east coast like us, you went directly from graduation to Fort Dix. First, there were six months of active duty; then six years of reserves, I think. Anyway, it was a ball! There were 200 people in my unit, and 198 of us had just graduated from some Ivy League school, and 100 of them were from my class at Yale. So we were all friends, and we did nothing but laugh and sing and joke. We had to get up early, and we had to do mess and all the other shit, but it was fun. After your time at Fort Dix you got assigned to a job. Well, one of our group got assigned to Governor's Island in the office that cut orders. So everybody who was his buddy, including me, was reassigned to Governor's Island. Which meant you could come into New York every night. And somebody there donated a pair of fourth-row seats to the old Met, for every single performance. So, since nobody wanted to go, I went to the Met all the time and saw all those divas from that era—Zinka, Antoinetta Stella, *et al*. Then, after the opera, I'd go to Julius's before catching the last ferry back. After being discharged, I got my job in London and never had to do the six years of reserves. So that was the Army.

Mass: Makes you want to go right out and enlist. In the interview with Tony, you also said that you didn't do well in school.

Kramer: Well, I did well in high school, but not at Yale. I was so miserable there. I tried to kill myself during my freshman year, and one of the reasons was because I was getting terrible grades. In high school, I'd been this big fish in a little pond; but at Yale, it was the opposite. The things I was supposed to be doing well in I was getting bad grades in, especially English. I had no idea what *The Waste Land* was about.

My freshman year I didn't do well. I had to take psychology, geology, then astronomy—all these hideous things. I was terrible in math, and I couldn't figure out the constellations. The thing I did best in was art history, which was taught by Vincent Scully. At one point, I even decided to major in architecture.

Mass: You mentioned *The Waste Land* by T. S. Eliot, whose anti-Semitism is only now being seriously weighed. What other writers did you stumble over?

Kramer: I didn't do well with most of them. We had to read Proust, Henry James, James Joyce, all those people, and . . . I'm afraid I was out to lunch. I had a great difficulty concentrating, because I was so unhappy. I was also in psychoanalysis. I felt so overloaded; I didn't know what I wanted to do. And I was surrounded by classmates and roommates and friends, all of whom knew exactly what they wanted to do. They were going to be bankers or they were going to be lawyers, or they were going to be doctors, and I didn't have the fucking vaguest idea what I was going to be.

Mass: During that time, did you have any sense about becoming a writer?

Kramer: No, I didn't know from writing and I had no sense that I wanted to be a writer, though I did write. I tried to get into an honors course by writing a very long short story, about my psychoanalysis, and I was in a play at the same time—*Home of the Brave*, directed by some guy from the Drama School.

I wrote the short story for Professor Charles Napoleon Feidelson, a very distinguished Melville scholar and authority on *Moby Dick*. He called me into his office and said "About this story, Mr. Kramer. I hear you're in this play downstairs, and I hear you're very good in it. Have you ever considered a life in the theater? As an actor?' In other words, he hated the story, and wouldn't accept me for the course. So even the few times I tried to write were failures.

Mass: You paint such a bleak picture of yourself, but you must have exceeded in some things to get into Yale.

Kramer: Well, my father and brother had gone to Yale, and I had two uncles who went to Yale. That meant a lot then. And, as I say, I did well in high school. I didn't get the scholarship to Yale my parents needed, though I was offered one to the University of Pennsylvania; but my father wouldn't hear of my going anywhere else but Yale.

Mass: You did say at one point that you heard Ed White teach at Yale, and that you were very impressed.

Kramer: Yes, but that was years later. He asked me to come up for a seminar he was doing. He's a wonderful teacher; he's so well read, always able to cite quotations from Chekov, or whomever, to illustrate a point. And he's obviously very knowledgeable about literature and writing.

Mass: Yes, I've heard from others that he's a wonderful teacher; and in my own experience, I've certainly found him to be an engaging speaker and panelist, though there can sometimes seem to be a fine line between the literary facility—all the allusions and references he so skillfully utilizes and that are always so prominent in his work—and name-dropping.

Now, speaking of graduation, did you ever "graduate" from analysis?

Kramer: No. (laughter) I continued individual therapy on-and-off over the years. Now, David and I sometimes do couples therapy together.

Mass: I want to go back to that CLAGS interview you did with Tony Kushner. What was most striking about your encounter was the amiability and good will between you. He adores you and respects you beyond measure, and you're a great admirer of his work. Though there was no anger or confrontation, probably to the disappointment of more than a few, there were some interesting differences that emerged. One had to do with Tony's feeling that it was very important for him to publicly identify himself as socialist, which he did and which he qualified by saying that these days, identifying yourself as socialist is as risky as it is unfashionable. Though no one said this, what occurred to me is that the reality is precisely the opposite, at least in literary and academic circles, where being socialist is widely regarded as politically correct. The truly politically incorrect thing to do in any gay academic, literary or political forum would be to identify yourself as a capitalist! As I pointed out earlier, I think the contrast between the embracement of Genet and the rejection of you by a lot of establishment gay literati (what else can we all them? Is there any writer with more clout in the gay literary world than Edmund?) is revealing in this regard. In any case, you responded that you don't identify yourself with any of these labels. Is that correct?

Kramer: You have to define your terms more because being involved in social causes and being socialist are clearly not always the same things. But I guess what you're saying, that I never was a politically identified person, is largely true. When I lived in England, so many people my age who were involved in making movies were Marxist; it was the first time I had ever come in contact with people who lived by such strict orthodoxy. The truth is that I didn't know what the fuck a Marxist was. And I doubt that I could pass the test on it today.

And I don't know for sure what a socialist is. I mean there are all these gradations. Are Tony's political views the same as Marty [Duberman]'s? I have no idea.

I grew up in and around Washington, and Washington is not, in the sense that we're talking about it, a political town. There, you're either a Democrat or a Republican, and you don't even talk about that very much. It's not a town where you have political opinions that you speak out loud because that's the nature of government and bureaucracy. I remember when my Latin teacher in high school wore an "I Like Ike" button, and we were all so shocked because nobody wore any kind of political buttons for either party.

As for being a socialist, I'm just not sure what it means, how it's defined.

Mass: This is a big subject; it's complicated, important and controversial. We can't cover it all here. Let's just say for now that it means not just that you respect gender parity and racial and ethnic equality as worthy and important goals, which no sane and decent person could possibly disagree with, but that you give them top priority in whatever organization or endeavor it is that you're involved with.

Kramer: Well, I don't believe in gender parity *per se*; I believe in finding the best person for the job; in fact, there's more than one essay in *Reports* in which I talk about all of that; I'm sorry, but I think that giving gender and color parity overriding priority has tended to ruin more organizations than it's helped.

Having that opinion has, of course, gotten me in trouble. People label me an elitist, but I don't think I'm that. I just feel that when you're dealing with emergencies, especially a health emergency like AIDS, you have to go for the best qualified people you can get. That's where the priorities have to be. As you will recall, we got a lot of flack for not having people of color in GMHC in the beginning. Well, we *did* try. The very first person we hired, the first paid employee, was Phil Patrick, an African–American, but it's still hard getting people of color involved.

Mass: Well, I think the socialist perspective would say that any failure in that area was ours entirely, and totally unacceptable.

On the other hand, having these priorities and perspectives was a real achievement of ACT UP (much more so than GMHC in its early years), which from the beginning featured this thrilling blend of gay, bisexual, straight, transgender and multicultural peoples. However you did it—or didn't!—you achieved what socialists accuse you of being insensitive to, and better than any of the endeavors they were involved in, or all of them combined, at least with regard to the gay and AIDS movements.

Kramer: I guess I've never felt like I belonged to any movement, group, organization or label. In any case, I don't see how you can rigidly subscribe to any one set of principles across the board. You know, there are different things in all the different philosophies, religions, creeds, some of which contradict each other. The thing to do is to take the best from all of them.

The diversity that made ACT UP so successful in the beginning is what helped destroy it in the end. Initially, the reason it was so successful is because of the really high caliber of the people who joined up. They were smart and they had skills and energy. It wasn't so much that they were committed to any philosophy. In fact, it was the opposite; the willingness to overlook differences to work for common goals. Not that differences weren't acknowledged. For example, the women demanded that we treat them with respect in a way that some of the men weren't used to. But it was all done really quite remarkably, in a friendly way. We realized that the emergency was so big that we had to work together. Whatever abrasivenesss, whatever the differences and disagreements we may have had with each other, we put aside. But as the early folks dropped by the wayside, the people who took over were more concerned about creed than the crisis. And the atmosphere became very schizo and paranoid. There were Asians who were against blacks, and blacks who were against Hispanics, and so forth. The fighting was more with each other than toward achieving that shared goal.

So it's a complicated issue, but I would certainly say that in the case of AIDS, we're not going to get anywhere until the best people, whoever they are, are participating in the process. But a lot of these people don't want to participate when they feel like they're going to be trod upon by extremists. Urvashi and I have talked about this a lot.

Mass: You gave a very nice blurb for Urvashi's book, *Virtual Equality*, so I take it you do agree with a lot of what she has to say.

Kramer: My relationship with Urvashi is an interesting one. We disagree on a great deal philosophically and tactically, and yet we're good friends, which shows that it's possible for different strokes to come together. I think her work is more interesting because it grapples with so many political issues than for any conclusions she draws. She talks an awful lot about grassroots organizations being the answer for everything; but if she believes it so much, how come it hasn't worked for her? I mean, why wasn't NGLTF [The National Gay and Lesbian Task Force], which she spent a lot of energy being a grassroots organizer for, ever able to increase its membership or its financial base? ACT UP was a grassroots organization, but we didn't really take off until we were able to raise substantial amounts of money. So I don't know how you get anywhere without the money, mostly from rich and/or successful people, and I don't know that you can get it through a grassroots approach.

These differences are what emerged with the leadership conference we tried to put together, and which she talks about in the book. It was my idea to have a leadership summit conference, but by the time it came to pass, which was a year later, it had turned into such a free-for-all—it was so far away from what I had envisioned—that I decided not to go. It turned out to be a real mess, except that it was there that Urv met her lover, Kate [Clinton]. It seemed like such a good idea for people to meet and talk, but it became very hard to bring off, to decide whom you're going to invite, how you're going to divide up without offending anybody, and so on. Before you know it, it's gotten too big and out-of-hand. There are 800 people there, all of whom don't get along with each other.

Mass: But they had the conference.

Kramer: They did, but nothing came of it. It was utterly useless.

Mass: Was there ever another?

Kramer: Not so far as I know, though I think John D'Emilio [former director of policy for NGLTF] has backed subsequent attempts for another.

Mass: In your interview with *HGLR* [*Harvard Gay and Lesbian Review*], you talk about how important money is for a constituency to secure political power. You mention David Geffen and note that he gave a million dollars to APLA [AIDS Project Los Angeles] so blindly it made you want to cry. Then, within weeks of the publication of the interview, he gave two and a half million dollars to GMHC's new HIV testing program. Was this timing a coincidence?

I mean, should he have donated that money elsewhere—to ACT UP or TAG [Treatment Action Group] or NGLTF?

Kramer: Well, he has said what I've said, which is that all these organizations would do best to meld into one, that we'd be better off having one strong organization than a bunch of weak ones. He and I have talked about this, and I wrote about it in one of my *Advocate* articles: that NGLTF and HRCF and the AIDS Action Council, and the others, that they should coalesce.

Mass: I never would have imagined that the two of you—you and David Geffen—would be in contact after some of what's gone between you in the past.

Kramer: Oh, we never stopped talking. I like David. He's very smart and certainly smart enough to know that even adversaries—especially adversaries—should never cut off contact with each other.

I just wish that if he were going to give a big sum of money, that it would go for research—that it would go to David Ho or the Salk Institute . . .

The thing about the testing program is that it's a money-making proposition. The main reason GMHC is doing it is to increase their cash flow, and I think that's slightly ... smelly. They get paid so much by the government, the state, I guess, for each person that gets tested, which is basically more than it costs them to do it; so they'll be making a profit. That's fine, I guess, except when organizations like Whitman Walker, which has been doing this for some time, try to keep home testing kits from going into existence, for no other reason than because it takes money away from them. I think that's tacky.

Mass: Do you get a lot of pressure to contribute to all these organizations?

Kramer: Sure! Don't you? Some are more aggressive than others, but I've never been part of the big boys' network of givers—you know, the Fred Hochbergs, Jeff Sorefs and David Geffens. That kind of charitable giving is part of their lives, as are the perks that go with it, like meeting with Clinton or whatever. I'm not in that league. And I don't want to meet Clinton with a dozen or 100 others.

Mass: Commensurate with your wealth, whatever that is, are you contributing to gay organizations and causes to the extent that you are asking others to do?

Kramer: Well, part of me should say that that's none of your business. I don't think that I ask people to give to specific gay organizations. In fact, I often say something like the opposite: that I don't know which gay organization I would give to. But I do give a lot of money for AIDS research, and I do encourage people to do that. Currently, I give a substantial amount of money to the Salk Institute because I believe in what they're trying to set up out there. [In 1996 Arthur Kramer, Larry's brother, became a vice-president of the Salk Institute's Board of Directors.]

It's a very impressive scientific think tank in La Jolla [California]. Basically, it's a group of scientists who are free to study whatever they want to study in their particular area, and many of them are funded by rich places like the Howard Hughes Medical Foundation, which funds a number of what are called Howard Hughes Fellows. Now, it so happens that the last director died from AIDS and they hadn't been doing too much on AIDS prior to that; but since that time, they've hired three very smart scientists who are doing very interesting work, particularly in connection with the combination of HIV and HBV (hepatitis B), which, as you know, is my problem. I firmly believe that the next round of discoveries, the next round of AIDS research, is probably going to have to come out of private funding because the government is such a mess, and the NIH [National Institutes of Health] is such a mess, and don't look to be getting any better soon. So the discoveries are going to have to come out of places like the Diamond Institute, Rockefeller, the Salk Institute, the Howard Hughes Institute, Cold Spring Harbor, places like that, which basically are all privately funded, certainly also with government grants, but privately run. And it's going to be up to us to see that they get as much help as they can, which will involve a complete shift of focus from all the attention activists have paid to the NIH. It's interesting that in the last couple of years, the NIH has really contributed very little to our knowledge of what's going on. The drugs like the proteases are coming out of the pharmaceutical houses; even the trials are not being done through the NIH, which, as you know, would have been unheard of four years ago. The major discoveries that have been made about viral replication—that's all out of David Ho's lab, which is privately funded by Irene Diamond. So it's a different ball game from what it was and as we understood it when we started GMHC and certainly when we started ACT UP. That's why it's so important for the David Geffens and the Barry Dillers and the Calvin Kleins to get involved. That's the whole thing about naming and confronting these people. It's not just about outing. We desperately need their support.

Mass: Confronting the rich and famous has been fruitful, unquestionably. In recent years Geffen has been extremely generous. Very fittingly, at the conclusion of that HGLR interview, you talk about two other very prominent public figures in this context. You were reflecting on what's happened to the Harvard AIDS Institute—how it started out as this vital, promising organization with a "dynamite" newsletter and then faded into obscurity. You note that, for a number of years, the president of their Board of Directors was Maurice Templesman. Did Max Essex [who heads the Harvard AIDS Institute] or anyone else there ever try to get Mrs. Onassis to lend her name, you asked? Now, we all know that Mrs. Onassis was very private and didn't lend her name to too many public things; but she did have a number of gay friends and acqaintances—the Warhols and Nureyevs—and must have been touched by AIDS. Yet such is her aura and mystique, her legend in the gay world as everywhere else, that no one except you has ever implied any disappointment with her absolute silence and disconnection from AIDS. Certainly not Wayne Koestenbaum, though I say that without having read his book.

Kramer: But my point was different. What upsets me even more is that I doubt that she was ever asked. So far as I know, no one ever even tried to approach her! Max Essex didn't. All I'm saying is that Essex could have said something to Templesman, who then could have taken it to her. Talk about missed opportunites!

Mass: On the other hand, perhaps Templesman's directorship *was* her connection. We are, after all, talking about someone whose every gesture had the diplomatic impact of the Queen of England.

Kramer: What I've found is that a lot of these people *will* respond, if you can get to them; but you usually can't, and one of the main reasons you can't is that they're surrounded, "protected" by, all those closet cases, the Jerry

Zipkins. Instead of being on our side, they're the opposite because they're still trying to prove they're not one of *those* people, not the raging queens everyone knows they are and that they hate themselves for being.

Mass: And I'll bet Zipikin was as "discreet" about being Jewish as he was about being gay.

Kramer: How can you be discreet about being Jewish with a name like Zipkin?

Mass: We've talked about your own experience of growing up Jewish in the Washington area and how it was remarkably free of any overt/serious anti-Semitism, though it did affect your father and brother. On the other hand, when you and I did that panel in London on "Jewish Sexuality," the designating of which as such (without the quotes) you were so articulate in criticizing, you told a little story of an encounter you had with a certain Lady Ely. She was an aristocrat who was a friend. One day, you said, you were speaking casually with her and her husband and she confided that, "We don't much care for Jews." But I don't think you told us what your response was.

Kramer: You mean did I get up and leave?

Mass: Is that what happened?

Kramer: She said, "You're Jewish, aren't you?" So I said "Yes, I am." So, that was all that was said. I think I went to dinner at their house a few times and the friendship sort of faded from lack of either one of us pursuing it with any avidity. I stayed friends with one of their kids; but, I mean, I don't know what was supposed to happen. At the time, I think I thought the whole thing was funny in the sense that it was so typically British. Certainly, this was anti-Semitism, but when I've told you I've never really experienced anti-Semitism, I've had in mind the much more virulent forms, like when you're a kid and they call you a kike and beat you up.

I was in my thirties when I had this little encounter with Lady Ely, and my intuitive sense of what happened and what it meant was very different. I actually recall that her saying it to me in public was somehow more courageous than hateful. She was trying to communicate, to be intimate, to say what she really thought, or had thought.

Mass: I can appreciate that. In any case, you didn't call her on it, or talk to her about it further?

Kramer: You mean, did I say something like, "What a terrible thing to say"? . . . I might have; I don't know. I wasn't so gutsy in those days.

Mass: Does your novel have much on Jewish Washington during the war years?

Kramer: Yes. The novel does have a lot about Jews and Washington, perhaps too much . . . I think I want more of a balance with other peoples, although you could say that Jews, like gays, can be represented disproportionately because they've contributed more to the world than their numbers would seem to indicate. But my problem right now isn't in understanding Jews or Jewishness. If anything, it's the opposite.

Mass: What do you mean?

Kramer: So many of my characters [in *The American People*] are Jewish and I've become so involved with them. At a very deep level, I guess I feel I really understand Jews. On the other hand, one of my characters is this nun, and because I'm not as immersed in her world, I don't know if I understand her as well. I guess I know more of the minutiae of what it means to be Jewish than I do about what it means to be a nun.

Mass: The chapter you gave me, "The Bloods," is all about this multigenerational Washingtonian Jewish family, the Masturbovs, and is filled with little details of daily life and superstition. So, is this woebegone family milieu what you think your father grew out of?

Kramer: No, there's another side of the family where he actually is a character. Larry, I don't know where they came from.

Mass: The characters?

Kramer: The Masturbovs. There are aspects of different people in my real life that I've used, of course, but I don't know where that story came from. I mean, all that business about her bleeding—I never had any experience with menstruation, or dealing with it. It wasn't until after I'd written it that I found out—I was talking to a doctor friend of mine in Washington—that there is such a disease (that causes women to bleed all the time). It may be that I'd picked it up without realizing it, but I have no memory of any such. As for the name Masturbov, which is very important in the novel, I think it was a name that Milan Kundera used in one of his books. I just saw it in an excerpt that ran in the *New Yorker*, and I thought, oh, what a great name.

Mass: Having said all that I have about anti-Semitism, I don't get that sense at all from this chapter, even though what comes through is this searing indictment of religious orthodoxy and fanaticism. It's typically Kramer-esque in being blisteringly critical and satirical, but I'd say it's no more anti-Semitic than *Faggots* is homophobic. On the contrary, underneath all the indictment is Love.

Kramer: Certainly, the book is very much a criticism of religion in general, but there are representatives from every major ethnic and religious group and they all get the same scrutiny; there's no discrimination there! There are nuns, Mormons, native Americans. I've even got this made-up religion, Furstwasserarianism.

Mass: We've been touching on the Jewish world of your new novel. In "The Bloods," there's all this fascinating history of Jewish lore, superstition and tradition. Also in your short story, "Mrs. Tefillin," several characters are aroused while laying the phylacteries. Is this something that was common?

Kramer: Who knows? As I was telling you earlier, I was out there in the Hamptons writing all this stuff and getting terrified because I didn't know where the hell it was coming from. The main point is that it represented this utter passion, a giving over to something else, that something else being something unknown. What happens in the fullness of prayer is what happens during arousal. It's the same process of giving over, of surrender.

I bought all these phylacteries, and had to keep them because you can't throw them away! (laughter)

Mass: One of the things that intrigues me in your work is the vigorous sexuality of the many middle-aged or elderly characters. This is especially true in "Mrs. Tefillin." I can't remember reading anything where the sexuality of comparably elderly folk is treated so uninhibitedly.

Kramer: I don't think people stop feeling sexual as they get older.

Mass: But why is this so salient in your work? To what extent is it autobiographical, if that isn't too dumb a question for another writer to ask?

Kramer: I'm not sure that it is. Maybe you're noticing it so much is more a reflection of you than my work. (laughter)

Of course, these things do touch my life. I guess I always felt the sadness of the situation with my parents, that they seemed to have so little ... affection. Instead, so much of the time it was this sort of armed warfare; and my mother had this other person—who I deal with in "Mrs. Tefillin"— who she must have had fantasies about. After my father died, she actually started going out with a number of men who she felt wanted to marry her. I doubt that they had sex, but they certainly were very warm and loving relationships. I don't know how "sexual" Mrs. Tefillin is ... Maybe what you're talking about is more their physicality. I think most writers are very aware of people's bodies—their smells, all that physical stuff. And old people have special smells, and special ways that their bodies respond to their clothing, and things like that. I just think I'm conscious of that stuff in a writerly kind of way. But "Mrs. Tefillin" is also a lot about their youths, and sexual youths, during times when people didn't know what to do with sex.

... I just drowned three thousand syphilitics last night.

Mass: What are you talking about?

Kramer: . . . in my novel. There's so much fascinating and important new history. There's a new book out about Roosevelt, Sumner Welles and Cordell Hull. Did you know Welles was gay?

Mass: I know the name, but can't remember who he was.

Kramer: He was Assistant Secretary of State, a very powerful government official. Cordell Hull, who was Secretary of State, got him fired. Sumner Welles was very close to Roosevelt, and . . . Now, I haven't read the book, but he evidently had a great deal to do with influencing him to run again. Evidently, he was known as the honorary member of the Railroad Porters or something because he liked black railroad porters. (laughter) . . . Anyway, I can't wait to read it.

Mass: Now I remember. I believe Welles was a major figure in Roosevelt's handling of the question of Jewish refugees. I think this is in David S. Wyman's book, *The Abandonment of the Jews.*

Kramer: So what we're seeing is that the sex lives of people are finally entering into history as they should, which is really what I was espousing in *Just Say No.*

Mass: Jerry Zipkin and Nancy Reagan. The real history of this country! How Krameresque . . . (laughter) Thinking of you writing this kind of historicity is like thinking of Callas as Medea—seems so natural!
    Was this drowning of the syphilitics something that actually happened?

Kramer: Of course it happened! Around 1800. Did you know that George Washington had syphilis?

Mass: No.

Kramer: He and Martha never had sex.

Mass: Fascinating. You come to realize that the so-called history we learned has no reality whatsoever.

Kramer: Oh, none!

Mass: Zero!

Kramer: That's what the book is about. Nothing we were told about anything is true. So why do we think that anything we learn in science or disease or anything else is true?

Mass: Well, it may not be, and I think you're one of the people who has helped us to see this. But as you've also been one of the leading people of our age to help us see, progress must be based on some combination of expanding our horizons of what's possible and utilizing the best we have, and that certainly extends to scientific methods and principles as we currently understand them.

What is that you're fiddling with on the computer?

Kramer: Fonts! How many fonts do you have?

Mass: I don't know and I don't care. I want to know as little about my computer as possible.

Kramer: There are all these fonts you can add. Pages of them! I love it.

Mass: Just as you are fascinated by the accouterments of writing—papers, pens—you've become fascinated by the universe of the computer. Bill Hoffman, too. He's into graphics!

Kramer: Ask me something threatening.

Mass: OK. In that *HGLR* interview you were asked if you had any regrets about comparing GMHC to Auschwitz and you said no.

Kramer: And I still say NO. More so now than ever!

Mass: But you yourself admit that that's rhetoric and that it's made enemies . . .

Kramer: How do you try to have an impact and not make enemies somewhere along the way?

Mass: True enough, but also, I guess it touches this deeper issue of what you're really trying to say. You know, David Bergman's essay, "Larry Kramer and the Rhetoric of AIDS," concludes with this vision of the great quilt, the silence of which is tacitly contrasted with the strident Larry Kramer of "Silence = Death." Likewise tacit in this conclusion is the fact that this was a phenomenon you weren't involved with. Larry, why didn't you have any connection with the Names Project or the Quilt?

Kramer: Nobody asked me. I was a name-reader at its New York unveiling. At some point, I was approached about the umpteenth display in Washington, and I think I said, "Enough already!"

Mass: (laughter) Larry, that's *appalling*—making me laugh about something so gravely serious and earnest. But I do see both viewpoints. Arnie and I went to all of the displays, where we saw the patches with Vito and cried when we heard his name named more than anybody else's—and where we ran into David Bergman!

So when you were in London, did you go to that medical history museum you told me about?

Kramer: Yes. The Wellcome Museum. It was started by the founder of Bourroughs-Wellcome.

Mass: Did they have any idea who their visitor was?

Kramer: I was the only one in the whole place. When they asked for my name, I thought, oh, my God, I must be on some computer list of unfriendly persons. But it wasn't that, and it's a great place, filled with fascinating exhibits and information.

Mass: ... Larry Kramer, invited to wander solo through galleries of history ... hmmmm ... that's light years from the Dracula's Castle Ned Weeks is told about at the conclusion of *The Normal Heart*.

But wait a minute. Didn't we just say that we don't, can't believe any history; or, at the least, that nearly all the history we've learned is suspect? Even the Holocausts of World War II and Larry Kramer's *Reports*?

Kramer: Perhaps each of us has to create our own history of the world. One that we can live with. And learn how to accept that my history of the world is different from your history of the world. It might put a lot of colleges and professors out of business!

Notes on Contributors

Christopher Bram's most recent novels are *Father of Frankenstein* (which has been made into a movie starring Ian McKellen and Brendan Fraser) and *Gossip*. He lives in New York City.

John Clum is Professor of English and Professor of the Practice of Drama and Theater at Duke University. He is the author of a number of books and essays on twentieth-century American and British drama and gay studies. His most recent books are *Acting Gay: Male Homosexuality in Modern Drama* (Columbia, 1992; rev. ed., 1994), and the anthology *Out On Stage: An Anthology of Contemporary Gay Male Drama* (Westview–Harper Collins, 1996). He is also a playwright whose work has been performed recently in Washington, Baltimore, his native Durham, NC, and London. Four of his plays have been published by DIALOGUS Play Service and Publishing.

Alfred Corn is a poet, novelist and critic. His seventh book of poems, titled *Present*, appeared in 1997, as well as his first novel *Part of His Story*, and he is the author of a collection of critical essays titled *The Metamorphoses of Metaphor*. He teaches creative writing at Columbia University in New York City.

John D'Emilio is the author of *Sexual Politics, Sexual Communities: The Making of a Homosexual Minority in the United States*, of *Making Trouble: Essays on Gay History, Politics and the University*, and (with Estelle B. Freedman) of *Intimate Matters: A History of Sexuality in America*. He is currently writing a biography of Bayard Rustin, the civil rights leader and pacifist. He has served as the Director of Policy of the National Gay and Lesbian Task Force in Washington, DC.

Michael Denneny is senior editor at St. Martin's Press, where he pioneered the publishing of gay and lesbian writing and founded the Stonewall Inn Editions line of trade paperbacks. He is the author of *Lovers: The Story of Two*

Men and *Decent Passions: Real Stories About Love*, as well as numerous essays. He lives in New York City.

Anthony S. Fauci, M.D., is Director, National Institute of Allergy and Infectious Diseases, National Institutes of Health (NIH). He is widely regarded as one of the world's pioneering AIDS researchers and has been a major force in driving the US government's biomedical research efforts in the AIDS epidemic.

Andrew Holleran is the author, most recently, of *The Beauty of Men*.

Arnie Kantrowitz is associate professor of English at the College of Staten Island, CUNY. He is the author of *Under the Rainbow: Growing Up Gay*, an autobiography; his essays, poems and stories have appeared in the *New York Times*, the *Village Voice*, and numerous gay publications and anthologies, and he has recently completed a biography of Walt Whitman. He lives in New York with his lover, Lawrence Mass.

Tony Kushner is the author of *Angels in America, Part One (Millenium Approaches)* and *Part Two (Perestroika)*, *Stars!*, and other plays, as well as numerous essays and reviews.

Lawrence D. Mass, M.D., is a co-founder of Gay Men's Health Crisis and the author of *Dialogues of The Sexual Revolution, Volumes I and II*, and of *Confessions of a Jewish Wagnerite: Being Gay and Jewish in America*. He lives in New York City where he is a medical director of Greenwich House, Inc. He is at work on *Musical Closets: Homosexuality, Judaism, Music and Opera*, forthcoming from Cassell.

Rodger McFarlane is co-author of *The Complete Bedside Companion: No-Nonsense Advice on Caring for the Seriously Ill* (Simon & Schuster, 1997). He is former executive director of Gay Men's Health Crisis, Inc. (GMHC) and of Broadway Cares/Equity Fights AIDS. Portions of his essay first appeared in the *Journal of the International Association of Physicians in AIDS Care*, November 1995, Medical Publications, Inc., Chicago, IL.

Patrick Merla as the editor of the *New York Native* from 1984 to 1988, worked with Larry Kramer on some of his best-known AIDS writings published during that period. His biography is based on Kramer's published and unpublished writings, research in the publications and media cited in the text, interviews and conversations with Kramer, Rodger McFarlane, and others, and the author's personal observation of many of the events. Like Kramer, Merla has worked in both show business and publishing. He is author of *The Tales of Patrick Merla* (Available Press/Ballantine) and the editor of *Boys Like Us: Gay Writers Tell Their Coming-Out Stories* (Avon).

Mark Merlis's *American Studies* (Houghton Mifflin, Penguin) won the *Los Angeles Times* book prize for first fiction and the Ferro/Grumley award for gay writing.

Michael Paller is a dramaturg and literary manager. He has written extensively on theater and books for *Outweek, Village Voice, Washington Post, Cleveland Plain Dealer, Theater Week* and *New York Native*. Current projects include a book about the plays of Tennessee Williams and an anthology of profiles of gay playwrights.

Gail Merrifield Papp was Director of Play Development for the New York Shakespeare Festival Public Theater from 1965–91. She developed and commissioned many new works by writers, among them Larry Kramer's *The Normal Heart* and, the same year, the Tony-award musical *The Mystery of Edwin Drood*. In 1988 she received the Arts and Communication Award from the Human Rights Campaign and in 1990 a Women's History Month Citation from the City of New York. She married Joseph Papp in 1976. She is on the Board of Trustees of the Joseph Papp Public Theater and is currently working on two books.

Canaan Parker is the author of two novels, *The Color of Trees* (1992) and *Sky Daddy* (1997) from Alyson Publications. His work also appears in *Flesh and The Word 4*. He works with the Publishing Triangle, the Lesbian and Gay Community Center Literary Program In Our Own Write and Outmusic. Parker is a native New Yorker, retransplanted to Chelsea from Boston.

Gabriel Rotello is the author of *Sexual Ecology* (Dutton). He lives in New York City.

Douglas Sadownick is the author of *Sacred Lips of The Bronx* and *Sex Between Men: An Intimate History of the Sex Lives of Gay Men Postwar to Present*. He has an M.A. in Clinical Psychology from Antioch University, is pursuing doctoral studies at Pacifica Graduate Institute, and counsels gay men and lesbians at the Los Angeles Gay and Lesbian Center.

Michelangelo Signorile is the author of *Queer in America* and *Outing Yourself*. His most recent book is *Life Outside: The Signorile Report on Gay Men: Sex, Love, Family and the Passages of Life* (HarperCollins). He lives in New York City.

Calvin Trillin is the author of *Remembering Denny* and, most recently, of *Messages From My Father*. He writes for the *New Yorker*.

Sarah Trillin is a graduate student in social work. She lives in Los Angeles.

David Willinger is a Professor of Theatre at City College and the Graduate Center, CUNY. His most recent book is an anthology titled *Three Fin-de-Siècle Farces*, published by Peter Lang. A two-time Fulbright Award winner, he has brought out four earlier anthologies of his translations of Belgian plays as well as essays about Belgian theatre and American playwrights Adrienne Kennedy and Eduardo Machado. In addition to his scholarly work, Willinger is an established playwright and director. Among his works are *Andrea's Got Two Boyfriends* and his adaptation of *The Heart is a Lonely Hunter*.

Maxine Wolfe has been an organizer of many ACT UP actions and campaigns. She co-founded its Women's Caucus and the ACT UP National Women's Committee. She was also a co-founder of the Lesbian Avengers and is a coordinator of the Lesbian Herstory Archives. Her writing about ACT UP and AIDS activism has been published in *Women, AIDS and Activism* (South End Press, 1990) and *AIDS Prevention and Services: Community Based Research* (Bergin and Garvey, 1994).

Index